HOLLYWOOD MUSICALS

HOLLYWOOD

HOLLYWOOD MUSICALS

THE 101 GREATEST SONG-AND-DANCE MOVIES OF ALL TIME

KEN BLOOM

FOREWORD BY JANE POWELL

BLACK DOG
& LEVENTHAL
PUBLISHERS
NEW YORK

To my movie-loving friends Michael Shoop and Marcie Agmon;
and Jay and Dixie Morse.

Copyright © 2010 by Ken Bloom

All rights reserved. No part of this book, either text or illustration, may be used or
reproduced in any form without prior written permission from the publisher.

Published by
Black Dog & Leventhal Publishers, Inc.
151 West 19th Street
New York, NY 10011

Distributed by
Workman Publishing Company
225 Varick Street
New York, NY 10014

Manufactured in China

Cover and interior design by Scott Citron

ISBN-13: 978-1-57912-848-7

h g f e d c b a

Library of Congress Cataloging-in-Publication Data available upon request

CONTENTS

Foreword **6**
Introduction **7**
All That Jazz **8**
American Hot Wax **10**
An American in Paris **12**
Animated Musicals **15**
Babes in Arms **16**
The Band Wagon **18**
Beach Blanket Bingo **20**
Beauty and the Beast **22**
Belle of the Nineties **24**
Born to Dance **26**
Broadway Melody **28**
Cabaret **30**
Cabin in the Sky **32**
Calamity Jane **34**
Carmen Jones **36**
Chicago **38**
College Swing **41**
The Court Jester **44**
Damn Yankees **46**
A Damsel in Distress **48**
Dangerous When Wet **50**
Dumbo **52**
Easter Parade **54**
42nd Street **57**
Funny Face **60**
Funny Girl **64**
The Gang's All Here **67**
Gentlemen Prefer Blondes **70**
Gigi **73**
Girl Crazy **76**
Gold Diggers of 1933 **78**
B Musicals **80**
Good News **81**
Goodbye Mr. Chips **84**
Grease **86**
The Great Caruso **88**
The Great Waltz **90**
The Great Ziegfeld **92**

Hallelujah! **94**
A Hard Day's Night **96**
Behind The Scenes **99**
The Harvey Girls **103**
Hedwig and the Angry Inch **106**
High School Musical 3 **108**
Hollywood Hotel **110**
The Jazz Singer **112**
The King and I **115**
King of Jazz **118**
Kiss Me Kate **120**
T & A: The Women **123**
Lady Sings The Blues **124**
Li'l Abner **126**
Living It Up **128**
Love Me Or Leave Me **130**
Love Me Tonight **132**
A Salute to the Chorus Girl **135**
Mad About Music **136**
Mary Poppins **138**
Singing Cowboys **141**
Meet Me in St. Louis **142**
The Merry Widow **146**
Moulin Rouge! **148**
The Muppet Movie **150**
The Music Man **152**
My Fair Lady **154**
Nashville **157**
Foreign Musicals **158**
A Night at the Opera **160**
The Nightmare Before Christmas **162**
Oklahoma! **164**
Oliver! **168**
On The Town **171**
One Hour With You **174**
The Pajama Game **176**
Big Band Musicals **179**
Pinocchio **180**
Poor Little Rich Girl **182**
Road to Morocco **184**
The Rocky Horror Picture Show **186**

The Rose **188**
Rose-Marie **190**
Saturday Night Fever **192**
Scrooge **194**
Seven Brides For Seven Brothers **196**
Great Numbers from Musicals **199**
Show Boat **200**
Singin' in the Rain **204**
Snow White and the Seven Dwarfs **208**
Sons of the Pioneers **212**
The Sound Of Music **214**
The Worst Movie Musicals **218**
A Star is Born **220**
Star Spangled Rhythm **224**
State Fair **226**
Stormy Weather **228**
Black Musicals **231**
Summer Stock **232**
Sun Valley Serenade **234**
Sunny Side Up **236**
Swing Time **238**
T & A: The Men **241**
This is Spinal Tap **242**
Tin Pan Alley **244**
Top Hat **247**
Jewish Musicals **250**
Viva Las Vegas **251**
We're Not Dressing **254**
West Side Story **256**
Country Musicals **259**
White Christmas **260**
Whoopee! **264**
Willie Wonka And The Chocolate Factory **266**
The Wizard of Oz **268**
Yankee Doodle Dandy **272**
You Were Never Lovelier **276**
Index **280**
Chronology of the 101 Greatest Broadway Musicals **279**
Acknowledgements & Photo Credits **288**

The street set of *Hello, Dolly!*

FOREWORD
BY JANE POWELL

SINCE I WAS A LITTLE GIRL BACK IN PORTLAND, OREGON—TWO years old, to be exact—I have loved musicals. At that age, I was already singing and tap dancing on the radio, so what would you expect? All those glamorous, beautiful ladies dancing in their beautiful gowns—even then it seemed so exciting! Oh, how I loved Ginger Rogers and Sonja Henie! I would put on a long skirt of my mother's and twirl and smile until I was blue in the face. How I wanted to be Sonja Henie! I loved her dimples so much that I even took the end of a pencil and pressed it into my cheeks for days, thinking I might get some of my own. Needless to say, it didn't work.

We lived in a little apartment house, the Banbury Cross, and in the basement laundry room there were sheets that I would use as a curtain. I would put on my roller skates, run on my toes, try an arabesque, spin, and smile. I was Sonja Henie! Coincidentally, much, much later, I married one of her skating partners. Can you believe it?

I thought I knew a lot of stories already—but I learned so many new things from this book. For instance, I was very happy to finally learn the name of the girl who sang for Snow White, Adriana Caselotti. She had such a charming voice. And I had no idea that it was the great dancer Marge Champion who did the physical moves for the animation. As a little girl, "Some Day My Prince Will Come" was in my repertoire. Now he finally has come—my prince, Dickie Moore.

If you are like me, you often hear a song in a movie and wonder where it came from. This is the book for you—because every song is listed, along with who wrote it. And the layout of each page is quite unique, never dull. Photo after glorious photo brings each movie to life and I happen to know that a lot of them are quite rare.

How right Ken Bloom is about Ann Miller, my good friend. She was as good a singer as she was a dancer. How she could belt a song! We were traveling companions to South America many years ago, where we became known by the studio contingent as Mutt and Jeff. Of course, I was Mutt. I loved Ann. She was one of a kind, and here's an opportunity for you to learn a little more about her and see some lovely photos of her in action.

Dancing with Fred Astaire in *Royal Wedding* was a thrill, and also frightening—but he put me at ease very quickly. Since I was the third in line for the part—June and Judy had bowed out, for different

reasons—the dances had already been set, so I learned all of them in three weeks. It was a great lesson in saying, "I think I can."

The honesty of so many of the stars, regarding their ability to do their jobs, was quite an eye-opener for me. I was reminded of that as I read through the text here. I remember Deborah Kerr in *The King and I*. She didn't think she could sing so Marni Nixon was asked to do it, and she sounded just exactly like Deborah. She was perfect. For more about Marni and her unsung (to use the wrong word!) contributions to so many musical films, see the chapter about *The King and I*.

The story told in these pages about the making of *Seven Brides for Seven Brothers* is too true. The studio was definitely planning to do the film, but it had also bought and paid a lot of money for the rights to another show—*Brigadoon*. So, they cut our budget for *Seven Brides*—a lot. What a coup it was when we went to Radio City Music Hall and *Brigadoon* was left at the gate. *Seven Brides* is timeless, and thanks to TCM, it is on television often—especially on my birthday.

The older pictures are fascinating…all those stars with their overdone makeup, hair always perfectly put in place, and beautiful clothes. How artistic it was to dress the star in a costume that would make her stand out in a crowd. Sometimes, the difference between the star and everyone else was subtle, but it was always there.

This is not your usual "motion picture" book. It is fascinating, educational, and a wonderful trip through the history of the movie musical. To see the past from different angles is enlightening, and even an insider like me learned a lot of new things. You'll find that the silver screen wasn't all sweetness and light. The wonderful people we loved in the movies were not always so perfect in their private lives—and you'll read some unvarnished stories here, along with a lot of little-known facts and anecdotes.

Hollywood Musicals is a must—to read and to own—for all those who love the form. It is a great history lesson, a great escape, and a great reference. Not having seen all the old, old films, it makes me want to run out and see every one I missed. I'm sure you will feel the same way.

How privileged I am to have been a part of it all, and to be represented in this exquisite book. Enjoy it—and keep going to the movies!

INTRODUCTION

MUSICALS HAVE BEEN A PART OF THE MOVIES SINCE film first learned to talk and sing. The great success of *The Jazz Singer* and early sound shorts led to an explosion of musical films, and the tradition continues some eighty years later.

This book is a celebration of all the studios, performers, technicians, musicians, writers, and artists who have added their artistry to the screen from the earliest black-and-white musicals through Cinemascope and today's newest wave of 3-D.

Before we go any further, we'd like to point out that our subtitle specifies the "greatest" musicals, not necessarily the "best." In selecting films for inclusion, we used a variety of criteria, including but not limited to overall excellence. Box office success, awards, cult status, innovation—these and other factors were considered as we painstakingly (emphasis on pain) narrowed decades of films down to a mere 101. Of course, most of the movies that made the final cut can stand up to the term "best," in our opinion, anyway. Lists are by nature subjective—that's part of the fun of lists! By all means, compile your own—no hard feelings.

We did impose several limitations when making our list. One could argue that all or most of the Astaire-Rogers films are among the greatest. The same might be said of the Dubin and Warren films directed by Busby Berkeley or the films of Shirley Temple in her heyday. But we've chosen representative films by these artists and others. We've also attempted to choose films from every era, since we believe that the greatest films speak to their audiences at the time they're released and throughout the decades.

In addition to the 101 films, we've included a plethora of special chapters examining subjects that aren't covered in the main chapters. For example, we pause to look at cowboy musicals, black and Jewish musicals, animated musicals—even movie posters and advertisements. That's in addition to the numerous biographical articles throughout the book that celebrate the actors, directors, composers, and others who put the "great" in greatest.

When choosing the photos, we tried hard to avoid any that were overly familiar. As a result, among the almost 1,000 included are many that have never before been published, including lots of color images of scenes from black-and-white films. As an extra treat, we've reproduced a great poster from nearly every musical, and added a chapter covering foreign posters. As much as the film stills themselves, these images are part of the world's love affair with the movies.

Unlike live stage plays and musicals, which exist only in real time, most film musicals are still available via broadcast television, DVD and VHS recordings, or the Internet. With a few exceptions, there's not a film in this book that you couldn't take a look at if reading about it whets your appetite or stimulates your memory.

We set out to make this book an overview and celebration of the film musical, not a lecture. If you find yourself wanting more information on specific films, artists, or genres (and we hope you do), there are good books, documentaries, and websites out there on topics large and small. And if we seem a little snarky or irreverent, well, we are. How serious can we be when dissecting films that include ladies playing neon violins, flying nannies, merry widows, dancing scarecrows, and dozens of kids putting on dozens of shows? Yes, there are serious musicals, but for the most part, sheer, blissful entertainment is their primary goal. We hope that this book inspires you to seek out a few movies you haven't seen or revisit old favorites with a new perspective.

And about those lists...we're showing you ours and we'd love to see yours. We'd also like to hear your opinions. E-mail or write us care of Black Dog & Leventhal. Who knows? You might even change a snarky author's point of view. Let the wrangling over great musicals begin!

—*Ken Bloom*

Judy Garland in A Star is Born.

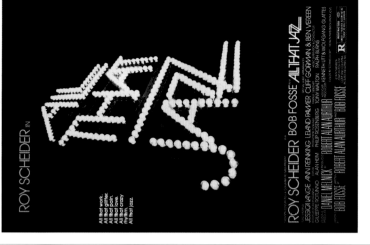

ALL THAT JAZZ

PRODUCER: Robert Alan Arthur
DIRECTOR: Bob Fosse
SCREENWRITER: Robert Alan Aurthur
CHOREOGRAPHER: Bob Fosse

Synopsis

Girls, gams, and the angel of death—they're all in a day's work when a great but flawed choreographer reviews his life.

Cast

Roy Scheider	Roy Gideon
Jessica Lange	Angelique
Leland Palmer	Audrey Paris
Anr Reinking	Kate Jagger
Cliff Gorman	David Newman
Ber Vereen	O'Connor Flood

Behind the Screen

- The pill bottle labeled "Joe Gideon" has Fosse's actual home address on it.
- The original title of *All That Jazz* was *Dying*.

ALL THAT JAZZ

COLUMBIA PICTURES/20TH CENTURY FOX—DECEMBER 20, 1979

ABOVE: Roy Scheider and Ben Vereen match egos.

OPPOSITE TOP: Bob Fosse proves he's still got it, as he teaches the chorus some steps.

OPPOSITE BOTTOM: Roy Scheider gives the audience a show-biz high five.

L IKE EUROPEAN FILMMAKERS WHO DRAMATIZE THEIR OWN LIVES IN THEIR FILMS (Woody Allen, François Truffaut, and Federico Fellini foremost among them), Bob Fosse turned the camera on his own life and experiences in *All That Jazz*. Fosse used film as a means of self-examination and a way of explaining his excesses to his audience—if not excusing them. He told the *New York Times*, "I wanted music and dancing in it. I wanted to try and move people in different directions. I wanted to show the fear and anxiety a person goes through in the hospital, and the stress of someone under business pressure. Many people are under this stress. They are trying to do something with their lives but instead become self-destructive with pills, alcohol, or in psychological ways."

All That Jazz is really about Fosse making the Broadway musical *Chicago*. It's funny because the film version of *Chicago* was made by director/choreographer Rob Marshall in an extreme Bob Fosse style.

Showing his usual fearlessness, Fosse had the nerve to create a movie musical in which the songs and dances don't uplift the audience with romance or laughter. There is little conventional joy depicted in the dances of *All That Jazz*—but the overall effect, while sometimes hard to watch and sometimes quite brutal and unforgiving, is fascinating in a certain "don't try this at home" way. Whether Fosse was excusing himself or offering a cautionary tale about his own excesses is unknown. Obsession is the order of the day and the Fosse character's reliance on medications swallowed and smoked is the ultimate car crash from which we simply can't avert our eyes.

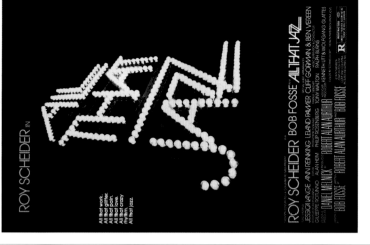

The layers of self-reflection and the mix of truth and fiction can sometimes be overwhelming. The Leland Palmer character is based on Fosse's then wife and star of *Chicago*, Gwen Verdon. Reinking was Fosse's mistress while working on the Broadway show and basically plays herself. The songwriters are disguised version of *Chicago*'s John Kander and Fred Ebb. And the real-life Fosse suffered a heart attack during rehearsals of *Chicago*, just as his character does in the movie. (He is played by Roy Scheider, in a bit of casting that mimicked Fosse's diminutive height as well as his oversized personality.) The title of the film (titles can't be copyrighted) is the same as the hit song from *Chicago*, though Fosse couldn't obtain the rights to the stage score.

Joe Gideon dies in *All That Jazz* whereas Fosse survived *Chicago*'s Broadway opening. One can only assume that the prospect of directing his own death was attractive to Fosse's controlling (i.e., choreographer) side. *All That Jazz* wants to have it both ways, and it succeeds. It has old-fashioned musical numbers in the best vaudeville/burlesque style, as well as surrealistic episodes. Its depiction of theater is spot-on. Its audition sequence is better than any other ever filmed. Ultimately, it is a painful and thrilling wrap-up of a brilliant career, a great commentary on artists in general, and an absolutely unique film musical. ■

SONGS

"After You've Gone" (Henry Creamer and Turner Layton) ■ "Bye Bye Love" (Boudleaux Bryant and Felice Bryant) ■ "Everything Old Is New Again" (Peter Allen and Carole Bayer Sager) ■ "On Broadway" (Barry Mann, Cynthia Weil, Jerry Leiber, and Mike Stoller) ■ "A Perfect Day" (Harry Nilsson) ■ "Some of These Days" (Shelton Brooks) ■ "Take Off with Us" (Fred Tobias and Stanley Lebowsky) ■ "There'll Be Some Changes Made" (W. B. Overstreet, B. Higgins, and H. Edwards) ■ "There's No Business Like Show Business" (Irving Berlin) ■ "Who's Sorry Now" (Ted Snyder, Bert Kalmar, and Harry Ruby)

Bob Fosse

Arms cocked, hips thrust, bowler hats doffed, and pelvises grinding—those are the hallmarks of Bob Fosse's choreography. His work composed of half burlesque moves, half vaudeville, and another half good old musical comedy, Bob Fosse's overflowing gifts translated into a unique style. Sexuality was always on view in abundance but so, too, was vulnerability juxtaposed with brashness. His greatness is best exemplified in a story about the stage musical *Chicago*, which was set in the 1920s. Before starting the directing assignment, Fosse asked his assistant to make sure that he never ever used a Charleston step in his choreography. The easy shorthand or cliché was not for him. The second-best example of his greatness is that by the end of his career he had invented his own clichés. Others tried to imitate his style, but none succeeded in capturing his magic—because they only copied the surface and never the intent or the emotion behind the dance. His film credits include choreography for *The Pajama Game*, *Damn Yankees*, *Sweet Charity*, and *The Little Prince*. Fosse, along with Jerome Robbins, Onna White, and Michael Kidd, was a master of American show choreography. Each of them had his or her qualities, but of them all, Fosse's style was the most brazenly showbizzy.

"It usually took me about two years to recharge my batteries after working with Fosse. He was a very intense and demanding man."

—Designer Tony Walton

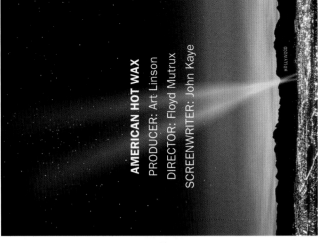

AMERICAN HOT WAX

PRODUCER: Art Linson
DIRECTOR: Floyd Mutrux
SCREENWRITER: John Kaye

Synopsis

Ripped from yesterday's headlines: Disc jockey and record producer Alan Freed endures harassment by the FBI, which considers his music a danger to American morals.

Cast

Tim McIntire................*Alan Freed*
Fran Drescher.............*Sheryl*
Jay Leno....................*Mookie*
Laraine Newman.........*Teenage Louise*
Carl Earl Weaver.........*Chesterfield*
Al Chalk.....................*Chesterfield*
Sam Harkness.............*Chesterfield*
Arnold McCuller..........*Chesterfield*
Jeff Altman................*Lennie Richfield*
Moosie Drier...............*Artie Moress*
Jerry Lee Lewis
Chuck Berry
Screaming Jay Hawkins
Frankie Ford

1959.
New York City.
The battleground
was Rock and Roll.
It was the beginning
of an era.

You shoulda been there.

AMERICAN HOT WAX

PARAMOUNT—MARCH 17, 1978

How do we know this is a period film? (a) Tim McIntire (as Alan Freed) is smoking indoors. (b) There are turntables for playing LPs—discs that had music in grooves that a needle tracked over to make sound.

W E WAS THERE. BABY BOOMERS WHO ARE NOW MIDDLE AGED (IF YOU PLAN TO live till 120) remember the heady early days of rock and roll: the thrill of discovering music that spoke only to us; the frowns on our parents faces; the 45 rpm record format especially made for our kind of music; the snide reactions of culture snobs who derided the insipid lyrics (well, they had a point); and most of all, the virulent reaction of the so-called moral majority, which encouraged their strait-laced kids to throw their 45s on bonfires.

The worst affront against the devil's music came from the federal government, which mounted an organized campaign to destroy rock and the people who promoted it. Number one on their hit list was disc jockey and promoter Alan Freed. Freed was a champion of black musicians and rhythm-and-blues music, a direct precursor to rock. He popularized the term *rock and roll* on his radio show and brought black music to the attention of white teens. All of this coincided with the nascent civil rights movement, an even bigger thorn in the side of conservative government officials.

Freed had gotten his start on the radio in Cleveland in the early 1950s, promoting his first concert—the first rock-and-roll concert ever—in 1952. Needless to say, it was a success—too much of a success, in fact. So many people tried to get into the Cleveland Arena that a riot began, the concert was canceled, and Freed's star ascended. He moved to New York and spun discs at a series of radio stations and even introduced rock to Europe's teens through Radio Luxembourg.

Eventually, Freed turned to television, where he hosted the ABC dance show *The Big Beat*—but the show was canceled when Frankie Lymon (of Frankie Lymon and the Teenagers) danced with a white girl on camera. Freed went on to appear in a series of important rock movies, beginning with *Rock Around the Clock* in 1956, which also featured

RIGHT: The Chesterfields and Laraine Newman. Carl Earl Weaver is the short one.

MIDDLE LEFT: Screamin' Jay Hawkins.

MIDDLE RIGHT: Chuck Berry.

BOTTOM RIGHT: Tim McIntire greets two film novices, Fran Drescher and Jay Leno. Whatever became of them?

Bill Haley and the Comets as well as the Platters. Other outings included *Rock, Rock, Rock; Mr. Rock and Roll; Don't Knock the Rock;* and *Go, Johnny, Go.*

During the "payola" scandals of the early 1960s, Freed was convicted of accepting money from record companies to play particular songs. Unable to find radio or TV work in New York, he tried California and then Miami, but he was completely washed up by 1962. He died of alcoholism in 1965.

American Hot Wax dramatizes the period of Freed's life from the height of his fame as a New York DJ and concert promoter through his involvement in the payola scandal. Although his story is fictionalized, the spirit of those years, the excitement of the fans, the possibilities open to black artists for the first time, and the relationship between whites and blacks in the music industry are artfully and realistically explored. The characters' enthusiasm and optimism are spot on and the guest artists bring real verisimilitude to the proceedings. If the film is a little skittish about integration and a bit loosey-goosey with the facts, well, so was early rock and roll. Plus, watching it makes for a real who-will-be-who fest: look for Fran Drescher in her second picture (after *Saturday Night Fever*), Jay Leno in his first credited film role (he'd make three more film appearances before decamping for good to television and animated character voices), and Laraine Newman in her second film (before ending her stint on *Saturday Night Live* for a future in voice work). Heck, at age fourteen, Moosie Drier had more acting experience than all of them put together. As Alan Freed, Tim McIntire gives a suitably driven performance that captures Freed's obsession with spreading rock to the masses. Of all the actors in the film, he showed the most promise but—ironically—alcohol and drugs cut his life short just eight years after making this picture.

It's too bad that *American Hot Wax* has never come out on DVD (or even VHS) so audiences might have an opportunity to enjoy its energy and its evocation of the early years of rock, before the genre was discovered by corporations. ■

Behind the Screen

■ Norman Lear wanted to build a sitcom around the Chesterfields but the four members couldn't agree among themselves whether to take the gig.

■ The great Carl Earl Weaver, who plays a thinly veiled Frankie Lymon in the film, would soon play the real Lymon on Broadway—and sing "Why Do Fools Fall in Love"—in *Rock and Roll: The First 500 Years*, a show that was truly ahead of its time.

SONGS

"The ABC's of Love" (Morris Levy) ■ "Church Bells May Ring" (Morty Craft and the Willows) ■ "Come Go with Me" (C. E. Quick) ■ "Great Balls of Fire" (Jack Hammer and Otis Blackwell) ■ "Hello Mary Lou" (Gene Pitney and Cavet Mangiaracina) ■ "Hushabye" (Doc Pomus and Mort Shuman) ■ "I Put a Spell on You" (Jay Hawkins) ■ "I Wonder Why" (Richard Weeks and Melvin Anderson) ■ "Little Star" (Vito Picone and Arthur Venosa) ■ "Maybe" (R. Barrett) ■ "Mr. Lee" (Heather Dixon, Helen Gathers, Emma Ruth Pought, Laura Webb, and Jannie Pought) ■ "Reelin' and Rockin'" (Chuck Berry) ■ "Rock and Roll Is Here to Stay" (David White) ■ "Speedo" (Esther Navarro) ■ "That Is Rock and Roll" (Jerry Leiber and Mike Stoller) ■ "That's Why" (Berry Gordy Jr. and Tyran Carlo) ■ "Why Do Fools Fall in Love" (Frankie Lymon and Morris Levy)

AN AMERICAN IN PARIS
COMPOSER: George Gershwin
LYRICIST: Ira Gershwin
PRODUCER: Arthur Freed
DIRECTOR: Vincente Minnelli
SCREENWRITER: Alan Jay Lerner
CHOREOGRAPHER: Gene Kelly

Synopsis

Should a starving but tune-filled painter fall for the beautiful dancer or become a kept man? This is an MGM musical, so we all know the answer. Lucky for us, we get to watch it unfold on a cloud of great art anc choreography.

Cast

Gene Kelly ....Jerry Mulligan
Leslie Caron....................Lise Bouvier
Oscar Levant....................Adam Cook
Georges Guétary.........Henri Baurel
Nina Foch....................Milo Roberts

AN AMERICAN IN PARIS

MGM—NOVEMBER 11, 1951

ABOVE AND FAR RIGHT:
Gene Kelly and Leslie
Caron lose themselves
in the whirl of Paris.

THE MOST POWERFUL PERSON AT MGM WASN'T LOUIS B. MAYER, THE SECOND "M" IN the title. The true power behind the studio wasn't even in Hollywood. It resided with the man who held the purse strings, Nicholas Schenck, at corporate headquarters in New York City. Schenck was the money man and, in the 1950s, he was instrumental in ousting Mayer, MGM's founder. Dore Schary was promoted to run the studio with a tight rein. Mayer could be ruthless but he really believed in his role as the father of MGM, and so was sometimes a softie. MGM's coffers had diminished in the years following the war. Audiences moved to the suburbs in droves, leaving the great downtown movie palaces little more than echo chambers. In 1951, the year *An American in Paris* was released, ten million television sets were broadcasting the *Late Show* to rapt audiences. So, Schary was brought in. Mayer was out.

Schenck kept his eye on the bottom line and he couldn't for the life of him understand why the new picture, *An American in Paris*, needed an almost twenty-minute-long ballet. What did it have to do with the plot of the picture? The ballet would add almost $500,000 to the cost of a production on which he had already spent two million dollars. But Schary stood up for Arthur Freed who, in turn, stood up for Gene Kelly and Vincente Minnelli. Still, even after a preview, Schenck felt that the ballet needed to be cut. They responded that it was a bad idea, because the film *The Red Shoes* had had a seventeen-plus-minute ballet in it and it was a success. The ballet stayed.

The film was one of the rare musicals to win the Academy Award for Best Picture—and no one would dispute the fact that the ballet was exquisitely art directed, photographed, choreographed, and danced. Dore Schary said, "I told Schenck this picture is going to be great because of the ballet—or it'll be nothing. Without the ballet it's just a cute and nice musical. So that's what we're gambling on." And he was right. The ballet gave the picture a weight and seriousness of purpose that elevated the music hall–styled numbers that preceded it. Honestly, are you caught up in the characters in a real, personal way prior to the ballet?

Irene Sharaff, Broadway and Hollywood costume designer, sketched out the elements of the ballet, the artists who would be represented in each scene, the color schemes, and the characters that would populate the story. She invented the *pompiers* (firemen) and the furies who would act as tour guides for Kelly and Caron through the different artists' visions. While the movement and style expressed the dancers' emotions, Kelly's choreography were inspired by the work of the artists depicted in the backgrounds. Kelly made sure that there was lots of emotion. He wrote, "We wanted to do a ballet without an actual story line or plot, a ballet that *suggested* rather than narrated, a ballet which said more with things unsaid, than with things said."

He said, "If the camera is to make any contribution to dance, the focal point must be the pure background, giving the spectator an undistorted and all-encompassing view of dancer and background. To accomplish this end, the camera must be made to move with the dancer, so that the lens becomes the eye of the spectator, *your eye*. . . . We tried to make a *ballet*, not just merely a dance, not a series of beautiful, moving tableaux, but an emotional whole, consisting of the combined arts which spell ballet, whether on the screen or the stage."

"There were other ballets in musicals: Fred Astaire and Lucille Bremer in the confusing *Yolanda and the Thief*; Astaire and Cyd Charisse in *The Band Wagon*'s "The Girl Hunt Ballet"; Kelly in "A Day in New York" from *On the Town*; the "Broadway Melody" finale of *Singin' in the Rain*; "Slaughter on Tenth Avenue" in *On Your Toes* (featuring Eddie Albert and Vera Zorina); and in *Words and Music* (Gene Kelly and Vera-Ellen). There was also the "Little Mermaid" ballet in *Hans Christian Andersen*, and the whole of Kelly's *Invitation to the Dance*. But none had the impact or the quality of the ballet in *An American in Paris*. ■

SONGS

"By Strauss" ■ "I Got Rhythm" ■ "I'll Build a Stairway to Paradise" (lyric by B. G. DeSylva and Ira Gershwin) ■ "Love Is Here to Stay" ■ "S'Wonderful" ■ "Tra-La-La"

RIGHT: Gene Kelly mans the camera as director of *Hello, Dolly!* It seemed like a good idea at the time.

Gene Kelly

W hy can't we ever talk about Gene Kelly without comparing him to Fred Astaire? When we talk about Astaire, we don't automatically bring up Kelly. That said . . . Fred Astaire liked full-body shots, nearly stationary cameras, and long takes. He wanted the experience of the film to mimic that of the stage. Astaire was slightly effete, spare in his extravagances, and sophisticated. Gene Kelly was none of the above. He wouldn't be seen in a tux or tails. He was the man's man, a virile, athletic dancer who swung down a ship's sail in *The Pirate*, jumped from a double-decker bus into Debbie Reynolds's convertible in *Singin' in the Rain*, and danced around the beams of a house under construction (shades of *Seven Brides for Seven Brothers*) in *Living in a Big Way*. Kelly wasn't much of a props dancer, as Astaire was, though he did dance with a mop in *Thousands Cheer* and performed a memorable soft shoe with a newspaper and squeaky floorboard in *Summer Stock*. Among Kelly's partners was Jerry Mouse, of Tom and Jerry fame. Astaire was fond of film tricks such as dancing in slow motion or having lots of other Fred Astaires backing him up, but Kelly instead relied on the camera as part of the choreography. He and his sometime collaborator Stanley Donen put the camera on a boom for the end of the "Singin' in the Rain" number, so it could literally dance along with him. Like Astaire, Kelly loved to rehearse until every dance was perfect. He was a naturally genial guy, but his temper could overtake him during rehearsal or filming. The primary contribution that Kelly made to movie musicals was his embrace of ballet in such films as *Words and Music*, *On the Town*, *Singin' in the Rain*, *An American in Paris*, and the seldom seen *Invitation to the Dance*. After his days at MGM were over in 1958, Kelly directed Rodgers and Hammerstein's *Flower Drum Song* on Broadway, made some screen appearances (notably in the courtroom drama *Inherit the Wind*), and directed several films, including *A Guide for the Married Man* and *Hello, Dolly!*

Johnny Green

Lela Simone, MGM's premier pianist and more, said of Johnny Green, "He is an impossible person to work with. On the scoring stage he would make take after take just because he was aggravated with a flute player . . . or because the orchestra hadn't laughed at his jokes." Johnny Green was a popular songwriter with a huge hit song, "Body and Soul," under his belt before he came to Los Angeles as a foil for Jack Benny on Benny's radio show. He had worked for Paramount in the late 1920s and, after a stint writing shows in London, started his own orchestra. For decades, "Body and Soul" was the most recorded song in popular-music history. He joined MGM in the early '40s and immediately made a mark for himself. "I was now general music director and executive in charge of music," Green recalled. "The reason I'm stressing that point is that when I came back in '49 with those two jobs, and the enormous administrative work that I had, the opportunity for me to be part of anything as inbred and as constantly together, not only together physically, but together in terms of mental preoccupation as that Freed Unit, was impossible. . . . You see, I had powers that nobody had ever had before or after." Green reconstituted the MGM orchestra, getting rid of less-than-stellar musicians and bringing in some of the best instrumentalists from throughout the country. He also rearranged the seating of the orchestra, thus improving its recorded sound. In the 1940s, when MGM was at its peak, Green was able to amass a brilliant company of arrangers and orchestrators. Not everyone liked Green, of course. When Saul Chaplin was about to start work on *West Side Story*, Robert Wise warned him, "When I was at Metro and had appointments with [Green], he kept me waiting in his outer office for hours. He never stops yapping and telling dialect jokes and wasting a lot of time." But Chaplin knew that Green's talents were enormous and both won Oscars for their work on the film.

"I'm not a prodigy, just impertinent."
—Johnny Green

ABOVE: Leonore Gershwin, Oscar Levant, Ira Gershwin, and producer Arthur Freed at a 1951 screening of *An American in Paris*.

RIGHT: It's very clear, their love was here to stay. Gene Kelly and Leslie Caron's mutual admiration society.

Behind the Screen

■ The big ballet sequence is danced to Gershwin's sublime "American in Paris." There was to be an additional ballet danced to "Somebody Loves Me" (lyric by B. G. DeSylva), but it was never filmed.

■ When, in Oscar Levant's "Ego Fantasy," we see the conductor from the back, it's lyricist Adolph Green wielding the baton.

ANIMATED MUSICALS NOT MADE BY DISNEY

ANIMATED MUSICALS NOT MADE BY DISNEY

LEFT: 1997's *Anastasia* with songs by Stephen Flaherty and Lynn Ahrens.

W HILE WALT DISNEY DOMINATED THE AMERICAN ANIMATED FILM market (and for good reason), other studios attempted to equal Disney's success. We've got to warn you that all but one of the movies we talk about here created the scores. In 1941, Fleischer Studios, creators of the Betty Boop and Popeye cartoons, produced *Mr. Bug Goes to Town* with a score by Frank Loesser. It opened a few days before the bombing of Pearl Harbor and was a massive failure, shuttering the studio for good. The classic Broadway musical, *Finian's Rainbow*, by Burton Lane and E.Y. Harburg, went into production in 1951. Musical tracks were recorded by Frank Sinatra, Ella Fitzgerald, and Louis Armstrong, but production ceased soon after animation began. In 1962, Chuck Jones secretly wrote and produced *Gay Purr-ee* while under exclusive contract to Warner Brothers. Judy Garland starred alongside Robert Goulet and Red Buttons. Garland's favorite songwriting team, Harold Arlen and E.Y. Harburg, wrote the score, as they had done for *The Wizard of Oz*. Joe Darion, George Kleinsinger, and none other than Mel Brooks saw their Broadway musical, *Shinbone Alley*, become an animated film in 1971. The story was based on the archy and mehitabel stories by Don Marquis. Eddie Bracken and Carol Channing starred but, despite the excellence of the underlying material, it was a failure. The year 1977 saw the release of *Raggedy Ann and Andy: A Musical Adventure* with a score by Muppets favorite, Joe Raposo. The movie was a bomb. Interestingly, Broadway lyricist Sheldon Harnick and his wife Margery Gray had roles in the film.

Henry Mancini and Leslie Bricusse supplied the score to the 1992 Hanna-Barbera production of *Tom and Jerry: The Movie*. It was not well received. We're happy to report that there was the occasional hit. In 1989, Don Bluth directed *All Dogs Go to Heaven*, with a score by Broadway's Charles Strouse. While the movie wasn't a success in its theatrical release, it did amazingly well on VHS and spawned a sequel and a television series. Randy Newman, who achieved fame with a whole new generation through his songs for Pixar films, wrote the score for *Cats Won't Dance* in 1997. It was a no go. In 1999, the animated film of Rodgers and Hammerstein's classic musical *The King and I* was released. Musical theatre aficionados deemed it an abomination; the general public ignored it. In 2002, Adam Sandler had the bright idea of writing and starring in an animated Hanukkah musical for adults called *Eight Crazy Nights*. The *geld* didn't pour in. So, the question remains: despite the talents involved in all these movies, why is it that only the Disney studios have reliably successful animated musicals??

THE SCREEN'S FIRST FULL-LENGTH MUSICAL COMEDY CARTOON

Mr. BUG GOES TO TOWN

in Technicolor

Produced by MAX FLEISCHER • Directed by DAVE FLEISCHER • A PARAMOUNT PICTURE

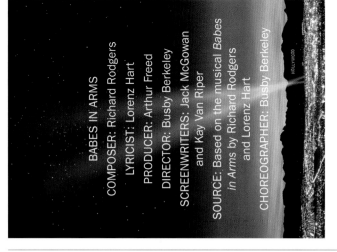

BABES IN ARMS
COMPOSER: Richard Rodgers
LYRICIST: Lorenz Hart
PRODUCER: Arthur Freed
DIRECTOR: Busby Berkeley
SCREENWRITERS: Jack McGowan and Kay Van Riper
SOURCE: Based on the musical *Babes in Arms* by Richard Rodgers and Lorenz Hart
CHOREOGRAPHER: Busby Berkeley

Synopsis

The oldsters can't hack it anymore so the whippersnappers put on a show and save the day . . . and just like that, a cliché is born.

Cast

Mickey Rooney	Mickey Moran
Judy Garland	Patsy Barton
Charles Winninger	Joe Moran
Guy Kibbee	Judge John Black
June Preisser	Rosalie Essex
Grace Hayes	Florrie Moran
Betty Jaynes	Molly Moran
Douglas McPhail	Don Brice
Rand Brooks	Jeff Steele
Leni Lynn	Dody Martin
Johnny Sheffield	Bobs
Margaret Hamilton	Martha Steele

BABES IN ARMS

MGM—OCTOBER 31, 1939

I F THE FIRST SHOW YOU TURNED TO AFTER BUYING THIS BOOK (OR WHILE SITTING AT THE coffee bar in Barnes & Noble perusing its pages) is *High School Musical*, then this chapter isn't for you. However, if you first checked out *42nd Street* or *The Pajama Game*, read on.

You see, if you're past forty, it's all over for you. You might as well climb into your Snuggie with Netflix and a hot toddy while shameless music that'll grab your sons and your daughters is being foisted on the youth of America. We've been told this for years. Every generation has rebelled against the one that came before. The flappers of the '20s scared the Victorian generation. When kids hit their late teens, they naturally want to find their own identity, and that means their own music, among other things.

Babes in Arms is a quintessential example of kids wanting to find themselves and their place in society. In fact, this movie, and the Broadway show that inspired it, started it all. Way back in 1939, Mickey and Judy's characters were rebels. Their parents tried to keep them down, so they and their friends and pet dogs marched through the streets, through backyards, over fences and into a playground, where they made a gigantic bonfire and threatened to burn down the town with their parents in it. No, wait. I'm wrong. It was worse than that. They threatened to . . . put on a show! That's right. They rebelled for a chance to put on a big musical show.

By the late 1950s, with the discovery of teenagers' spending power, consumer-driven entertainment sought to create a whole new market. Americans of a certain age were told they were out of touch with the times and, for the first time, teenagers had whole subdivisions of entertainment devoted to their tastes. In the late '50s, rock and roll was the sound of rebellion and the previous generations' taste was deemed irrelevant. In came cool and

ABOVE: The Babes take to the streets to protest being treated like children. They'll show their parents and put on a show!

FAR RIGHT: Mickey Rooney hides behind Judy Garland.

hipness. Some old fogies, including Frank Sinatra, managed to assume the mantle of coolness alongside such newcomers as Bobby Darin and Sammy Davis Jr. But the nation was undergoing a seismic change in culture. It was scary times for the oldsters. The young whippersnappers were calling the musical shots.

Yet, when we actually look back at the '50s, those were still innocent years, when Hollywood and Broadway musicals still produced many of the song hits of the day. Even the early rock movies were more jazz than actual rock and roll. Take the 1958 Columbia picture *Senior Prom*. Twenty-three-year-old pop singer Jill Corey played the lead. And the big musical numbers were sung by, making their feature film debut as a team, Louis Prima and Keely Smith, making their feature film debut backed by Sam Butera and the Witnesses. Other big musical names included Mitch Miller and Connee Boswell of Boswell Sisters fame. Ed Sullivan even makes an appearance.

"Come on . . . we need you . . . to save the show!"

Elvis Presley's early films, immensely shocking at the time, can be viewed today as blandly tame romances. Elvis was the cleanest-cut boy you could ever want your parents to meet. In the satire *Bye Bye Birdie*, when the Elvis character (Conrad Birdie) swivels his hips and sings "One Last Kiss," all the females of Sweet Apple, Ohio, swoon . . . but that's just about all he and they do. Elvis (and Pat Boone) took the truly sexy music of black singers and musicians and denatured it for white audiences. Elvis wiggled his aforementioned hips (banned from television) and Pat took his shirt off a lot in movies and the white girls drooled, but their songs were a far cry from the graphic imagery seen and heard on the mildest segments of MTV.

So . . . what are the big hit musicals of today's younger generation? Guess what? The "LPOAS" concept is alive and well in *High School Musical* and its progeny, on screens big and small: *Glee*, where even the black kids act whiter than white; Nickelodeon's *HSM* wannabe *Spectacular!* starring Nolan Gerard Funk (who played Conrad Birdie in the Broadway revival of *Bye Bye Birdie*); and another satire of '50s soft rock, *Hairspray*. Pretty tame stuff. Suddenly, the nerds are the cool ones, eager to show up those elders who just don't understand. Well, kids, sorry to break it to you, but those elders do understand. They've been in that barn themselves.

Mickey Rooney, meet Zac Efron. Judy Garland, meet Vanessa Hudgens. Sixty-seven years have passed between *Babes in Arms* and the first *High School Musical*. We bet that in the year 2073, sixty-seven years after Zac and Vanessa first expressed themselves through song and dance, two other kids, perhaps living on a space station circling the globe, will rebel against the older generation and insist on putting on a show. But *Babes in Arms* did it first . . . in a classic form that has never been beaten. ■

Behind the Screen

■ When we talk about the enduring cliché of the "Let's put on a show" musical, it's difficult to assign credit. The original Broadway script of *Babes in Arms* was written by Rodgers and Hart, so they get credit for the idea. But a host of MGM scribes fleshed it out and made its naif "LPOAS" aspect endearing and enduring (and remember, the cliché largely came later, with *Babes* its model). Jack McGowan adapted the Broadway original; he was followed by writers Noel Langley, Florence Ryerson, Edgar Allan Woolf, Anita Loos, Sid Silvers, and Joe Laurie; and finally, Kay Van Riper and director Busby Berkeley made their contributions. So it is with Hollywood.

Georgie Stoll

Musical director, conductor, mentor to the young André Previn, and Louis B. Mayer's pinochle partner, Georgie Stoll was one of the most important cogs in the MGM musical factory. In his memoir, *No Minor Chords*, Previn describes Stoll's office as filthy: "The carpet was torn and stained, the piano scarred and burnt and so desperately out of tune as to make it the object of derision in a whorehouse. There were production schedules of movies that had been made ten years earlier Scotch-taped to the walls, and his desk was the only one I have ever seen in my life that had ants on it." Sweet and supportive, he was described by Hugh Martin as "greatly loved by everyone, including me." A firm believer in equality, Stoll brought black arranger Calvin Jackson to MGM, where they worked on *Anchors Aweigh*. Stoll won an Oscar for his score for that film—he would be nominated a total of nine times in the course of his career. A favorite of producers Arthur Freed and Joe Pasternak, Stoll worked for thirty years, with every one from Mickey and Judy to Elvis (on *Viva Las Vegas* and others). His first assignment was on *Go West Young Man* in 1936, and almost one hundred films later, his last assignment was to score the 1966 *Made in Paris*.

THE BAND WAGON

COMPOSER: Arthur Schwartz
LYRICIST: Howard Dietz
PRODUCER: Arthur Freed
DIRECTOR: Vincente Minnelli
SCREENWRITER: Betty Comden and Adolph Green
CHOREOGRAPHER: Michael Kidd

Synopsis

Girls, gams, and laughs triumph over pretension in the making of a Broadway show. Along the way, we get lots of great revue numbers.

Cast

Fred Astaire	Tony Hunter
Cyd Charisse	Gabrielle Gerard
Oscar Levant	Lester Marton
Nanette Fabray	Lily Marton
Jack Buchanan	Jeffrey Cordova
James Mitchell	Paul Byrd

THE BAND WAGON

MGM—AUGUST 7, 1953

Talk about your sixth floor walk-up! Fred Astaire in "The Girl Hunt Ballet" from The Band Wagon.

PROPERTIES THAT HAD FOUND THEIR WAY INTO THE HEARTS OF THE PUBLIC IN ANOTHER form were and still are attractive to Hollywood. Think about it. Most of the great Hollywood musicals are based on a previous movie, Broadway show, novel, or (in the case of biomusicals such as *Night and Day* and *Till the Clouds Roll By*) a songwriter's catalog. But it is tough to dip into the biographical well twice—and sometimes even once, if the songwriter in question doesn't have an interesting backstory that can be embellished at will.

And so, the catalog musical was born, in which songs from the '30s are integrated (or shoehorned) into a brand-new story. The songwriting team of Howard Dietz and Arthur Schwartz had created a string of highly successful revues on Broadway in the '30s and '40s. Their book shows weren't nearly as successful. So, there were lots and lots of Dietz-and-Schwartz songs that had become popular hits without ever appearing in movies. They could all be pressed into service, once a story was constructed around them. Comden and Green's screenplay is their second funniest after *Singin' in the Rain.*

Chief among these songs-without-a-story was their most famous one, "Dancing in the Dark," which they'd written for an original Broadway revue also called *The Band Wagon* (no relation to the movie except for some songs and Fred Astaire). In the film, it occupies a prime spot as Astaire and Charisse's big number, though, surprisingly, the lyric is never sung. The remainder of the film score is a rundown of Dietz and Schwartz's greatest hits from *Three's a Crowd*, *The Little Show*, *Flying Colors*, and other shows. Ingeniously, MGM managed to craft a coherent musical comedy around the songs it wanted to use.

There are a few other catalog shows on our list of ten: *Funny Face*, *Singin' in the Rain*, *Tin Pan Alley*; *Easter Parade*, and *White Christmas*. The scores of the last two are by the king of the genre, Irving Berlin. He was there when talkies first began to sing: "Blue Skies" was crooned by Al Jolson in *The Jazz Singer*. Berlin's hits woven into new scores more than those of any other songwriter. *On the Avenue*, *Alexander's Ragtime Band*, and *Blue Skies*, as well as *Easter Parade* and *White Christmas*, all feature songs from the

Berlin catalog with a new song sprinkled in here and there. Berlin's last proposed film, *Say It with Music*, would have been yet another catalog musical—but MGM dropped it in the 1970s. And with its cancellation another era ended, as Arthur Freed left the studio.

In recent years, following the mega-success of *Mamma Mia*, Broadway has revived the idea of creating musicals around song-writers' catalogs, but nearly all of their attempts—including such gems as *Good Vibrations* and *All Shook Up*—have failed. But if you look over the list of Hollywood musicals constructed in this manner, the track record is remarkably good. *The Band Wagon* is among the best of them. ■

"Oh, that's perfectly all right, Fred, I drive everybody crazy."

—Vincente Minnelli to Fred Astaire on the set of
The Band Wagon

Cyd Charisse

Legs. That's what comes to mind when you think of Cyd Charisse. She may have been born Tula Ellice Finklea, but even as a small child she was Cyd Charisse inside. Dancer Gwen Verdon took dance classes with the preteen Charisse, er . . . Finklea, and remembered that the class was "in awe of her beauty and appalled by her underwear." Charisse wore pink undies. Shocking! Even then there was fire under the cool, cool surface. Charisse couldn't sing and was always dubbed, but she was a knockout in the dance and looks departments. And though she came across as slightly bionically beautiful—almost too perfect, which matched her sometimes chilly, almost robotic, demeanor—she was well suited to some roles. Her frigid Communist emissary in *Silk Stockings* simply needed Fred Astaire to defrost her. When she ultimately let down her hair (as in *Silk Stockings* and *It's Always Fair Weather*), she let loose in dance. For some of her career Charisse didn't have speaking parts, relegated to individual dance numbers such as in *Deep in My Heart* and *Singin' in the Rain's* "Broadway Melody" sequence. Dance partner expert Fred Astaire loved dancing with her, and his description of her is apt—"beautiful dynamite."

SONGS

"By Myself" ■ "High and Low" ■ "I Guess I'll Have to Change My Plan" ■ "I Love Louisa" ■ "Louisiana Hayride" ■ "New Sun in the Sky" ■ "A Shine on Your Shoes" ■ "Something to Remember You By" ■ "That's Entertainment" ■ "Triplets"

TOP: Pyramid scheme. Jack Buchanan, Nanette Fabray, Oscar Levant, and Fred Astaire have plans to save a flop show.

CENTER: Arthur Schwartz (at piano) and Howard Dietz (standing)perform the songs that Cyd Charisse won't be singing (she was dubbed) in *The Band Wagon*.

LEFT: Va va voom!! Charisse demonstrates the proper way to sit on a bar stool in a tight dress in *Meet Me in Las Vegas*.

"Cyd was an inch taller and had longer legs; and her long legs made her look steamlined like the Chrysler building. Fred was General Motors."

—Howard Dietz

BEACH BLANKET BINGO

AMERICAN INTERNATIONAL—APRIL 14, 1965

BEACH BLANKET BINGO

PRODUCERS: James H. Nicholson and Samuel Z. Arkoff

DIRECTOR: William Asher

SCREENWRITER: William Asher

CHOREOGRAPHER: Jack Baker

Synopsis

Frankie and Annette live the American dream day and night on the beach without ever getting sand in their bathing suits.

Cast

Frankie Avalon	Frankie
Annette Funicello	Dee Dee
Deborah Walley	Bonnie Graham
Harvey Lembeck	Eric Von Zipper
John Ashley	Steve Gordon
Jody McCrae	Bonehead
Donna Loren	Donna
Marta Kristen	Lorelei
Linda Evans	Sugar Kane
Don Rickles	Big Drop
Paul Lynde	Bullets
Donna Michelle	Animal
Buster Keaton	Buster

Annette poses with Frankie Avalon. No, wait, that's a surfboard.

GIRLS JUST WANT TO HAVE FUN—AND BOYS, TOO, ESPECIALLY TEENS WHO, IN THE early '60s, were really feeling their oats, newly empowered by a culture that was putting the spotlight on their tastes. *Bye Bye Birdie* was the first important cultural showcase of the growing chasm between teens and adults and the new teen aesthetic. "Why can't they be like we were?" chanted the parents, but once the teen bandwagon (or should we say the American Bandstand) got rolling there was no stopping it. Hollywood, following the lead of the record companies and radio stations, saw there was money to be made from America's callow youth with their utterly disposable incomes.

Which brings us to Samuel J. Arkoff, Roger Corman, and others who invented an entirely new genre of movies, the teen flick. Corman specialized in the quickie movie made fast and loose and on the cheap. If the film failed, nothing much was lost, but if it succeeded, there were great profits to be had. And the postpubescent audience seemed undemanding in its tastes.

Arkoff, for his part, realized the golden (as in ticket sales) virtues of sun, sand, and partial nudity. He revived the California dream that had been born years before, when the movies first began.

In the early '30s would be stars from Sheboygan, Oshkosh, and points west flocked to Hollywood with the dream of being discovered by MGM or Fox. Some, like Janet Gaynor, star of the first and best *A Star Is Born*, realized that dream. In the 1950s, people were still trying to make it big in Hollywood but thousands more were traipsing to California simply for a radical change in lifestyle. The looming threat of the Russians and "the bomb" fueled a sense of paranoia and a desire to live for the moment. If we were all going to die, better to do it on a sunny beach than in a basement fallout shelter.

And that brings us, if overly seriously, to the trifle *Beach Blanket Bingo*, the best of a mindless genre of films whose charms completely eluded anyone over twenty-five and vexed cinematographers with all that sun, surf, and glare. To fulfill the bitchin' formula, producers had to start with one cute, perpetually horny but sexually unthreatening pop singer, preferably of Italian-American extraction with bonus points if the came from South Philadelphia. To that they added a pretty, vivacious girl who could fill out a bikini but keep her virtue intact. It was all the better if she could sing and swivel convincingly. Neither of these youngsters had to have the talent of young stars of the past, like Deanna Durbin or Jane Powell. They just had to remind you of the boy and girl in your senior class that you had a crush on—but even more so.

These living and breathing Barbie and Ken dolls flirted and kissed and had summer flings but like those dolls, underneath their bathing suits there was nothing. At all. There were no protests from the Bible Belt about these two. (Elvis, on the other hand, was proper and polite on screen but there was no question that he had something going on . . . down there. Heck they had to cut him off at the waist for television!)

We admit that though they were no Clark Gable and Claudette Colbert, Frankie Avalon and Annette Funicello were eminently watchable. They acted just fine, sang well enough, looked good, and could carry on conversations while surfing the waves (thanks to the miracle of rear projection). Most important, they clicked, becoming the Nelson Eddy and Jeanette MacDonald of their generation. It was a pleasure to be in their company.

The songs were boppy affairs, as lightweight as the plots. No one remembered either one after the film was over. But it was all a lark, and best of all, fulfilled the fantasy that we might save up from our paper route or lawn mowing to spend a summer living on the beach, surfing by day, and singing and dancing around a campfire by night. There'd be kissing and cuddling and, best of all, no adults (read parents) to tell us to come in before we caught our death of cold.

Strangely, though there were no parents in these movies, there were adults around. And what an odd lot they were. Some were biker dudes, equally as unthreatening as the kids on the beach. Harvey Lembeck, an underrated talent, put considerable energy into stirring things up along with Don Rickles in manic mode. Paul Lynde, who had previously asked the question, "What's the matter with kids today?" in *Bye Bye Birdie*, only added to the weirdness. And then there was the most unlikely adult you'd ever expect to see on the beach at Malibu in 1965—Buster Keaton, silent screen star, old enough to be the kids' grandfather. He'd be goofing around, falling down—adding a bit of surrealism to paradise. If the kids were bland, the adults were bizarre and charged with supplying the comic relief—hey, adults were made to be laughed at, right?

The casts comprised a homogeneous group: no blacks, no homosexuals (unless you count Paul Lynde), no foreigners, no one different. But it should be noted that blacks, homosexuals, and foreigners all liked these films fine. Today, when everything is teen culture is sex and irony, *Beach Blanket Bingo* and others of its ilk seem remarkably naïve. I suppose we like them for exactly that reason. ■

Annette Funicello

Like Judy Garland in *The Wizard of Oz*, Annette Funicello, Mouseketeer, was bound for glory. Bound in the sense of having her breasts cinched so she wouldn't look so . . . mature. Even when she was loaned out to American International by Uncle Walt, he asked that she wear a one-piece bathing suit, not one of those Commie-inspired bikinis. Annette was pretty, good natured, likeable and, well, perfect. She was always up for a good time and seemed to have a ball on the beach with Frankie Avalon.

Unlike that other all-American girl, Farrah Fawcett, Annette never graduated into dramatic roles; she stayed eternally sunny—though not in a cloying, sticky way. When she showed up in commercials as a mother hawking peanut butter, it seemed she hadn't aged a bit. As the American equivalent of a French gamine (though more voluptuous and self-sufficient), we could see her playing an Americanized version of *Gigi* or *Lili*. To those of us who grew up watching her, Annette will always be our favorite Mouseketeer.

SONGS

"Beach Blanket Bingo" ■ "Cycle Set" (Gary Usher and Roger Christian) ■ "Fly Boy" ■ "Follow Your Leader" ■ "I Think You Think" ■ "I'll Never Change Him" (Gary Usher and Roger Christian) ■ "It Only Hurts When I Cry" ■ "New Love" ■ "These Are the Good Times"

ABOVE: This rockin' press conference features Earl Wilson (with pad), Paul Lynde (with tie), Annette Funicello (peeking out), Frankie Avalon (in bathing suit), and future *Dynasty* star Linda Evans (in stripes).

RIGHT: Frankie and Annette, America's fun couple in the 1960s.

Behind the Screen

■ Note future *Dallas* star Linda Evans in the cast list. Her character was named Sugar Kane, the same as Marilyn Monroe's in *Some Like It Hot*.

BEAUTY AND THE BEAST

COMPOSER: Alan Menken

LYRICIST: Howard Ashman

PRODUCER: Don Hahn

DIRECTORS: Gary Trousdale and Kirk Wise

SCREENWRITER: Linda Woolverton

SOURCE: Based on the story *Beauty and the Beast* by Jeanne-Marie Leprince de Beaumont

Synopsis

Beastliness, it turns out, is only skin deep—especially when it involves a spell that can be broken by the love of beautiful girl and a half-dozen decent songs. Can you say, "Happily ever after"? Don't forget to visit our gift shop.

Cast

Paige O'Hara.............Belle
Robby Benson ....Beast
Richard White.............Gaston
Jerry Orbach ....Lumiere
David Ogden Stiers ......Cogsworth
Angela Lansbury ....Mrs. Potts
Bradley Michael Pierce...Chip
Rex Everhart...............Maurice
Jo Anne Worley...........Wardrobe

Behind the Screen

- Only Belle and Beast wear the color blue, distinguishing them from the rest of the characters.

BEAUTY AND THE BEAST

DISNEY—NOVEMBER 22, 1991

ABOVE: Belle (that's "Beauty" *en français*) and the Beast.

BOTTOM RIGHT: David Ogden Stiers, Angela Lansbury, and Jerry Orbach voicing Cogsworth, Mrs. Potts, and Lumiere.

W ITH DISNEY'S PASSING IN 1966, THE STUDIO SEEMED TO LOSE ITS ARTISTIC footing. Disney's last animated feature under his supervision was *The Jungle Book*, which, typically, had little or nothing to do with its original source but was entertaining nonetheless. Then followed a very dark period. The first cartoon release following Walt's death was *The Aristocats* in 1970, a sort of a *101 Dalmatians* with felines. *Robin Hood* was next up, and featured caricatures rather than characters and an overdose of slapstick. *The Jungle Book* had been the first Disney film to feature the voices of name actors, and *Robin Hood* continued that dubious practice. The name actors didn't always have distinctive voices. Think, on the other hand, of Verna Felton in *Dumbo* and *Cinderella*, Cliff Edwards as Jiminy Cricket, and even Adriana Caselotti's Snow White. Those were *voices*.

The Rescuers (1977) brought new animation talent to Disney and an entirely delightful picture in the old Disney tradition. Even the score reflected the mix of old and new, with Sammy Fain of *Alice in Wonderland* supplying the music and Carol Bayer Sager, a contemporary songwriter, providing the lyrics.

The Fox and the Hound, *Mickey's Christmas Carol*, and *The Black Cauldron* (Disney's first PG animated film) all had excellent animation but suffered in the storytelling. Then came *The Great Mouse Detective*, an altogether entertaining film. *Oliver and Company* was also a success—and then came the revolution.

The Little Mermaid hit the screen in 1989, over fifty years after *Snow White*, and exhibited the same kind of artistic integrity. The strength of *The Little Mermaid* lay in its inception as an animated musical comedy in the Broadway style, just like the big five Disney classics—*Snow White, Pinocchio, Dumbo, Fantasia,* and *Bambi.*

Broadway songwriters Howard Ashman and Alan Menken supplied the songs and they fulfill the same function they would in a well-made Broadway show. Their numbers delineate characters, advance the plot, and entertain in a grand manner.

Following Disney's next animated feature, *The Rescuers Down Under,* came *Beauty and the Beast.* For the first time in Disney history, the story was completely scripted before animation or recording began. Interestingly, the new generation of Disney creators continued the tradition of featuring a young woman as the protagonist, but with a decidedly up-to-date, dare we say feminist, twist.

But Belle's admirable nature plays only a minor role in the success of a picture loaded with interesting characters, especially the servants of the Beast. Cogsworth the clock, Lumiere the dashing candelabra, and especially Mrs. Potts the teapot and her son, Chip, are unique characters with lots and lots of personality. The voice casting was spot on. Yes, David Ogden Stiers, Jerry Orbach, and Angela Lansbury happen to be well-known actors and were able to use their voice to create memorable characters, bringing to life the beautifully crafted drawings.

Beauty and the Beast was in itself groundbreaking, thanks to developments in computer technology. The ballroom sequence celebrating the waltz between Belle and the Beast is exquisite. The ballroom was "drawn" entirely in the computer, whereas Belle and the Beast were hand-drawn. Surprisingly, the two techniques complement each other well. The film's opening shots, reminiscent of Peter Pan's flight, has a three-dimensional quality that borders on the realistic. In the old days of Disney, animators used the Disney-patented multiplane camera to create a sense realistic depth; nowadays, computers can achieve the same effect for much less cost.

Menken and Ashman's score has the old Broadway pizzazz, just as *The Little Mermaid's* does—but *Beauty's* ballads are better and more deeply emotional. Perhaps because Ariel is every inch a teenager whereas Belle is more of a young woman, the songs are more adult in tone. Sadly, Howard Ashman died of AIDS before the film was released. He had started work on Disney's next cartoon feature, *Aladdin,* but was unable to finish the picture.

Disney's animation unit was in its second golden age. Menken and Ashman won Academy Awards, and the film was nominated in the Best Picture category—the first time ever for an animated film. Since then, there has been a stage version of the film on Broadway, which may have seemed odd at the time but now is a natural part of the Disney life cycle. Its great success provided the Disney Corporation with a solid foothold in the Broadway market.

Beauty and the Beast's success proved that the success of *The Little Mermaid* was not a fluke. The studio went on to produce *Aladdin* and *The Lion King,* two more blockbusters. It also sparked an interest on the part of other studios in animation—but others' tries at traditionally animated musicals were all failures. Today, computer-generated films such as *Toy Story* and its Pixar cousins, *Ice Age* and its sequels, *Horton Hears a Who,* and the Oscar-winning *Up* dominate the animation field. ■

SONGS

"Be Our Guest" ■ "Beauty and the Beast" ■ "Belle" ■ "Gaston" ■ "The Mob Song" ■ "Something There"

Alan Menken and Howard Ashman

The songwriting team of Alan Menken (composer) and Howard Ashman (lyricist) began with the Off-Broadway musical *God Bless You, Mr. Rosewater.* That one didn't make much of an impact but their next show, *Little Shop of Horrors,* was a huge hit, the biggest of their theatrical careers. Neither writer's other shows amounted to much but when the team went to Hollywood and Disney animation, their talents bloomed. *The Little Mermaid* was followed by *Beauty and the Beast* and *Aladdin.* After Ashman's death during production of *Aladdin,* Menken went on to write the music for *Pocahontas, The Hunchback of Notre Dame, Hercules,* and *Home on the Range.* But he never again achieved the success of his Hollywood work with Ashman.

ABOVE: Alan Menken (at piano) and Howard Ashman at the start of their greatest success.

BELOW: Lumiere channels Maurice Chevalier.

BELLE OF THE NINETIES

PARAMOUNT—SEPTEMBER 21, 1934

ABOVE: Libby Taylor looks askance as John Miljan offers Mae West a small token of his esteem.

BELOW RIGHT: Mae with Mickey Hargitay in her 1954 nightclub act. What do you think Hargitay's talents were?

Let us direct you to the hit song from this film, "My old flame." It was often covered by other artists but Mae West's original was never equaled, starting with the line, "My old flame, I can't even remember his name." That, in two simple lines, sums up Mae West's enduring image. She was an original, unlike any actress before or since. She came out of a tradition that included Anna Held and Lillian Russell, voluptuous yet impermeably corseted, proper-mouthed leading ladies at the turn of the century. Imagine the shock to the Victorian and Edwardian morals of the country when audiences were confronted by Mae West, with her sashaying hips and sexy drawl of double and even single entendres. She was a feminist in an age when women were expected to aspire to be pure and untouchable upon an unreachable pedestal. Mae West projected experience and the promise of palpable pleasures . . . but on her own terms.

George Jean Nathan wrote of West, "What the 'movie' audiences had uniformly been privileged to see before, over the years, had been nothing but an endless succession of imported lesbians, spindle-shanked, flat-chested flappers, forty-year-old Baby Dolls, beauty parlor imitations of women, and Sylvia-massaged stringbeans, in not one of whom there was any real, genuine, honest-to-God female quality to interest even a vegetarian cannibal. In the midst of this dearth, the Mlle. West came like a rainfall, a veritable torrent, upon a dry desert. Here, unmistakably, whatever one might think of her art, was a woman, a female. No little dried-up cutie, no pretty little narrow-shouldered skeleton of a chicken, no parched and skinny pseudo-vamp, no trumped-up, artificial siren, but a good, large, full, round, old-time 1890 woman, with 'woman' up and down and sidewise written plainly on her every feature—and all other places."

SONGS

"Memphis Blues" (W. C. Handy, George A. Norton, and Sam Coslow) ■ "My American Beauty" ■ "My Old Flame" ■ "Troubled Waters" ■ "When a St. Louis Woman Comes Down to New Orleans" (Arthur Johnston, Gene Austin, and Sam Coslow)

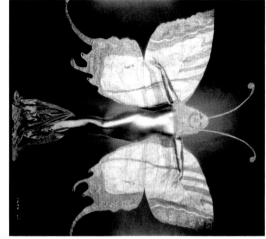

TOP LEFT AND RIGHT: Two of Mae West's little outfits: just little somethings to wear to the beach.

Mae West

Heavy lidded, her hourglass figure a throwback to the days of Lillian Russell, with her soft, seductive drawl, Mae West always lived her private and professional life on the edge of established morality (sometimes crossing the line). She was a supremely confident and intelligent actress and writer whose considerable assets kept her in the public eye for sixty-seven years. Her outspoken ideas were dramatized in controversial plays, some of which were either banned outright or closed by the police. Her plays dealt with homosexuality, cross-dressing, women's rights, and feminist issues (though she denied being a feminist) decades before general acceptance. She was also an early supporter of African-American equality; even the black maids in her movies had their dignity and a special relationship with the character West played. Because of her outspokenness she found herself in jail on morals charges on at least one occasion. It could easily have been more—but she developed a method for avoiding the censors when she moved from Broadway to film at age thirty-eight: the double entendre. During her reign at Paramount, she earned the studio millions of dollars and at least one of her pictures, *She Done Him Wrong*, saved the studio from bankruptcy. After her stint at Paramount, she was enticed by Universal Pictures to star opposite W. C. Fields in *My Little Chickadee*, a tremendous hit. Then it was on to Columbia and 1943's *The Heat's On*. After that, West left the movies and concentrated on touring in stage productions, especially her play *Diamond Lil*. In 1937, her quips on a radio show with Charlie McCarthy drew the ire of the morality police and the FCC, whereupon she took a thirteen-year break from the medium. After conquering Las Vegas and the rest of the country in a famed nightclub act and making several television appearances, she returned to the screen in the 1970 campfest *Myra Breckenridge*. Her figure remained remarkably intact but by then her face had become a caricature. Her last picture was 1978's *Sextette*; however, by this time, her career had clearly passed its date of expiration. She was the last of her breed, managing the remarkable feat of remaining relevant (or at least an object of curiosity) long after the cultural ideal of femininity had changed. Certainly no one could equal her in her prime, and her persona remains unique in the history of entertainment. ■

It was those qualities, of course, that drew the ire of self-proclaimed protectors of the nation's morals—the Legion of Decency, the Seamen's Institute, the YWCA, the YMCA, the Campfire Girls of America, the Boy Scouts of America, the American Association of University Women, the National Council of Catholic Women, the Young Ladies' Institute, the Council of the Methodist Episcopal Church, the National Council of Jewish Women, the American Citizenship Council, the Federation of Women's Clubs, and so on. Hollywood's answer to the conservative uproar was to set up the code of ethics under the control of Will Hays in New York and Joseph I. Breen in Hollywood. The Hays Office set down the rules of engagement and every studio was forced to sign on to their list of dos and don'ts. Although the code was entered into the books four years earlier, it was not until 1934—the year *Belle* was produced—that every film script, every lyric, every property—including fictitious characters and those who portrayed them—came under their control and approval.

Mae West came under particular scrutiny, *Belle of the Nineties* was, according to the Hays Office, "a yarn which is quite patently a glorification of prostitution and violent crime. From the outset, the leading character is established as a person with a long and violent criminal record who displays all the habits and practices of a prostitute and aids in the operation of a dishonest gambling house, drugs a prizefighter, robs her employer and deliberately sets fire to his premises and in the end goes off scot-free in the company of her illicit lover who is a self-confessed criminal, thief and murderer."

Paramount had the script rewritten and retakes were undertaken according to the objections of the Hays Code. But no one could stop West from inserting her own sly digs and wisecracks into the screenplay. And Breen understood the problems with any picture that starred West. He wrote to his staff, "Just so long as we have Mae West on our hands, with the particular kind of story she goes in for, we are going to have trouble. Difficulty is inherent with a Mae West picture. Lines and pieces of business, which in the script seem to be thoroughly innocuous, turn out when shown on the screen to be questionable at best, when they are not definitely offensive." Local censorship boards took their scissors to prints of the film or banned it outright from their communities.

Despite or perhaps due to the hubbub, Paramount was making a fortune off West. Sure, it cost extra for retakes and rewrites but the films were still good, their star a celebrity. Still, Hollywood's atmosphere of lascivious-minded suppression took its toll on West. Although she later stated that the interference by the Hays Office was "much ado about nothing," she eventually quit movies, tired of the censorship and picking-apart of her writing and performing.

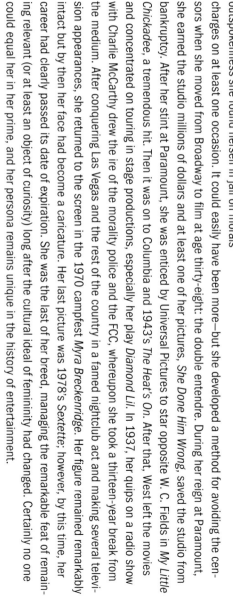

BORN TO DANCE

COMPOSER: Cole Porter
LYRICIST: Cole Porter
PRODUCER: Jack Cummings
DIRECTOR: Roy Del Ruth
SCREENWRITERS: Jack McGowan
and Sid Silvers
CHOREOGRAPHER: Dave Gould

Synopsis

Boy meets girl and a nice, low-key romance unfolds as they stroll through the park. Girl gets boy but more important, girl gets show. And what a show! Among other things, it's got hundreds of dancers on the deck of a battleship and three huge cannons shooting overhead.

Cast

Eleanor Powell	Nora Paige
James Stewart	Ted Barker
Virginia Bruce	Lucy James
Una Merkel	Jenny Saks
Sid Silvers	"Gunny" Saks
Frances Langford	"Peppy" Turner
Raymond Walburn	Captain Percival Dingby
Alan Dinehart	James "Mac" McKay
Buddy Ebsen	"Mush" Tracy
Juanita Quigley	Sally Saks

BORN TO DANCE

MGM—NOVEMBER 27, 1936

J AMES STEWART COSTARRED WITH ELEANOR POWELL IN THIS SINGING AND DANCING extravaganza. Yes, James Stewart—an unlikely choice, as he himself admitted. But he didn't shrink from the job of putting across the big ballad "Easy to Love." He was charming and natural and seemed to be feeling no pain—even if the audience felt a twinge or two. Stewart had appeared in Princeton variety shows (in drag, we think), but that was pretty much the extent of his musical experience. Really—didn't MGM have any established singers and dancers on their roster who could've filled the bill? Apparently not. MGM insisted on trying to make musical stars out of their leading men (and some women), usually with indifferent results.

Metro cast Robert Montgomery in the wonderful trifle "Love in the Rough," where he was forced to sing and dance. While he was appealing in the part, his musical talent was close to undetectable. Clark Gable did a song-and-dance routine to "Puttin' on the Ritz" with a bevy of chorus girls in *Idiot's Delight.* He gave it his all but didn't have a song-and-dance man's physical gifts, and gravity definitely had the upper hand. Nonsingers sounded good after audio engineers pieced together many takes into an acceptable performance. It's rumored that Gene Kelly and Lili Pons benefited from this technique.

Over at RKO, Joan Fontaine partnered with Fred Astaire in *A Damsel in Distress.* It must be said that she's utterly delightful and sweet and almost apologetic in her performance. (The surprise of the picture is what terrific hoofers George Burns and Gracie Allen are absolutely holding their own with Astaire.) Hats off to all of those brave souls whose seven-year contracts forced them to embarrass themselves in musicals.

ABOVE: Eleanor Powell gets out the big guns in *Born to Dance.* (Those same guns would later appear in the finale of *Hit the Deck.*)

OPPOSITE: Eleanor Powell and the gangly Jimmy Stewart.

SONGS

■ "Easy to Love" ■ "Entrance of Lucy James" ■
"Hey Baby Hey" ■ "I've Got You Under My Skin" ■
"Love Me, Love My Pekinese" ■ "Rap Tap on
Wood" ■ "Rolling Home" ■ "Swingin' the Jinx
Away"

Eleanor Powell

Eleanor Powell was known as the female Fred Astaire. Like that other great dancer, she choreographed her own tap routines, but her talents stretched far beyond tap to include ballet, acrobatics, and prop work. She could seemingly do anything and do it all better than anyone. If you are surprised that she isn't better known, perhaps it is because she retired in 1945 after her son was born. Powell certainly wasn't demure in her routines. Whereas Ginger Rogers brought sex appeal to Fred Astaire and let him lead the way in their dances together, Eleanor Powell danced as an equal to the men who partnered her. She had an almost masculine style in such films as *Broadway Melody of 1936*, *Rosalie*, and *Ship Ahoy*. Having started her career on Broadway in such hits as *Follow Thru*, *Hot Cha!* and *At Home Abroad*, Powell excelled in dances that had little character development or even relation to the plot. So it was in her movies as well. In the final analysis, the only thing her solos lacked was emotion. They were all erect posture, concrete smile, remarkable technique, and astounding stamina. Like Astaire, Powell believed in rehearsing and then rehearsing some more. For her appearance with Red Skelton in *I Dood It!* Powell and choreographer Bobby Connelly (with whom she had worked on Broadway) devised a difficult dance that employed a lariat. She spent sixteen weeks learning to throw the thing, under the tutelage of expert ropesman Sam Garrett. Always an arresting presence, in *Born to Dance* she held the complete attention of the audience—even with hundreds of sailors and a battleship behind her.

Cole Porter

Cole Porter liked the good life and he was lucky enough to have been born with the bankroll to support his high living. Unlike such other high livers as lyricists Al Dubin or Mack Gordon, Porter always exhibited class. Although he seemed shallow to some, his deeply emotional lyrics reveal great depth and complexity. He could write the most devastating songs (both music and lyric, thank you very much) as well as the most ribald and hilarious ones for the great clowns of Broadway and Hollywood. He wrote about high society ("Miss Otis Regrets," "Thank You So Much, Mrs. Lowsborough-Goodby") and low ("Friendship" and "Love for Sale"). His songs about the rich and pampered depicted them as unfulfilled despite their luxuries. To him, the lower classes had more fun and were happier. As Porter put it, "Even the janitor's wife has a perfectly good love life." He never put down anyone because of their place on the social ladder. A most facile writer, Porter was happy to write new music and lyric if a song—even a good one—wasn't working in a show. He wrote "It's Delovely" for *Born to Dance* but it was rejected, so Porter simply wrote another song and put "It's Delovely" into his Broadway show *Red, Hot and Blue!* Porter's lyrics could be as intricate as those of anyone writing or silly and simple. While composers such as Harry Warren were writing simple songs for films, Porter wrote a Gilbert and Sullivanesque operetta sequence into *Born to Dance's* "Entrance of Lucy James," concluding with the song "Love Me, Love My Pekinese." The song is supremely wacky and satirical. "I've Got You Under My Skin," also written for *Born to Dance*, has an especially long melodic line, making it very sophisticated while the lyric is supremely sophisticated and satirical. No surprise that it is a classic in the canon of American standards.

All-star wartime revusicals (revues masquerading as musicals) forced lots of straight performers to exit their comfort zone, and audiences were in on the joke. *Thank Your Lucky Stars* was Warner's entry into the field. In that film, Bette Davis pulled off "They're Either too Young or Too Old" through sheer muscle and grit. No sooner did she get through it than she was forced into a jitterbug version of the song. What a gal! Apparently a glutton for punishment, later in her career she appeared on Broadway in the musical revue *Two's Company*. Also appearing in *Thank Your Lucky Stars* were musical neophytes Olivia de Havilland, Ida Lupino, and George Tobias, who sang the eminently forgettable song "The Dreamer." It wasn't entirely their fault that the song never made it: Dinah Shore sang it subsequently and it still stank. Ann Sheridan wasn't a musical star but, to her credit, she did an excellent job with "Love Isn't Born (It's Made)." And Errol Flynn talk/sang "That's What You Jolly Well Get" without a hint of embarrassment, long before Rex Harrison made an art out of not holding a note. But the biggest surprise of the film is Hattie McDaniel, who performed "Ice Cold Katie" opposite the shuffling stereotype of Willie Best. Man, could that hot mama (Mammy?) swing!

More recent films have continued the proud tradition of casting leading men and women who just couldn't hack it. They tried their best, failed miserably, and had egg on their face in musical film kamikaze missions. Take Elizabeth Taylor in *A Little Night Music*. Her performance would have been wonderful if she had been dubbed—but she wasn't, and Hal Prince's film career went down with the film (unfortunately, as he showed evidence of talent for the medium with the stylish *Something for Everyone*).

Sure, Richard Burton proved he could pull it off magnificently in Broadway's *Camelot*, but every British actor isn't Burton or even Rex Harrison (what hath Rex wrought?). Peter O'Toole was enrolled in *Goodbye Mr. Chips* but flunked out of Musical Comedy 101 trying to hold his own opposite Petula Clark. Even more unlikely was the casting of Peter Finch in *Lost Horizon*. (After that one, audiences stormed out of the theater crying, "We're mad as hell and we're not going to take it anymore!") Joan Collins proved herself a game gal in a variety of roles but try as she might, and she's tried mighty hard, she just can't sing! *The Road to Hong Kong* and *Heronymous Merkin* are but two attempts that prove "try, try again" doesn't always work.

Just in case, dear reader, you think that Hollywood has learned its lesson, we leave you with four words: Renée Zellweger in *Chicago*. ■

THE BROADWAY MELODY

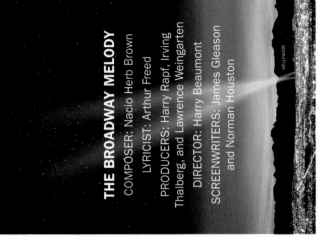

THE BROADWAY MELODY

COMPOSER: Nacio Herb Brown

LYRICIST: Arthur Freed

PRODUCERS: Harry Rapf, Irving Thalberg, and Lawrence Weingarten

DIRECTOR: Harry Beaumont

SCREENWRITERS: James Gleason and Norman Houston

Synopsis

A Duncan Sisters type act wants to hit the big time on Broadway. The show goes on but only one of the sisters wins the love of the song-and-dance man, to the chagrin of the other.

Cast

Charles King	Eddie Kearns
Anita Page	Queenie Mahoney
Bessie Love	Hank Mahoney
Jed Prouty	Uncle Jed
Kenneth Thomson	Jock Warriner
Edward Dillon	Stage Manager
Mary Doran	Flo
Eddie Kane	Francis Zanfield
J. Emmett Beck	Babe Hatrick

Behind the Screen

■ This was MGM's first musical and the first all-talking musical ever. It was also the first musical to win the Academy Award, and the first in which the cast lip-synched to an already produced soundtrack. (This became necessary when the "Wedding of the Painted Doll" number was reshot after a disappointing preview.)

■ MGM didn't cast their biggest stars in the film in case it was a terrible failure.

Mary Doran, Bessie Love, Anita Page, and Charles King. Bessie Love's career, one of the longest in film history, spanned from *Georgia Pearce* in 1915 to *Ragtime*, *Reds* (both 1981), and *The Hunger* (1983).

A FTER THE PREMIERE OF *THE JAZZ SINGER*, SOUND FILMS BECAME THE RAGE AND STUDIOS geared up to produce them. Unfortunately, the studio heads were former scrap metal salesmen (Louis B. Mayer), garmentos (Samuel Goldwyn), and shoe repairer/bicycle seller/grocer/bowling alley owners (Harry Warner) before they became nickelodeon operators. None of them had any experience with putting together a musical film—or putting any sound on film, for that matter—and that complicated matters greatly.

Thus began the great stampede from the East Coast to the West Coast, as the film companies scoured Broadway and quickly signed (to limited contracts) the best composers and lyricists—or, rather, the best white composers and lyricists. Black artists such as Eubie Blake and James P. Johnson were not welcome. Just as their immigrant forefathers had pictured New York streets paved with gold, the luckier composers and lyricists envisioned a land of plenty amidst the Pacific breezes.

Some, including Harry Warren and the Gershwins, embraced the new world. Others, such as Rodgers and Hart, made a fast retreat after a few tries at Hollywood. Later, Johnny Mercer would try his hand, only to be summarily dismissed.

MGM found itself needing composers who were available immediately. They turned to homegrown talents Arthur Freed and Nacio Herb Brown, who named them the *Hollywood Music Box Revues*, a series of musical revues in Hollywood that they named the *Hollywood Music Box Revues*, a nod to the revues produced back East in Irving Berlin's Music Box Theater.

"Boy Friend" ■ "Broadway Melody" ■ "Harmony Babies from Melody Lane" ■ "Love Boat" ■ "Truthful Parson Brown" (W. Robertson) ■ "Wedding of the Painted Doll" ■ "You Were Meant for Me"

Once the songwriters were in place, the studios turned to their talent roster. It had been tough enough for the silent stars to talk on screen. Some had made the transition easily but others were hamstrung by their potent accent or a voice that didn't match their image. Who could sing?

Since the studios had little experience with book musicals, they sidestepped the conventional book show and created revues. That solved the problem of integrating songs into the stories (such as film stories were in those days). Besides, the revues could serve as expensive talent shows, helping the studios determine who might serve them best in for future musical productions. MGM produced the *Hollywood Revue of 1929*, Paramount put out *Paramount on Parade*, Fox presented the *Movietone Follies*, and Warner Brothers stepped up with *The Show of Shows*.

Of course there were some original book musicals, as well as some transfers from Broadway. *The Jazz Singer* was a kind of hybrid: it had a strong story but didn't include any numbers sung in character; rather, the songs were sung by Jolson at the piano, for his mother, or onstage at the Winter Garden Theater. This first backstage musical became the template for a whole subgenre of the musical film.

Universal's *Broadway*, Warner Brothers' *On with the Show* (with the added bonus of two-strip Technicolor), and MGM's *The Broadway Melody* (also with an early Technicolor sequence) were but three early entries in this genre. You could argue that *The Broadway Melody* wasn't the best of the backstage musicals—but it did win the Academy Award for Best Picture.

Today, *The Broadway Melody* might seem static and clichéd—but perhaps you can envision why it was such a huge success in its time. MGM's excellent production values and the film's exemplary score, featuring three future standards guaranteed its immortality. The film stoked the momentum toward talkies that had begun with *The Jazz Singer*, and movies would never be quiet again. ■

Nacio Herb Brown and Arthur Freed

The backbone of MGM musical movies, the team of composer Nacio Herb Brown and lyricist Arthur Freed began life with MGM's first musical films and ended it with the studio's last significant ones. The two began their long collaboration in 1921 but they were launched in earnest when their song "The Doll Dance" was interpolated into the 1927 stage show *Hollywood Music Box Revue*. It was for that show that they wrote their greatest hit, "Singin' in the Rain"—which made no impact whatsoever. MGM's Irving Thalberg convinced the team to come to work for MGM on the studio's first all-talking, all-singing, all-dancing musical, *The Broadway Melody*, for which they wrote the standard "You Were Meant for Me." Except for a brief breakup in 1932, the team continued writing together until 1939, when Freed became an associate producer for the studio. Of course, that didn't stop the studio from featuring their songs in subsequent musicals, and even in dramatic films with interpolated songs. For example, the aforementioned "You Were Meant for Me" was featured in *Hullabaloo*, *Forty Little Mothers*, and *Singin' in the Rain*. Brown's melodies were simple but memorable. Freed's lyrics were straightforward. There was little wordplay, little development of a theme, and even less sophistication. But the lyrics fit the music perfectly and the simple melodic and lyric lines made the songs stick in audiences' mind.

TOP RIGHT: And they say a woman is bad luck on a ship.

CENTER RIGHT: Nacio Herb Brown and Arthur Freed, the most successful songwriting team in film history.

LEFT: Harry Beaumont directs a scene from *The Broadway Melody*.

CABARET

ALLIED ARTISTS/ABC—FEBRUARY 13, 1972

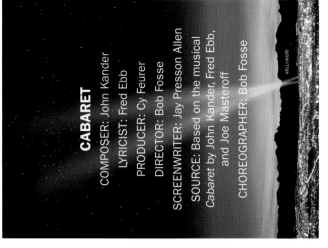

CABARET

COMPOSER: John Kander

LYRICIST: Fred Ebb

PRODUCER: Cy Feurer

DIRECTOR: Bob Fosse

SCREENWRITER: Jay Presson Allen

SOURCE: Based on the musical *Cabaret* by John Kander, Fred Ebb, and Joe Masteroff

CHOREOGRAPHER: Bob Fosse

Synopsis

Poor, talent-deprived Sally Bowles is singing in Berlin at the Kit Kat Club. Writer Brian Roberts is looking for inspiration. He sleeps with Sally and with his friend Maximilian. Sally's sleeping with Max, too. Whee!!! Then those perverted Nazis come in and ruin everything!

Cast

Liza Minnelli	*Sally Bowles*
Michael York	*Brian Roberts*
Helmut Griem	*Maximilian Von Heune*
Joel Grey	*Master of Ceremonies*
Fritz Wepper	*Fritz Wendel*
Marisa Berenson	*Natalia Landauer*
Elisabeth Neumann-Viertel	*Fraulein Schneider*
Helen Vita	*Fraulein Kost*

Joel Grey as the Emcee and the girls of the Kit Kat Club.

WAY BACK IN 1929, IN THE EARLY YEARS OF "ALL TALKING! ALL SINGING! ALL Dancing!" movies, Universal Pictures released a film version of the stage play *Broadway* as a musical. Director Paul Fejos and designer Charles Hall musicalized and Hollywoodized the original. In place of the seedy nightclub, the film's Paradise Club was an immense, impossible Art Deco behemoth. Critics castigated the film for going against the spirit of the original.

Now to *Cabaret*. In the stories by Christopher Isherwood and the subsequent stage musical, the lead character, Sally Bowles, is a self-deluded amateur talent. For the film, her talent was supersized to accommodate Liza Minnelli's larger-than-life talents.

Bob Fosse understood the world of small-time cabaret, burlesque, and vaudeville. His Kit Kat Club might have had spectacular lighting but the stage itself wasn't opened up for the movie à la *Broadway* or Busby Berkeley. Fosse kept the chorus small and the musical numbers within the boundaries of the little stage. His Kit Kat Club was nothing like *Broadway*'s Paradise Club, described by one critic as "the Cathedral of St. John the Divine." Rather, it was extraordinarily realistic for a big-budget musical.

With the exception of the anthem, "Tomorrow Belongs to Me," all the musical numbers in the film *Cabaret* take place on the Kit Kat stage. Director and auteur (we really mean it) Fosse explained, "I had to break away from movie musicals that just copy the Broadway show. Or movie musicals that copy conventions of the stage. *Singin' in the Rain*, *An American in Paris*, all the Gene Kelly, Fred Astaire musicals—they're classics. But they represent another era. Today I get very antsy watching musicals in which people are singing as they walk down the street or hang out the laundry. . . In fact, I think it looks a little silly. You can do it on the stage. The theater has its own personality—it conveys a removed reality. The movies bring that closer."

"You never thought I could direct this movie, did you? You hired me only for the fucking choreography."

—Bob Fosse to producer Cy Feuer

SONGS

"Cabaret" ■ "If You Could See Her" ■ "Maybe This Time" ■ "Married" ■ "Mein Herr" ■ "Maybe"
■ "Tomorrow Belongs to Me" ■ "Money" ■ "Two Ladies"
"Wilkommen"

ABOVE RIGHT: S·E·X. Michael York and Liza Minnelli get in the swing of decadent Berlin.

ABOVE LEFT: Joel Grey contemplates his career as the chorus walks all over him.

Fosse's choreography and movement reflect the world of the cabaret. As he put it, "I tried to make the dances look not as if they were done by me, Bob Fosse, but by some guy who is down and out. You think, 'Oh I can't really have them do *that*.' That's so embarrassing; it's so bad, so cheap.' But you think, 'But if I were the kind of guy who works with cheap cabarets and clubs, what else would I do?' So I worked from that."

Fosse's rethinking of *Cabaret* has little in common with the stage musical. He and screenwriter Hugh Wheeler (who worked uncredited) went back to the original source for inspiration, the 1939 book *Goodbye to Berlin* by Christopher Isherwood. So, the usual question of how faithful a screen adaptation is to the Broadway original isn't relevant. Fosse's *Cabaret* is its own entity, and while the rushes brought the director tsuris from the front office, just as anything radically new does, the film was a smash hit both artistically and financially. ■

Behind the Screen

■ Back in 1963, Kaye Ballard was a regular on Perry Como's *Kraft Music Hall* television variety show. Ballard found John Kander and Fred Ebb's song "My Coloring Book" but wasn't permitted to sing it on the air because the producer said, "You're the comedian." So, Sandy Stewart sang it on the show and her subsequent recording became a big hit. Disappointed, Kaye went back to the songwriters and asked them for another song, pointedly suggesting the title "Maybe Next Time I'll Be Lucky." Kander and Ebb wrote the song to Ballard's specifications and she performed it successfully in her club act. Years later, they put it into the movie version of *Cabaret*, never telling Ballard. She didn't speak to Fred Ebb for years afterward.

CENTER RIGHT: The young and innocent Liza Minnelli.

RIGHT: Liza in one of her soon-to-be-a-cliché movements..

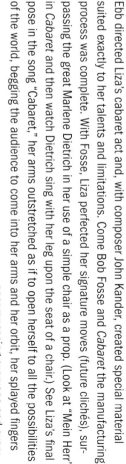

Liza Minnelli

L iza Minnelli is a product; a spectacular piece of talent formed by a series of Svengalis and a genetic boost from her parents. First came her mother, who taught her how to interpret a song and how to capitalize on those doe eyes, that shyness, and that nervous laugh. Then came Kay Thompson, Judy Garland's coach. Thompson took Liza in hand and taught her the same movements of arms and legs that she'd taught her mother. Liza next teamed up with Fred Ebb, the lyricist of her first Broadway show *Flora, the Red Menace.* Ebb directed Liza's cabaret act and, with composer John Kander, created special material suited exactly to her talents and limitations. With Fosse, Liza perfected her signature moves (future clichés), surpassing the great Marlene Dietrich in her use of a simple chair as a prop. (Look at "Mein Herr" in *Cabaret* and then watch Dietrich sing with her leg upon the seat of a chair.) See Liza's final pose in the song "Cabaret," her arms outstretched as if to open herself to all the possibilities of the world, begging the audience to come into her arms and her orbit, her splayed fingers encompassing everyone and everything. Now, after years of various addictions, illnesses, and mental battles, Minnelli's voice and stamina may be a fraction as powerful as they once were, but she's still a star, thanks to the training and talents of her teachers. They helped her create a *persona*—and that's what being her kind of star is all about.

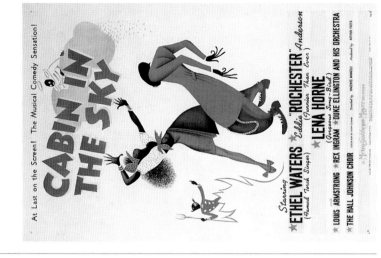

Ethel Waters and Eddie Anderson share a quiet moment in *Cabin in the Sky*.

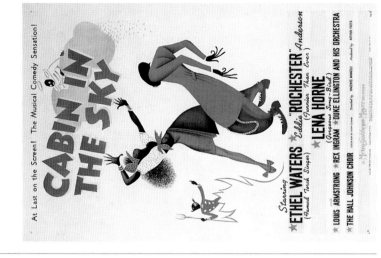

CABIN IN THE SKY
MGM—APRIL 9, 1943

CABIN IN THE SKY

COMPOSER: Harold Arlen
LYRICIST: E.Y. Harburg
PRODUCER: Arthur Freed
DIRECTOR: Vincent Minnelli
SCREENWRITER: Joseph Schrank
SOURCE: Based on the musical *Cabin in the Sky* by Vernon Duke, John Latouche, and Lynn Root

Synopsis

Little Joe wants to be good and stop gambling but the devil makes him do it. Really, the devil.

Cast

Ethel Waters	Petunia Jackson
Eddie "Rochester" Anderson	"Little Joe" Jackson
Lena Horne	Georgia Brown
Louis Armstrong	The Trumpeter
Rex Ingram	Lucifer Jr.
Kenneth Spencer	The General
John Bubbles	Domino Johnson
Oscar Polk	The Deacon
Mantan Moreland	First Idea Man
Willie Best	Second Idea Man
Butterfly McQueen	Lily
Ruby Dandridge	Mrs. Kelso
Nicodemus	Dude
Duke Ellington, Hall Johnson Choir	Themselves

I T'S NO SURPRISE THAT RACISM EXISTED IN HOLLYWOOD THROUGHOUT THE LAST CENTURY, and still exists today. Anti-Semitism was also a problem: the mainly Jewish studio heads preferred to downplay their Jewish background. People who consistently cast blacks as slaves, porters, or maids didn't think they were being racist at all. In fact, the issue never entered their mind. They simply knew nothing about black life and had no black friends or acquaintances. It was as if black people lived on another planet—and, in a way, they did, in ghettos in major cities of the Northeast and Midwest. Few blacks came in contact with whites except in subservient roles. Although stereotyping in film is most obvious in relation to blacks, other groups were subject to it as well, including Italians, Jews, and the Irish. For screenwriters, stereotyping served as a convenient shorthand for character development.

The problem is alleviated a bit when there is another side to the coin. Hollywood presented a rounder view of Hispanics, for example, balancing hot-blooded characters like Lupe Valez and that South American bombshell Carmen Miranda with the suave, sexy leading men Ricardo Montalban and Caesar Romero. Both were stereotypes but at least the men came across as serious characters.

As we said, ignorance was a prime cause of racist stereotyping. Take this memo from the famed black musician and chorus director, Hall Johnson, to *Cabin in the Sky's* associate producer Albert Lewis: "You are to be commended for your desire to include nothing which might give offense to the Negro race—a consideration too often overlooked in this

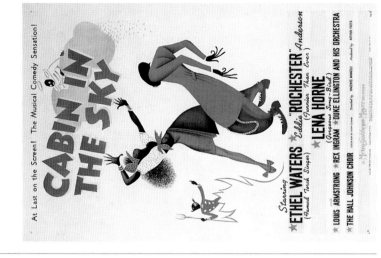

business of motion-picture making. I have been unable to detect anything in this script which could possibly offend anybody....

"At the moment, the dialect in your script is a weird but a priceless conglomeration of pre-Civil War constructions mixed with up-to-the-minute Harlem slang and heavily sprinkled with a type of verb which Amos and Andy purloined from Miller and Lyles, the Negro comedians; all adding up to a lingo which has never been heard nor spoken on land or sea by any human being, and would most certainly be 'more than Greek' to the ignorant Georgia Negroes in your play. The script will be immeasurably improved when this is translated into honest-to-goodness Negro dialect."

At least Lewis sought feedback from an actual black person. For the most part, Hollywood didn't care how blacks would perceive their screen counterparts. Major Hollywood pictures were made by white people for white people. Blacks might enjoy them, of course, though they saw themselves reflected only in minor roles. But sometimes a screenwriter and actor could make magic with a black character; take for instance Hattie McDaniel's performance as Mammy in *Gone with the Wind.* The character is crucial to the story, powerful, respected by the family, and takes no lip from anyone.

Black audiences who wanted to see black performers in leading roles could go to their local movie theaters and see films made especially for them. These films were popular, in spite of their technical and artistic shortcomings. Here's the irony, though: the films made by black artists for black audiences contained just as many stereotypes as the films made by whites. The same is true today of many black movies and television series.

Cabin in the Sky represented a sincere effort by MGM to present a first-class all-black film, the studio's first since *Hallelujah* in 1929. Producer Arthur Freed proclaimed, "I will spare nothing and will put everything behind it. It will be a picture on a par with any major film under the MGM banner." He kept his word. The technical and design aspects were up to the studio's high standards and the film marked Vincente Minnelli's directing debut. The score, including new songs by Harold Arlen and E. Y. Harburg, was better than many MGM A-list musicals. The cast featured Ethel Waters, the greatest black star of her day; the sultry beauty Lena Horne; the lighthearted John Bubbles; all accompanied by the greatest black musicians of the time, Duke Ellington and Louis Armstrong among them.

For Minnelli, the picture was a kind of trial by fire. Ethel Waters was intensely jealous of the up-and-coming Lena Horne, and accused her costar of stealing her style of singing and attracting too much attention. Unspoken was Waters's realization that Horne was the sexier one of the two. Waters ranted and raved on the set, ending her hurricane of vitriol with an anti-Semitic diatribe. She would hate Horne even more when *Stormy Weather* premiered that same year. In that film, Horne sang the title tune and made it her own for all time; it had been Waters's greatest hit at the Cotton Club. Think of someone recording "People" to great acclaim and making audiences forget Streisand's original version.

The story of *Cabin in the Sky* is a hoary one—the whole thing's a dream sequence and at the end, Eddie Anderson, playing the Judy Garland role, wakes up to declare that there's no place like home. Despite the problems on the set, the film is a beauty and extremely exciting. Today we can't help being aware of the stereotyping even in this well-intentioned picture, but it is still terrific entertainment that shows off its performers beautifully. ■

Lena Horne, sporting the Daisy Mae look, doesn't see any reason to get excited.

Ethel Waters

Growing up in the early years of the twentieth century and appearing in the blacks-only burlesque and vaudeville circuits informed all of Ethel Waters's subsequent life. Racism and stereotyping followed her throughout her career, but she overcame many hardships to become a star of recordings and Broadway. Slowly she worked her way up the entertainment ladder. She was the first black artist to make records and when Black Swan Records, a race label, folded, she was signed by Columbia Records, one of the leading record companies. Waters appeared at the Plantation Club in New York and graduated to Broadway in the musical revue *Africana.* She sang at New York's famed Cotton Club, where she introduced what would become her theme song, "Stormy Weather." That led to an appearance on Broadway in Irving Berlin's *As Thousands Cheer,* where she shared equal billing with the stars, Clifton Webb and Marilyn Miller, and sang the scathing ballad "Supper Time." She played Carnegie Hall twice, in 1938 and 1939, and sang with the bands of Duke Ellington, Benny Goodman, and Jack Teagarden. Although she had appeared on screen in 1929's *On with the Show* and a handful of other shorts and features, her first starring film role was a reprise of her Broadway turn in *Cabin in the Sky.* It would be her next to last appearance in a musical film. Never a happy woman, Waters caused trouble on stage and off. Late in her life she became devoutly religious, but it didn't seem to mellow her personality.

At first we thought this was Ethel Waters watching Lena Horne vamp her way through the film, but in fact, it's Ethel singing Irving Berlin's "Heat Wave" in the Broadway revue *As Thousands Cheer.*

SONGS

"Cabin in the Sky" (Vernon Duke and John Latouche) ■ "Happiness Is Just a Thing Called Joe" ■ "Honey in the Honeycomb" (Vernon Duke and John Latouche) ■ "Li'l Black Sheep" ■ "Life's Full of Consequence" ■ "S-H-I-N-E" (Cecil Mack, Lew Brown, and Ford Dabney) ■ "Taking a Chance on Love" (Vernon Duke, John Latouche, and Ted Fetter)

CALAMITY JANE

COMPOSER: Sammy Fain
LYRICIST: Paul Francis Webster
PRODUCER: William Jacobs
DIRECTOR: David Butler
SCREENWRITER: James O'Hanlon
CHOREOGRAPHER: Jack Donohue

Synopsis

Calamity Jane travels to Chicago to pick up a singer for her pals back in Deadwood. Unfortunately, she gets the wrong gal. But she gets the right guy.

Cast

Doris Day	Calamity Jane
Howard Keel	Wild Bill Hickok
Allyn Ann McLerie	Katie Brown
Philip Carey	Lt. Danny Gilmartin
Dick Wesson	Francis Fryer
Paul Harvey	Henry Miller
Chubby Johnson	Rattlesnake
Gale Robbins	Adelaid Adams

CALAMITY JANE

WARNER BROTHERS—NOVEMBER 4, 1953

Calamity's frustrated. She's got Frank Butler as her costar but she's not Annie Oakley.

IMITATION IS THE SINCEREST FORM OF HOLLYWOOD MUSICAL. HAS YOUR COMPETITION HAD a big success with a musical revue such as MGM's *Hollywood Revue of 1929*? Then you must produce *Paramount on Parade*, or *Fox Movietone Follies*, or Universal's *King of Jazz*. Backstage musicals? No problem. Biopics? There's a million biographies to musicalize. You get the idea.

Well, here's another variation on the theme. Back in 1946, Irving Berlin, Dorothy Fields, and Herbert Fields came up with a doozy of a show, *Annie Get Your Gun*, which scored a terrific success on Broadway with Ethel Merman and became a smash hit in London a year later, with Dolores Gray in the lead. Jack Warner attempted to buy the rights to the stage musical but lost out to MGM.

In 1950, the MGM film version opened with Betty Hutton as Annie. The part had been meant for Judy Garland, who had laid down all the prerecords of the songs and started filming her scenes. But Judy got sick and MGM fired her from the film. Mary Martin toured the country with the show, which was a musical comedy star's dream: a surefire hit with a great score and book. What star wouldn't have wanted to play Annie Oakley?

Everyone did, as it turned out. And that included Doris Day, who was distraught when MGM won the rights to the show and doubly disappointed when the role went to Judy Garland. When Garland was fired and MGM sought to fill the role outside their studio, Day hoped she would be chosen—but as far as Metro was concerned, she still wasn't a big enough star having only made one movie thus far in her career. Ginger Rogers offered to play the part for nothing; Betty Garrett was briefly considered but wasn't a big enough

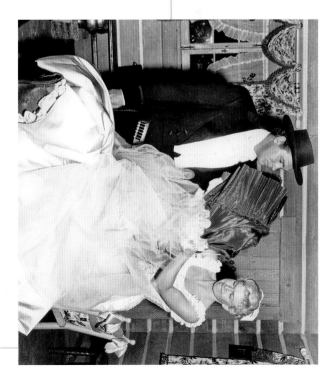

RIGHT: Doris Day rassles with a whole heap of finery while Howard Keel looks on.

ABOVE: Chubby Johnson minds the team on the Deadwood stage while Doris Day sings about it.

Behind the Screen

- When Doris Day went in to prerecord "Secret Love," she sang the song once through with the orchestra and musical director Ray Heindorf said, "That's it."

star; and June Allyson tested for the part. MGM borrowed Hutton instead, on loan from Paramount.

In an attempt to placate Day, Warner offered her *Calamity Jane*, a film that was more than inspired by *Annie Get Your Gun*. Let's see, a film that was more than inspired by *Annie Get Your Gun*. Let's see, a film that was more than inspired by *Annie Get Your Gun*. A love affair with a competitive man who's also handy with a gun? Check. A wedding knot to tie up the story? Check. Other than that, the story of *Calamity Jane* is completely unique.

Which brings us to the score. Sammy Fain and Paul Francis Webster were instructed to model their score after that of *Annie Get Your Gun*. "I Can Do Without You" is similar to "Anything You Can Do." "I Just Got Back from the Windy City" is musical ringer for "Doin' what Comes Natur'lly." Annie's ballad, "I Got Lost in His Arms" is mirrored by Calamity's "Secret Love."

Given the assignment, Fain and Webster managed to produce a terrific score that, perhaps not surprisingly, is more like a Broadway score than a movie score. The songs are much more theatrical than most movie songs and of a higher, less pop, quality. It helps, of course, that Doris Day is singing them. She's marvelous and it makes us as sad that she never got to play Annie Oakley. She did, however get to costar opposite MGM's Frank Butler, Howard Keel. Day also sang the score of *Annie Get Your Gun* on vinyl along with Robert Goulet and they are both excellent. ∎

Howard Keel

More manly than Nelson Eddy, MGM's previous star of musicals and operettas, Howard Keel began his career with MGM at the top, starring in the big-screen version of *Annie Get Your Gun*. Although he appeared in other notable musicals, including *Show Boat*, *Kiss Me Kate*, *Seven Brides for Seven Brothers*, and (last but least) *Kismet*, Keel became a casualty of the end of the musical film era—and the star system itself. A better than fair actor, if a bit stiff in that grand baritone way, he alternated between musicals and straight movies. But soon, even those roles disappeared and Keel turned to stage tours and nightclub appearances. It's interesting to note that many stars of that era thought nothing of tramping around the country to little theaters. Keel, on the other hand, was smart enough to leap at the chance to work on the small screen and later found work on the hit series *Dallas*. A big man in the Rock Hudson mode, he made a believable millionaire oil man. Even after *Dallas* finally hung up its spurs, Keel remained a big star in England, travelling extensively and profitably throughout the United Kingdom and even making recordings there that were never available in the States. Keel might not have been the greatest actor or even the greatest baritone—but he was talented enough to span the media and enjoy a long-lasting career.

Sammy Fain

Like most Tin Pan Alley songwriters, unsung master Sammy Fain spent all of his waking hours with potential music running through his mind. Fain came to Hollywood at the start of the musical era and worked on such films as *The Big Pond* and *Footlight Parade*. For the former movie, he, Irving Kahal, and Pierre Norman gave Maurice Chevalier one of his signature tunes, "You Brought a New Kind of Love to Me." It was Fain's music and Irving Kahal's lyrics that accompanied Busby Berkeley's extravaganza "By a Waterfall" in the latter picture. But, really, with all that water and feminine pulchritude on camera, who was listening to the song? Fain and Kahal decamped to Broadway in the midthirties and came up with one of the greatest hits of the war years, "I'll Be Seeing You," for the otherwise unremarkable show, *Right This Way*. That score also included another smash hit, "I Can Dream Can't I?" Fain then returned to pictures to write a series of marvelous scores for Disney cartoon features. In 1951, he and Bob Hilliard wrote the songs for Disney's *Alice in Wonderland*, whose score has become a favorite of jazz instrumentalists through the years. He also contributed to Disney's *Peter Pan*, *Sleeping Beauty*, and *The Rescuers*, his last work for the movies. In 1953, he wrote the music for *Calamity Jane*; the hit song was "Secret Love," which won Fain and Paul Francis Webster the Oscar. Later, the team wrote successful title tunes for *April Love* and *Love Is a Many Splendored Thing*. And if you think writing words and music to that latter title is easy, you try it!

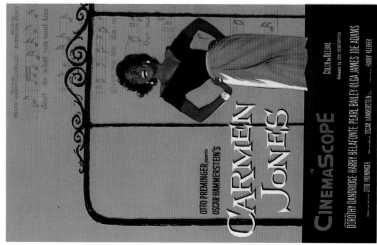

CARMEN JONES

COMPOSER: Georges Bizet
LYRICIST: Oscar Hammerstein II
PRODUCER: Otto Preminger
DIRECTOR: Otto Preminger
SCREENWRITER: Harry Kleiner
SOURCE: Based on the musical *Carmen Jones* with lyrics by Oscar Hammerstein II
CHOREOGRAPHER: Herbert Ross

Synopsis

Carmen Jones has a hold over the young army corporal Joe and it ain't good. Thanks to her, they both meet tragic ends. If only he'd had season tickets to the Met, he'd have seen it coming.

Cast

Harry Belafonte...........Joe
Dorothy Dandridge.......Carmen Jones
Pearl Bailey................Frankie
Olga James..................Cindy Lou
Joe Adams...................Husky Miller
Brock Peters................Sergeant Brown
Roy Glenn...................Rum Daniels
Nick Stewart................Dink Franklin
Diahann Carroll............Myrt

Behind the Screen

■ The success of *Carmen Jones* got Preminger the green light on *Porgy and Bess.*

CARMEN JONES

20TH CENTURY FOX—OCTOBER 28, 1954

Dorothy Dandridge and Harry Belafonte steam up the set in *Carmen Jones.*

A N ETERNAL QUESTION OF FILM LOVERS IS, WHY CAST NONSINGERS IN A MOVIE MUSICAL? It may make no sense to us commoners—but the studios have their reasons. A star may already be attached to a project. And of course there is the issue of box office—big stars sell tickets, whether they can warble or not. After all, they can always be dubbed.

Which brings us to *Carmen Jones*. Here was a movie musical based on a stage hit, in turn based on a famous opera, cast with a variety of fine singers, including Dorothy Dandridge and Harry Belafonte. Yet they and many others were dubbed. In fact, only Brock Peters and Pearl Bailey did their own singing. Apparently, the decision was made that pop and jazz singers couldn't handle the musical ranges called for by the music.

Nearly all of the brides and brothers in *Seven Brides for Seven Brothers* were dubbed, but that made sense since it was largely a dance movie, with Jane Powell and Howard Keel handling the central vocal chores. Then there was the controversial dubbing of Audrey Hepburn in *My Fair Lady*. Why hire a nonsinger when the original Eliza, Julie Andrews, was ready and willing? We'll never understand it.

Here's the most remarkable story of all. Alan Jay Lerner was working with André Previn on the film *Paint Your Wagon*, and they needed to dub Jean Seberg's voice (as well as the other leads, Lee Marvin and Clint Eastwood). Frederick Loewe suggested that they use a woman named Anita Gordon to sing the song for Seberg, but nobody seemed to know what had happened to her. The Screen Actors Guild finally produced an address but no phone number, so Previn decided to send her a telegram. He called Western Union and said, "I want to send a telegram to Anita Gordon." There was a pause and the operator responded, "I'm Anita Gordon." Mystery solved. Gordon came in and dubbed for Seberg.

The vocal swapping in *Carmen Jones* is done so expertly that our enjoyment of the film isn't hampered at all. For starters, all of the actors, whether they could sing a note or not, look as if they're singing the songs full out. (Too many performers don't put any energy into their songs when they're lip-synching.) You can see Dandridge and Belafonte's throat muscles straining and their breaths measuring the cadence of the songs.

Considering the subject matter and tragic ending, it's a remarkably enjoyable film. Preminger gives his cast permission to act out the strong emotions of the characters with brio, yet they manage to avoid the pitfalls of overacting. Opera stories can be creaky and overblown, but Preminger guides his cast along the fine line between melodrama and realism.

The director also allows his camera great latitude (especially compared to his later handling of *Porgy & Bess*, where most of the scenes are shot with a stationary camera and no cuts to indicate changes of viewpoint).

Hammerstein's original stage version of *Carmen Jones* was greeted with apprehension before it opened, but won over audiences and critics because of the seriousness of its intent and its first-rate production. The film adaptation is entirely true to the original play, and provides yet another example of the breadth of talent available among black performers. Sadly, as in the Broadway production, further opportunities for the cast were limited by their color. Belafonte, to take just one example, as handsome and talented as he was, made only a handful of mostly disappointing movies after *Carmen Jones*.

For once, the hype about the stars heating up the screen was true. Belafonte and Dandridge make a great-looking couple and act as if they'd rather spend the entire time enjoying each other carnally. Dandridge even wears zebra patterned underwear. It's a strange sort of reverse racism in an era when women in film couldn't be seen in a bra.

Otto Preminger holds forth while Roy Glenn, Diahann Carroll, and Joe Adams look on. In the background, Harry Belafonte (in white t-shirt) seems unconcerned.

Of course, the prevailing feeling was that blacks were hotter, jazzier, and sexier than whites so latitude was given to the characters. If the film had been cast with white performers it would have had a completely different tone.

In *Carmen Jones* we have an excellent record of a truly unique property, realized brilliantly for the screen. ∎

"If you were in your right mind, would you sit down and write Bizet's *Carmen* as a modern American musical with an all-black cast?"

—*Howard Dietz*

Something tells us Carmen Jones isn't in the café for the Blue Plate Special.

SONGS

"Beat Out Dat Rhythm on a Drum" ∎ "Blow on 'em Sugar" ∎ "Card Song" ∎ "Carmen Jones is Goin' to Jail" ∎ "Dat's Love (Habanera)" ∎ "Dere's a Café on de Corner" ∎ "Dis Flower" ∎ "Lift 'Em Up and' Put 'Em Down" ∎ "Final Duet" ∎ "My Joe" ∎ "Send Along Anudder Load" ∎ "Stan' Up an' Fight" ∎ "String Me High on a Tree" ∎ "Toreador Song" ∎ "Whizzen' Along de Track" ∎ "You Talk Jus' Like My Man" ∎ "You Go for Me"

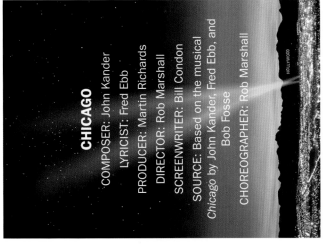

CHICAGO

COMPOSER: John Kander
LYRICIST: Fred Ebb
PRODUCER: Martin Richards
DIRECTOR: Rob Marshall
SCREENWRITER: Bill Condon
SOURCE: Based on the musical *Chicago* by John Kander, Fred Ebb, and Bob Fosse
CHOREOGRAPHER: Rob Marshall

Synopsis

Wanna make it big without any talent? Get in the headlines! Is this the synopsis of *Chicago* or a plot torn from today's headlines?

Cast

Renee Zellweger.............Roxie Hart
Catherine Zeta-Jones.....Velma Kelly
Richard Gere...............Billy Flynn
Taye Diggs...................Bandleader
Queen Latifah..............Matron Mama Morton
John C. Reilly..............Amos Hart
Dominic West................Fred Casely
Christine Baranski.........Mary Sunshine
Chita Rivera.................Nickie
Scott Wise ....Ezekial Young
Lucy Liu......................Kitty Baxter

CHICAGO

MIRAMAX—JANUARY 24, 2003

Few moviegoers knew Catherine Zeta-Jones could sing and dance, but she had starred on London's West End in *42nd Street*, among other shows.

GOOD STORIES NEVER SEEM TO GO OUT OF FASHION.

In the mid-'20s, reporter Maurine Dallas Watkins recognized that some of the people she came across on the crime beat would make good characters in a play. One woman, Beulah Annan, particularly caught her eye. It seems that Annan was sharing a bottle of wine with her boyfriend when they both reached for the gun. After changing her story a few times, Annan was acquitted; all the while her husband steadfastly supported her, emotionally and financially. After her acquittal she promptly divorced him—and, to capitalize on her notoriety, went on a vaudeville tour.

This wasn't as farfetched as it seems. During the dying days of vaudeville, all sorts of headline grabbers trod the boards, however dubious their talents. In the years before reality television and so-called entertainment news shows, audiences were thrilled to see people they had read about in the papers live on stage.

Watkins' play, *Chicago*, opened on Broadway in 1926, just as America was nearing the end of the Roaring Twenties. A cautionary tale and a satirical one, *Chicago* caught the anything goes atmosphere of its time. A year later, a silent film version premiered that hewed to the basic plot of the play. The story was revived in 1942, when Ginger Rogers, before she was grand and dull, took the title role in the film *Roxie Hart*.

Flash forward to Broadway, 1975. John Kander and Fred Ebb, along with director-choreographer Bob Fosse, opened their new musical, *Chicago*. Framed by a vaudeville show conceit, the musical was dark and daring. There was lots of razzamatazz provided by Gwen Verdon, Chita Rivera, and Jerry Orbach, but the show was darker than either of the preceding versions. This was Kander and Ebb at their most cynical and Fosse at his sleaziest, *Chicago* was a hit, running almost one thousand performances (substantial by the standards of the time).

Broadway's *Chicago* remains beloved in the hearts and minds of aficionados. The cast album went in and out of print without much notice. And Fosse made the film *All That Jazz* about his experiences bringing the show to Broadway, and it wasn't a pretty sight.

That would probably be the end of the story, if it weren't for two events. In 1995, what was dubbed "The Trial of the Century" began in Los Angeles. We're referring to the O.J. Simpson affair, which was televised as the ultimate in reality television. When O.J. was acquitted the country went crazy. Some perceived it to be a win for minorities who'd been frequent victims of injustice, but for most, it was a travesty. In any case, it was incredibly entertaining. A year later, a revival of *Chicago* opened at the Richard Rodgers Theatre, the same in which the original had played. With the memory of the O.J. trial fresh in our mind and our view of justice shaken, the musical had a special resonance. Then, just when ticket sales were slipping, the film opened.

Essentially a great big overblown music video, the film certainly captured the spirit of the story. Jettisoned was Fosse's original conceit that each song reflect a different kind of vaudeville number. Instead, director Rob Marshall, reflecting the modern moviemaker's view that audiences won't accept characters randomly breaking into song, made the musical interludes flights of imagination. We don't know why that was necessary, since today's younger generation was brought up watching *The Wizard of Oz* and *The Sound of Music* on television and video. But . . . Marshall's concept worked.

Like many music videos, quick cutting and lots of close-ups hid the flaws, or, rather, limitations, in the performers' talents. Fred Astaire's dictum that he should always be filmed full figure and that, whenever possible, the numbers should be shot in one complete take was thrown out the window. The approach in *Chicago* was quite the opposite.

Even the dimmest audience member drooling into his popcorn could follow the plot and get the humor, because there was little going on beneath the surface. Subtlety and depth of character were not the point. Some critics complained that there wasn't any breathing space between numbers, and maybe they were right. Momentum is a good thing, but with the runaway-train pace and the hyperactive editing, audiences never got a chance to catch their breath. This technique all started with Baz Luhrman's *Moulin Rouge*, in which the spectacle overwhelmed the story. Still, *Chicago* was certainly successful as eye candy, and although the director and cast didn't have a particularly original point of view on the proceedings, the resulting film was respectable and a great success, even winning a Best Picture Oscar.

The success of the film jolted the box office for the Broadway revival and it became the Olive Garden of Broadway shows. Tourists coming to New York are a bit leery of stepping outside their comfort zone, so they flock to restaurants they know, such as the Red Lobster, Hooters, and the Olive Garden. Same with shows. They saw the movie of *Chicago* so they know what they're getting.

The film also inspired a mini boom in film musicals, such as *Hairspray*, *Dreamgirls*, and *Nine*, some of which were quite satisfactory—and for that, at least, we are extremely grateful. ■

TOP: Renee Zellweger and Catherine Zeta-Jones shoot up the screen in *Chicago*. BOTTOM: Lawyer Richard Gere gets wrapped up in another case.

John Kander and Fred Ebb

Kander and Ebb are certainly the most theatrical of Broadway's songwriters. Many of their songs fall into the "special material" category, as opposed to simple character songs. Perhaps for this reason, their film excursions have been spotty. The screen adaptations of their Broadway hits *Cabaret* and *Chicago* were huge successes but their original film scores, *New York, New York* and *Funny Lady*, were less successful. (Certainly, the title song for *New York, New York* was a mega-hit, thanks to both Liza Minnelli and Frank Sinatra, but the film never took off.) Given the inherent theatricality of their Broadway shows, it's surprising that more of them haven't been translated into film but the songwriting team may just be victims of the cyclical nature of movie musicals. Bob Fosse chose to eject all of *Cabaret*'s songs that didn't take place on the stage of the Kit Kat Klub and Rob Marshall set *Chicago*'s musical numbers in the imagination of the characters. Here's a thought: *The Act, Kiss of the Spider Woman,* and *Curtains* would make excellent films in the right hands. Are you listening, Hollywood?

ABOVE: Lyricist Fred Ebb and composer John Kander dream up another hit musical.

RIGHT: Eugene Pallette and Phyllis Haver in the 1927 version of *Chicago.*

BELOW: Catherine Zeta-Jones as murderess Velma Kelly

Behind the Screen

■ Rob Marshall's direction and choreography are based on Bob Fosse's work in *Cabaret.*

■ Martin Richards, who produced the show on Broadway, tried to get the movie made for years but nobody could find a way to translate the material to film. Rob Marshall suggested that the musical numbers could take place in the characters' imagination.

■ At an early screening, Kander and Ebb saw a print of the film with a new song over the end credits, a song they hadn't written. Their lawyers informed the producers that their contract forbade this. The prints were all pulled, the offending song removed, and Kander and Ebb wrote the song "I Move On" to take its place.

SONGS

"All I Care About" ■ "And All That Jazz" ■ "Cell Block Tango" ■ "Funny Honey" ■ "I Can't Do It Alone" ■ "I Move On" ■ "Mister Cellophane" ■ "Nowadays" ■ "Razzle Dazzle" ■ "Roxie" ■ "We Both Reached for the Gun" ■ "When You're Good to Mama"

COLLEGE SWING

PARAMOUNT—APRIL 29, 1938

COLLEGE SWING

LYRICIST: Frank Loesser
PRODUCER: Lewis E. Gensler
DIRECTOR: Raoul Walsh
SCREENWRITERS: Walter De Leon, Francis Martin, and Preston Sturges
CHOREOGRAPHER: LeRoy Prinz

Synopsis

A bunch of actors whose only educational experience was on the vaudeville stage play students ten or so years younger than themselves. Luckily, songs and humor abound, giving them an A for all-round entertainment.

Cast

George Burns	George Jonas
Gracie Allen	Gracie Alden
Martha Raye	Mabel
Bob Hope	Bud Brady
Edward Everett Horton	Hubert Dash
Ben Blue	Ben Volt
Betty Grable	Betty
Jackie Coogan	Jackie
John Payne	Martin Bates
Skinnay Ennis	Skinnay
The Slate Brothers	Themselves
Jerry Colonna	Prof. Yascha Koloski

D URING THE 1930s AND '40s, SONGWRITERS PRODUCED TONS OF SONGS THAT WEREN'T ultimately used in a given project. At Paramount, where scores and films were more loosey-goosey than at other studios, songwriters didn't necessarily write for plot or characters; rather, they tossed their songs into the mix, hoping that they would be chosen by the producers, stars, and music supervisors. Because they churned out a wide range of pieces from which the production team could choose, including love songs, comedic songs, production numbers, torch songs, music for dance sequences, novelty numbers, and so on, the value of songwriters was diminished in the studio suits' minds. The songwriters' very versatility worked against then—how low could they go to get their work in a film? Songwriters were treated with little more respect than (gasp!) screenwriters.

College Swing is a good example of a show that could boast an embarrassment of musical riches. At least thirty songs were considered for inclusion in the film, probably the record for any musical. Most had lyrics by Frank Loesser and the majority had music by Burton Lane. But other staff writers, including Leo Robin and Ralph Rainger, as well as Frederick Hollander and Ralph Freed, also submitted songs.

Songwriters at the big studios, with the exception of megastar Irving Berlin, wrote for hire. That is, they were drones onstaff and the songs they wrote while under contract belonged to the studios. They did get royalties from sheet music sales and recordings, but the studios were free to do what they pleased with the songs. There's a funny story about Jule Styne and Frank Loesser working at B-movie studio Republic on a rare A-musical, *Sis Hopkins*. They were in their office on the studio lot working on a new song. Styne played the melody for Loesser, who responded, "Stop! Don't play that here. Never play that here again. Don't you ever play that for anyone else. We'll write that song at Paramount." They held on to the song and "I Don't Want to Walk Without You" was sung in the Paramount musical, *Sweater Girl*. It became one of the top hit songs of the war years.

Rah! Rah! Rah! John Payne, Gracie Allen, George Burns, Martha Raye, Bob Hope, Florence George, Ben Blue, Betty Grable, and Jackie Coogan give it the old college try. Not that they'd really know what that was, since the closest most of them came to higher education was playing Loew's Pitkin Theatre near Brooklyn College.

Tea time on the set. Cecil Cunningham looks on while Gracie Allen and Martha Raye have a little pick-me-up.

SONGS

"College Swing" (music by Hoagy Carmichael) ▪ "Howd'ja Like to Love Me?" (music by Burton Lane) ▪ "I Fall in Love with You Every Day" (music by Manning Sherwin and Arthur Altman) ▪ "I'm Tired (of Carrying Plates Around)" (The Slate Brothers) ▪ "Moments Like This" (music by Burton Lane) ▪ "The Old School Bell" (music by Manning Sherwin) ▪ "What a Rumba Does to Romance" (music by Manning Sherwin) ▪ "What Did Romeo Say to Juliet?" (music by Burton Lane) ▪ "You're a Natural" (music by Manning Sherwin)

All film songs are prerecorded and then lip-synched while the cameras are rolling (a notable exception is "How'dja Like to Love Me" in *College Swing*, but more on that in this chapter's Behind the Scenes). Fox's *Three Little Girls in Blue* included the Harry Warren and Mack Gordon song "This Is Always," which was prerecorded by June Haver and George Montgomery (who was dubbed by Ben Gage). The song appears in the film as underscoring but the number itself wasn't used. However, the song was published and even the underscoring got some interest. The song has survived as a semistandard for pop and jazz musicians and singers. Such artists as Chet Baker, Benny Carter, Nat King Cole, Sammy Davis Jr., Cab Calloway, Errol Garner, Frank Sinatra, and Charlie Parker recorded it. One of the earliest recordings was the Harry James Orchestra's with Kitty Kallen vocalizing.

Another of Harry Warren's loveliest melodies, "Spring Isn't Everything," was written for the MGM musical version of *Ah! Wilderness*, called *Summer Holiday*. Walter Huston prerecorded the song for the movie, which was filmed in 1946 but not released for two years. The song wasn't included in the film but luckily, Margaret Whiting recorded the Ralph Blane lyric as a Capitol Records single. This led to a number of recordings over the years, notably one by Maxine Sullivan (and she'll be back again later in this essay) in the 1980s.

In 1938, the Dick Powell film *Going Places* featured Warren and Mercer's song "Jeepers Creepers," as performed by Louis Armstrong and Maxine Sullivan. Maxine also had a terrific song, "Say It with a Kiss" that, unfortunately, only made it onto the soundtrack as an instrumental. Fortunately, Maxine recorded it commercially in 1938, as did Count Basie, Billie Holiday, and Artie Shaw's Orchestra with a Helen Forrest vocal.

Sometimes a cut song will appear in a later picture. That was the case for "Pass That Peace Pipe," by Hugh Martin and Roger Edens. It was prerecorded in 1944 by June Allyson, Gene Kelly, and Nancy Walker for the musical *Ziegfeld Follies*, which was eventually released in 1946 but without "Pass That Peace Pipe." The tune finally showed up in MGM's *Good News* in 1947, performed brilliantly by Joan McCracken in the dance highlight of the film.

And, speaking of Hugh Martin, in some cases a prerecorded song may appear by the same artists in a later film. Such is the case of "Who Do You Think I Am?" sung by Gloria DeHaven and Kenny Bowers and intended for MGM's 1943 *Best Foot Forward*. The song was eventually filmed by the same performers and with the same prerecord for 1944's *Broadway Rhythm*.

One song started its life written for a Broadway musical in 1943 and finally resurfaced in another Broadway show almost fifty years later. In the intervening years, the song was intended for two motion pictures but not used. "Boys and Girls like You and Me"

"Studios should stop trying to keep up plot appearances in musicals of this type and advertise them frankly as variety shows."

—*The New York Times review of* College Swing

Martha Raye

Some feared that Martha Raye's oversize personality (and mouth) would overwhelm audiences when projected on the big screen, but she knew exactly how far to go. Like all the great clowns, including Bob Hope, Bert Lahr, Fanny Brice, and others, Raye could also show a gentler, emotional side. She was considered by aficionados to be a great jazz singer who never had the opportunities to shine. Rumor has it that she was basically illiterate and had her scripts read to her over and over just as Shirley Temple did. She made her Broadway debut during a 1967 run of *Hello, Dolly!* and was considered one of the best women to have played the role. When her Hollywood career slowed down, Raye devoted herself to entertaining the troops in Vietnam. She didn't politicize the war like right-wingers Bob Hope and John Wayne, preferring to focus her attention and resources on the soldiers. For nine years, she toured the battlefields, entertaining and keeping up morale for six months at a time with little or no fanfare, venturing into areas where no other entertainer would dare go. Raye even pitched in with first aid when necessary. During an especially dangerous attack on a camp she was visiting, she worked for thirteen hours straight in the aid station without asking for evacuation or any special attention. Raye's personal life was a different kind of battlefield: she was married seven times and estranged from her daughter—but she became the substitute mother to thousands of GIs.

was written by Rodgers and Hammerstein for the stage musical *Oklahoma!* It was cut from that show when MGM picked it up and had it prerecorded by Judy Garland for *Meet Me in St. Louis* (1944), which had a Hugh Martin score. It was dropped from the final print. Five years later, MGM filmed it with Frank singing to Betty Garrett in *Take Me Out to the Ball Game*, but the number was excised from the final print. The song did not reappear until the 1996 Broadway stage version of the 1945 Fox film *State Fair*.

We end with one of the strangest of all Hollywood song stories. India Adams was a well-known dubber in the halls of MGM. She sang on the soundtracks of loads of films while the stars lip-synched to her singing. Adams recorded the Dietz and Schwartz song "Two Faced Woman" for Cyd Charisse to sing and dance to in *The Band Wagon*. Well, that didn't work out so well since the number was shot and then dropped. Never known to waste anything, MGM took the prerecord over to the Joan Crawford weeper *Torch Song*, where the star performed the number in a West Indian blackface! All of which helps explain why *College Swing* had thirty songs considered for inclusion in the picture. There were eventually nine songs used in the final print. Of the twenty-one songs not used for one reason or another, almost all were eventually placed in other Paramount Pictures. And five of the numbers that did appear in the film were used again in at least one other Paramount film. ∎

Burton Lane

Most composers are the unsung heroes of American popular song. Other than such blockbuster teams as Rodgers and Hammerstein and Lerner and Loewe, the authors of the hit songs we love remain unknown to most Americans. Burton Lane had some Broadway hits but only *Finian's Rainbow* is known today, and barely at that. But Lane was considered by his peers to be one of our greatest songwriters. Indeed, the composer of "How Are Things in Glocca Morra," "Too Late Now," "How About You?" "On a Clear Day You Can See Forever," "I Hear Music," and lots of other great standards never got his due. Writing with top-notch lyricists such as E. Y. Harburg, Frank Loesser, and Alan Jay Lerner, Lane made mighty contributions to the American songbook.

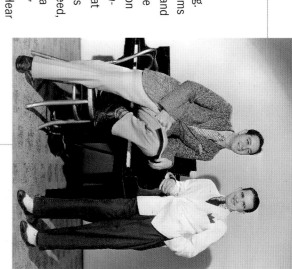

Frank Loesser

Frank Loesser was one of the most versatile of America's popular songwriters. He began his career as a lyricist writing for Hollywood films. Collaborators Jule Styne and Burton Lane, as well as musical supervisor and composer Saul Chaplin, urged him to write both music and lyrics to his songs—and they were right to do so. He was one of the rare breed who could effectively supply both words and music. His fame grew when he began his Broadway career, penning songs for such successful shows as *Guys and Dolls* and *How to Succeed in Business Without Really Trying*. Among his hit songs are "Luck Be a Lady," "A Bushel and a Peck," "I Believe in You," "Heart and Soul," "How About You?" "Standing on the Corner," "I Don't Want to Walk without You," and "Spring Will Be a Little Late This Year."

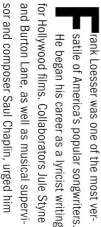

Behind the Screen

■ Perhaps the funniest musical number in all of screen history is the "Howd'ja Like to Love Me" scene in this film, featuring Bob Hope and Martha Raye. Obviously filmed live without prerecords and with damned little rehearsal, the exuberance of the stars and their obvious surprise at what the other is doing is infectious. Bob Hope even looks off camera at the crew as if to say, "Can you believe this? She's nuts. You're not going to say 'cut'?" They both have lines to say but they can't keep a straight face. It's a rare unguarded movie moment and that makes it all the more hilarious.

TOP: Burton Lane strikes a jaunty pose but it's no match for lyricist Ned Washington's mustache.

CENTER: Martha Raye is despondent because Bob Hope won't go pettin' in the park.

LEFT: Marlon Brando shows Frank Loesser how he would have composed the score to *Guys and Dolls*.

THE COURT JESTER

COMPOSER: Sylvia Fine

LYRICISTS: Sylvia Fine and Sammy Cahn

PRODUCERS: Melvin Frank and Norman Panama

DIRECTORS: Melvin Frank and Norman Panama

SCREENWRITERS: Melvin Frank and Norman Panama

CHOREOGRAPHER: James Starbuck

Synopsis

A valet pretends to be a rebel who pretends to be a minstrel to regain the throne for its rightful heir.

Cast

Danny Kaye..............Hubert Hawkins
Glynis Johns................Maid Jean
Basil Rathbone..............Sir Ravenhurst
Angela Lansbury...........Princess Gwendolyn
Cecil Parker...............King Roderick I
Mildred Natwick.............Griselda
Robert Middleton...........Sir Griswold
John Carradine.............Giocomo
Edward Ashley..............Black Fox
Alan Napier...............Sir Brockhurst

Behind the Screen

■ The "Vessel with the Pestle" and the duel were rewritten from a sequence in Bob Hope's 1939 film *Never Say Die*, with Martha Raye.

THE COURT JESTER
PARAMOUNT—JANUARY 27, 1956

ABOVE: Glynis Johns cozies up to Danny Kaye. There's nothing like a nice suit of armor to warm a fair maiden up on a cold night.

OPPOSITE TOP RIGHT: If Errol Flynn can beat Basil Rathbone in a duel, so can Danny Kaye. Or so he thinks.

OPPOSITE BOTTOM RIGHT: Norman Panama (left) and his partner Melvin Frank (right) watch Cary Grant and Danny Kaye go nose-to-nose.

SOMETIMES IT'S NOT THE MUSIC OR THE DANCES THAT MAKES A MUSICAL MEMORABLE. On a few occasions, it is the least appreciated element of the film: the script. Why is it that straight dramas and comedies have lots of quotable lines, while musicals have so few?

One exception is *The Court Jester*, a hilarious picture featuring Danny Kaye's best role. The most famous sequence comes when Danny Kaye's character, Hawkins, is given instructions on how to poison his opponent and avoid a duel with the formidable fellow. The gist of the lengthy exchange runs as follows:

Witch: Listen. I have put a pellet of poison in one of the vessels.

Hawkins: Which one?

Witch: The one with the figure of a pestle.

Hawkins: The vessel with the pestle?

Witch: Yes. But you don't want the vessel with the pestle, you want the chalice from the palace! . . .

Jean: Don't you see? The pellet with the poison's in the vessel with the pestle.

Witch: The chalice from the palace has the brew that is true! . . .

Hawkins: The pestle with t . . . the pellet with the poison's in the vessel with the pestle, the palace from the chalice has the brew that is blue. Eh, no . . . The pellet with the poison's in the vessel with the pestle. The cha- eh, the pellet with the plip . . . the pellet with the poisle's in the vessel with the plazzle. Eh, the plazzle with the vlessle. Eh, the the bless . . . The vessel with the plozle is the plazzle with the . . . I've got it! I've got it. The pellet with the poison's in the vessel with the pestle, the chalice from the palace has the brew that is true, right?

Witch: Right. But there's been a change. They broke the chalice from the palace.

Hawkins: They broke the chalice from the palace?

Witch: And replaced it with a flagon.

Hawkins: Flagon.

Witch: With a figure of a dragon.

Hawkins: Flagon with a dragon.

Witch: Right. . . .

Hawkins: The chalice with the pa . . . the flagon with the cha . . . the floizle with the flagon is the chalice with the poison. . . . The pellet with the poison's in the flagon with the dragon!

While we're calling up memorable lines, the world's first talkie, *The Jazz Singer*, gave rise to the first great movie quote, "Wait a minute, wait a minute. You ain't heard nothin' yet." Another well-known quote from the movies originated live on stage as well, spoken by George M. Cohan. After he took a bow he liked to inform audiences, "My mother thanks you. My father thanks you. My sister thanks you. And I thank you." But it was James Cagney in in the Cohan biopic *Yankee Doodle Dandy* who made it a nationally known catchphrase.

The Wizard of Oz has the most often quoted lines from any movie, musical or not: "Toto, I've got a feeling we're not in Kansas anymore"; "Unusual weather we're having"; "I'd turn back if I were you"; "Oil can"; "I'll get you, my pretty, and your little dog too!"; "I'm melting! Melting! Oh, what a world! What a world!"

Mae West, in *She Done Him Wrong*, asked, "Why don't you come up sometime and see me?" Which, morphed somehow into, "Why don't you come up and see me sometime?" West was usually her own screenwriter so most of her great lines are her own. In *I'm No Angel*, she tells the audience, "It's not the men in your life that count, it's the life in your men."

The comics most often quoted out of context have to be the Marx Brothers. Their jokes were so much a part of their musical that we tend to forget that their films *were* musicals. Did you think Groucho wrote the line, "One morning I shot an elephant in my pajamas. How he got in my pajamas, I don't know."? Nope. The genius behind that and a lot of other quotable quips was screenwriter Morrie Ryskind. The saddest thing about movie quotes is that they're associated with the actors who recited the lines rather than the screenwriters who wrote them.

Modern musicals have some standout lines, too. In 1968's *Funny Girl*, Barbra Streisand greets her own reflection with, "Hello, gorgeous." Roy Scheider, as Bob Fosse's alter ego in *All That Jazz*, announces, "It's showtime!" And in *Dirty Dancing* Patrick Swayze's character tells us, "Nobody puts Baby in the corner."

The 1930s and 40s were the golden days of Hollywood screenwriting, when language was as important as visuals. In more recent decades, concept and effects have ruled the movies and language, with few exceptions, has become secondary. It's a pity since famous lines live on even after their movies are forgotten. ■

It would only be a few years after sound came in that Hollywood came up with another long-lasting line, "You're going out a youngster but you've got to come back a star!" Ruby Keeler was commanded thusly by Warner Baxter in *42nd Street* and a cliché was born.

SONGS

"Baby, Let Me Take You Dreaming" ■ "Life Could Not Better Be" ■ "The Maladjusted Jester (Nobody's Fool)" (lyric by Sylvia Fine) ■ "My Heart Knows a Lovely Song" ■ "Outfox the Fox" ■ "Pass the Basket"

Danny Kaye

O ne of the great comics, Danny Kaye had a series of films specially tailored to his unique talents. Both Kaye and Jerry Lewis were often bewildered by the opposite sex, modern appliances, and contemporary mores. Both were bumblers, but Lewis destroyed whereas Kaye merely upset the apple cart. Lewis gave in to his more immature side and was childish; in contrast, Kaye remained simply childlike. In *Hans Christian Andersen*, and *The Secret Life of Walter Mitty*, Kaye escapes the responsibilities and realities of his disappointing adulthood by daydreaming, in fact. With his slightly feminine demeanor and sensitivity, he embodied the man-child. He gained fame on stage in the Kurt Weill–Ira Gershwin musical, *Lady in the Dark*. After the Cole Porter romp, *Let's Face It*, Hollywood beckoned and Kaye was headlined in 1944's *Up In Arms*. A number of his films have become classics *White Christmas* (1954), *The Five Pennies* (1959). Kaye decamped to television when his film career petered out. He was married to songwriter Sylvia Fine, who supplied the often tongue-twisting songs for his pictures. In 1970, he returned to the Broadway stage as Noah in the Richard Rodgers musical *Two By Two*.

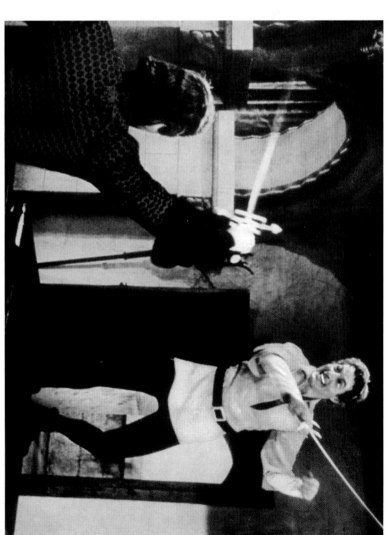

Norman Panama and Mel Frank

T he team of Panama and Frank specialized in hilarious farces where the language was precise and the routines bordered on the ridiculous without falling into the realm of impossibility. They kept a tight rein on stupidity. In fact, *Li'l Abner*, which they originated on Broadway, is one of the smartest musicals ever written about uneducated people. Panama and Frank met in school and began a thirty-year collaboration, writing, producing, and directing films high (*White Christmas*) and low (*Not with My Wife You Don't*). Panama wrote about their pairing, "We were a composite of almost the same personality, strangely enough—a composite talent." After college, the team began writing for radio. Bob Hope put them on his personal staff and took them to Hollywood, where they wrote their first picture, *My Favorite Blonde*.

THE COURT JESTER **45**

DAMN YANKEES

WARNER BROTHERS—MARCH 6, 1959

DAMN YANKEES

COMPOSERS: Richard Adler
and Jerry Ross

LYRICISTS: Richard Adler
and Jerry Ross

PRODUCERS: George Abbott
and Stanley Donen

DIRECTORS: George Abbott
and Stanley Donen

SCREENWRITER: George Abbott

SOURCE: Based on the musical Damn
Yankees by George Abbott, Richard
Adler, and Jerry Ross

CHOREOGRAPHERS: Bob Fosse and
Pat Ferrier

Synopsis

An old baseball fan with regrets over never making it to the mound makes a pact with the devil to become a smash hit (is that a pun?) baseball player. When he has a change of heart, the devil tries to tempt him with S-E-X and musical numbers. Calling Dr. Faustus.

Cast

Tab Hunter	Joe Hardy
Gwen Verdon	Lola
Ray Walston	Mr. Applegate
Shannon Bolin	Mrs. Meg Boyd
Rae Allen	Gloria Thorpe
Robert Shafer	Joe Boyd
Jean Stapleton	Sister Miller
Nathaniel Frey	Smokey
James Komack	Rocky
Russ Brown	Benny Van Buren
Albert Linville	Vernon
Bob Fosse	Dancer in "Who's Got the Pain"

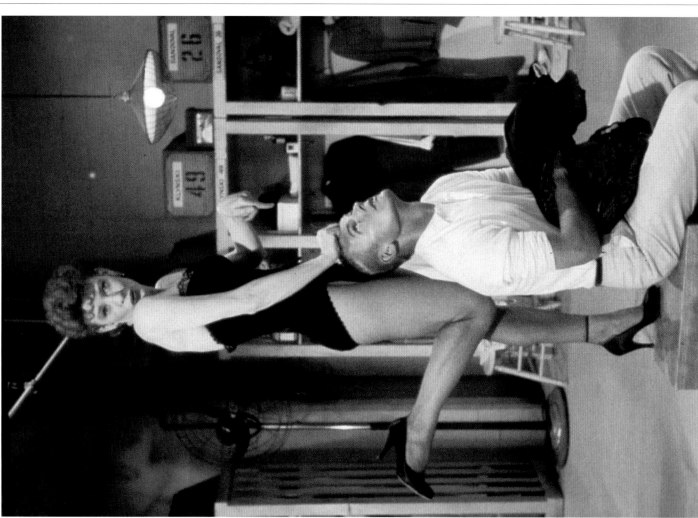

Whatever Lola wants Lola gets. Except Tab Hunter, that is—to the relief of thousands of girls (and boys) watching *Damn Yankees*.

EVERY TIME A BROADWAY WAG SEES THE FILM VERSION OF HIS FAVORITE (OR ANY) musical, he complains, "It's not the same as it was on Broadway." He has a point, of course, as Hollywood has historically shown little respect for the Broadway originals. (See our thoughts in *The Pajama Game* chapter for some tales of horrific recasting, alongside a few examples where Hollywood got it right.)

Well, there have been a few shows that are basically filmed versions of the stage originals. *Top Banana* (which was actually filmed in 3-D but never issued that way), *Li'l Abner*, the aforementioned *The Pajama Game*, and *Damn Yankees* are all extremely faithful to their respective stage incarnation—the last one perhaps to a fault. Film versions of *The*

Pirates of Penzance and *Rent* featured most of their original stage casts; *Top Banana* and, more recently, *Passing Strange*, were actually filmed live in theaters.

The Pajama Game and *Damn Yankees* sprang from the same creative minds. Both had scores by Jerry Ross and Richard Adler; were produced by Harold Prince, Robert E. Griffith, and Frederick Brisson; directed by George Abbott; and choreographed by Bob Fosse. The film versions were codirected by Abbott and Stanley Donen. The studios needed box-office names. Nobody was going to pay to see non-film stars. They replaced one Broadway cast member for *The Pajama Game*—Janis Paige was shut out in favor of Doris Day. Since that switch worked so well, they decided to swap out one original cast member for *Damn Yankees*, too.

Out went Stephen Douglass in favor of Warner contract player Tab Hunter. If it had been hard for Doris Day to step into *The Pajama Game* among cast members that had worked together on Broadway, Hunter didn't seem to worry about such things. He was undaunted by George Abbott, though the man was considered a god on Broadway, and referred to by all as "Mr. Abbott." (As Gwen Verdon remembered, "He'd say, 'Oh, that's fine. Just get up and say the words. Say them fast and let's get out of here.'") Hunter often disagreed with Mr. Abbott's directorial notes. Finally, Abbott threw up his hands and told Hunter, "Oh, do what you want."

That was a problem—but not the only one. The shoot was plagued by a musicians' strike, so there wasn't the usual orchestral playback on the set when filming. (Because of the strike Ray Heindorf got no credit for his musical supervision.) Soon, the directors were threatening to join their fellow union members, so the movie's shooting schedule was speeded up, echoing *The Pajama Game* foreman's edict to "Hurry up!"

Luckily for us, Gwen Verdon's exciting performance as Lola is preserved forever. Sadly, it was her only leading role in a musical, though she made a comeback of sorts very late in her career, in the oldster ensemble picture *Cocoon*. Ray Walston came to the attention of Hollywood that same year, with his double play of *South Pacific* and *Damn Yankees*. But we are the real winners here, bagging a well-preserved version of a Broadway hit. ∎

> "Stanley [Donen] was very gentle with me, because he felt I didn't know what I was doing. Which was true."
>
> —*Gwen Verdon*

SONGS

"Goodbye Old Girl" ▪ "Heart" ▪ "Shoeless Joe from Hannibal, Mo." ▪ "A Little Brains, a Little Talent" ▪ "Six Months out of Every Year" ▪ "There's Something About an Empty Chair" (Richard Adler) ▪ "Those Were the Good Old Days" ▪ "Two Lost Souls" ▪ "Whatever Lola Wants (Lola Gets)" ▪ "Who's Got the Pain"

Stanley Donen

Struth 24 times a second. Because in my opinion, film is a lie 24 times a second. Everything is pre-arranged, pre-digested, rehearsed, thought out, worked out, written down, and eventually photographed." (Goddard was a huge fan of Donen's, especially of his work on *Seven Brides for Seven Brothers* and *The Pajama Game*.) Donen collaborated with George Abbott on both *Pajama Game* and *Damn Yankees*—but the great collaboration of his career was with Gene Kelly, on a series of films that exploited the possibilities of film and changed the way dance was depicted in movies. In *Cover Girl*, Gene Kelly performed a dance duet with his alter-ego, in *Anchors Aweigh*, he partnered with an animated Jerry Mouse from *Tom & Jerry* fame. *On the Town*, in which dance was as important as the score, provided ample opportunities for Donen/Kelly invention. Vera-Ellen's character was introduced in a dance montage that revealed the disparate aspects of her personality. In that film, too, Donen took the camera onto the streets of New York, giving it a sense of excitement, drive, and realism that hadn't been achieved since Rouben Mamoulian's *Applause* in 1929. Donen said, "We never told ourselves, 'Now we're going to do something no one has ever done before.' We simply thought that this was the way one should deal with, one should conceive, musical comedy. This is the way we felt—we didn't realize we were making any innovations." That was Stanley Donen's strength. He was never a show-off, never schematic, but always natural and inventive in service of the needs of his films.

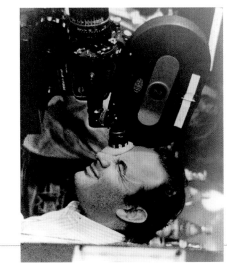

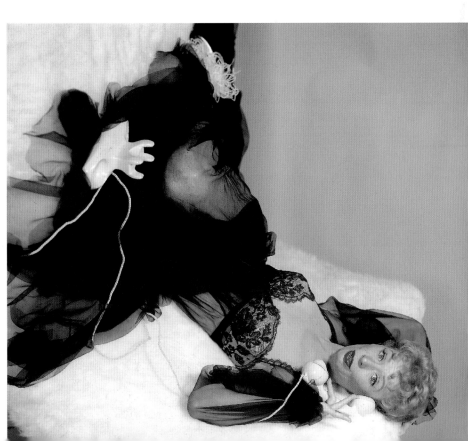

ABOVE: Gwen Verdon calls her agent to see if there are any other offers on the horizon. There aren't.

BELOW LEFT: Bob Fosse and Gwen Verdon explain "Who's Got the Pain?"

BELOW RIGHT: Stanley Donen on the set of *Bedazzled*.

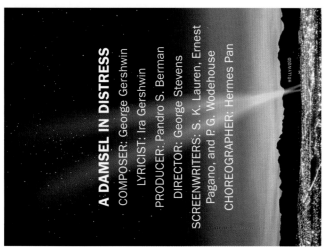

A DAMSEL IN DISTRESS

COMPOSER: George Gershwin
LYRICIST: Ira Gershwin
PRODUCER: Pandro S. Berman
DIRECTOR: George Stevens
SCREENWRITERS: S. K. Lauren, Ernest Pagano, and P. G. Wodehouse
CHOREOGRAPHER: Hermes Pan

Synopsis

In a plot we can all identify with, Lady Alyce Marshmorton will lose her inheritance unless she marries—but fast! She runs into Fred Astaire, who attempts to teach her to dance. They get married anyway.

Cast

Fred Astaire..............*Jerry Halliday*
George Burns..............*George*
Gracie Allen..............*Gracie*
Joan Fontaine..............*Lady Alyce Marshmorton*
Reginald Gardiner..............*Keggs*
Ray Noble..............*Reggie*
Constance Collier..............*Lady Caroline*
Montagu Love..............*Lord John Marshmorton*
Harry Watson..............*Albert*
Jan Duggan..............*Miss Ruggles*

A DAMSEL IN DISTRESS

RKO—NOVEMBER 19, 1937

George Burns, Gracie Allen, and Fred Astaire take a spin in the fun house sequence.

HERE'S THE FIRST RKO FILM WITH FRED BUT NO GINGER. HIS NEW PARTNER? JOAN Fontaine—charming and delightful, yes, but imagine the disappointment to audiences at the time.

With Astaire at center screen, there had to be dancing—but Fontaine couldn't be expected to fill the void left by Rogers. It took two additional pros to make up for her absence: those stalwart stars of vaudeville, radio, and film (and later television) George Burns and Gracie Allen. The duo even made their own choreographic contribution. Burns recalled a whisk broom dance that he'd seen done in vaudeville by the team of Evans and Evans; he flew Evans (but not Evans) to Hollywood to teach the dance to Fred, Gracie, and himself, and it became a highlight of the film.

If you thought George and Gracie couldn't really dance, take a gander at the fantastic funhouse sequence set to the song "Stiff Upper Lip," where Fred and Gracie reenact a sequence from Fred and his sister Adele's old vaudeville act. Called the "Oompah Trot/ Runaround Dance," the two follow each other in a circle, round and round and round, Gracie partnering delightfully with her masterful partner.

It's like this: with their years of stage experience, vaudevillians (the great ones, anyhow) could do anything: sing, dance, act, you name it. The Marx Brothers, Jimmy Durante,

"The poor girl couldn't even walk."

—Hermes Pan on Joan Fontaine

Eddie Cantor, and Al Jolson all got their start in vaudeville. So did the multitalented Jack Benny, Bob Hope, and Milton Berle. These great performers and others like them enjoyed extremely long, successful careers.

Some of these versatile performers, including Burns and Allen, appeared in early talkie short subjects, notably the Vitaphone shorts. Some, like the Three Stooges (originally named Ted Healy's Stooges), barely strayed from their two-reel roots. Feature films in the 30s, especially musicals, provided work for former vaudeville artists with more specialized talents as well, in countless scenes set in theatrical agents' offices. For ten minutes or so, the movie would stop dead while these novelty artists strutted their stuff before the cameras, finally achieving some degree of immortality.

George and Gracie might have been luckier than most—but then they were more talented than most. Having created their own unforgettable persona, they could sing, dance, act, and write their own material. Given George's vaudeville history with the likes of Fink's Mules, it's surprising he didn't also team up with Donald O'Connor on the Francis the Talking Mule series at Universal. But seriously, vaudeville was a priceless training ground for all sorts of performers with all sorts of talents, and the movies were richer for them. ■

ABOVE: Fred looks incredulous when Joan Fontaine admits she can't dance.

BELOW: Choreographer Hermes Pan, Fred Astaire, director Mark Sandrich, Ginger Rogers, Ira Gershwin, and musical director Nat Shilkret listen attentively as George Gershwin plays the score of *Shall We Dance?*

SONGS

"A Foggy Day" ■ "I Can't Be Bothered Now" ■ "The Jolly Tar and the Milkmaid" ■ "Nice Work If You Can Get It" ■ "Sing of Spring" ■ "Stiff Upper Lip" ■ "Things Are Looking Up"

Behind the Screen

- George Gershwin died before the film was released.

- Adele Astaire was asked to come out of retirement to do the film, but she turned it down. Also considered were Carole Lombard, Katharine Hepburn, Ida Lupino, Jean Arthur, Eleanor Powell, Alice Faye, Ruby Keeler, and Jessie Matthews.

George and Ira Gershwin

Right off the bat, we'd like to clear up one thing. George and Ira Gershwin were brothers, not husband and wife. Composer George was the outgoing, gregarious, enthusiastic one. At parties he'd be the one at the piano, joyously trying out his newest song. Lyricist Ira was the quiet bookworm. Although he enjoyed the constant stream of visitors that trooped through the brothers' apartments, he was outwardly the more sensitive of the two. They came to Broadway fame in the early 1920s. As it did to many Broadway songwriters, Hollywood beckoned and they went to Fox in 1931 to try their hand at the movies. *Delicious* was the result and the score was . . . well, delicious. But Broadway had the stronger pull and George had classical aspirations. After George's opera/musical (take your pick), *Porgy and Bess* opened in 1935, they went west again, landing RKO. With films such as *A Damsel in Distress* and *Shall We Dance*, the brothers proved themselves equally at home in Hollywood and New York. Tragedy came when George died of a brain tumor in 1937, at age thirty-eight. Ira was devastated, as were the many Americans who loved George's music. An unfinished score for *The Goldwyn Follies* was completed with the help of the George's friend Kay Swift and two ballet scores by Vernon Duke. Four years later, Ira felt up to returning to Broadway with 1941's *Lady in the Dark*, and collaborating with Jerome Kern on the 1944 score to *Cover Girl*. The following year, Hollywood saluted the team with a typically idiotic biopic, *Rhapsody in Blue*. Two more original scores of George's would premiere in movies: Ira wrote the lyrics for *The Shocking Miss Pilgrim* using musical sketches George had left behind. And, after Ira penned the brilliant lyrics to Harold Arlen's equally brilliant music to *A Star Is Born*, yet another original George and Ira score hit the screen, when Billy Wilder's 1964 *Kiss Me, Stupid* featured three new songs by the Gershwins.

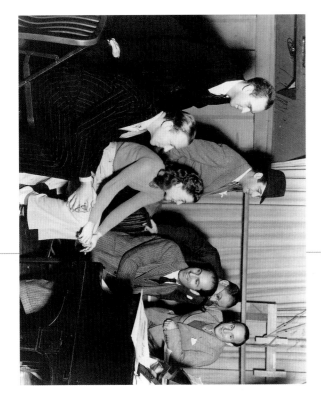

DANGEROUS WHEN WET

MGM—JULY 3, 1953

DANGEROUS WHEN WET

COMPOSER: Arthur Schwartz
LYRICIST: Johnny Mercer
PRODUCER: George Wells
DIRECTOR: Charles Walters
SCREENWRITER: Dorothy Kingsley
CHOREOGRAPHERS: Billy Daniels and Charles Walters

Synopsis

Esther Williams swims with a cartoon cat and mouse and Fernando Lamas. She chooses the last, after she conquers the English Channel.

Cast

Esther Williams	Katie Higgins
Fernando Lamas	André Lanet
Jack Carson	Windy Weebe
Charlotte Greenwood	Ma Higgins
Denise Darcel	Gigi Mignon
William Demarest	Pa Higgins
Donna Corcoran	Junior Higgins
Barbara Whiting	Suzy Higgins
Tom and Jerry	Themselves

Behind the Screen

■ Esther Williams met Fernando Lamas on the film. They'd eventually marry.

■ Jerry the mouse also danced with Gene Kelly in *Anchors Aweigh* but he and his partner Tom's tight schedule made other feature appearances impossible.

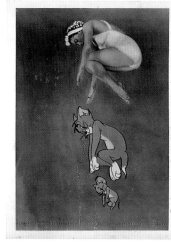

Esther Williams and her costars, Tom and Jerry.

MGM HAD CLOWNS SUCH AS RED SKELTON, GIRLS NEXT DOOR SUCH AS JUNE ALLYSON and Judy Garland, youngsters such as Mickey Rooney and Elizabeth Taylor, and oldsters such as C. Aubrey Smith and Lewis Stone. Other studios matched them categorically. But only MGM had two swimming stars, Esther Williams and Johnny Weissmuller, though not at the same time. Weissmuller got out of the jungle only once in his career but Williams was more versatile and spent at least some of her film career drying out. She was beautiful, could sing well enough, and her acting was equal to her singing. She had the MGM zip, a projection of self-confidence and energy that masked other deficiencies. Acting with confidence

Esther Williams

When someone grew tired of her. After all, how much variety can you get when the star spends most of her time waterlogged? Here's a list of Esther Williams's musical movies.

There were some terrific individual numbers and some of the movies were actually good, but overall it's a pretty sorry record. She began with the definitely minor offering *Fiesta* with Ricardo Montalban as her costar. She followed it up with *This Time for Keeps*, another so-so film. *On an Island with You* had Peter Lawford and Ricardo Montalban vying for Esther's attention. They certainly got the attention of women in the audience (and some men, too) with their beautiful physique and charm. Williams then spent some time one on dry land in *Take Me Out to the Ball Game*, a rare assignment with the Freed unit. It wasn't one of their best, but it's stylish and slickly produced. That film seemed to briefly lift her status at MGM and she followed it with *Neptune's Daughter*, a pretty good film. But then came four pretty much unwatchable films: *Duchess of Idaho, Pagan Love Song, Texas Carnival* (with a fine score by Arthur Schwartz and Dorothy Fields, and strong support by Howard Keel), and *Skirts Ahoy!* Finally, MGM seemed to wake up and provided Esther with one of her strongest films, the biopic of Annette Kellerman, *Million Dollar Mermaid*. *Bathing Beauty*, a huge hit, is another great film with Williams, rivaling *Dangerous when Wet* as her best. As the '50s went on, the caliber of MGM's musicals sagged precipitously. The final one featuring Williams is her only flop, *Jupiter's Darling*. It contains one of the greatest film dances ever—Marge and Gower Champion dancing around and under some very compliant pachyderms. Director George Sidney said that audiences had grown tired of her. Despite what Williams said of her own acting abilities, she turned into a pretty good actress and singer by the time she was done. After her movie career went down the drain (hah!), she tried a little television and retired to tend to a line of swimwear and a swimming pool company, both bearing her name. Her autobiography was published in 1999 and in it, she claimed that her one-time beau Jeff Chandler was a cross-dresser. In private conversations with friends, she admitted that she'd made the story up to sell books.

"I am a swimmer, not an actress."
—Esther Williams, when asked if she'd replace Lana Turner in a picture

brought the audience along for the ride. Other studio's stars had it, too. Paramount's Bob Hope and Martha Raye had that the same zip, but they were looser, less reined in than their Metro counterparts. Fox stars didn't have that get-up-and-go. Musical stars such as Alice Faye were more measured in their performances, but MGMers, including Judy Garland, Mickey Rooney, Debbie Reynolds, Betty Garrett, Nanette Fabray, Gene Kelly, Red Skelton, and Esther Williams employed a certain attack that propelled them, their plots, and their characters from the first frame to the end titles. In *Dangerous When Wet*, Williams gives the impression that crooning songs, dancing wildly, snogging Fernando Lamas, swimming the English Channel, and costarring with Tom and Jerry are nothing but fun.

In the early '50s MGM made a lot of Technicolor films. Other studios saved color for their A-list films, but MGM was the proudest of studios and, with the encroaching threat of television, felt that glorious Technicolor set their product apart from the black-and-white TV offerings. This benefited Williams in particular. Her production numbers were made for color (just look at the Busby Berkeley extravaganza in *Million Dollar Mermaid*). The sight of Williams swimming in gray water just wouldn't be as sumptuous or appealing.

Stars with specialties graced other studios as well. Sonja Henie at Fox and Vera Hruba Ralston at Republic were Olympic skaters. Though their production numbers were quite large and elaborate, they didn't have the advantages of Williams's best numbers. Being ice-bound didn't lend itself to the flights of imagination that were possible with a swimming star.

Although *Dangerous When Wet* isn't the most outrageous of Williams's many films, it's among the tightest, plot-wise, and the most charming. It has a terrific score, a wonderful supporting cast of characters, a whimsical rather than eyeball-assaulting fantasy sequence, and a hunky leading man. What more could one want in escapist entertainment? ■

SONGS

"Ain't Nature Grand" ■ "Fifi" ■ "I Got Out of Bed on the Right Side" ■ "I Like Men" ■ "In My Wildest Dreams" ■ "Liquapep"

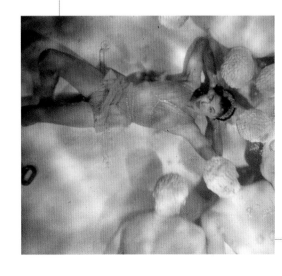

ABOVE: Two cameramen join Esther Williams for a dip. Note the contraption on the floor that keeps her at the bottom of the pool. We love this photo from *Jupiter's Darling*.

RIGHT: Esther underwater while filming *Jupiter's Darling*. She's surrounded with adoring Roman statues come to life. Notice the handle behind her.

DUMBO

COMPOSER: Frank E. Churchill
LYRICIST: Ned Washington
PRODUCER: Walt Disney
DIRECTOR: Ben Sharpsteen
SCREENWRITERS: Joe Grant and Dick Huemer
SOURCE: Based on the book by Helen Aberson and Harold Pearl

Synopsis

Dumbo is a nerd among elephants and teased incessantly—until Timothy the mouse teaches him that the very things that make him different might just make him soar.

Cast

Edward Brophy	Timothy Q. Mouse
Verna Felton	Mrs. Jumbo
Sterling Holloway	Mr. Stork
Jim Carmichael	Crow
Cliff Edwards	Jim Crow
James Baskett	Crow
Herman Bing	Ringmaster

Behind the Screen

- The first ten minutes is nearly continuous music. This sequence almost certainly inspired the creators of the 2008 film *Wall-E*.
- RKO, Disney's distributor at the time, was upset that the picture was only sixty-four minutes long.

DUMBO

DISNEY—NOVEMBER 23, 1941

Defying gravity, Dumbo and Timothy soar over the circus lot.

IS THERE ANYTHING AS TOUCHING IN ALL MOVIE HISTORY AS THE SCENE IN WHICH DUMBO'S mother, locked in the jail car, reaches her trunk through the bars to cradle her young son? Is there any tour de force of animation that equals the psychedelic, drunken dreams of Dumbo and Timothy?

Is there anything more terrifying than the *Tyrannosaurus rex* in *Fantasia* or as hilarious as Elmer Fudd and Bugs Bunny romping through Wagner in the animated short *What's Opera, Doc?* Are there set designs more beautiful than those in *Sleeping Beauty*, or scenes as warmly romantic as that of *Lady and Tramp* sharing a plate of spaghetti and meatballs? We ask these loaded questions because, for decades, the animated film has been treated simply as children's fare. Yes, a couple of songs and scores might have been nominated for Oscars—and some cartoon shorts have even won their categories. But, until quite recently, feature cartoons have been second-class citizens in Hollywood. This in spite of the fact that Disney's directors have always been just as adept as their live-action counterparts at choosing camera angles, coaxing out great performances, and creating on-screen emotions.

Disney's resurgence with *Beauty and the Beast* in 1991 was an undeniable affirmation of the skill and artistry of cartoons—but they continue to be slighted at Oscar time, bagging mainly songwriting nominations with an occasional Best Picture thrown in. We would aver that the screenplay to *Dumbo* is as tight and well constructed as any. The editing, lighting, and effects in the "Song of the Roustabouts" is equal to those of any Spielberg film. And the humor of "Look Out for Mister Stork" is funny, imaginative, and—get this—charming. In today's era of crass, cynical, and sophomoric humor, "charming" is practically unknown.

Brad Bird, Pixar Studios' brilliant director, recognized this irony when he said, "When *Snow White* came out, it was at the forefront of cinema, not just at the forefront of animation. If you look at the best scenes in *Snow White* and compare them with the best filmmaking in 1937, it's up there." Perhaps it is not surprising, then, that Pixar has taken up the Disney mantle and is producing films with many of the Disney hallmarks and values. And we mean artistic values as well as social ones. Bird explained, "When you're given a film, you're given a whole package of tools—the same tools that Chaplin and Welles and Kubrick and the other great filmmakers use. If you use every single one of them in concert, it nails you?"

We're pleased that animated films (including Pixar's *Toy Story, Finding Nemo, Ratatouille,* and the exquisite *Wall-E*) are finally getting their due. The wide range of artists at work in animation may still be underappreciated in relation to their live-action brethren, but we're sure their moment is coming. Meanwhile, those of us who appreciate great work on the screen, no matter what the medium, have great movies like *Dumbo* to cherish forever. ∎

SONGS

"Baby Mine" ∎ "Casey Junior" ∎ "Look Out for Mr. Stork" ∎ "Pink Elephants on Parade" (music by Oliver Wallace) ∎ "Song of the Roustabouts" ∎ "When I See an Elephant Fly" (music by Oliver Wallace)

Mrs. Jumbo loves her son, ears and all—or is it all ears?

Frank Churchill

When Carl Stalling left Walt Disney Studios, Disney was left with a giant hole in its music department. Composer Frank Churchill, a Down-Easter who had moved with his family to the central California coast as a child, helped fill the gap. He joined the Disney organization in 1931 as a pianist and arranger. After working for a couple of years on the *Silly Symphony* shorts, he made his first real mark on the music business when he dashed off a catchy little tune for the Disney short *The Three Little Pigs*. Lyricist Ted Sears had written the title line, "Who's Afraid of the Big Bad Wolf," as part of a dummy lyric. Ann Ronell, also a neophyte in Hollywood, would complete the lyric. On the soundtrack, it's Carl Stalling playing the piano for one of the little pigs. During the Second World War, the song became a symbol of America's fortitude, with the Big Bad Wolf standing in for Adolf Hitler. Following that success, Churchill was assigned to the studio's first full-length feature, *Snow White*. He and Larry Morey, one of the directors on the film, wrote twenty songs for the film and eight were ultimately used. The team was then set loose on *Dumbo* and, next, *Bambi*. Churchill's underscoring for *Bambi* was mostly discarded, sending the composer into a depression. Even winning the Academy Award (along with Oliver Wallace) for the score to *Dumbo* didn't help his mood and, a month after the Oscars, Churchill took his own life.

Ned Washington

Ned Washington began his professional career on Broadway, where he contributed exactly one song to *Earl Carroll's Vanities of 1928*. Then it was off to Hollywood. It was a smart move: in 1928 his song "Singing in the Bathtub," written with Michael Cleary and Herb Magidson, became a hit. When movie musicals went briefly out of style, Washington turned to popular songs ("I Don't Stand a Ghost of a Chance," "Got the South in My Soul," and "I'm Getting Sentimental over You"). Washington returned to Hollywood and, with Bronislau Kaper and Walter Jurmann, provided "Cosi Cosa" for the Marx Brothers vehicle *A Night at the Opera*. Hoagy Carmichael provided the lyrics to "The Nearness of You" for the film *Romance in the Dark*. Disney beckoned and Washington provided the music to Leigh Harline's music for *Pinocchio*. He joined his lyrics to Frank Churchill and Oliver Wallace's music for *Dumbo*, and the result is a very sophisticated and emotional score for a cartoon feature. Washington didn't usually contribute complete scores for films but he had some smash hit single songs, including "Stella by Starlight," a promo song based on a theme from the move, and great title songs for *High Noon* and *Town without Pity*.

EASTER PARADE

COMPOSER: Irving Berlin
LYRICIST: Irving Berlin
PRODUCER: Arthur Freed
DIRECTOR: Charles Walters
SCREENWRITERS: Frances Goodrich.
Albert Hackett, and Sidney Sheldon.
CHOREOGRAPHER: Robert Alton

Synopsis

Two couples sing and dance their way through a great American's song catalog, accompanying us on a stroll down the avenue, Fifth Avenue . . .

Cast

Frec Astaire.................Don Hewes
Judy Garland..............Hannah Brown
Peter Lawford............Jonathan Harrow III
Ann Miller...................Nadine Hale
Jules Munshin.............Headwaiter François

EASTER PARADE

MGM—JULY 8, 1948

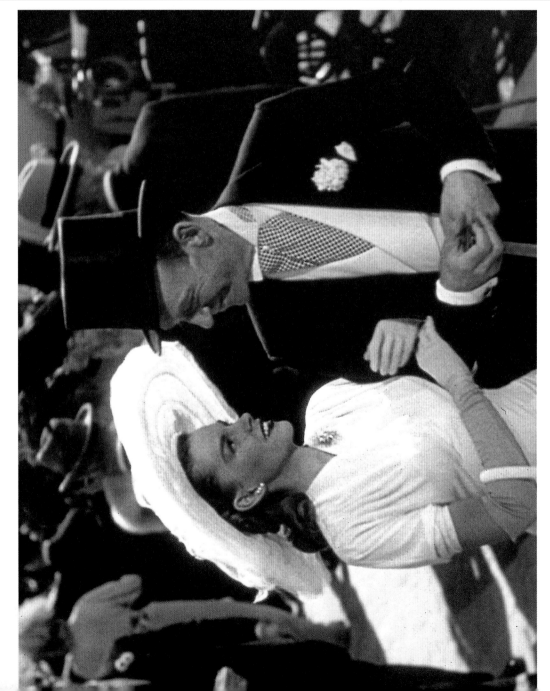

Judy Garland and Fred Astaire stroll down the avenue, Fifth Avenue, while the photographers snap them for the rotogravure.

A PRIME EXAMPLE OF SLICK, SOPHISTICATED, FAULTLESS MOVIE MAKING, *EASTER PARADE* is a hallmark of MGM and what became known as the Freed Unit. MGM's musicals were produced within an inch of their lives. Not for them the quickie production schedules of Universal, the anything-for-a-laugh philosophy of Paramount, or the slangy zip of Warner Brothers. MGM musicals were conceived and executed to be the best in the business and many times they were.

Arthur Freed, Jack Cummings, and Joseph Pasternak were the main producers of MGM musicals but Freed was the big deal, first-string producer. Lots has been written about Freed's reliance on his associate, Roger Edens, in all matters of taste, but Freed had the business smarts and knew how to talk to the MGM execs. And he went to bat for his productions, too. When *Gigi* needed expensive retakes, it was Freed who found a way to free up the money. Pasternak and Cummings made hit A-budget movies but they were more formulaic—not ambitious, Broadway-influenced projects like Freed.

Freed left artists alone to be as creative as they could be. And if problems arose, as they certainly did, on *Easter Parade*, Freed made sure that the resulting picture didn't show any of the stress and strain of production. Gene Kelly was supposed to be the lead in the film but he broke his ankle while playing touch football–skiing–playing volleyball (take your pick—they've all been cited) and had to be replaced by Fred Astaire. Now, you must admit that excellent as they both were, their styles are wildly divergent and this made for a very different film than it might have been. Cyd Charisse was cast as the second female lead but *she* had the nerve to tear a ligament in her foot. She was replaced

Ann Miller shakes the blues away as only she can.

by Ann Miller. Again—a substitution that was excellent but wildly divergent. When Freed was asked by Irving Berlin what he was going to do about the tragic loss of Kelly, he calmly replied, "Don't worry. I'll handle it." He brought Astaire out of one of his occasional retirements and the show went on. The result? *Easter Parade* seems perfectly suited to the talents of Astaire and Miller. It is a high compliment to Freed that we can't even imagine Kelly and Charisse in the parts.

There's one common denominator in such classics as *An American in Paris, Gigi, Meet Me in St. Louis, The Harvey Girls, On the Town, Royal Wedding, Singin' in the Rain, Show Boat,* and *Easter Parade,* and that is producer Arthur Freed. ∎

"Ann Miller would always ask to do everything 'one more time,' and after she reached a certain point, she never improved."

—Saul Chaplin

Ann Miller

Ann Miller got her start in films at RKO at age thirteen (she said that she was eighteen). Four years later, in 1940, she moved over to Columbia Pictures. She was all of seventeen. Did the studios not know she was underage—or did they just not care? Miller employed the always stick-a-smile-on style of dancing. She'd tap her heart out—she was supposedly the fastest tapper on earth—grinning the whole time, her dance personality consisting of one emotion: efficiency. But she was a good actress and a seriously underappreciated singer. On top of it all, she had a lot of camp value. Like a lot of performers, Donald O'Connor, for example, she did her best work at MGM where she was mostly placed in secondary roles. They felt she was brassy, hard, and coquettish to play leads. After movie musicals dried up in the late '50s, Miller turned to the theater and television. In every role, no matter what the piece, she managed to find a reason to whip off her skirt, flash her long gams, and tap till there was no tomorrow. Miller and another MGM musicals outcast, Mickey Rooney, teamed up for the 1979 Broadway musical revue *Sugar Babies,* a smash hit. In it, Miller stopped the show cold with her rendition of "Don't Blame Me." Her last stage role was in a revival of the musical *Follies* at the Paper Mill Playhouse in New Jersey. In it she sang Stephen Sondheim's "I'm Still Here," a song that aptly summed up her incredible career.

LEFT: Ann Miller strikes a sultry pose in this publicity shot for MGM. But really, was Ann Miller ever sultry?
BELOW: Judy accompanies Fred on her violin. (Of course, she's not playing and he's not singing.)

Irving Berlin

His deft lyrics made up of equal parts schmaltz and sass and his music employing counterpoint and syncopation like no other songwriter, Irving Berlin remains the most successful songwriter in American history. Berlin's career spanned the popular music century; for over 60 years, his songs were sung on vaudeville stages, in Broadway revues and musicals, on radio, film, television, and recordings. There was no theme or style of popular music that Berlin didn't conquer. His contributions to Hollywood were immense. He wrote terrific scores through the '30s and '40s for America's top stars. Later in his career, his film scores consisted mainly of recycled tunes—but nobody seemed to mind or notice; they remained great audience favorites. Berlin was a patriotic American and something of a contradiction. A generous man, he donated millions of dollars in royalties to deserving groups but if a colleague or even his wife needed money, he refused. Berlin remained insecure about his songs, despite his great fame. "As a writer gets successful," he once said, "he sharpens his tools and sometimes they're a little *too* critical and what comes out is a good *songwriter's* song but not a natural song." In reality, Berlin was the master of the "natural song," the song that everyman could whistle and hum and think, "Hey! I could write that."

Behind the Screen

- Broadway actress Benay Venuta plays a bar customer. Jimmie Dodd, later host of *The Mickey Mouse Club*, plays the taxicab driver.
- It was decided that in Ann Miller's dancing scenes with Fred Astaire, they would never be seen in a full body shot, because Miller was forced to wear flat ballet shoes so she wouldn't be taller than him.

SONGS

"Better Luck Next Time" ▪ "A Couple of Swells" ▪ "Drum Crazy" ▪ "Easter Parade" ▪ "A Fella with an Umbrella" ▪ "The Girl on the Magazine Cover" ▪ "Happy Easter" ▪ "I Love a Piano" ▪ "I Want to Go Back to Michigan (Down on the Farm)" ▪ "It Only Happens when I Dance with You" ▪ "Steppin' Out with My Baby" ▪ "Ragtime Violin" ▪ "Shaking the Blues Away" ▪ "Snookey Ookums" ▪ "When the Midnight Choo-Choo Leaves for Alabam'"

TOP LEFT: Irving Berlin in 1928, helping to dedicate the new Los Angeles City Hall.

ABOVE RIGHT: Irving Berlin in the 1950s, the grand old man of American popular song.

LEFT: Irving Berlin plays the score to *Top Hat* (1935) for Fred Astaire and Ginger Rogers. Ginger seems to think her cane is a flute!

42ND STREET

WARNER BROTHERS—MARCH 11, 1933

FS-29

H ERE'S THE RARE POPULAR ENTERTAINMENT THAT CREATED A CLICHÉ, AND NOT just a cliché, but perhaps the greatest of all plot clichés. Do we have to tell you that it's all about, "You're going out a [whatever] and coming back a star?" The trope is right up there with Mickey and Judy's, "Let's put on a show!" (and Hamlet's, "There's something rotten in Denmark").

But the great thing about *42nd Street* and other Warner Brothers musicals is their energy. One critic described the backstage antics of chorus girls running up and down the spiral staircase to their dressing rooms as a bunch of especially comely pirates cavorting up and down the rigging of their ship.

It's not an exaggeration to say that *42nd Street* revived the film musical as an art form. And it was exactly that up-to-date, streamlined momentum that felt so fresh after the stilted dialogue (we have to be close to that newfangled microphone) and leaden camerawork (we can't move a two-ton box of sound-proofing around the camera) of early sound films. Improvements in sound technology and Busby Berkeley's sweeping camera antics, including shooting through the legs of chorus girls or far above a bevy of geometrically choreographed females, made the Warner's musicals thrilling to watch. Marry that with dialogue written in short bursts, devoid of long romantic speeches (save the most important speech in movie history, the aforementioned, "You're going out there a...") and you get a whole new form of entertainment.

Ginger Rogers as Anytime Annie, Ruby Keeler as Peggy Sawyer, and Una Merkel as Lorraine Fleming. Quiz: Which character will date just about any guy?

42ND STREET

COMPOSER: Harry Warren
LYRICIST: Al Dubin
PRODUCER: Hal B. Wallis
DIRECTOR: Lloyd Bacon
SCREENWRITERS: Rian James and James Seymour
SOURCE: Based on the novel *42nd Street* by Bradford Ropes
CHOREOGRAPHER: Busby Berkeley

Synopsis

Two dreamers, one who yearns to be a big Broadway star and another who wants to be a big Broadway songwriter, realize their dreams—and find each other in the process! Everything's great until the leading lady is forced to drop out of the show because of an injury. Who will save the day?

Cast

Dick Powell................Billy Lawler
Ruby Keeler................Peggy Sawyer
Warner Baxter................Julian Marsh
Bebe Daniels................Dorothy Brock
George Brent................Pat Denning
Guy Kibbee................Abner Dillon
Una Merkel................Lorraine Fleming
Ginger Rogers................Ann
Ned Sparks................Barry
Allan Jenkins................Mac Elroy

These were movies whose plots went by at breakneck speed, buoyed along by fast cuts, snappy dialogue with plenty of slang, and an attitude that combined cynicism and romanticism, sometimes softening the hard edge of the characters while desweetening the sappy love story. It was a hard thing to accomplish.

How hard? Think of MGM's *A Night at the Opera*, where the Marx Brothers' explosion of pretense stood well apart from the schmaltzy romance between Kitty Carlisle's character and that of Allan Jones. The humor stopped dead whenever the lovers broke into unashamedly sentimental operetta-styled numbers such as "Alone." These moments were gloriously over the top, but many blocks from *42nd Street*.

Warner lyricist Al Dubin was a cigar-chomping, whoring, binge-eating, and drinking reprobate. His songs reflect his hard-boiled attitude toward life and that that informed all the Warner Brothers musicals. When you think about it, Warner musicals had exactly the same artistic ethos as the studio's tough-guy gangster films starring James Cagney and Humphrey Bogart—lacking only the bloodshed, which was replaced by armies of beautiful girls.

You'll notice, especially in Dubin and Warren songs, that even the ballads have an energy that drives them forward. And . . . were there any more socially significant statements made in films than "Remember My Forgotten Man," "We're in the Money," and "Lullaby of Broadway?"

Beyond its value as entertainment, *42nd Street* reputedly saved Warner Brothers from bankruptcy and set the template for a whole subgenre of films. There aren't too many movies that can make that boast. ∎

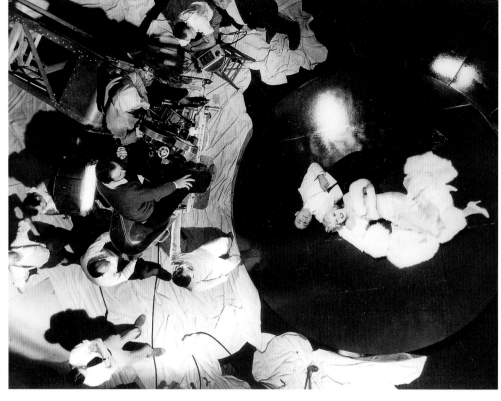

LEFT: Joan Blondell and Dick Powell enjoy the state of holy matrimony. Three years later they were divorced.

ABOVE: Toby Wing and Dick Powell sing "Young and Healthy" (which they are) as Busby Berkeley (in dark sweater) looks over them.

Dick Powell

Baby-faced Dick Powell was the ultimate male musical juvenile, appearing in lots of Warner musicals. He broadened his acting and had a quick mind that lent itself to film producing and directing. But for our purposes, never mind those accomplishments. Let's concentrate on his years of indentured servitude to the brothers Warner. Squiring Ruby Keeler around a series of Horatio Alger-esque musicals, he played would-be songwriters who just needed pluck, luck, and a comely girl to make it big on Broadway. Funny that none of the aspiring tunesmiths he played wanted to break into pictures. Even then Hollywood writers knew that Broadway was the apex of it all. (Of course, Harry Warren might have disagreed—but back to Dick Powell.) Warner featured him in films such as *42nd Street*, *Gold Diggers of 1933*, *Footlight Parade*, *College Coach*, *Wonder Bar*, *20 Million Sweethearts*, *Flirtation Walk*, *On the Avenue*, *Hollywood Hotel*, and *Going Places* but they suited him to a T. He was charming, bright, humorous, and had a winning way with a song. He broke out of the musicals grind to become one of the best (and darkest) of film noir actors in films like *Murder My Sweet*, *Cornered*, and *Pitfall*. We should have known that Powell had more to him than just boyish charm. He first married fellow Warner toiler Joan Blondell, a smart, brassy gal, and then moved on to MGM's June Allyson.

ABOVE: Director Lloyd Bacon (far left) looks on, as Guy Kibbee is surrounded by pretty chorines. Guy Kibbee? What did they see in him?

■ Producer David Merrick saw the film of *42nd Street* and decided it would make an ideal Broadway musical. He was right: the show was an immense hit, following a turbulent out-of-town tryout. It gave even greater impetus to the adaptation of movie musicals for Broadway, though none was as successful as *42nd Street*.

"Sawyer, you're going out a youngster but you've got to come back a star!"

—*Director Julian Marsh*

Ruby Keeler

Ruby Keeler was sweet. She came across as a little dim but game, which made for a nice combination. She didn't have a lot of range, but no matter. She was married to Al Jolson, which helped her behind the scenes (and probably accounted for her anti-Semitism). She was pliable, and that came in handy when she was surrounded by hundreds of tapping feet and far more conventionally pretty girls. We'll defend her here as a dancer. She gets a bad rap for her tap dancing but critics are missing the point, which is that there were two styles of dancing back in vaudeville days: soft shoe and hard shoe. The latter could be heard in the biggest theaters, even in the days before microphones. Hard shoe dancing gave way to tap dancing, but Keeler was a hard shoe dancer—which made her look flat-footed. After appearing on Broadway (where Ziegfeld himself wanted to make her a star), she came to Warner in 1933, made *42nd Street*, and a series of classic films including *Gold Diggers of 1933*, *Footlight Parade*, *Dames*, *Flirtation Walk*, *Go Into Your Dance*, and *Shipmates Forever*. She retired after only eight years yet had a big impact on film culture.

TOP LEFT: Even the skyscrapers have rhythm when Ruby Keeler is on *42nd Street*.

TOP RIGHT: Julian Marsh delivers the big line about coming back a star to Peggy Sawyer, while her fellow chorines wonder, why *her*?

ABOVE: Ruby walks in on Dick while he's adjusting his garters. Yes, I said garters.

LEFT: Busby Berkeley and Ruby Keeler are reunited on the stage of the 1971 revival of *No, No, Nanette*.

FUNNY FACE

COMPOSER: George Gershwin
LYRICIST: Ira Gershwin
PRODUCER: Roger Edens
DIRECTOR: Stanley Donen
SCREENWRITER: Leonard Gershe
CHOREOGRAPHERS: Fred Astaire and Eugene Loring

Synopsis

Audrey Hepburn plays a dowdy bookworm startled to find herself on the road to supermodel stardom. In Paris, she puts her books aside and learns to love the camera, as well as a photographer thirty-one years her elder. He's Fred Astaire—can you blame her?

Cast

Audrey Hepburn............Jo Stockton
Fred Astaire...................Dick Avery
Kay Thompson..............Maggie Prescott
Michel Auclair...............Professor Emile Flostre
Robert Flemyng............Paul Duval
Dovima.........................Marion

FUNNY FACE

PARAMOUNT—FEBRUARY 13, 1957

ABOVE: The Venus de Milo had nothing on Audrey Hepburn.

RIGHT: Kay Thompson in full swagger. *Très chic, n'est pas?*

F UNNY FACE STARTED ITS LIFE IN 1927, AS A BROADWAY MUSICAL STARRING FRED AND Adele Astaire, with a score by George and Ira Gershwin. Thirty years later, Fred (without his sister Adele) starred in the film version. Since none of the original plot and only four songs were retained from the original, there's little else that links the two properties.

Roger Edens deserves a lot of the credit for the success of *Funny Face*—and perhaps for its very existence. The film was conceived in London, where screenwriter Leonard Gershe and British composer Richard Addinsell were working together on revues and wanted to write a book show. Gershe thought a musical about famed photographer Richard Avedon

and his reluctant model-wife would make a good subject. He wrote a script and titled it *Wedding Day*.

Nothing came of the project until Gershe returned to America and talked Vernon Duke and Ogden Nash into writing some songs for it. Producer Clinton Wilder optioned the property and director-choreographer Robert Alton said he'd take it on if Kay Thompson would play the magazine editor. A while later, when Alton was at MGM and so was Thompson, Alton advised Gershe to approach her about the script. She turned him down.

Two years later, Gershe gave his boyfriend Roger Edens at MGM a copy of the script and score of *Wedding Day*. Edens loved the script but wasn't interested in Duke and Nash's contributions. Then he had a brainstorm: the songs from the Broadway musical *Funny Face* would fit right into the story. All they'd need were a couple of new numbers. Gershe took another crack at the script

and inserted the Gershwin songs. The revamped project attracted the attention of director Stanley Donen, then making musicals for MGM.

Edens wanted Broadway dancer Carol Haney for the "funny face," but she wasn't a big enough name. Cyd Charisse had the name and the talent, but while Metro was considering her, Gershe read an interview in a movie magazine in which Audrey Hepburn said, "I'd love to do a musical one day." Edens and Donen contacted Hepburn's agent, Ketti Frings, who told them to get him a copy of the script and send another one to Hepburn in Paris. Frings read the script, despised it, and told Edens and Donen that Hepburn would never appear in the picture. Luckily, they had already mailed her copy to Paris and she read it and loved it. She contacted Frings and ordered him to make the deal.

Meanwhile, at a cocktail party at Clifton Webb's house, Roger Edens told Fred Astaire to drop his plans for doing *Papa's Delicate Condition* for Paramount and come on board this exciting new picture. After all, he'd costar with Audrey Hepburn. Astaire was thrilled.

"I could have shot Fred ... but didn't." —*Kay Thompson*

Flash to Richard Avedon cavorting with Marlene Dietrich. The diva had Avedon's fortune told and it was predicted that his life would take a turn. Avedon was in Jamaica when a telegram came from Edens and Donen asking him to work on the film. Fred Astaire would be playing a character based on him. Avedon was smart enough to jump on board.

You'd think the rest would be easy. Fred Astaire and Audrey Hepburn, Stanley Donen, Gershwin songs . . . what could stop them? Well, by that time, Dore Schary had come into power at MGM and the studio had cooled on movie musicals. Hepburn was

under contract to Paramount and so was Astaire. The Gershwin songs were owned by Warner Brothers and they weren't about to let a competing studio capitalize on their property.

Here's how it finally worked out. Donen was asked by George Abbott to codirect *The Pajama Game* over at Warner Brothers,

though he was under contract to MGM. MGM agreed to let Donen go in exchange for the Gershwin songs. Donen convinced Metro to sell their services and the rights to the material to Paramount for a goodly sum of money, and because Metro didn't want the picture anyway and badly needed cash, the deal was set and the project moved to Paramount, where Hepburn and Astaire were already under contract.

And that, folks, is how to get a brilliant movie into production. Piece of wedding cake. ■

Kay Thompson, Fred Astaire, and Audrey Hepburn sing "Bonjour Paree" while on the Eiffel Tower.

AUDREY HEPBURN · FRED ASTAIRE

PRESENTED IN A REAL NEW DIMENSION IN MOTION PICTURE ENTERTAINMENT.

FUNNY FACE

KAY THOMPSON with MICHEL AUCLAIR ROBERT FLEMYNG

TECHNICOLOR · A PARAMOUNT PICTURE · VISTAVISION

Behind the Screen

- Fred Astaire was unhappy with "Clap Yo' Hands," as he thought Kay Thompson was pulling focus from him. He hardly looks at her during the whole number.
- In the Parisian nightclub scene, the quarrelling couple is played by Roger Edens and Audrey Hepburn's mother, Baroness Ella Van Heemstra.
- Fred Astaire ascends the same staircase that Gene Kelly descended in *An American in Paris* in the song "Bonjour Paree."

SONGS

"Bonjour Paree" (Roger Edens) ■ "Clap Yo' Hands" ■ "Funny Face" ■ "He Loves and She Loves" ■ "How Long Has This Been Going On" ■ "Let's Kiss and Make Up" ■ "On How to Be Lovely" (Roger Edens) ■ "'S Wonderful" ■ "Think Pink!" (Roger Edens)

ABOVE RIGHT: Roger Edens coaches Lena Horne for *Ziegfeld Follies*.

RIGHT: Taking his role as a photographer to heart, Fred Astaire snaps a bemused Audrey Hepburn.

Roger Edens

Kay Thompson said of Roger Edens, "He was a darling man. Absolutely peaches and cream." He began his career on Broadway, where he was the pit pianist for *Girl Crazy*, starring Ethel Merman. On the second night, Merman's onstage accompanist was unable to continue and Edens assumed the role. He followed Merman to Hollywood and Paramount Pictures, but when she left in 1935, he remained. He subsequently moved to MGM, where he hooked up with his mentor and associate, Arthur Freed. Screenwriter Leonard Gershe said of Edens, "Roger was responsible for the 'class' of the Freed Unit, and the Freed Unit was the Rolls-Royce of Hollywood. No one was ever quite certain of what Roger did, but whatever he did was quite crucial to the picture." Adolph Green clarified things when he said that Edens was "absolutely indispensable to Arthur. He worked on the script, the music, he coached Judy Garland, wrote for her—Roger did it all." If Edens didn't like a design, song, or take, Freed acted accordingly. Irving Berlin, a notable curmudgeon and tough guy to please, said, "Listen, you can't say enough about Roger Edens as far as I'm concerned!" Edens also supplied a variety of songs for MGM productions, including "Our Love Affair" (with Arthur Freed), "Dear Mr. Gable," and "It's a Great Day for the Irish."

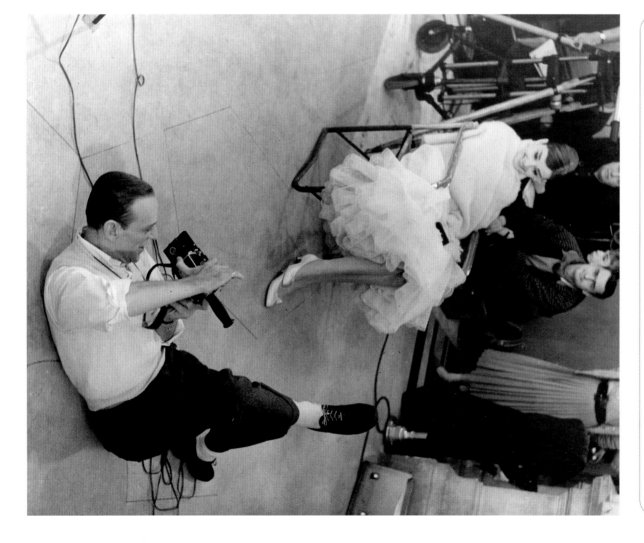

FUNNY GIRL

COLUMBIA—SEPTEMBER 19, 1968

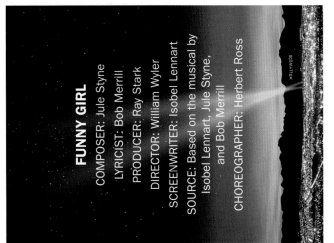

FUNNY GIRL

COMPOSER: Jule Styne
LYRICIST: Bob Merrill
PRODUCER: Ray Stark
DIRECTOR: William Wyler
SCREENWRITER: Isobel Lennart
SOURCE: Based on the musical by
Isobel Lennart, Jule Styne,
and Bob Merrill
CHOREOGRAPHER: Herbert Ross

Synopsis

Oy! A girl with such a punim should end up with a handsome nogoodnik? On the stage, only, can she be happy.

Cast

Barbra Streisand..........*Fanny Brice*
Omar Sharif ....*Nick Arnstein*
Kay Medford ....*Rose Brice*
Anne Francis.................*Georgia James*
Walter Pidgeon.............*Florenz Ziegfeld*
Lee Allen......................*Eddie Ryan*
Mae Questal.................*Mrs. Strakosh*
Frank Faylen................*Keeney*

Barbra Streisand makes a beautiful, beautiful bride—except for one small thing.

U NDERSTAND AT THE OUTSET THAT, LIKE ALL MOVIE BIOPICS, *FUNNY GIRL* SHOULD not be construed as slavishly truthful—which is ironic as producer Ray Stark was Fanny Brice's son-in-law. Of course, it's almost impossible, even for an enormously gifted performer, to portray a legend accurately. By definition, the talents of the original were unique. Some biopics, such as those about Marilyn Miller and Lillian Russell, work because the subjects left us few relics of their great talents. (Miller made only two films and Russell can be heard on fewer than a handful of recordings.)

By contrast, Eddie Cantor, and Al Jolson were fresh in audiences' mind when their biopics came out. For that reason, it made sense that Al Jolson himself dubbed (and secretly appeared) in *The Jolson Story*. It just wasn't possible for anyone to reproduce his special talents. Perhaps James Cagney came closest to doing justice to a popular entertainer when he appeared as George M. Cohan in *Yankee Doodle Dandy*. Cagney had seen Cohan perform and could mimic his swagger and drive. He definitely captured the song-and-dance man's essence—but naturally, his performance was as much Cagney as Cohan.

Similarly, Barbra Streisand captured the essence of Fanny Brice, who was a smart cookie, just as Streisand made her out to be. But Brice had a warmth that Streisand didn't exude—and she was more of a ham. Put Brice in front of an audience and she'd do practically anything for applause. Streisand is funny in "Roller Skate Rag," but it's as if she's *acting zany rather than being zany.*

Still, Streisand's is a totally mesmerizing performance in a role that is perfectly tailored to her talents. She's dynamic and totally theatrical in attacking every scene. It's a remarkable motion picture debut with not a single misstep. How great was it? Other than

Streisand, only Julie Andrews has won a Best Actress Oscar for a debut film. It is Streisand's complete ease that makes her the equal of Brice, who was at home in every musical situation, from a serious torch song such as "My Man" to a comedy number such as "Mrs. Cohen at the Beach."

In one way, Streisand even outdoes Brice. Fanny was never a success in pictures. Her earliest ones were disappointments. She took a breather from films for six years, returning as herself in 1936's *The Great Ziegfeld.* She played a supporting role in *Everybody Sing* two years later, then waited eight more years until *Ziegfeld Follies.* Films were clearly not her métier.

Also making his film musical debut with *Funny Girl* was director William Wyler. His stormy relationship with Streisand undoubtedly arose from the fact that both felt they were in charge of the production. (Even then, Streisand was never shy about asserting herself artistically.) Any tension on the set was worked through somehow and the film has many exciting moments.

So, though she may not have captured Fanny Brice precisely, Streisand launched her film career with her greatest role. With the excellent support of Omar Sharif as ne'er-do-well husband Nicky Arnstein, Kay Medford as Mrs. Brice, and a bevy of great songs by Jule Styne and Bob Merrill, *Funny Girl* is one of the best movie musicals of its time. ∎

"They interpolated a few old songs, and that was the fatal mistake that caused the destruction of that movie. They destroyed the drama; that's why it didn't win an Academy Award. They made the leading character self-pitying, whereas on the stage she was a strong woman." *—Jule Styne*

TOP: Is Barbra Streisand pondering William Wyler's direction—or asking herself why she's wearing that schmatta sweater?

ABOVE: Barbra Streisand washes Nicky Arnstein out of her hair and everywhere else.

LEFT: Omar Sharif and Barbra Streisand prove that Arabs and Jews can coexist quite comfortably.

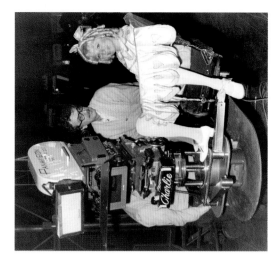

Behind the Screen

- Rumor has it that Barbra Streisand had Anne Francis's part reduced considerably. Kay Medford also had more screen time before it was determined that Streisand could indeed carry the film.

- Ray Stark wanted "My Man" to go into the Broadway production but this was nixed by Styne and Merrill. He got his way for the film because the composers didn't have contractual veto power.

- Streisand insisted that the Broadway designer, Irene Sharaff, do her costumes for the film version.

ABOVE: Barbra celebrates her movie debut.

ABOVE RIGHT: Dressed as Baby Snooks, Barbra confers with director Herbert Ross during the filming of Funny Lady (1975). Obviously comfortable behind the camera, she would go on to direct several films.

LEFT: Interesting... Barbra's sits in producer Ray Stark's chair as she talks to director William Wyler.

BELOW RIGHT: Barbra is obviously sickened by Funny Lady's art direction.

Barbra Streisand

Barbra Streisand graduated from small Greenwich Village boîtes to Broadway, television, Hollywood, arenas—and just lately, back to small Greenwich Village boîtes. (She appeared at the Village Vanguard in 2009.) She was almost immediately a star—no—a supernova. She appeared in only two shows on Broadway before decamping to Hollywood and the film version of Funny Girl, soon switching from filmed musicals to comedies to dramas—and to film directing—with aplomb. Sometimes her choices in film musicals didn't turn out so well (On a Clear Day You Can See Forever and A Star Is Born) or were successful (Yentl, which she also directed, and Hello, Dolly!). Strangely, with the possible exception of Funny Girl, she has never appeared in a totally successful movie musical. Perhaps it's because she overwhelms the material (although other larger-than-life personas, including Marilyn Monroe, have blended into film musicals quite nicely). Her "farewell appearances" have been recorded regularly since 1995, but to many, she remains the most popular living interpreter of the American Songbook.

THE GANG'S ALL HERE

20TH CENTURY FOX—DECEMBER 24, 1943

Carmen Miranda has clearly just heard the joke about the guy with a banana in his ear.

W HEN IT COMES TO FOX'S CARMEN MIRANDA EXTRAVAGANZAS, THE PLOTS DON'T matter at all. Honestly, can you tell one Carmen Miranda number from another? They're never integrated into the plot; they simply exist on their own, numbers performed in front of a band in some incredibly large nightclub. We've seen the movies more times than we care to admit, but even we had to look up the synopsis of this film. (Well, we did remember something about bananas, bananas, bananas.) They may be interchangeable, but the fact remains: they are hugely entertaining, featuring great scores and often spectacular sequences by Busby Berkeley.

If we partook of illegal substances, this film would send us on a trip from which we'd never return. Maybe it's because the often alcoholic Busby Berkeley was practically certifiable. Certainly his id took over when conceiving the finale. Add color, bright color, to Berkeley's signature cinematic excesses and you've got a positively psychedelic experience.

It was always thus with Berkeley. In *Footlight Parade's* "By a Waterfall" number, over a hundred women cavort for fifteen minutes in, out, and around water in Berkeley's famous kaleidoscopic patterns, diving into pools and sliding down a five-story series of waterfalls before becoming part of a huge human fountain themselves. As Berkeley tells it, "The mountain wilderness and the pool covered almost an entire sound stage. The pool measured eighty feet by forty, and while the number was being shot we pumped twenty thousand gallons of water a minute over the falls and into the pool. I had them build me plate-glass corridors underneath the pool so I could light and shoot it from the bottom." The whole setup cost almost $40,000—a huge expense for one musical number.

THE GANG'S ALL HERE

COMPOSER: Harry Warren
LYRICIST: Leo Robin
PRODUCER: William LeBaron
DIRECTOR: Busby Berkeley
SCREENWRITER: Walter Bullock
CHOREOGRAPHER: Busby Berkeley

Synopsis

A playboy meets a showgirl and gets sent overseas, courtesy of the army. He returns in time for a party celebrating his engagement to a girl he doesn't love. Somewhere in there is a crazy woman with a fruit stand on her head.

Cast

Alice Faye.................Edie Allen
Phil Baker.................Phil Baker
Carmen Miranda.........Dorita
Eugene Pallette...........Andrew Mason Sr.
Charlotte Greenwood ....Mrs. Peyton Potter
Edward Everett Horton...Peyton Potter
James Ellison..............Andy Mason
Sheila Ryan................Vivian Potter
Tony de Marco
Bando da Lua
Benny Goodman and His Orchestra

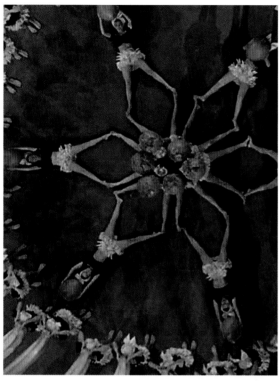

For the "Don't Say Goodnight" number in *Wonder Bar*, Berkeley had the construction crew build sixty tall, white moveable columns on individual tracks. One hundred dancers cavorted with the columns. When the columns disappeared, in their place was a huge forest of silver trees with reindeer (not real ones) running around them. After that came a huge octagonal mirror, each side of which was twenty-eight feet high and twelve feet wide. Naturally, this held a huge platform that revolved! The dancers reappeared, seemingly in the thousands, stretching back as far as the eye could see, thanks to the mirrors. For *Fashions of 1934*, Berkeley dressed the fifty-girl chorus in feathers and attached others to giant harps. This led to a quip that made the rounds in Hollywood. "I didn't raise my girl to be a human harp."

We could go on and on about Berkeley's fever dreams, but you get the point. Perhaps you have seen the dancing grand pianos, the neon-lit violins, the chorus all eerily wearing Ruby Keeler masks, or the phalanx of fifty huge (they had to be huge, didn't they?) rocking chairs each with a loving couple rocking to "Let's Put Our Heads Together."

In the '30s, the studios had the kinds of budgets that allowed for hundreds of extras rehearsing for weeks and then sitting around for days between takes. In the '40s, Berkeley's staging of the numbers in Fox's *The Gang's All Here* was right up there with his work at Warner. When the bottom started to fall out of the studio system after the war, budgets were slashed. Instead of spectacle, audiences

were treated to special effects—as in the 3-D *Kiss Me, Kate* and *The French Line*; Esther Williams swimming with Tom and Jerry in *Dangerous When Wet*; and Fred Astaire dancing on the floor, walls, and ceiling in *Royal Wedding*. Berkeley had the last word, though. His work with Esther Williams in 1952's *Million Dollar Mermaid* was one of the last of the musical spectacles.

Roger Edens, remarking on making *On the Town*, said. "I began to realize my idea of making musicals without overelaborate production numbers. Intimate musical numbers are the only way to get true entertainment. People are not entertained by chorus lines anymore."

Luckily, these magnificent excesses are available for our amazement and enjoyment anytime we wish, through DVDs and television broadcasts. We'll never see their like again. The great dramatic spectacles such as *Ben-Hur*, *El Cid*, and *Lawrence of Arabia* were astounding in their scope but they had to be, given their plots. Movies such as the 1997 *Titanic* may amaze us for their sheer scale but they don't provoke that perfect mixture of awe, astonishment, glee, and guilty pleasure boasted by the spectacular movie musicals of the past. ∎

ABOVE: Eugene
Pallette, Edward Everett
Horton, and Charlotte
Greenwood are also in
The Gang's All Here.

LEFT: Carmen Miranda,
all decked out for
Copacabana (1947).

"Honey, they're not Brazilian—they're Italian.
But don't tell anybody."

—*Harry Warren, explaining his songs to Carmen Miranda*

SONGS

"A Journey to a Star" ■ "The Lady in the Tutti Frutti Hat" ■ "Minnie's in the
Money" ■ "No Love, No Nothin'" ■ "Paduca" ■ "The Polka Dot Polka" ■ "You
Discover You're in New York"

Carmen Miranda

mmigrants are funny, aren't they? What with their funny accents, funny looks, and the fruit on their heads? At least that's how Carmen Miranda represented them. Despite her antic image, Miranda was one of the most talented singers in film. She had been a big star in Brazil before coming to Broadway for *The Streets of Paris*, and it didn't take long for Hollywood to discover her. It was there that she established the persona of a ditzy, sexy Brazilian bombshell.

Miranda signed with 20th Century Fox, where her first film was *Down Argentine Way*. (Already she was losing her Brazilian identity!) Over the course of fourteen films, she sambaed and rumbaed through a mix of authentic Brazilian and South American tunes and those composed by the finest Italian composer in Hollywood, Harry Warren. Brazilians felt that Miranda had sold out to Hollywood and she was deeply hurt by the criticism. This was ironic, since President Franklin Roosevelt considered her an important proponent of his Good Neighbor Policy, an attempt to strengthen the alliance between Latin America and the United States. In 1946, Miranda was the highest paid performer in Hollywood—but she yearned to be taken more seriously as a singer and actress. She grew tired of repeating the same role in film after film. The stresses associated with her career and a bad marriage took their toll and she turned to alcohol and barbiturates to forget her problems and keep her weight down. Although she never managed to escape her Hollywood persona, she remained a beloved figure and a totally unique part of motion picture history.

"If you want to kill me, why don't you use a gun?"

—*Carmen Miranda to Busby Berkeley, after an out-of-control
camera boom knocked the fruit off her headdress*

GENTLEMEN PREFER BLONDES

COMPOSER: Jule Styne
LYRICIST: Leo Robin
PRODUCER: Sol C. Siegel
DIRECTOR: Howard Hawks
SCREENWRITER: Charles Lederer
SOURCE: Based on the musical
Gentlemen Prefer Blondes by Joseph
Fields, Anita Loos, Jule Styne,
and Leo Robin
CHOREOGRAPHER: Jack Cole

Synopsis

OMG, Lorelei is a gold digger and goes on a cruise w/ her BFF. She tells her boyfriend she's GTG but she'll BRB. BTW, she meets a guy who is gr8 but she doesn't know he's rich. Diamonds r a grrrl's best friend, LOL.

Cast

Marilyn Monroe...........*Lorelei Lee*
Jane Russell...............*Dorothy Shaw*
Charles Coburn...........*Sir Francis "Piggy" Beekman*
Elliott Reid................*Ernie Malone*
Tommy Noonan..........*Gus Esmond*
George Winslow...........*Henry Spofford III*

GENTLEMEN PREFER BLONDES

Climbing that ladder of success, Marilyn Monroe and Jane Russell perform a number ultimately cut from *Gentlemen Prefer Blondes*.

FOLKS, NO MATTER IF YOU WRITE THE GREATEST MUSICAL ON EARTH, WITH NUMEROUS hit songs and brilliant dialogue, the Hollywood powers that be will still barge in and interpolate songs by other writers. Only Rodgers and Hammerstein, Irving Berlin, and Lerner and Loewe escaped what many theatergoers view as this heinous crime.

Imagine that you've loved a Broadway show, sung and danced along to the original cast album, and looked forward to the film version. Then the reality. Not only is your favorite star not included—you get Ann Southern instead of Ethel Merman, for example—but your favorite songs aren't in the film, either. You're lucky if the plot has any relationship at all to the original.

It would be understandable if the songs that were deleted or replaced were bad, or the new ones better. No. The reason that songs were changed is that the major studios all owned their own music publishing companies and if a movie was a success, they wanted to control the publishing of the hit songs. Besides, they had lots and lots of songwriters under contract and wanted to get their money's worth out of them.

Cole Porter probably had it worse than any other songwriter. Porter saw complete scores jettisoned by Hollywood. *Panama Hattie, DuBarry Was a Lady, Let's Face It,* and others premiered with the majority of their scores shorn. Only *Kiss Me, Kate's* score was left intact—and even had and additional Porter song interpolated, "From This Moment On." (It had been cut from the Broadway show *Out of This World*.)

Kurt Weill and Ira Gershwin fared badly when *Lady in the Dark* was movieified. Their hit "My Ship," crucial to the plot, was an especially perverse exclusion. The hit from the film was "Suddenly It's Spring," not by Weill and Gershwin. *One Touch of Venus* retained Weill's "That's Him" and "Speak Low," and the song "West Wind" was there with a new lyric by Ann Ronell.

When *Funny Girl* was on Broadway, producer Ray Stark wanted to interpolate "My Man" into it. Songwriters Jule Styne and Bob Merrill were completely against this. Well, Stark got a second chance when he produced the film version—and because the film was a pretty faithful to the show.

Using instrumental versions of cut songs as underscoring is a common practice, but Harold Rome's *Fanny* was an extreme example. The wonderful if quirky songs were used in Josh Logan's film version (he had directed the Broadway show, too) only as underscoring. There were no vocals. Likewise, the similarly French-set *Irma la Douce*.

On the Town was a unique situation (save the one below). Leonard Bernstein wasn't interested in contributing new songs to the MGM film, so, with Bernstein's blessing, Betty Comden and Adolph Green, who had worked on the Broadway production, wrote additional songs with Roger Edens. When *Anything Goes* went into production at Paramount in 1938, Cole Porter was asked to update some of his lyrics and clean up others, due to concerns about Hays Code censorship. Porter declined, but gave his blessing to Ted Fetter's adaptations.

It's not that Hollywood producers and directors didn't respect the contributions of Broadway songwriters and librettists, or value the properties they bought. But they felt they understood the particular needs of their film adaptations and the taste of their audiences. No hard feelings—just business as usual. ■

ABOVE: Marilyn Monroe copies Madonna singing "Diamonds Are a Girl's Best Friend." Or do we have that backwards? Future Oscar winner George Chakiris is seen all the way right.

BELOW LEFT: Jane Russell plaintively asks, "Ain't There Anyone Here for Love?"—and soon gets knocked in the pool for her troubles.

BELOW: Ethel Merman and Betty Hutton, stage and screen Annie Oakleys, make nice over Jule Styne.

Jule Styne

Jule Styne was a brilliant composer who was perfectly happy being exactly who he was. His brashness, his ego, and his zest for life kept him from being a diva, like many. He was just secure in his talents. A man whose brain worked faster than his mouth, Styne was a fount of good ideas and great tunes. He admitted, "Most people don't hear everything because they're thinking what they're going to say. I don't think what I'm going to say. That's why I have to talk so much. Because there's so much I want to say." He was invested in each project completely, always assuming that the next one would be his greatest hit. Sometimes it didn't work out quite as he thought but, no bother, there were plenty more terrific melodies where those came from. He was brilliant at writing for specific performers. He crafted songs for the talents of Barbra Streisand in *Funny Girl*, Judy Holliday in *Bells Are Ringing*, and Carol Channing in *Gentlemen Prefer Blondes*. The first two ladies repeated their stage successes for the movies but poor Carol had to watch Marilyn Monroe take over the role of Lorelei Lee. You couldn't find two more different performers than Channing and Monroe, but Styne and Robin's score suited each perfectly. And that's the miracle of great songwriting and great performing. When listening to Channing sing "Diamonds Are a Girl's Best Friend," you can't imagine anyone else singing the song as well. So, too, it was with Monroe. Each became just as well known singing the song as the other. Styne began his Hollywood career as a vocal coach at Fox, teaching the likes of Alice Faye and Shirley Temple. He went to Republic Pictures and started writing songs for the studio. As soon as he could, he moved to Paramount and, later, Columbia. His songs were immensely popular, especially those written in collaboration with Sammy Cahn for Sinatra, but you won't find any of Styne's original movie musicals in this book of the greatest 101. But, although he never wrote a great score for a movie, he wrote plenty of smash hit songs for pictures. He left Hollywood in the late '40s for Broadway, and spent the remainder of his career there, with occasional forays back West.

ABOVE: Leo Rubin (center) with Tony Martin and Vic Damone.

CENTER RIGHT: Choreographer and Svengali Jack Cole with his obedient acolyte, Marilyn Monroe, working on 1960's *Let's Make Love.*

BOTTOM LEFT: Marilyn Monroe and Jane Russell learn their songs.

BOTTOM RIGHT: Marilyn Monroe and Jane Russell make Elliott Reid's most private dream come true.

Leo Robin

Leo Robin is one of the many (excuse the pun) unsung lyricists whose work is known by most Americans but whose name is not. Like many of his contemporaries, Robin came to Hollywood during the great land rush of 1928, when seemingly every hit songwriter was summoned to Hollywood (except for the black ones, but that's for another time). His first film hit was "Louise," which he and Richard Whiting wrote for Maurice Chevalier to sing in *Innocents of Paris* in 1929. Somehow, writing for a plot, even if the song had nothing to do with that plot, inspired Robin. His first Tin Pan Alley hit was 1926's "My Cutie's Due at Two-to-Two-Today." The next year, Robin, Whiting, and W. Frank Harling contributed "Beyond the Blue Horizon" for *Monte Carlo.* Robin and Rainger became Bing Crosby's songwriters of choice when they were signed to Paramount. They produced "Please," "Here Lies Love," and "Love in Bloom," among other hits for the crooner. Perhaps the biggest hit Robin and Rainger wrote was for Bob Hope and Shirley Ross: "Thanks for the Memories." After Rainger was killed in a plane crash, Robin went on to collaborate with Harry Warren on *The Gang's All Here.* Jerome Kern soon called Robin in to work on the Fox hit *Centennial Summer.* Robin then went on to work with Arthur Schwartz and Harold Arlen. After a stint on Broadway with *Gentlemen Prefer Blondes* in 1948, he returned triumphant to Hollywood, but his output was slowing down. Another Broadway show, *The Girl in Pink Tights,* was not successful although it featured a wonderful score, including the beautiful "Lost in Loveliness." In 1955, after Robin and Jule Styne completed work on the film *My Sister Eileen,* and television's *Ruggles of Red Gap,* he retired. Proof of Robin's excellence is his ability to write both serious ballads and humorous numbers, including funny songs that actually contained jokes within their lyrics—a very difficult thing to do. Along with Robin, Cole Porter, Irving Berlin, and Howard Dietz were among the very few who could write a truly funny song. Robin was a sold craftsman as well as an extraordinary artist.

Behind the Screen

■ Both George Chakiris and Larry Kert are dancers in the "Diamonds Are a Girl's Best Friend" number.

■ It wasn't planned for Jane to fall into the pool in "Ain't There Anyone Here for Love." She was bumped by one of the athletes and in she went! It was such a good button on the number that it was left in the film.

SONGS

"Ain't There Anyone Here for Love" (Hoagy Carmichael and Harold Adamson) ■ "Bye Bye Baby" ■ "Diamonds Are a Girl's Best Friend" ■ "A Little Girl from Little Rock" ■ "When Love Goes Wrong (Nothin' Goes Right)" (Hoagy Carmichael and Harold Adamson)

Leslie Caron yearns to be all grown up. It'll happen before she knows it.

MY FAIR LADY IS THE MOST ERUDITE AND SOPHISTICATED OF BROADWAY MUSICALS and *Gigi* is the original Hollywood musical equivalent. That makes sense, because the same team—Lerner and Loewe—created both. In fact, when you think about it, the two films have pretty much the same plot: a young, inexperienced girl gets a makeover, becomes a woman, and captivates her teachers. A lot of *Gigi's* allure and its sense of realism arise from the fact that it was shot on location throughout Paris.

Screenwriter and lyricist Alan Jay Lerner has written, "For some unfathomable and marvelously mysterious reason, even if one is shooting an *interior scene*, if it is in its authentic setting something of the outside atmosphere creeps through the wood work and on to the film. *An American in Paris* had been made at the studio, but the sets had been designed to give an artist's impression of Paris. It had never been the intention to hoodwink the audience into believing it was actually Paris. But *An American in Paris* was anything but a French story; *Gigi* was, Paris was as much a character as Gaston and Gigi themselves."

Jean Genet wrote, "*Gigi* may well be the most authoritative Parisian movie so far filmed, as well as the most sensuous, effective, and respectful one yet made from any of Colette's writings." And that was all due to Vincente Minnelli's stunning eye for design and the extensive Parisian locale.

Location shooting was frowned upon by studio bigwigs as it was extremely expensive; audiences, they felt, were just as happy with films shot entirely on soundstages and back-lots. Of course, many nonmusicals had been filmed on location, going as far back as the

GIGI

COMPOSER: Frederick Loewe
LYRICIST: Alan Jay Lerner
PRODUCER: Arthur Freed
DIRECTOR: Vincente Minnelli
SCREENWRITER: Alan Jay Lerner
SOURCE: Based on the novel *Gigi* by Colette

Synopsis

Amid the eye candy of Paris, wealthy Gaston sees the courtesan-in-the-making Gigi grow up before his very eyes. Seizing his golden opportunity, he picks her for his own.

Cast

Leslie Caron............*Gigi*
Louis Jourdan............Gaston Lachaille
Maurice Chevalier............Honoré Lachaille
Hermione Gingold............Madame Alvarez
Eva Gabor............Liane d'Exelmans
Jacques Bergerac............Sandomir
Isabel Jeans............Aunt Alicia

THE FIRST LERNER-LOEWE MUSICAL SINCE "MY FAIR LADY"

M-G-M Presents AN ARTHUR FREED PRODUCTION

LESLIE CARON
MAURICE CHEVALIER · LOUIS JOURDAN
HERMIONE GINGOLD · EVA GABOR · JACQUES BERGERAC · ISABEL JEANS
Screen Play and Lyrics by ALAN JAY LERNER
Music by FREDERICK LOEWE
Directed by VINCENTE MINNELLI
Gowns and Scenery Production Designed by CECIL BEATON
CinemaScope · METROCOLOR

silent era, and parts of the 1929 musical *Applause* were filmed in New York City. Westerns, especially, needed to be shot on location. But the cumbersome sound equipment required for musicals made location shooting the rare exception. MGM, always the most adventurous studio, filmed some of the MacDonald and Eddy operetta *Rose Marie* in spectacular natural settings. But the film that proved that location shooting in a big city was feasible was *On the Town*. Stanley Donen and Gene Kelly filmed brief but impressive sequences at, among other sites, the rooftop of the Loew's State

Theater, Rockefeller Center, and on Fifth Avenue. It wasn't easy but the results were impressive and, coming in the "New York, New York" section at the beginning of the film, made the audience forget that the rest of the film was shot on soundstages. As in *Gigi*, the city became a main character in the film.

When television began to erode Hollywood's box office, studios strove to come up with ways to keep film special and differentiate between the two media. Since the TV picture was a black-and-white medium, many more films were shot in color. Since the TV picture was essentially square, various widescreen processes came into fashion. Special effects such as 3-D and Cinerama hit theaters, though the gimmicks didn't last very long. And the budgets of many films were increased to make location shooting possible.

Gigi took full advantage of the availability of good, genuine sites. Because so much of nineteenth-century Paris still exists, locations were easy to find; still, shooting was still tricky, what

with modern signage, cars whizzing around, and crowds following the filmmakers. The opening scenes in the Bois de Boulogne were relatively easy to achieve, but when Gaston walks the streets pondering his relationship to Gigi (the "aha moment," as Lerner called it), the task was more difficult. Among the solutions was to shoot him from below, framing the statuary and great buildings above him while avoiding the telltale signs of modern times.

Even when crowd control could be maintained and the correct period evoked, problems arose. In the "Thank Heavens for Little

"If I were a sissy I would be in love with you." —*Maurice Chevalier to Vincente Minnelli*

Girls" opening, filmed in the Bois de Boulogne, the ground on which the camera's tracks needed to be laid was uneven and had to be smoothed out. Minnelli decided there weren't enough trees in the shots, so fake trees and branches were added. Giant speakers were set up for playback. Electrical generators had to be brought in to power the lighting and their wiring had to be camouflaged. And once all of the technical aspects were ready, the weather had to cooperate. Rehearsals and shooting had to be finished before dusk. The horses had to be calmed and cleaned up after, wind stirred up dust, and water trucks were needed to keep the roadbed wet so it would look better on film. The one song took four days to film.

Location shooting has its difficulties but for *Gigi*, as well as for another film set in Paris, *Funny Face*, there would have been no other way to achieve the same magical results. Nowadays, studio backlots are largely gone, necessitating location shooting—though Vancouver often substitutes for New York, or Rome, or even Paris. ∎

Leslie Caron

Was the word *gamine* invented for Leslie Caron or vice versa? Why is it some of the most petite and delicate women in movies are the strongest? On the musical side, look at Shirley Jones and Leslie Caron. Both were beautiful, innocent ingenues yet both summoned up surprising strength—Jones in *Elmer Gantry* and Caron in *The L-Shaped Room*. But in musicals, both Jones's and Caron's personas enchanted audiences. Perhaps it's exactly that combination of vulnerability and single-mindedness that made them so attractive. Caron was discovered by Francophile Gene Kelly and put into her first picture, *An American in Paris*, in a starring role. (This probably says more about the esteem in which MGM held Kelly and the intelligence and trust of producer Arthur Freed than about Caron's talents.) But she more than repaid their faith. Her first picture was a trial by fire, or rather, a trial by sore, bleeding feet, as Kelly was a severe taskmaster when it came to rehearsals. Caron continued in both straight films and musicals. Of the latter, *Gigi* was the best showcase of her skills, though she barely dances in the film, and her character's transition

from little girl to woman is an amazing testament to her natural abilities (plus the MGM hair and makeup departments, Cecil Beaton's costumes, Alan Jay Lerner's script, and Vincente Minnelli's sensitive direction). Five years earlier, she played a similar role in *Lili* and again was utterly charming. Some of her pictures, as good as they are, have been forgotten. She partnered with Fred Astaire in *Daddy Long Legs*. Her turn as Cinderella seemed to be a natural; however, although *The Glass Slipper* has much to recommend it, it's mostly forgotten today. Caron continues to perform on stage, screen, and television but her first films are the ones that have maintained her renown.

"The picture was twenty minutes too long, the action too slow, the music too creamy and ill-defined, and there must have been at least five minutes (in the theatre that can seem like five hours) of people walking up and down stairs."

—Alan Jay Lerner, on the first preview of Gigi

TOP LEFT: Leslie Caron has a ball with Fred Astaire in *Daddy Long Legs*.

TOP RIGHT: Roland Petite and Leslie Caron wait for filming to commence on *Lili*.

LEFT: Leslie Caron in the dream ballet from *Lili*.

SONGS

"Gaston's Soliloquy" ■ "Gigi" ■ "Gossip" ■ "I Remember It Well" ■ "I'm Glad I'm Not Young Anymore" ■ "It's a Bore" ■ "The Night They Invented Champagne" ■ "The Parisians" ■ "Say a Pray for Me Tonight" ■ "She Is Not Thinking of Me" ■ "Thank Heavens for Little Girls"

Behind the Screen

■ Because of the tight schedule, prerecordings with an orchestra were not done before filming. The cast sang to a piano track and the orchestra recorded the soundtrack back in Hollywood after the filming. Then the cast came in and looped their singing to the orchestral track.

■ Lerner was not happy with the way "She Is Not Thinking of Me" was shot, so a reproduction of Maxim's was built in Culver City and Charles Walters directed the reshoot. (Minnelli was unavailable as he was to begin filming on *The Reluctant Debutante*.) Walters also reshot "The Night They Invented Champagne," "I Remember It Well," portions of "Gaston's Soliloquy," and bits and pieces of other scenes.

Synopsis

Bad little rich boy Mickey thinks he knows it all, so he's sent out west to grow up a little. He intends to tame the Wild West—but guess what? The Wild West ends up taming him.

Cast

Judy Garland...............Ginger Gray
Mickey Rooney.............Danny Churchill Jr.
Gil Stratton................Bud Livermore
Robert E. Strickland......Henry Lathrop
Rags Ragland..............Rags
Nancy Walker..............Polly Williams
Guy Kibbee.................Dean Phineas Armour
Henry O'Neill..............Mr. Danny Churchill Sr.
Tommy Dorsey and His Orchestra, June Allyson,
Six Hits and a Miss, the Music Maids
...........As Themselves

GIRL CRAZY

MGM—NOVEMBER 26, 1943

Mickey Rooney (left) and Tommy Dorsey (right) serenade Judy Garland, much to her amusement.

IF YOU WANT TO STUDY THE HISTORY OF THE HOLLYWOOD MUSICAL IN ONE SHOW, LOOK NO further than *Girl Crazy*. The stage play opened in 1930. The first film version was made in 1932, with the now sadly forgotten comedy team of Wheeler and Woolsey in the leads. The second cinema incarnation was the MGM film with Mickey and Judy (to this day, those two don't need last names). The absolute end of the line came in an adaptation titled *Where the Boys Meet the Girls* in 1966, starring the wildly mismatched Connie Francis and Harve Presnell.

Of course this wasn't the first film to be made, remade, and remade again. The straight film *Three Blind Mice* became the 1941 musical *Moon over Miami* and then the song-and-dance treat *Three Little Girls in Blue*. *Folies Bergère* (1936) was remade as *That Night in Rio* (1941), which became Danny Kaye's *On the Riviera* ten years later. The 1943 *Coney Island* was relocated to Chicago as *Wabash Avenue*—and both versions starred Betty Grable. *The Jazz Singer* was made three times: the original in 1927; the first remake, with Danny Thomas and Peggy Lee, in 1952; and the ultimate version (so far), starring Neil Diamond.

But while many remakes aren't particularly better or worse than their predecessors (okay, the last *Jazz Singer* is a joke), the best version by far of *Girl Crazy* is the middle one, with Mickey and Judy. (No surprise—since that's the one featured here.) The talent behind the scenes was superior, the songs are better presented, and the stars exhibit a chemistry that cannot be beat.

Mickey began his career as a youngster and grew up at MGM. Judy, on the other hand, was a relative neophyte when they began working together. In 1937, Judy first appeared with Mickey in *Thoroughbreds Don't Cry*, her third feature film. Mickey had appeared in

109—yes, 109!—shorts and features by that time. The next year, after appearances in two musicals, Judy joined Mickey's screen family, the Hardys, for *Love Finds Andy Hardy*. They had yet to become a team in MGM's eyes, but that would change with their next picture, *Babes in Arms*.

Finally, MGM woke up to the possibilities of teaming the two youngsters. From the beginning, Mickey played the more mature (but not too mature) of the duo, leading Judy through the trials of adolescence. In real life, Mickey was only two years older than Judy—but he did have those years of film experience. On their first picture together, he advised her, "Honey, you gotta believe this, now. Make like you're singing it."

It seemed that Mickey could do anything—comedy, drama, musicals. He was a terrific singer, could play the drums, and was athletic. But most of all, he had seemingly endless stores of energy. So much in fact, that he needed someone less manic to play against. In the Hardy pictures, it was his screen father, Lewis Stone, who toned him down. But when Judy entered the scene, her shyness and seeming insecurity somehow gave focus to Mickey's energies. And she could certainly keep up with him in the acting, singing, and dancing departments.

With *Babes in Arms* such a great hit that it inspired its own cliché (the "let's put on a show" picture), MGM prevailed on Judy to join the Hardys for two more pictures and then delivered what it called a sequel to *Babes in Arms: Strike Up the Band*. Their next musical together was *Babes on Broadway*.

The two were simpatico on and off the screen, though never romantically attached (to Judy's dismay). Their love and admiration for each other radiate from the screen into the hearts of audiences. It is always a pleasure to be in their company, no matter the fluff or contrivance of the pictures' plots. The country was still in Depression during their heyday, but Mickey and Judy provided a welcome sense of resilience, optimism, and youthful vitality. Certainly, there must be hope for the country with such good, honest, clean-cut kids working to make their big dreams come true.

There have been lots of other movie partnerships but none have had the truthfulness of Mickey and Judy. That is undoubtedly due to the fact that, for once, what was on the screen was a true reflection of two actors' mutual admiration and sympathetic talents. If you want to see Mickey and Judy at their best, there's no better vehicle than *Girl Crazy*. Sure, their relationship in the film is a cliché—but they believe in that hambone script and we admire them for it. And they make us believe in it, too. *Girl Crazy* is a movie we can root for, and what's better than that? ■

"I have always loved Judy without ever being *in love* with her."

—Mickey Rooney

ABOVE: Judy Garland, Tommy Dorsey, Mickey Rooney, and company.

BELOW: Esther Williams is ready for her closeup as Charles Walters lies in wait during the filming of *Easy to Love* (1953).

SONGS

"Bidin' My Time" ■ "But Not for Me" ■ "Could You Use Me" ■ "Embraceable You" ■ "I Got Rhythm" ■ "Treat Me Rough"

Charles Walters

Charles Walters was one of the great unsung talents of the musical film. He doesn't have the pop-culture cred of Busby Berkeley or Vincente Minnelli (for whom he reshot some numbers in *Gigi*). In fact, his first assignments in Hollywood began in 1942 with *Seven Days Leave*, *Presenting Lili Mars*, and redding Seymour Felix's choreography in MGM's *DuBarry Was a Lady*. Walters had appeared in the Broadway stage production of *DuBarry* as well as *Jubilee* and *I Married an Angel*, among others. He choreographed *Meet Me in St. Louis* and *The Harvey Girls*, the latter with Robert Alton. Walters once said, "I think I'm the only dance director who ever read a script to find out what the characters were all about." That sensitivity, and his understanding of the role of choreography, led to his upgrade to director. It seemed like a natural transition to Walters. "I'll never understand why more choreographers haven't made it as directors," he wrote. "After all, dialogue is movement and rhythm." In such films as *Easter Parade, Good News, The Barkleys of Broadway,* and *Summer Stock*, Walters directed and choreographed some of MGM's biggest stars in their best pictures—but he drew the line at directing *Royal Wedding* with Fred Astaire and Judy Garland. As he said to Arthur Freed after directing Garland in *Easter Parade* and *Summer Stock*, "I'm terribly sorry, but I can't go through it again. I've just spent a year and a half with her, and I'm ready for a mental institution." Although he worked with big stars and bigger budgets, none of his choreographic pieces were show-offy. Unlike Berkeley, he preferred to deal in what he called, "intimate numbers." One of his best, and one of the best musical numbers in any musical by any studio at any time, is the trio of Mickey, Judy, and a jalopy in "Could You Use Me?" It's a model of simplicity that perfectly expresses the lyric of the song, the characters, and the situation, with a distinctive flow and a build from start to finish.

GOLD DIGGERS OF 1933

WARNER BROTHERS—MAY 27, 1933

There's a certain Dr. Seuss quality to the set for "The Shadow Waltz." Note the ceiling peeking into the top of the frame—oops.

GOLD DIGGERS OF 1933

COMPOSER: Harry Warren
LYRICIST: Al Dubin
PRODUCER: Robert Lord
DIRECTOR: Mervyn LeRoy
SCREENWRITERS: Erwin Gelsey, James Seymour, David Boehm, and Ben Markson
SOURCE: Based on the play *The Gold Diggers* by Avery Hopwood
CHOREOGRAPHER: Busby Berkeley

Synopsis

Four typical Warner Depression-era gals want to get into a show in the worst way. Their buddy, a producer, wants to oblige—but he needs the scratch. The aspiring composer next door gets the moolah and the show goes on with one twist. Instead of Ruby Keeler getting her big break by replacing an ill performer, it's the composer who steps in to stardom. Still, the composer's snobby family wants to break up the show—"show business" being beneath their station in life. Surprise, surprise: everybody falls in love and lives happily and wealthily ever after.

Cast

Warren William............J. Lawrence Bradford
Joan Blondell...............Carol King
Aline MacMahon..........Trixie Lorraine
Ruby Keeler.................Polly Parker
Dick Powell..................Brad Roberts
Guy Kibbee..................Fanuel H. Peabody
Ned Sparks..................Barney Hopkins
Ginger Rogers..............Fay Fortune
Busby Berkeley.............Call boy
Etta Moten...................Singer of "Remember My Forgotten Man"

S CREEN MUSICALS WERE DIFFERENT FROM BROADWAY SHOWS IN ONE IMPORTANT REGARD. Whereas, after the success of *Show Boat* in 1927, many shows strived to include integrated numbers that advanced the plot, delineated characters, or were written in the voice of a particular character, film scores remained a collection of pop songs written with filmic possibilities in mind. *Gold Diggers of 1933* represents a move toward the Broadway method, with its merging of revue-style, stand-alone numbers and songs tailored to the plot.

There's no doubt that the film features one of the top-notch song scores of any picture ever. It was ripe with filmic potential for Busby Berkeley. In fact, as was the case for almost all the Warner Brothers backstage musicals, the entire score was meant to be set on a theater stage or behind the scenes, where the songwriter characters were composing the songs. Understandably, films set in the world of the theater can be humongous affairs that no Broadway producer could ever realize onstage—so they make perfect fodder for Hollywood.

Even in shows-within-films, there are few numbers that have anything to do with the plots—if such plots exist. Take *Gold Diggers*. The show around which the film revolves is described as having actual roles for the actors, but we see them only in stand-alone numbers. And who cares, really? These shows have nothing on their minds except to entertain, and that they do that brilliantly. For a few years in the early 1930s there was a perfect melding of songwriters (usually Dubin and Warren), cast (usually Dick Powell and Ruby Keeler), and choreographer (usually Busby Berkeley). When they were doing their stuff, plot was the last thing on the audience's mind.

RIGHT: The chorus isn't lying when they proclaim, "We're in the money." Why can't today's Broadway shows look like this?

BELOW: Dick Powell and Ruby Keeler share an intimate moment.

CENTER: Harry Warren (at piano) and Al Dubin.

BOTTOM RIGHT: The magnificent set for "Remember My Forgotten Man."

SONGS

- "Gold Diggers Song (We're in the Money)" ■ "I've Got to Sing a Torch Song" ■ "Pettin' in the Park" ■ "Remember My Forgotten Man" ■ "The Shadow Waltz"

Behind the Screen

- "We're in the Money" includes a chorus sung by Ginger Rogers in pig latin, Darryl Zanuck's brainstorm.

Gold Diggers wasn't supposed to be a musical in the first place. But after shooting was completed, *42nd Street* opened and was a giant success. So, Dubin, Warren, and Berkeley were drafted to write songs for the film, the show went back into production and interpolations were made.

Because the studio powers loved the "Forgotten Man" number, it was moved from the middle of the film to the closing spot, where "Pettin' in the Park" was meant to be. Other changes were of a more mercenary kind. State censorship boards were the bane of Hollywood, one reason the Hays Bureau as a central clearinghouse for smut of all kinds. Still, the studios worried that localities might either ban their films outright or subject them to cutting by local projectionists (many of whom kept reels of censored film in their homes!). So, alternative scenes and dialogue were filmed and inserted into prints bound for troublesome areas of the country.

The Warner musicals of Dubin and Warren and their songwriting brethren definitely followed a template, but the ingredients in each were so strong that there was a sense of variety from film to film. So too are the RKO Astaire/Rogers musicals. They all have basically the same plot, and even, as in the Warner musicals, a stock company of performers playing stock characters. But we don't mind, as each member of the team adds his or her special brilliance. ■

Al Dubin and Harry Warren

Dubin and Warren were as unlikely a pair of collaborators as you'll ever find, but maybe that accounts for their success. Harry Warren was a serious, dour composer who felt he never got the acclaim he deserved, and he was right! Al Dubin, on the other hand lived a life of excess. He was prone to disappearing on his composers. (Burton Lane had to write the lyric to "Feudin' and Fussin' and Fightin'" with the help of Frank Loesser, when Dubin went on one of his "vacations.") But the team of Dubin and Warren couldn't be beat when it came to jazzy, smart, attitudinal songs that were also honest and truthful. Really, it was an unbeatable partnership that perfectly matched the wisecracking, soft-hearted, no-nonsense Warner Brothers musicals on which they worked. The partnership split up in 1939. Dubin's grandiose appetites accounted for his early death in 1945. Warren soldiered on, working at almost every major studio, including Warner Brothers, MGM, 20th Century Fox, and Paramount. His collaborators included Billy Rose, Leo Robin, Mack Gordon, Ira Gershwin, and Johnny Mercer, and he wrote hits with all of them. But it was with Al Dubin that Warren wrote his most spirited numbers and his catchiest ballads.

"I was nineteen forever. In the meantime, I had married, had a baby, and divorced."

—Peggy Ryan on her long on-screen partnership with Donald O'Connor

B MUSICALS

RISE AND SHINE HAS A SCORE BY ROBIN AND RAINGER AND STARS GEORGE MURPHY; JOHN BARRYMORE and George Murphy headline Hold That Coed; Sweater Girl's score by Jule Styne and Frank Loesser includes the hit song "I Don't Want to Walk without You; Torch Singer stars Claudette Colbert; Buck Privates is the "Boogie Woogie Bugle Boy" movie with Abbott and Costello and The Andrews Sisters; Hooray for Love has Ann Sothern, Gene Raymond, and Bill Robinson performing Jimmy McHugh and Dorothy Fields songs; McHugh and Ted Koehler wrote a catchy score for King of Burlesque's Alice Faye and "Fats" Waller; MGM's Athena stars Jane Powell, Debbie Reynolds, and Vic Damone singing superior Hugh Martin music and lyrics; Everything I Have Is Yours features Marge and Gower Champion—and they all have one thing in common. They were considered "B movies."

B movies were not devoid of talent, nor were they substandard entertainment. While they weren't all successes (or even good), a lot of them were fun romps. To tell the truth, some of the films, such as Athena, could be dubbed A-minus films—but the line between As and Bs is a shadowy one. Ann Miller was probably the queen of the Bs, with appearances in Carolina Blues, Eadie Was a Lady, Reveille with Beverly (a Columbia Picture that also features Frank Sinatra, the Mills Brothers, and Duke Ellington and His Orchestra), Priorities on Parade (which boasts a Styne and Loesser score), and Hit Parade of 1941, in which Miller appears with Frances Langford, Kenny Baker, and Borrah Minnevitch and His Harmonica Rascals. Now, that's entertainment!

Universal also specialized in B movies. Their Abbott and Costello line contained a few musicals and another Universal team, Donald O'Connor and Peggy Ryan, provided a lot of terrific musical moments. It's sad that their movies aren't available for viewing now. Almost by definition, all singing cowboy movies were B musicals, and although they don't get their due today, they were among the most popular films with audiences of all ages when they came out. What we're trying to say is that B musicals might have been made on the cheap but they packed a lot of entertainment into 90 or so minutes.

TOP LEFT: The Andrews Sisters in Buck Privates.

TOP RIGHT: Peggy Ryan and Donald O'Connor in Patrick the Great.

LEFT: Kay Kyser.

GOOD NEWS

MGM—DECEMBER 26, 1947

June Allyson admires Peter Lawford as he trips the light fantastic. Or is it just "trips?"

Good News is an example of MGM at its best, a silly little piece of fluff done brilliantly. You might think it's easy to pull off a breezy musical but there are hundreds of films in the musical comedy graveyard that took one fatal misstep over the precipice into cliché and overly cute situations, on the one hand, or dead seriousness on the other.

Screenwriters Betty Comden and Adolph Green excelled at good-natured musicals, as exemplified by *Singin' in the Rain* and *The Band Wagon.* (When they got too serious, as in *It's Always Fair Weather,* the festivities turned bitter.) Good spirits, a sunny disposition, sky wit, and the ability to laugh at oneself are hallmarks of their best writing. In their day, they and the rest of the MGM crew could do what some might think impossible—make a creaky, old Broadway musical acceptable to film audiences decades after the stage premiere.

GOOD NEWS

COMPOSER: Ray Henderson
LYRICISTS: B. G. DeSylva and Lew Brown
PRODUCER: Arthur Freed
DIRECTOR: Charles Walters
SCREENWRITERS: Betty Comden and Adolph Green
SOURCE: Based on the musical *Good News* by B. G. DeSylva, Lew Brown, Ray Henderson, Frank Mandel, and Laurence Schwab
CHOREOGRAPHER: Robert Alton

Synopsis

Rah, Rah! and Boola, Boola! Peter Lawford goes down on his heels and June Allyson goes up on her toes, they kiss and find they are lucky in love.

Cast

June Allyson	Connie Lane
Peter Lawford	Tommy Marlowe
Patricia Marshall	Pat McClellan
Joan McCracken	Babe Doolittle
Ray McDonald	Bobby Turner
Mel Tormé	Mel
Robert E. Strickland	Peter Van Dyne III
Donald MacBride	Coach Johnson
Tom Dugan	Pooch

Kay Thompson

All legs, elbows, and mouth, Kay Thompson was a huge force in American music though, through every fault of her own, she's practically unknown except to the cognoscenti. She was a singer, arranger, pianist, and choral director on Broadway, in movies, and on television and radio, but she spent the last decades of her life as a recluse, refusing interviews. Thompson wrote special material that fully lived up to the term. How special was it? Ask the audiences of her legendary nightclub act, in which she was backed by the Williams Brothers, the best of which was Andy (with whom she apparently had an affair). She appeared in only four films; *Funny Face* is the most famous and offers us a glimpse of her genius. She was head of MGM's vocal department from 1943 to 1947, arranging and sometimes writing additional music and lyrics for such films as *Ziegfeld Follies*, *Till the Clouds Roll By*, *The Harvey Girls*, and *Good News*. Thompson met Judy Garland at MGM and helped the singer find the unique style she ultimately passed down to Thompson's goddaughter, Liza Minnelli. In the mid fifties, Thompson dreamed up the children's book character of Eloise, a little sprite who lived in the Plaza Hotel and got into lots of trouble. Drawn to a T by illustrator Hilary Knight, Eloise became a worldwide sensation. Thompson even had her own line of ladies' slacks at Saks Fifth Avenue (marketed by none other than Robert Evans, later the head of Paramount Studios). She also directed a number of influential fashion shows and mentored designer Anne Klein. Stephen Sondheim and Arthur Laurents wanted her to star on Broadway in their musical *Anyone Can Whistle*, but this wasn't to be. Kay Thompson was a true Renaissance woman and our list covers a mere fraction of her many accomplishments.

Behind the Screen

- Kay Thompson's vocal arrangements of the songs so altered them to fit the 1940s style that they sounded nothing like the 1920s originals.
- Robert Alton staged "Pass That Peace Pipe" and "The Varsity Drag."
- When Joan McCracken went to Kay Thompson for vocal coaching, Thompson remembered, "She wasn't the least bit interested in who I was or what I was going to do for her." McCracken came in the office and promptly took off her blouse and her bra, presumably to improve her lung power.

ABOVE: Kay Thompson models the wet look in Funny Face (1957).

ABOVE LEFT: Gus Shy and Bessie Love in the original 1930 MGM film version of Good News.

"You've got to get me out of this picture! I'll make an absolute ass of myself." —Peter Lawford to Comden and Green

If you need any proof, take a look at the original 1930 MGM film version of *Good News*. So, let us tell you about it. The Broadway show had opened in 1927, just as the Roaring Twenties were ceasing to roar. But the first MGM version took no notice of tough times. It was all about the raccoon coat-wearing, banner-waving students of Tait College and the big game. The hit songs from Broadway, including "Varsity Drag," "The Best Things in Life are Free," and the title tune, were there, but "Lucky in Love" and "Just Imagine" were nowhere to be found. The "Varsity Drag" number neatly encapsulated the energy of the times—but by 1930, the times had changed. The optimism and vitality of youth and the slavish devotion to mindless fun had given way to Prohibition and Depression. What's more, audiences had tired of film musicals. (If you see a whole bunch films from this period, you can hardly blame them.)

Here's the interesting thing—following the proud Hollywood tradition of "improving" stage shows, new songs were interpolated into the score—and guess who wrote those songs? Arthur Freed and his composing partner, Nacio Herb Brown, decided it would make a swell new musical. Seventeen years later, Arthur Freed, then MGM's lead musical producer, decided it would make a swell new musical.

Comden and Green, along with Freed's taste maker, Roger Edens, and arranger Kay Thompson, undertook the job of modernizing the old warhorse by streamlining the story, reworking some of the DeSylva, Brown, and Henderson songs, and making it into a 1940s musical, albeit set in the '20s.

Certainly, the acting of Peter Lawford, June Allyson, and company was firmly in the style of their time. The '20s-style, rife with funny voices, frisky flappers, and over-emoting, was replaced by a more serene, naturalistic style. (Well, except for the work of Joan McCracken, whose uninhibited exuberance in "Pass That Peace Pipe" matched that of the original film's Dorothy McNulty—latter known as Penny Singleton.) Allyson and Lawford provided a gentleness and concern that would have been foreign to the earlier filmmakers. And not least, there was the patented Comden and Green wit in place of the corny jokes of the original.

Needless to say, the production values were typically superb. Early film musicals often injected energy and brio to compensate for a lack of technical prowess. Perhaps, MGM could have used a little more of the former in exchange for just a tiny bit of the latter. But, while *Good News* isn't a classic, it's a fine example of the kind of filmmaking that audiences could trust. All they were expected to do was sit down, have some popcorn, and let the movie carry them along. That easy connection is deceptively difficult to achieve, and let in itself makes *Good News* enduringly valuable. ■

SONGS

"Best Things in Life Are Free" ■ "French Lesson" (Roger Edens , Betty Comden, and Adolph Green) ■ "Good News" ■ "He's a Ladies' Man" ■ "Lucky in Love" ■ "Just Imagine" ■ "Pass That Peace Pipe" (Roger Edens and Hugh Martin) ■ "Tait Song" ■ "Varsity Drag"

"Oh, shit!!!" —*June Allyson during "The Varsity Drag" number when the boys are swinging her around (Watch her lips!)*

DeSylva, Brown, and Henderson

This songwriting triumvirate had the most hits of any of them, but is the least well-known. B. G. "Buddy" DeSylva, Lew Brown, and Ray Henderson were men of the theater, writing hit after hit for revues and book musicals that are now mostly forgotten. More than any other songwriters, their output defined the Roaring Twenties. Some of their future standards also inspired smash-hit dances, the "Varsity Drag" and "Black Bottom," to name but two. In 1929, they joined the great exodus from Broadway to Hollywood. Landing at Fox, they came up with the Janet Gaynor–Charles Farrell vehicle *Sunny Side Up* in 1929 and *Just Imagine*, a bizarrely futuristic sci-fi musical the following year. DeSylva was smart enough to make himself producer on both films and thus establish his behind-the-screen creds. His partners left Hollywood. DeSylva stayed at Fox, where he produced Shirley Temple vehicles including *Captain January*, *Poor Little Rich Girl*, and *Stowaway*—all in 1936. He occasionally returned to Broadway as a producer, then it was back to Paramount from 1941 to 1945. DeSylva was responsible for bringing Betty Hutton to Paramount and produced or executive-produced Preston Sturges's pictures, *The Road to Morocco* and to *Utopia*, *Birth of the Blues*, and *The Stork Club*, among other films. Several of DeSylva, Brown, and Henderson's Broadway shows (both together and separately with other collaborators) were brought to the screen, with varying degrees of success. *Hold Everything*, *Good News*, *Queen High*, *Big Boy*, and *Flying High* are all largely forgotten but *Good News* remains a favorite.

RIGHT: The famed team of DeSylva, Brown, and Henderson.

GOODBYE MR. CHIPS

MGM—DECEMBER 9, 1969

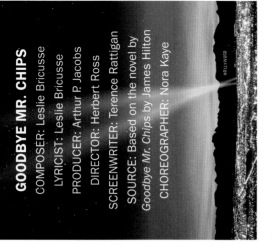

GOODBYE MR. CHIPS

COMPOSER: Leslie Bricusse
LYRICIST: Leslie Bricusse
PRODUCER: Arthur P. Jacobs
DIRECTOR: Herbert Ross
SCREENWRITER: Terence Rattigan
SOURCE: Based on the novel by *Goodbye Mr. Chips* by James Hilton
CHOREOGRAPHER: Nora Kaye

Synopsis

Don't be shocked, but this is a May-September romance between a dusty college professor and a music hall actress. Faster than you can say "Bob's your uncle," they marry, the second Great War begins, and all bets are off.

Cast

Peter O'Toole.............*Arthur Chipping*
Petula Clark..............*Katherine Bridges*
Michael Redgrave.........*The Headmaster*
Alison Leggatt............*The Headmaster's Wife*
Siân Phillips..............*Ursula Mossbank*
Michael Bryant............*Max Staefel*
George Baker.............*Lord Sutterwick*

The Musical that fills the world with love.
He is a shy schoolmaster. She is a music hall star. They marry and immediately have 283 children...all boys!

Peter O'Toole and Petula Clark run the gantlet of pre- and post-pubescent boys.

MARY RODGERS, COMPOSER OF *ONCE UPON A MATTRESS*, INVENTED A CATEGORY OF musicals that she calls the "why?" musicals, shows that make us wonder why songs are included at all. What role do the songs play in advancing the plot, establishing character, providing insights to the audience? As enjoyable and excellent as it is, we have to admit that *Goodbye Mr. Chips* is a "why?" musical.

The original novel by James Hilton, as well as the screenplay for the 1939 film by R. C. Sherriff, Eric Maschwitz, and Claudine West and the poignant Robert Donat in the title role, held up pretty well on its own. Readers and audiences got the point and bawled their eyes out on cue. So, why add songs, no matter how great and lively, no matter how well sung by Petula Clark?

Honestly, we can't answer the question. When MGM remade the property in 1969, big splashy musicals were the vogue and all the studios were jumping to make films like *Oliver!* and *Hello, Dolly!* (exclamation points were also really big in this period). So, why not *Goodbye Mr. Chips?* At least they didn't title it *Chips!* or *Goodbye, Chips!* so we guess they did have some taste and restraint.

Having decided to make it a musical, they cast Peter O'Toole—a singer in the vein of Rex Harrison, Lee Marvin, Walter Matthau, and Albert Finney, all of whom starred in big musicals of the period. Harrison and Finney didn't do so badly, actually, given their limitations of range and tone quality. There had to be a real singer in the cast somewhere, so Petula Clark, was chosen. She was pretty, a natural performer, had a big hit song, "Downtown," four years earlier, and was a child star on stage and screen in Great Britain. Spoiler alert! To be able to add the musical numbers, several plot points had to be changed from the book and original movie. The powers-that-be made the Clark character a music hall singer with a dubious past, whereas Greer Garson had played an ordinary woman who pursues Chips, unconcerned with the difference in her age and that of her paramour. The period was changed from pre-World War I to pre-World War II, and in the new version, Clark is killed in a bombing while entertaining the troops with the song "London Is London." There are other differences—but none of the changes in any way improved the story.

We can think of a few other movie musicals that didn't benefit from the inclusion of music. In fact, in most cases, the original stories were watered down when the musical numbers were introduced. Here's a partial list, in no particular order, of properties that suffered from unnecessary musicalization: *Lost Horizon*, *The Happiest Millionaire*, the Streisand/Kristofferson remake of *A Star Is Born*, *Yentl* (where the songs were mostly inner monologues sung in voiceover), *The Opposite Sex*, and *You Can't Run Away from It*. Elevating *Goodbye Mr. Chips* from the rest of the list is the fact that it was exceptionally well made and still carried an emotional wallop at the end. ■

SONGS

"And the Sky Smiled" ■ "Apollo" ■ "Fill the World with Love" ■ "London Is London" ■ "Walk Through the World" ■ "Schooldays" ■ "What a Lot of Flowers" ■ "What Shall I Do with Today" ■ "When I Am Older" ■ "Where Did My Childhood Go" ■ "You and I"

Leslie Bricusse

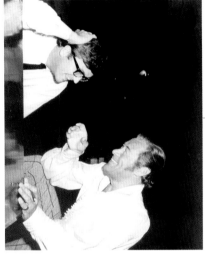

During the 1960s and '70s, composer-lyricist Leslie Bricusse seemed to be everywhere. He collaborated with Anthony Newley on two Broadway shows, *Stop the World—I Want to Get Off* and *The Roar of the Greasepaint, the Smell of the Crowd*, and the film score to *Willy Wonka & the Chocolate Factory*. He, Newley, and John Barry wrote the title song for the James Bond film *Goldfinger*, and Bricusse and Barry wrote the title tune to *You Only Live Twice*. Bricusse composed both music and lyrics for a series of musical films including *Doctor Dolittle*, *Scrooge*, and *Victor/Victoria*. That last one was with Henry Mancini. Bricusse also wrote the stage musicals *Pickwick* (with Cyril Ornadel) and *Jekyll and Hyde* (with Frank Wildhorn).

TOP: Peter O'Toole and the lads.

ABOVE: Peter O'Toole and Petula Clark.

BELOW: Leslie Bricusse discussing *Doctor Dolittle* with Rex Harrison.

Behind the Screen

■ Richard Burton and Rex Harrison were both offered the lead in the movie.

■ André and Dory Previn wrote a complete score for the film but it was never used. Instead, after *Doctor Dolittle*, producer Arthur Jacobs decided to call in Leslie Bricusse to write the songs. "London Is London" had been written for the unproduced film version of the Broadway show *Baker Street* (which was not going to use any of its stage songs).

GREASE

PARAMOUNT PICTURES—JUNE 16, 1978

GREASE

COMPOSERS: Jim Casey and Warren Jacobs

LYRICISTS: Jim Casey and Warren Jacobs

PRODUCERS: Allan Carr and Robert Stigwood

DIRECTOR: Randal Kleiser

SCREENWRITER: Bronte Woodard

SOURCE: Based on the musical by Jim Casey and Warren Jacobs

CHOREOGRAPHER: Patricia Birch

Synopsis

Bad boy Danny Zuko and good girl Sandy Olsson are destined to fall in love. But first . . . Sandy needs to cultivate her dark side and get a makeover in skintight leather.

Cast

Olivia Newton-John ......Sandy Olsson
John Travolta.........Danny Zuko
Stockard Channing.......Betty Rizzo
Jeff Conaway............Kenickie
Barry Pearl..............Doody
Michael Tucci ....Sonny
Kelly Wood.............Putzie
Didi Conn...............Frenchy
Jamie Donnelly..........Jan
Dinah Manoff.......Marty Maraschino
Eve Arden.............Principal McGee
Frankie Avalon..........The Teen Angel
Joan Blondell............Vi
Edd Byrnes.............Vince Fontaine
Sid Caesar..............Coach Calhoun

Pretty in pink. Olivia Newton John and John Travolta.

I F *SATURDAY NIGHT FEVER*'S STORY WAS ECLIPSED BY JOHN TRAVOLTA'S STRUTTING HIS STUFF on the mean streets and in the disco, why not make a movie musical with all strutting and no story at all? Enter *Grease*. This colossally successful film version of the Broadway musical was the ultimate nostalgia fest for people who hadn't actually lived through the 1950s. Hollywood did its thing, presenting iconic types from a fondly remembered period and cleaning them up for mass consumption.

Not only did John Travolta strut his stuff in this one, Olivia Newton-John matched him strut for strut. By the end of the picture, she has transformed herself from a goody-two-pumps sweetheart into a shiny little biker chick. And, in another great Hollywood tradition, she is surrounded by a supporting cast a decade older than the characters they're playing. Stockard Channing was the worst offender, thirty-four years old at the time of the film's release. (Hey, we've got nothing against Stockard Channing, but come on!)

In addition to the "kids," there was another generation on hand in the film. The nostalgia quotient skyrocketed with the inclusion of favorite old television and movie stars, including Sid Caesar, Eve Arden, and Joan Blondell, none of whom had much to do. They certainly weren't given funny material—but they did put smiles on the faces of some baby boomers. Two authentic 1950s teen stars also appeared in the film: Edd Byrnes, best/only known as Kookie in *77 Sunset Strip*, showed up as DJ Vince Fontaine (although most audience members of any age didn't recognize him); and Frank(ie) Avalon had a cameo as Teen Angel, complete with a song, and he acquitted himself well. Frankie Valli was heard but not seen, singing the title song over the credits.

That brings us to the score. The original stage production was a gentle spoof but the movie took the whole thing as seriously as it could, given the lightweight material. Toward that end, dramatic weight was added to the score that the piece just couldn't support. Barry Gibb, Louis St. Louis, and John Farrar rightly decided to ignore the fifties time period altogether and write catchy pop songs. Gibb supplied the title song and Farrar wrote "Hopelessly Devoted to You," the one song that wasn't a spoof twisted into something serious.

Nostalgia is, by definition, a celebration of the good clichés of an era. People nostalgic for the thirties think of Fred and Ginger, not the Depression or the ramping up to World War II. Nostalgic movies from Fox such as *Tin Pan Alley* and *Wabash Avenue* and MGM nostalgia fests including *Meet Me in St. Louis* and *Little Nellie Kelly* were steeped in period research. Not so much with *Grease*. But it didn't matter to audiences because, as we said at the beginning, it was all about attitude. The Olivia Newton-John–John Travolta's showdown, "You're the One That I Want," is a mega-attitude strut. And that's what the movie is all about. Kudos to first-time feature director Randal Kleiser for making such a smooth and slick production out of the material he was handed. ■

Italian American Heartthrob Singers

Frankie Avalon, Fabian, Bobby Rydell, and Bobby Darin . . . was it the cheese steaks that accounted for the boom in Italian-American singers from South Philly? All cute. All talented. All with great hair loaded with what today is known as "product" but that was then known as Brylcreem. And, like most stars, they all had big heads—and I mean that quite literally. Their heads were large in proportion to their bodies. Don't believe me? Check out Bobby Rydell in *Bye, Bye, Birdie*. Their Philly attitude and accent, reedy voices, and self-assured sexiness made them all incredibly appealing to teenage girls (and a few teenage boys, too). All of them took a stab at pictures and for the most part, they acquitted themselves with honor. Some, like Fabian, appeared in nonmusicals and did as well as could be expected. (We mean that as a compliment.) With the exception of Darin, who died young but probably would have had the longest run, their careers tapered off relatively quickly. Whether or not you think he had real talent, you must admit that Darin had "it." The others still appear in front of throngs of baby boomers at nostalgia shows, having never really left a business that has largely left them.

Behind the Screen

■ *Grease* was the highest-grossing movie of 1978 and surpassed *The Sound of Music* as the highest-grossing musical film to date.

■ The sequel, *Grease 2*, was a bomb, forcing Paramount to scuttle plans for more sequels and a TV series.

John Travolta and his rough-and-ready gang of greasers.

SONGS

"Alma Mater" ■ "Beauty School Dropout" ■ "Grease" (Barry Gibb) ■ "Born to Hand Jive" ■ "Greased Lightnin'" ■ "Hopelessly Devoted to You" (John Farrar) ■ "It's Raining on Prom Night" ■ "Look at Me, I'm Sandra Dee" ■ "Rock 'N' Roll Party Queen" ■ "Rydell Fight Song" ■ "Sandy" (Louis St. Louis and Scott Simon) ■ "Summer Nights" ■ "There Are Worse Things That I Could Do" ■ "Those Magic Changes" ■ "We Go Together" ■ "You're the One that I Want" (John Farrar)

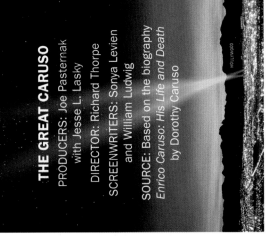

Synopsis

Life is tough for a brilliant tenor-in-waiting. His wife's father doesn't approve of him and his ego gets in the way of his fellow performers—but wow, what a voice!

Cast

Mario Lanza......................Enrico Caruso
Ann Blyth.........................Dorothy Benjamin
Dorothy Kirsten..................Louise Heggar
Jarmila Novotna.................Maria Selka
Richard Hageman................Carlo Santi
Carl Benton Reid................Park Benjamin
Eduard Franz....................Giulio Gatti-Casazza
Ludwig Donath...................Alfredo Brazzi
Alan Napier......................Jean de Reszke
Paul Javor........................Antonio Scotti
Nestor Paiva.....................Egisto Barretto
Peter Edward Price.............Caruso as a boy

THE GREAT CARUSO

ABOVE AND OPPOSITE TOP RIGHT: Two lobby cards advertising *The Great Caruso*. Even when the films were in black and white, the lobby cards were hand colored.

Admittedly, this isn't the greatest film ever. In fact, it's squarely in the mode of most Hollywood biopics: a lot of hooey and so-called "facts" surrounding some terrific performances. Although reviews of the film were mixed, it was MGM's highest-grossing picture of 1951 and extremely profitable for the studio, given its low production cost. The saving grace of *The Great Caruso*, and what got it into this book, was Mario Lanza's remarkable singing voice, his charming good looks, and the typically high-quality MGM production. Opera diva Dorothy Kirsten exclaimed, "Caruso never sang like that one day of his life!" She meant it as a compliment. Yes, Lanza could be difficult, crude, blustery, overbearing, and his weight fluctuated by more than 25 pounds during the filming—but that voice, and his sex appeal, made it all worthwhile.

Maybe it was fate that brought the movie to the screen. Lanza was born in 1921, the same year Caruso died. Lanza was baptized by a Reverend Caruso. And Jesse L. Lasky had produced Caruso's two silent films (yes, you read that right), *The Splendid Romance* and *My Cousin*. Not quite as stunning as the JFK–Abraham Lincoln coincidences, but it can't be denied that the Caruso mystique and the voice and acting of Lanza made for a potent combination at the box office.

The success of *The Great Caruso* came as a complete surprise to MGM, and to Hollywood as a whole. In the 1930s, with the advent of sound on film, opera singers Lily Pons, Grace Moore, Lawrence Tibbett, and Gladys Swarthout had headlined films. These usually featured a mix of opera standards and new songs by the likes of Jerome Kern, for example.

By the 1950s, opera had most often been inserted into a movie to add what the producers (primarily Louis B. Mayer) thought of as "class." Think of Jane Powell and Jeanette

"Caruso? That guy could not even whistle properly."

—Mario Lanza in 1958

SONGS

"The Loneliest Night of the Year" (lyric by Paul Francis Webster) was the only original song in the score. Others songs and arias included: "Magnificat" (Bach) ▪ "A Vucchella" (Tosti and D'Annunzio) ▪ "La Danza" (Rossini) ▪ "The Consecration Scene," "The Trio Finale," "Celeste Aïda," and "Numi Pietà" (Verdi's *Aïda*) ▪ "The Torture Scene" and "E Lucevan le Stelle" (Puccini's *Tosca*) ▪ "The Villification Scene" and "Brindisi" (Mascagni's *Cavalleria Rusticana*) ▪ "Cielo e Mar" (Ponchielli's *La Gioconda*) ▪ "La Donna è Mobile" and "Quartette" (Verdi's *Rigoletto*) ▪ "Torna a Sorriento" (De Curtis) ▪ "Che Gelida Manina" (Puccini's *La Bohème*) ▪ "Mattinata" (Leoncavallo); "Miserere" (Verdi's *Il Trovatore*) ▪ "Sweethearts" (Victor Herbert and Harry B. Smith); "Recitativo" and "Vesti la Giubba" (Leoncavallo's *Pagliacci*) ▪ "Ave Maria" (Bach and Gounod) . "Sextette" (Donizetti's *Lucia di Lammermoor*) ▪ "Because" (Guy D'Hardelot [pen name of Helen Guy Rhodes]) ▪ "M'Appari" and "Finale" (Flotow's *Martha*)

Behind the Screen

▪ Mario Lanza's recording *The Great Caruso* was actually issued before the film opened and includes only four of the film's numbers, none of them from the film's soundtrack. In fact, a soundtrack of the film was never released. The Lanza record became the first opera recording to sell over one million copies.

The real Enrico Caruso beating his own drum as Pagliacci.

MacDonald warbling operatic arias in their films, especially those produced by Joe Pasternak. In fact, Powell and MacDonald appeared together in MGM's *Three Daring Daughters*, whose soundtrack includes "Je Veux Vivre" from Gounod's *Romeo and Juliet*, "Passepied" by Delibes and Eristoff; light classics, including "Springtide" by Grieg and Dole; and newly honed "classical" songs such as "Where There's Love" by Richard Strauss with new words by Earl Brent. Deanna Durbin was a sunny young girl who just couldn't be stopped from singing and smiling through such films as *One Hundred Men and a Girl*, where she offered up "The Drinking Song" from *La Traviata* and Mozart's "Alleluia." Susanna Foster was featured in the Paramount biopic *The Great Victor Herbert* and Universal's *The Phantom of the Opera*.

The Great Caruso started a mini-cycle of other opera stars biopics: *Melba* starring Patrice Munsel as toast namesake Nellie Melba, *So This Is Love* starring Kathryn Grayson as Grace Moore, and *Interrupted Melody* starring Eleanor Parker as Marjorie Lawrence.

Remember Kitty Carlisle and Allan Jones in *A Night at the Opera*, singing arias from Verdi's *Il Trovatore*? Of course you do, because they annoyed you when they stopped the antics of the Marx Brothers. For many movie patrons, the operatic interludes provided perfect opportunities to run to the restroom or concession stand. Kitty Carlisle was actually a star of the light opera world, but her girlish charm and beauty made her accessible and appealing to movie audiences. Helen Traubel brought her infectious joie de vivre to another of MGM's dubiously historical biopics, *Deep in My Heart*—her one stab at musical films. In it, she had a ball singing Sigmund Romberg's music opposite José Ferrer.

The Great Caruso also featured actual stars of the Metropolitan Opera Blanche Thebom, Giuseppe Valdengo, Jarmila Novtona, and Nicola Moscona, as well as members of the Metropolitan Opera chorus. And unlike the films mentioned above, Caruso's opera scenes were integral to its plot, not just stuck in as filler. ▪

Mario Lanza

Mario Lanza was one of the greatest tenors in history, though his operatic career never amounted to much. His brief life (he died at age thirty-eight) was marked by successes in both records and films. There was no doubt that he was a brilliant singer with a remarkable instrument, but because he came to prominence through pictures and not the opera stage, Lanza was always insecure about his fame. MGM head Louis B. Mayer, heard Lanza at the Hollywood Bowl and immediately signed him to a contract. The singer's first two movies, *That Midnight Kiss* and *Toast of New Orleans*, were immense hits and his next film, *The Great Caruso*, his biggest success. But Lanza's insecurities led to bouts of binge eating and drinking, causing his weight to fluctuate between 170 and 270 pounds and putting a strain on his heart. When he was fired from the film *The Student Prince* after disagreements with the director (his prerecords were used on the soundtrack anyway), his already fragile self-esteem crumbled. He made the moderately successful film *Serenade* and then went to abroad to make *Seven Hills of Rome*. He concertized around Europe but his health continued to decline. His heavy drinking and yo-yoing weight finally led to a heart attack in April 1959. Pneumonia followed and in October of that year, Lanza died.

THE GREAT WALTZ

MGM—NOVEMBER 4, 1938

THE GREAT WALTZ

COMPOSER: Johann Strauss and Dimitri Tiomkin

LYRICIST: Oscar Hammerstein II

PRODUCER: Bernard H. Hyman

DIRECTOR: Julien Duvivier

SCREENWRITERS: Samuel Hoffenstein and Walter Reisch

CHOREOGRAPHER: Albertina Rasch

Synopsis

Johann Strauss II finds fame and love, all in three-quarter time.

Cast

Luise Rainer	Poldi Vogelhuber
Fernand Gravet	Johann 'Schani' Strauss
Miliza Korjus	Carla Donner
Hugh Herbert	Julius Hofbauer
Lionel Atwell	Count Anton "Tony" Hohenfried
Curt Bois	Kienzl
Leonid Kinsky	Dudelman
Al Shean	Cellist
Minna Gombell	Mrs. Hofbauer
Alma Kruger	Mrs. Strauss
Henry Hull	Emperor Franz Josef

Miliza Korjus, surrounded by the opulence of The Great Waltz.

A T THE BEGINNING OF *THE GREAT WALTZ*, MGM's BIOPIC OF JOHANN STRAUSS II, MGM placed a legend on the screen stating, "We have dramatized the spirit rather than the facts of his life, because it is his spirit that has lived—in his music."

At least they were honest—more so than they had been about their versions of the lives of Rodgers and Hart, Jerome Kern, Kalmar and Ruby, or any of the other composers they made films about.

This may be the only movie musical that can be called luscious. Duvivier's camera floats through the film as if it is waltzing along with the music. Near the beginning, during the "Artist's Life" waltz, a montage of failure turned to fame is brilliantly executed with only the rich music as accompaniment. Extreme closeups, shot from below or above, capture the swirling waltzes in perfect spirit. Has any other film made better use of the camera crane? We think not.

In the "Vienna Woods" scene, where the clip-clop of the horse and carriage, the bird calls, the trumpet of a passing carriage, the horseman's harmonica, and the tunes of shepherds all inspire Strauss to write a glorious waltz. When the waltz is later played by the full orchestra, the camera follows Strauss and Carla Donner around and around the bandstand, sharing the delirium of their love.

It's too bad that the principals made so few films in the United States. *The Great Waltz* was director Duvivier's first American film. Double Oscar winner Luise Rainer made two more films before retiring from the movies for over forty years. Watch her subtle and expressive performance during the song "One Day when We Were Young." The exceedingly beautiful Miliza Korjus made only three films in her notable career as an opera singer—sad, since her spirit and voice shine through *The Great Waltz*.

SONGS

"Artist's Life" (lyric by Dimitri Tiomkin) ■ "The Bat" ■ "Birth of the Vienna Woods" (lyric by Dimitri Tiomkin) ■ "Du und Du (Only You)" ■ "I'm in Love with Vienna" ■ "One Day when We Were Young" ■ "Polka" ■ "Revolutionary March" ■ "Tales from the Vienna Woods" ■ "There'll Come a Time

Mention must also be made of the film's two Oscar winners. Cinematographer Joseph Ruttenberg artfully captures the film's many moods, from the light shining through the Vienna Woods to the chiaroscuro of the scene between Count Hohenfried and Mrs. Strauss. Film editor Tom Held's cutting of the waltz scenes and many montages artfully captures the spirit of the film and of the waltz form itself. Watch especially the editing of the scene in which Luise Rainer enters the opera house. Of course, he was following the artful direction of Duvivier but the sequence is dramatic. Although she didn't win an Oscar, the choreography of Broadway favorite Albertina Rasch, in conjunction with the work of Duvivier and Held, makes the waltz seem the most exciting dance imaginable.

There have been many motion pictures celebrating classical music. They are usually punctuated by shots of orchestras and singers standing stock still, arms clasped in front. The reverence of these films makes them static and pompous, and none comes close to equaling The Great Waltz in its thrilling celebration of the music and its impact. ■

Behind the Screen

■ There were directorial contributions by Josef Von Sternberg and far more extensively, Victor Fleming. He was brought in to restructure the narrative.

THE GREAT ZIEGFELD

MGM—APRIL 8, 1936

THE GREAT ZIEGFELD

COMPOSER: Walter Donaldson

LYRICIST: Harold Adamson
PRODUCER: Hunt Stromberg
DIRECTOR: Robert Z. Leonard
SCREENWRITER:
William Anthony McGuire
CHOREOGRAPHER: Seymour Felix

Synopsis

A great producer's life interpreted by MGM, typified by an immense white wedding cake of a tower, chockablock with pretty girls who, by the way, are just like a melody . . . which is what that great producer has been telling everyone for years.

Cast

William Powell...............Florenz Ziegfeld Jr.
Myrna Loy ....Billie Burke
Luise Rainer....................Anna Held
Frank Morgan...................Billings
Franny Brice....................Herself
Virginia Bruce.................Audrey Dane
Reginald Owen.................Sampston
Ray Bolger ....Himself
Ernest Cossart.................Sidney
Joseph Cawthorn.............Dr. Ziegfeld
Nat Pendleton.................Sandow
Harriet Hoctor................Herself

Harriet Hoctor tames the savage beasts as a gaggle of gorgeous girls stand ready with spears.

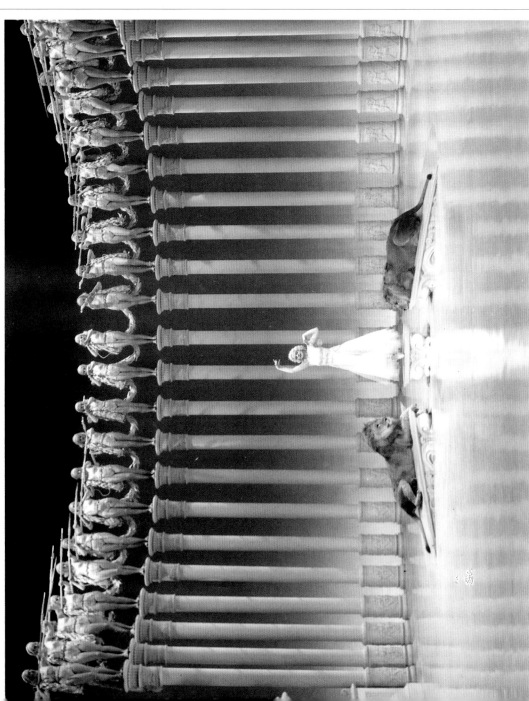

THERE ARE TWO MAINSTAYS OF HOLLYWOOD BIOGRAPHICAL MUSICALS—THE "AND-then-I-wrote" films about songwriters and the "and-then-I-sang" films about performers. Here's another variation—the "and-then-I-produced." Florenz Ziegfeld, producer of *The Ziegfeld Follies* revue series, was the greatest producer of the early twentieth century, so it seems only natural that MGM, the greatest studio in Hollywood, would have undertaken the daunting project of creating a fitting Ziegfeld biopic.

Ziegfeld's shows were lavish affairs with elaborate costumes and settings, so a picture about him required at least a taste of the Ziegfeldian production values. Warner Brothers and MGM were the studios most devoted to creating film spectacles. Warner had Busby Berkeley, and the first-act finale to *The Great Ziegfeld* was Seymour Felix's inspired and successful attempt to out-choreograph Warner's master.

You'll notice, when watching *The Great Ziegfeld* and any of Busby Berkeley's films, that the camera is choreographed to a greater extent than the dancers. In fact, Berkeley and Felix should have been titled "conceivers" rather than choreographers. They specialized in elaborate camera movements and effects while the set and company moved in geometric patterns. When actual dance steps were needed, they turned to assistants. (This is still a practice on Broadway today.) Gower Champion, Bob Fosse, and Michael Bennett conceived musical numbers but mostly left the creation of the actual steps to their assistants. Marge Champion, Gwen Verdon, and Bob Avian, respectively.

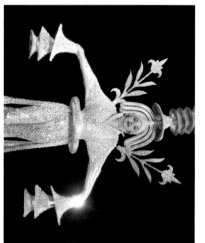

The whole of *The Great Ziegfeld* seems to move inexorably toward the grand finale, probably the most impressive and imaginative stage effect of all time. And to think it was all done for real with no camera tricks or special effects. The gigantic wedding cake of a set for "A Pretty Girl Is Like a Melody" seems large enough to hold the entire population of Toledo, Ohio; it actually held 180 performers. We'd like to see the Broadway stage that could hold that big a set or that many people! Ah, well, that's why we have the movies. And how about that curtain that rises to the heavens to reveal tier after tier of tuxedoed gentlemen, grand pianos, and a bevy of beautiful women (some seemingly out walking their dogs)? The curtain was made up of 4,300 yards of rayon silk. It's a magnificent sight—and it should be. It cost a whopping $220,000, a fortune in 1939.

Although it took weeks to set up the number and film it, reportedly photographer Ray June shot the entire number in one long take without any cuts. By the way, Virginia Bruce is the gal propped up at the apex of the "cake."

The Great Ziegfeld has just about as much truth in it as any Hollywood biopic but you've got to admit it's a marvelous entertainment for the heart as well as the eyes. ■

Robert Z. Leonard

A well-loved director of some of MGM's best musicals. He made a mini-career out of MacDonald/Eddy operettas and was a favorite of both performers. MacDonald said Pops was "one of the most loveable men I've ever had the joy to work with." (High praise from a mercurial star like MacDonald.) Good natured, efficient, and imaginative, Leonard made working a pleasure and even the roughest, most trite script shone under his classy direction.

Falstaffian man who began his career as an operatic baritone, "Pop" Leonard was a

TOP: A bevy of beauties exhibiting the latest in showgirl fashion.
ABOVE: Frank Morgan confers with William Powell as Florenz Ziegfeld.

HALLELUJAH!

MGM—AUGUST 20, 1929

HALLELUJAH!

PRODUCER: King Vidor
DIRECTOR: King Vidor
SCREENWRITERS: Ransom Rideout
and Richard Schayer

Synopsis

A poor black sharecropper has a run of bad luck. He finds redemption as a preacher but a woman threatens to bring him down again.

Cast

Nina Mae McKinney.......*Chick*
Daniel L. Haynes ....*Zeke Johnson*
William Fountaine.........*Hot Shot*
Harry Gray....................*Pappy "Parson" Johnson*
Fanny Belle DeKnight ....*Mammy Johnson*
Everett McGarity............*Spunk Johnson*
Victoria Spivey..............*Missy Rose*
Dixie Jubilee Singers ....

Behind the Screen

■ Nina Mae McKinney was the first black woman to be offered a contract by a major Hollywood studio.

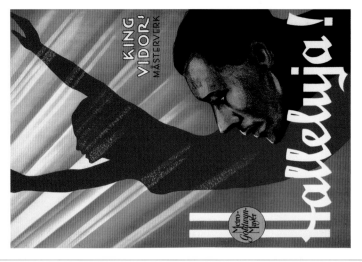

Hot stuff! Nina Mae McKinney is ogled by William Fountaine (far left) while Daniel L. Haynes (center right) can't believe his eyes.

IMAGINE THIS: SOUND FILMS ARE JUST COMING AROUND THE CORNER AND YOU'RE TRYING TO come up with musical subjects and themes suitable for the new medium. You want to avoid the cliché of the backstage musical and uneven musical revues. What's left? How about colored people and their simple but poor lives which they enrich with music? Now you're thinking like Fox, whose first musical film was *Hearts in Dixie*, and the folks at MGM, who gave us *Hallelujah!*

Although both films suffer from the inevitable stereotypes of the period and other insensitivities, they were both produced and directed by notable talents who made sincere attempts to capture the lives of black Southerners. Yes, Stepin Fetchit makes an appearance in *Hearts in Dixie*—but, after all, he was an audience favorite.

Of the two films, *Hallelujah!* is a bit nobler in its goals and thus a little more pretentious, but it crackles with authenticity, enthusiasm, and veracity. Director King Vidor sincerely felt sympathy toward his subjects though, perhaps inevitably, those old stereotypes crept into the proceedings.

Truth be told, the majority of white audiences coming to see the film had limited experience with blacks, except as maids or porters. Since the races didn't mix in everyday life, many white audience members, as well as some Northern blacks, didn't recognize the stereotypes as stereotypes. They took the characters at face value. Ironically, a film that tried to celebrate black culture honestly may have helped propagate stereotypes.

In New York, the film opened in Harlem for the black audience and downtown for the white audience (though technically, the city didn't segregate its theaters). Some Southern cities refused to play the film at all, and whites in the nonsegregated north felt uncomfortable mingling with black patrons. Still, those who did manage to see the film found favor with it. Yes, the story is melodramatic and clichéd but Vidor's respect and enthusiasm, not to mention the excellent performances, made people overlook the films' flaws. Although MGM lost money on the film, they were proud to have it on their roster. In fact, the company had such regard for the film that they reissued it in 1939, shorn of around ten minutes of footage.

In viewing early sound musicals, we have to ignore their sonic imperfections and somewhat stilted camerawork—the results of technical limitations of the day. *Hallelujah!* certainly isn't in high fidelity but many of the problems inherent in those times were made moot by Vidor's style of filming.

When sound came in to replace silents, more adventurous filmmakers embraced the new dimension and reveled in the possibilities it offered. Rouben Mamoulian, famous for using sound montages on Broadway, expanded the film pallet in *Applause* and *Love Me Tonight*. King Vidor also saw sound as integral part of his story. *Hallelujah!* features sound as a particularly important element. Vidor filmed silent footage (the MGM sound truck never showed up) of the cast in Memphis locations and then cut in the dialogue when back in Culver City. Surprisingly, the fact that the quality of the sound in *Hallelujah!* is not up to today's standards works for the film. The location filming and sound recording make the exterior scenes seem almost like documentary footage. This helps mitigate any uncomfortably over-the-top moments in the story.

Hallelujah! might not be a true reflection of Southern black life but there is some truth in its story and attitudes. Ignoring stereotypes and melodramatic plot machinations may not be easy for today's audience but there is a lot of exuberant filmmaking to be found here. ∎

TOP: William Fountaine holds a gun on prisoner Daniel L. Haynes.

MIDDLE: Fanny Belle DeMay, Daniel L. Haynes, and Harry Gray pray for salvation in a scene played out similarly in many black films of the era.

BOTTOM: Daniel L. Haynes stands up for the righteous in a dance hall.

A HARD DAY'S NIGHT

UNITED ARTISTS—AUGUST 11, 1964

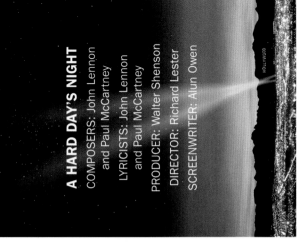

A HARD DAY'S NIGHT

COMPOSERS: John Lennon and Paul McCartney

LYRICISTS: John Lennon and Paul McCartney

PRODUCER: Walter Shenson
DIRECTOR: Richard Lester
SCREENWRITER: Alun Owen

Synopsis

John, George, Ringo, and the cute one have to get to a television station in time for their show—but crazed fans, high-spirited high-jinks, and kooky editing keep getting in the way.

Cast

John Lennon................*John*
Paul McCartney...........*Paul*
Ringo Starr.................*Ringo*
George Harrison...........*George*
Wilfrid Brambell...........*John McCartney*
Norman Rossington ......*Norm*
John Junkin..................*Shake*
Victor Spinetti...............*Richard*
Anna Quayle.................*Millie*
Richard Vernon..............*Man on Train*
Lionel Blair...................*Choreographer*

The Beatles try to elude their fans.

W HAT HATH RICHARD LESTER AND THE BEATLES WROUGHT? IN SHORT, A FILM that looked like no other. It has elements of the French New Wave, owing a particular debt to Godard's *Breathless*; echoes of a British comedy group the Crazy Gang; and its silliness is reminiscent of the Hope and Crosby's Road pictures. It also owes a nod to Tony Richardson's *Tom Jones*, released the year before. That film had a similar anything-goes quality, complete with snarky title cards, sped-up sequences, and a celebration of the unconventional. *A Hard Day's Night* takes it all a little further, though—and, with the quadruple star power of the fab four, it's irresistible.

If the film seems a bit slapdash, perhaps it is because the "true" story of the Beatles was still unfolding as it was being made, and the filmmakers were racing to stay ahead of it. The subject of the film, after all, is the exploding popularity of the group—but no one was quite sure how long Beatlemania would last. They managed to make the thing in six and a half weeks, leaving it unpolished and untouched by the kind of overthinking and exactitude associated with big studio productions. Sometimes it's preferable to just let the chips fall where they may. This was clearly one of those cases.

Screenwriter Alun Owen followed the boys around, hoping to catch a bit of their own language for the dialogue. Although he's denied it, there was clearly lots of ad libbing going on in front of the camera and behind. Thanks to him and mainly to American-

A Beatles-eye view of a concert.

John Lennon, with Richard Lester, gets his moptop made suitably moppy during production of *How I Won the War* (1967).

Ringo, John, George, Richard (Lester), and Paul wait to film a scene.

born Richard Lester, whom the Beatles had hand-picked for the assignment, it was certainly the most revolutionary—yes, we mean revolutionary—and free-form commercial movie ever made. Handheld cameras, spinning cameras, running and jumping cameras all made *A Hard Day's Night* the most delirious (as is fever dream delirious) and momentous (as in with the greatest momentum) film to date.

The film's great success guaranteed that it would be copied, as that's what filmmakers do best. A whole series of rock acts from Herman's Hermits (*Hold On!*) to the Dave Clark Five (*Catch Us If You Can*) jumped on the bandwagon and made knockoff films of their own. Richard Lester embroidered upon his own techniques in *Help!*, the Beatles next (and more self-conscious) film, as well as in *A Funny Thing Happened on the Way to the Forum* and the *Three Musketeers* trilogy.

A few years later, Bryan Forbes directed the hilarious farce, *The Wrong Box*, taking a page from Lester's playbook. Not to be left out, America appropriated some things—well, everything—from *A Hard Day's Night* for its television sitcom *The Monkees*. Not only did creators Bob Rafelson and Burt Schneider steal the techniques, but the Beatles' characters themselves were put through the American television mill, and out popped Mike, Peter, Mickey—and the cute one. The show was surprisingly successful—but *A Hard Day's Night* is a keeper. ■

"Alun hung around with us and was careful to try and put words in our mouths that he might've heard us speak, so I thought he did a very good script."

—*Paul McCartney on screenwriter Alun Owen*

Behind the Screen

■ It's a fine line between documentary and fiction in *A Hard Day's Night*. Some of the scenes, including those with the fans at the beginning of the film, are real.

■ Ringo came up with the phrase "a hard day's night" to describe a particularly grueling recording session. Producer Walter Shenson thought it would make a good title and Lennon and McCartney wrote the song that evening.

SONGS

"All My Loving" ■ "And I Love Her" ■ "Can't Buy Me Love" ■ "Don't Bother Me" (George Harrison) ■ "A Hard Day's Night" ■ "I Should Have Known Better" ■ "I Wanna Be Your Man" ■ "If I Fell" ■ "I'm Happy Just to Dance with You" ■ "She Loves You" ■ "Tell Me Why"

ABOVE: The Beatles get a touch up by some lucky girls, who will save the locks of hair for sale on eBay.

RIGHT: John Junkin and Norman Rossington look for inspiration.

BEHIND THE SCENES

In today's world of DVDs featuring "making of . . ." mini-documentaries, media magazines such as *Entertainment Weekly* and *Premiere*, and television shows such as *Entertainment Tonight* and *Inside Edition*, seeing stars on location, on the studio lot, and at home is a normal thing. Back in the dark ages, before the cult of so-called celebrity became a national obsession, seeing actors and actresses off the screen was a rare occurrence. While we might be blasé about seeing today's stars waiting for their closeups, we still get a thrill when we see stars from the past in unguarded moments. Here are some of our favorite photos from movie sets of yore.

ABOVE: The heather on the hill on the soundstage for *Brigadoon*.
RIGHT: Cinematographer Ray June shoots Judy Garland on the set of *Ziegfeld Girl*.

TOP LEFT: Esther Williams is all wet filming *Million Dollar Mermaid*.

TOP RIGHT: Annette Kellerman, Busby Berkeley, and Esther Williams on the set of *Million Dollar Mermaid*, the story of Annette Kellerman.

RIGHT: Busby Berkeley, Rudy Vallee, Rosemary Lane, Allan Jenkins, and Mabel Todd on the set of *Gold Diggers in Paris*.

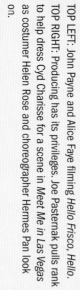

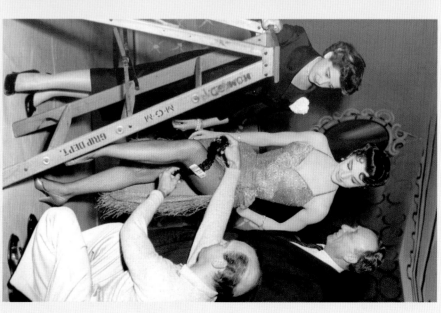

TOP LEFT: John Payne and Alice Faye filming *Hello Frisco, Hello.*
TOP RIGHT: Producing has its privileges. Joe Pasternak pulls rank to help dress Cyd Charisse for a scene in *Meet Me in Las Vegas* as costumer Helen Rose and choreographer Hermes Pan look on.
BOTTOM LEFT: Marge and Gower Champion work on their tans.
BOTTOM RIGHT: Lucky guy. Director George Sidney gets Rita Hayworth into bed on the set of *Pal Joey.*

TOP LEFT: Joan Crawford and Clark Gable share an intimate moment while the crew of *Dancing Lady* looks on.
TOP RIGHT: *Anchors Aweigh* director George Sidney gives Gene Kelly and Frank Sinatra some sage advice.
BELOW: H. Bruce Humberstone puts Betty Gable and the troops through their drills on the set of *Tin Pan Alley*.

THE HARVEY GIRLS

MGM—JANUARY 18, 1946

THE HARVEY GIRLS
COMPOSER: Harry Warren.
LYRICIST: Johnny Mercer
PRODUCER: Arthur Freed
DIRECTOR: George Sidney
SCREENWRITERS: Edmund Beloin,
Nathaniel Curtis, Harry Crane,
James O'Hanlon, Samson Raphaelson,
and Kay Van Riper
SOURCE: Based on the novel by
Samuel Hopkins Adams
CHOREOGRAPHER: Robert Alton

Synopsis

As the Atchison, Topeka, and the Santa Fe wends its way westward, an army of young girls tries to tame the wild, wild west—one restaurant at a time.

Cast

Judy Garland...............Susan Bradley
John Hodiak................Ned Trent
Ray Bolger................Chris Maule
Angela Lansbury ....Em
Preston Foster............Judge Sam Purvis
Virginia O'Brien..........Alma from Ohio
Kenny Baker...............Terry O'Halloran
Marjorie Main.............Sonora Cassidy
Chill Wills...............H. H. Hartsey
Selena Royle..............Miss Bliss
Cyd Charisse.............Deborah Andrews

Judy Garland on that fateful trolley ride to film immortality.

I F YOU'RE A STUDIO HEAD AND CAN'T GET THE RIGHTS TO A HIT BROADWAY SHOW, JUST appropriate some of the elements and make your own original musical. Hey, it worked for Doris Day when she and Warner Brothers lost out to MGM on *Annie Get Your Gun*; they concocted a close second, *Calamity Jane*. And it happened at MCM, too. *The Harvey Girls* was originally a novel and MGM bought the property as a possible vehicle for Lana Turner. But then the stage smash *Oklahoma!* came on the scene and associate producer Roger Edens wanted his own western-themed musical for Metro. He took control of *Harvey Girls*, convinced Judy Garland that she'd be a smash in the lead, and set the wheels in motion. (Garland had wanted to appear in *Yolanda and the Thief*, under the direction of her husband, Vincente Minnelli—good thing Edens talked her out of that one.)

Speaking of wheels in motion, the smash hit from Harry Warren and Johnny Mercer's score was "On the Atchison, Topeka and the Santa Fe," a paean to the train that helped open up the West. The number was inspired by another song about vehicular travel sung by Judy Garland in an MGM film, Hugh Martin's "The Trolley Song" from *Meet Me in St. Louis*. Like Martin's song, Warren and Mercer's driving ditty was an unlikely hit. Usually it was the ballads that got all the attention, but "On the Atchison, Topeka . . ." was a smash on the *Hit Parade*, broke the record for records, and was awarded the Academy Award for Best Song. What was even more amazing was that the hit recording was by the song's lyricist, Johnny Mercer, backed up by the Pied Pipers.

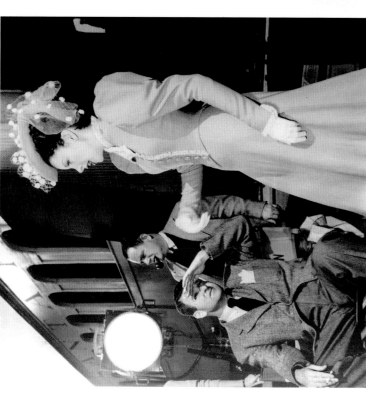

> "They're going to make me look like an idiot . . . everybody's going to think I wrote that junk."
>
> —*Johnny Mercer on Kay Thompson and Roger Edens's additions to "On the Atchison, Topeka and the Santa Fe"*

Before we continue, we'd like to mention that the irreplaceable Kay Thompson provided the vocal arrangement of the song and supplied some additional lyrics, along with Roger Edens, for when the girls introduce themselves. Ralph Blane (credited with cowriting "The Trolley Song" with Hugh Martin—though he didn't) also wrote some additional lyrics. Mercer hated the interpolated sections.

Rhythmic numbers that just won't let go are great, and although "OTATATSF" is undeniably a masterpiece, we believe that "It's a Great Big World" is just as good a song although it doesn't get the benefit of a huge production number to help it shine. It's not the kind of number that would ever be a showstopper—but the next time you're watching the movie on DVD, take a second to replay "It's a Great Big World" and listen to the way the music is perfectly wedded to the lyric. The overall sentiment of the song is both delicate and melancholy, and helps make *The Harvey Girls* the memorable musical it is. ∎

TOP LEFT: Angela Lansbury keeps the men occupied.

TOP RIGHT: Producer Roger Edens (seated), director George Sidney, and Judy Garland by the Atchison, Topeka, and the Santa Fe.

BOTTOM LEFT: Marjorie Main looks suitably tough as Chill Wills looks on.

BOTTOM RIGHT: Rubber-legged Ray Bolger.

SONGS

"In the Valley when the Sun Goes Down" ∎ "It's a Great Big World" ∎ "Oh, You Kid" ∎ "On the Atchison, Topeka and the Santa Fe" ∎ "Swing Your Partner Round and Round" ∎ "The Train Must Be Fed" (Roger Edens) ∎ "Wait and See" ∎ "The Wild, Wild West"

RIGHT: Fred Astaire and Ginger Rogers join Arthur Freed on the set of *The Barkleys of Broadway*.

BELOW: Producer Arthur Freed with Judy Garland.

BOTTOM RIGHT: Ray Bolger in the Rodgers and Hart Broadway musical, *By Jupiter*.

Arthur Freed

A few short paragraphs can't do justice to the astounding career of Arthur Freed. Along with his writing partner, composer Nacio Herb Brown, Freed supplied songs to a host of MGM musicals, including the studio's first sound musical, *Broadway Melody*. The team's greatest hit, "Singin' in the Rain," was a mainstay of the MGM catalog, appearing in several films but most impressively as the title song of *Singin' in the Rain*, a film whose score is drawn almost exclusively from the Brown and Freed songbook. Other Brown and Freed songs that achieved popularity beyond their respective musical were "You Were Meant for Me," "All I Do Is Dream of You," "You Are My Lucky Star," "Broadway Rhythm," and "Alone." After serving as an associate producer on *The Wizard of Oz*, which he brought to MGM from Samuel Goldwyn, Freed nabbed his first producing credit on *Babes in Arms*—and, as would become his pattern, proceeded to add some of his and Brown's songs to the proceedings after eliminating most of the Broadway score, in this case by Rodgers and Hart. But ego has its uses. Thanks to Freed, MGM would go on to produce the greatest series of screen musicals in motion picture history. An inordinate number of films in this book were produced by Freed, who was also responsible for assembling the greatest company within the MGM factory. Largely due to the entreaties of his lyricist brother Ralph Freed, he brought Vincente Minnelli, Comden and Green, Irene Sharaff, Charles Walters, Stanley Donen, Gene Kelly, Kay Thompson, Robert Alton, Johnny Green, Conrad Salinger, and many others into what became known as "the Freed Unit." He was a tough guy but not a despot, and that probably accounted for the loyalty of his collaborators. (This was not without trying their patience, however. Alan Jay Lerner commented that Arthur Freed started a sentence on Wednesday and finished it on Friday.) Freed became a mentor to hire Roger Edens after the latter left Paramount at the end of Ethel Merman's contract with that studio. Freed was smart enough to hire Roger Edens after the latter became the master—of style and taste, anyway; surprisingly, Freed was more than a little intimidated by Edens. Freed always remained his fellow artists' best friend, though, going to bat for his movies and representing them energetically to the bosses upstairs.

Alan Jay Lerner on Arthur Freed: Arthur was a strange and touching man, filled with contradictions, idiosyncrasies, and surprises. By any standard, he was an original. He was a hero worshipper of talent and if you were one of the fortunate ones whom he respected, his loyalty knew no bounds. He also had the ability to bring out the best in you when you were working; but you had to mete out your ideas with discretion so as not to overwhelm him and at times make him feel your ideas were his.

Hugh Martin on Arthur Freed: I actually felt sorry for him. I wanted to be his friend. He was very blocked; Roger Edens had the Southern charm—and the friends; he was popular and socially graceful—all the things Arthur was not. I tried to bond with Arthur, but after a particularly bad tongue-lashing, I just couldn't be comfortable with him again. I worked hard to pair him with Vincente [Minnelli]—also Stanley Donen. When the two teams became so successful I waited in vain for a pat on the head. It never came. I introduced him to Stanley when he was a chorus boy in *Best Foot Forward*. Arthur brushed him off cruelly. Later on, several awards later, I laughed but I laughed alone.

"If the barber wants to shave Freed, he has to lather Mayer's ass." —*Screenwriter Irving Brecher*

Ray Bolger

Eccentric dancer turned Broadway and Hollywood star, Ray Bolger achieved fame on Broadway and in film. After appearing in a few MGM pictures, sometimes as himself, he gained immortality—along with the rest of the cast—as the Scarecrow in the 1939 film, *The Wizard of Oz*. Bolger had had a burgeoning stage career prior to *The Wizard of Oz*, starring in the revue *Life Begins at 8:40* in 1934 along with future king of the forest Bert Lahr. He also danced the "Slaughter on Tenth Avenue" ballet as the lead in Rodgers and Hart's *On Your Toes*. He went on to star in two more Broadway hits: *By Jupiter* by Rodgers and Hart and Frank Loesser's Broadway debut, *Where's Charley?* from which he got his theme song, "Once in Love with Amy." After *Oz*, MGM didn't quite know what to do with Bolger. He wasn't leading man material and eccentric dancing wasn't exactly in demand (take a look at Buddy Ebsen's career, for example). He appeared in only seven more films through 1952, at which point he turned to television. *April in Paris*, *Where's Charley?* (repeating his Broadway success), and *The Harvey Girls* (by far the best of the bunch) were the highlights. Bolger returned to Broadway occasionally but without making much of an impact, and made a few more films—including a version of *Babes in Toyland* for Disney, the studio where aging stars (Ed Wynn, Fred MacMurray, Walter Pidgeon, etc.) revived their careers during their golden years.

Behind the Screen

- There is one other star in *The Harvey Girls*. The horse that Preston Foster rides in the film, "King Charles," also played the title role in *National Velvet*.

- Inspired by *Oklahoma!* Roger Edens wanted the *Harvey Girls* score to be similarly integrated into the action.

HEDWIG AND THE ANGRY INCH

COMPOSER: Stephen Trask

LYRICIST: Stephen Trask

PRODUCER: Pamela Koffler, Katie Roume., and Christine Vachon

DIRECTOR: John Cameron Mitchell

SCREENWRITER: John Cameron Mitchell

SOURCE: Based on the musical *Hedwig and the Ugly Inch* by John Cameron Mitchell and Stephen Trask

CHOREOGRAPHER: Jerry Mitchell

Synopsis

A shocking screed against public-option health care, *Hedwig* tells the story of an East German transsexual whose operation is one (angry) inch shy of success.

Cast

John Cameron Mitchell...Hedwig
Miriam Shor...............Yitzak
Andrea Martin.............Phyllis Stein
Stephen Trask ....Skszp
Theodore Liscinski........Jacek
Rob Campbell..............Krzysztof
Michael Aronov ....Schlatko

Behind the Screen

■ John Cameron Mitchell sang his songs live to a taped music track . . . just as Rex Harrison did on *My Fair Lady*.

Poor butterfly, John Cameron Mitchell as Hedwig.

TODAY'S MOVIE MUSICALS EXCEL IN ENERGY, THOUGH IT'S NOT ALWAYS FOCUSED ENERGY. Take *Chicago* or *Nine*, for example. They feature lots of strutting, posing, and hyperactive editing, but the considerable energy put forth is too diffuse to have much of an impact. The noise, quick cutting, and general mayhem are forced to compensate for the lack of directed energy coming from the cast.

In *Hedwig*, on the other hand, John Cameron Mitchell (starring in the piece he wrote and directed) shoots his energy out to the audience like a laser beam. Perhaps, because he comes from the theater—he was the only good thing in *The Secret Garden*—he knows how to aim it and hit the target.

Hedwig provides plenty of flash and glitter but also a surprisingly intelligent story, considering the basic shock value of its premise: a confessional concert delivered by an aging semitranssexual with a colorful past and a few axes to grind. The young folk can revel in the rock score and tawdriness while taking in its basically tender message of tolerance and self-love. Old fogies who can get past their inherent aversion to rock musicals (and the subject matter) can appreciate the craft and wit of the story and lyrics.

As an independently produced musical film, safe from the influence, "good ideas," and insistence on pleasing the lowest common denominator that hamper big studio productions, *Hedwig* could remain true to its source—a small, personal stage musical performed by its creator and a few close collaborators. The result is an intimate, personal movie. It a way, the film, like Hedwig herself, hides the morality of its story behind a spandex veneer.

Stephen Trask and John Cameron Mitchell in the original New York stage production of *Hedwig*.

Hedwig's success, both financial and artistic, should have opened the door to more independent musicals—but the musical is a difficult art form. With their high production costs and the public's basic indifference to musicals without huge stars, independent film musicals remain an oddity. The next major minor musical to come out of the independent tradition was 2006's *Once* . . . , the story of immigrant musicians trying to make their way in Dublin. The film is the opposite of *Hedwig* in tone but it shares themes of alienation, self-expression against all odds, and the importance of connecting with other humans. If *Once* . . . were an American movie, it certainly would have been included in this book. ■

SONGS

"The Angry Inch" ■ "Exquisite Corpse" ■ "Freaks" ■ "Hedwig's Lament" ■ "I Will Always Love You" ■ "In Your Arms Tonight" ■ "The Long Grift" ■ "Midnight Radio" ■ "The Origin of Love" ■ "Random Number Generation" ■ "Sugar Daddy" ■ "Tear Me Down" ■ "Wicked Little Town" ■ "Wig in a Box"

TOP LEFT: John Cameron Mitchell gets ready for his closeup.

TOP RIGHT: Drag queen and drag king.

BOTTOM LEFT: Hedwig in an early dinner-theatre appearance.

BOTTOM RIGHT: Michael Pitt and John Cameron Mitchell.

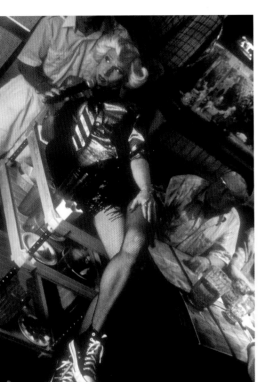

HIGH SCHOOL MUSICAL 3

WALT DISNEY—OCTOBER 24, 2008

Zac Efron and Vanessa Anne Hudgens spend their high school years singing and falling in love.

HIGH SCHOOL MUSICAL 3

COMPOSERS: Matthew Gerrard and Robbie Nevil

LYRICISTS: Matthew Gerrard and Robbie Nevil

PRODUCERS: Bill Bordon and Barry Rosenbush

DIRECTOR: Kenny Ortega

SCREENWRITER: Peter Barsocchini

CHOREOGRAPHER: Kenny Ortega

Synopsis

Troy, Gabriella, Sharpay, Ryan, and Chad are about to graduate and are worried about how they'll continue their careers after the franchise ends.

Cast

Zac Efron ....*Troy Bolton*
Vanessa Hudgens........*Gabriella Montez*
Ashley Tisdale............*Sharpay Evans*
Lucas Grabeel.............*Ryan Evans*
Corbin Bleu.................*Chad Danfort*
Monique Coleman........*Taylor McKessie*
Alyson Reed................*Ms. Darbus*
Bart Johnson..............*Coach Jack Bolton*

CTUALLY, WE WANTED TO INCLUDE *HIGH SCHOOL MUSICAL*, THE ORIGINAL, IN THIS book, but it was made for television and that was against our (admittedly arbitrary) rules. Luckily for us, *High School Musical 3: Senior Year* was released in cinemas.

Yes, it is bland, depthless, and ever so white. And while the pop songs didn't really rock anyone, the movie itself rocked tweens and teens like no other film since *A Hard Day's Night*. The *HSM* trilogy made stars of its leads (and we'll admit they are extremely talented, albeit in roles that don't call for a lot of acting). The choreography is traditional but inventive and the production values are top-notch if a bit plastic in the cinematography department. This is a movie that looks as if it has been airbrushed to make it as easy on the eyes as possible. We don't mean that it was shot through Doris Day lenses—just that the film's look (like its script) was shorn of all nuance.

We may sound a little critical but actually we don't mean to be. We celebrate all three *HSM* movies for their message of tolerance, friendship, and other positive values. Corny, yes, but worth drumming into kids' heads now and then. There is no irony, no subtext, no surprises, no confusion as to what is being said or sung. The action takes place in a fantasy world just as the films of Fred and Ginger or MacDonald and Eddy did, where poverty and gloom don't exist and everything always turns out ducky and beautiful in the end. Heck, the High School Musical films make Mickey and Judy look like Sid and Nancy.

And speaking of Mickey and Judy, kids today still want to put on a show—but they don't have to find a barn to do it in. They need not look any farther than their own high schools. It seems that high schools are the epicenter of musical expression in the United States these days, and that includes shows, marching bands, drum corps, color guard,

cheerleading, winter guard, drum line, and choir—not to mention glee clubs. You know where we're going now, right? That blazing hot TV musical series *Glee* is nothing if not a direct descendent of *HSM* 1, 2, and 3.

Those *Glee* kids may have more issues than the *HSM* kids do, but they're all trying to find themselves and express themselves through music, and that can't be a bad thing. After all, we Tin Pan Alley acolytes were raised to believe that there's a song to make every situation better and elevate every mood. So, too, do the kids of *HSM* and *Glee*. The only difference is that while we might turn to Judy Garland, they're in the thrall of Lady Gaga. Oh well, time marches on, we guess. ∎

ABOVE: Vanessa Anne Hudgens, Zac Efron, Ashley Tisdale, and Jason Williams strut their stuff on the school stage.

RIGHT: Ashley Tisdale and Lucas Grabeel start out the series insufferable but—surprise—they're swell by graduation day.

BELOW LEFT: Corbin Bleu and Monique Coleman may look a little old for high school, but so does the rest of the cast.

Behind the Screen

- Zac Efron is the dreamiest.
- Vanessa Hudgens is hot, hot, hot.
- Corbin Bleu is so delicious you just want to eat him up.

SONGS

"The Boys Are Back" (Matthew Gerrard and Robbie Nevil) ∎ "Can I Have This Dance?" (Adam Anders and Nikki Hassman) ∎ "Freaky" (Theodore Thomas, Theron Makiel Thomas, and Timothy Jamahli Thomas) ∎ "High School Musical" ∎ "I Want It All" (Matthew Gerrard and Robbie Nevil) ∎ "Just Getting Started" (Jaime Huston) ∎ "Just Wanna Be with You" (Andy Dodd and Adam Watts) ∎ "Last Chance" (Randy Petersen and Kevin Quinn) ∎ "Like Whoa" (Antonina Armato, Tim James, Amanda Joy Michalka, and Alyson Michalka) ∎ "My Shoes" (Arnthor Birgisson and Savan Kotecha) ∎ "A Night to Remember" (Matthew Gerrard and Robbie Nevil) ∎ "Now or Never" (Matthew Gerrard and Robbie Nevil) ∎ "Right Here, Right Now" (Jaime Huston) ∎ "Scream" (Jaime Huston) ∎ "Snareway to Heaven" (Bart Hendrickson and Stix Randolph) ∎ "Walk Away" (Jamie Huston) ∎ "We're All in This Together"

HOLLYWOOD HOTEL

COMPOSER: Richard A. Whiting
LYRICIST: Johnny Mercer
PRODUCER: Hal B. Wallis
DIRECTOR: Busby Berkeley
SCREENWRITERS: Jerry Wald,
Maurice Leo, and Richard Macaulay
CHOREOGRAPHER: Busby Berkeley

Synopsis

Hooray for Hollywood! Dick tries to make it big in film, doesn't gain any traction, but still ends up a star and gets the girl.

Cast

Dick Powell	Ronnie Bowers
Lola Lane	Mona Marshall
Rosemary Lane	Virginia
Hugh Herbert	Chester Marshall
Ted Healy	Fuzzy
Glenda Farrell	Jonesy
Johnnie "Scat" Davis	Georgia
Alan Mowbray	Alexander Dupre
Mabel Todd	Dot Marshall
Allyn Joslyn	Bernie Walton
Frances Langford	Alice
Louella Parsons	Herself

Behind the Screen

- Ronald Reagan made his second screen appearance (uncredited) as an interviewer outside Grauman's Chinese Theatre.

HOLLYWOOD HOTEL

WARNER BROTHERS—JANUARY 15, 1938

ABOVE: The delightfully demure Mabel Todd.
RIGHT: Dick Powell and Ted Healy.

Neatness, gentility, perfection—all have their place in movie musicals. And that place is Metro-Goldwyn-Mayer. If you want to feel that spirit of show business rough and tumble, then Paramount and Warner Brothers are the studios for you. Do their films top the all-time best lists? Not so much. Pound for pound of pure enjoyment, silliness, and joie de vivre, Warner's musicals are the top.

Warner Brothers was a top-drawer studio but its style was rough. Think of James Cagney, usually cast as a gangster, appearing in *Footlight Parade* and *Yankee Doodle Dandy*. Dick Powell, the mainstay of Warner's, was more of a classic male ingenue, but he had backbone—no Kenny Bowers was he. And the women he was paired with had some nerve, too (though Ruby Keeler was a bit of a drip).

For *Hollywood Hotel*, Busby Berkeley provided a great opening, complete with Benny Goodman and His Orchestra riding jeeps while Johnny "Scat" Davis and Frances Langford sang Johnny Mercer's irreverent "Hooray for Hollywood." Berkeley also created an utterly silly and delightful little dance in a fountain to the tune of "I'm Like a Fish Out of Water." There was no spectacle here, just good, simple, inventive ideas.

The reason there wasn't any spectacle in the film was that Warner's musicals in the late 1930s were no longer making the kind of money the studio had at the beginning of the decade, when it ruled Hollywood. The film that jump-started musicals after the public had grown weary, *42nd Street*, earned almost 2 million dollars at the box office. Dick Powell's first decade in film was spent at Warner and the story of his films exemplifies Warner's output in the '30s. From 1933 to 1935, Powell's musicals averaged around a half a million dollars profit each—and that's Depression dollars, very good returns indeed.

But cracks in Powell's drawing power, and that of Warner's musicals in general, began to appear in 1936, when *Stage Struck* only made $200,000 profit at the box office (the film cost $500,000). Powell's next film, the 1937 edition of the popular *Gold Diggers* series, made a respectable profit of $235,000, but nowhere near the million dollars earned by the first edition in 1933 or even the $400,000 earned by the 1935 follow-up.

After 1937's *The Singing Marine* made a $300,000 profit, none of Dick Powell's musicals made money. *Hollywood Hotel*, the best of Warner's musicals of the thirties (thus, its inclusion here), lost $200,000. With a year to go on his contract, Powell made four more films, including *The Cowboy from Brooklyn* and the wonderful *Going Places*—but they all ended up in the red. As for Powell, his musical film career may have petered out by the end of the decade but those thirty-one features earned the studio a total profit of just short of 8 million dollars.

When Powell moved on to Paramount, Warner pretty much shut down its musical-comedy machine. Berkeley left the same year and Powell later created a whole new film persona for himself as a hard-nosed dick in film noir classics. Harry Warren, the most important composer in Warner Brothers' history, had decamped to Twentieth Century-Fox, and his lyric partner, Al Dubin, would be dead in 1945. In 1939, MGM ascended to become the preeminent musical film studio with the release of *The Wizard of Oz*. And with the war in Europe beginning and the Depression ending, Warner's movie musical style went out of fashion.

But it had been a glorious decadelong run and *Hollywood Hotel*, with its snappy script, spot-on acting, and joyful tone, was the culmination of Warner's decade of dominance in musical movies. ∎

SONGS

"Hooray for Hollywood" ■ "I'm Like a Fish Out of Water" ■ "I've Hitched My Wagon to a Star" ■ "Let That Be a Lesson to You" ■ "Silhouetted in the Moonlight" ■ "Sing You Son-of-a-Gun"

TOP RIGHT: Dick Powell and Rosemary Lane wait for a shot.
RIGHT: Johnny Mercer (left) and Richard Whiting (right).

Richard Whiting

Sad. Very sad. Richard Whiting was a hit pop composer and sometime lyricist in the late teens and early twenties, the author of such typical Tin Pan Alley songs as "It's Tulip Time in Holland" and "Where the Black-Eyed Susans Grow." He also penned some big sellers that have become standards, including "Breezin' Along with the Breeze" and "Ain't We Got Fun." He chalked up some mildly successful Broadway shows, but his lasting fame didn't come until he joined the westward migration when sound pictures came in. In 1929, he went to Hollywood with lyricist Leo Robin and set up shop at Paramount Pictures. Some of his film music was exquisite—*Innocents of Paris* ("Louise"), *Monte Carlo* ("Beyond the Blue Horizon"), *One Hour with You* (title song)—and some less so, but even the lesser scores contained hit songs. When musical movies were briefly out of fashion, Whiting, like many of his contemporaries, returned to Broadway. But with the success of the film *42nd Street*, the studios were ready to jump on the musical bandwagon all over again. Whiting and Ted Koehler contributed "On the Good Ship Lollipop" to Shirley Temple's film *Bright Eyes* and Whiting stayed at Fox until 1935, when he decamped to Warner Brothers, then the leading producer of musical films. After turning out a hit with Walter Bullock, *Sing, Baby, Sing* ("When Did You Leave Heaven?"), he teamed with Johnny Mercer for a string of successful songs including "Too Marvelous for Words" for *Ready, Willing and Able*, "Have You Got Any Castles" and "We're Working Our Way through College" for *Varsity Show*, "Hooray for Hollywood" for *Hollywood Hotel*, and others. Here's the sad, very sad part. Whiting died of a heart attack in 1938, at age forty-seven. He did leave behind his daughter, Margaret, who became a great pop star and a person who really is too marvelous for words. The same might be said of the art of Richard Whiting.

THE JAZZ SINGER

DIRECTOR: Alan Crosland

SCREENWRITER: Alfred A. Cohn

SOURCE: Based on the play
The Jazz Singer by Samson Raphaelson

Synopsis

Little Jakie wants to sing jazz but his father wants him to continue in the family tradition and be a cantor at the local synagogue. Jake's in a quandary: Should he appear on Broadway as Jack Robin or conduct the High Holy Days service? But wait, there's another option. He could do both—and revolutionize the movies.

Cast

Al Jolson	Jakie Rabinowitz
May McAvoy	Mary Dale
Warner Oland	Cantor Rabinowitz
Eugenie Besserer	Sara Rabinowitz
Otto Lederer	Moisha Yudelson
Bobby Gordon	Jakie Rabinowitz
	(age 13)
Richard Tucker	Harry Lee
Cantor	Joseff Rosenblatt

THE JAZZ SINGER

WARNER BROTHERS—OCTOBER 6, 1927

Everything's Jake.
Eugenie Besserer as
Sara Rabinowitz and Al
Jolson as her son Jake.

WHEN AL JOLSON AD-LIBBED HIS "YOU AIN'T HEARD NOTHIN' YET!" SPEECH during the filming of *The Jazz Singer*, he made movie history. The powers that be had wanted to cut the dialogue, but Sam Warner insisted it remain in the film, thus assuring its spot in film textbooks.

The legend of the early years of sound movies, propagated by the film *Singin' in the Rain*, might lead you to suppose that sound on film quickly exploded as the 1920s moved into the '30s. In fact, it took a series of small steps for sound on film to reach wide acceptance.

For one thing, there were lots of technical problems to overcome. Competing scientists tried recording sound on cylinders, on discs, and on the film itself. Placement of microphones, sound fidelity, easy and cost effective reproduction, and the need for loudspeakers powerful enough to broadcast sound throughout a large auditorium all had to be dealt with before sound movies could gain a foothold.

There had been experiments before. Fox had collaborated with Lee DeForest on a series of short subjects featuring sound recorded on film. Warner Brothers had better luck when it teamed with Western Electric on the Vitaphone system. The sound was recorded on 33⅓ records and synchronized to the film, with a single machine operating both the player and projector. Beginning in 1926, Warner Brothers used this system to present experimental shorts featuring stars of the vaudeville and musical comedy stage recorded in their New York studios.

For these Vitaphone shorts, a single, stationary camera was used, capturing the performances as if the artists were on the stage of the motion picture theater. They simply performed their acts, speaking to the film audience just as they did to live audiences, even bowing to presumed applause at the end. To accommodate a few cuts and camera angle changes, the performances were usually recorded by three cameras simultaneously. At the time, even the phonograph recordings weren't edited: if a singer or band made a mistake, the director simply scratched the take and they started the performance over from the beginning.

Between 1926 and 1930, Vitaphone produced over one thousand shorts, leaving us a unique view into the world of vaudeville. Exhibitors loved programming the shorts, as it meant they could bring stars such as Al Jolson, Eddie Cantor, Burns and Allen, Ruth Etting, and Willie and Eugene Howard into their theaters

"Wait a minute, wait a minute, you ain't heard nothin' yet! Wait a minute, I tell ya! You ain't heard nothin'!" —*Jack Robin to the audience at the Winter Garden Theater*

for four, five, six, or more shows a day. And audiences thrilled to see performers that they had heard only on recordings.

Western Electric rented the Vitaphone equipment to theaters on a five-year lease, at a cost of $12,000 per venue. Soon, other sound on disc competitors turned up, including Mellaphone, Bristolphone, and Cineophone, but they never achieved anywhere near the success of Vitaphone.

In 1926, twelve theaters were wired for Vitaphone. The next year, that number rose to 157 and, by 1928, more than four thousand cinemas boasted Vitaphone sound-on-disc presentations. By

1930, when Vitaphone stopped making the discs, almost fourteen thousand theaters featured the Vitaphone setup in their projection booths.

Unfortunately, the records sometimes cracked and the film sometimes broke, making the playback awkward at best. Fox's Movietone sound-on-film process worked better and studios other than Warner Brothers tended to use it instead, though they issued their films in both formats so theaters could have their choice.

In 1930, even Warner Brothers switched over to sound-on-film, for by then the audio quality of optical sound had caught up with the fidelity of the discs. But many theaters resisted scrapping the equipment they'd leased, and until 1936, Vitaphone discs were

made available to them. (As late as 1930, some cinemas in the South and Midwest still weren't wired for any sound format at all!)

Fast-forward to 1991, when a group of concerned collectors and film buffs formed the Vitaphone Project to track down as many of the films and discs as possible and preserve them for future generations. In conjunction with Turner/Warner Brothers, several important film archives and major private collectors have discovered and preserved more than 3,500 discs, many of which are one-of-a-kind. Having raised half a million dollars for the purpose, the group has restored some one hundred shorts and twelve features for posterity. ∎

The lady or the tallis? Richard Tucker, May McAvoy (in the far left corner, representing Broadway), Otto Lederer, and Eugenie Besserer (in the far right corner, representing religious tradition). In the middle of the ring, Al Jolson.

Al Jolson

The World's Greatest Entertainer. That's what they called Al Jolson—among other less flattering things concerning his personality. Everyone, but everyone, who saw Jolson on Broadway agreed that he was the greatest. It was only natural that he'd turn to the movies, and after committing his *Plantation Act* to sound film, courtesy of Vitaphone, he was hired for *The Jazz Singer*, in a part that had been turned down by George Jessel. If a lesser talent (Jessel, for example) had starred in the film, sound movies wouldn't have gotten the immediate jolt that Jolson gave the new invention. He went on to a series

of highly successful films for Warner Brothers before audiences' tastes changed and Jolson turned to radio. But the movies catapulted him to fame once again with the premiere of Columbia Pictures' biopic *The Jolson Story* in 1946 and its sequel, *Jolson Sings Again*, in 1949. His role was played by Larry Parks, but Jolson recorded new vocals for both pictures. His star rose and he was again called one of the greatest performers of all time (though still not such a nice guy).

ABOVE: Al Jolson in full blackface singing "Mammy."

RIGHT: Spoiler alert!! Don't look at this picture if you don't want to know how the film ends.

BELOW: One of the most important photos in the history of cinema. The world premiere of *The Jazz Singer*. Hollywood, the movies, and entertainment would never be the same after this night.

ABOVE: Yul Brynner, Deborah Kerr, Martin Benson, Rita Moreno, and some testy guards after the ball is over.

OPPOSITE LEFT: Yul Brynner and Deborah share a few choice words.

OPPOSITE RIGHT: Brynner is a puzzlement—did he use an Abmaster?

THE KING AND I

20TH CENTURY FOX—JUNE 29, 1956

THE KING AND I

COMPOSER: Richard Rodgers
LYRICIST: Oscar Hammerstein II
PRODUCER: Charles Brackett
DIRECTOR: Walter Lang
SCREENWRITER: Ernest Lehman
SOURCE: Based on the stage musical *The King and I* by Richard Rodgers and Oscar Hammerstein II
CHOREOGRAPHER: Jerome Robbins

Synopsis

Long before "No Child Left Behind," Englishwoman Anna travels to Siam to teach its king's children geography, manners, and how to whistle.

Cast

Deborah Kerr................Anna Leonowens
Yul Brynner.................King Mongkut
Rita Moreno.................Tuptim
Martin Benson...............Kralahome
Terry Saunders..............Lady Thiang
Rex Thompson................Louis Leonowens
Carlos Rivas................Lun Tha
Patrick Adiarte.............Prince Chulalongkorn
Alan Mowbray................Sir John Hay
Geoffrey Toone..............Sir Edward Ramsay

WE THINK *THE KING AND I* IS THE SECOND GREATEST OF THE RODGERS AND HAMmerstein adaptations (*The Sound of Music* is the first, of course). The film's production design is exceptionally beautiful, Alfred Newman's rich underscoring is magnificent, and the performances are all excellent, especially those of stars Yul Brynner and Deborah Karr.

So what if the star of the musical can't sing? He or she can always be dubbed. Some are shocked at this notion, most don't even know it is happening, and many couldn't care less. When it came time to mount *The King and I* for the screen, Marni Nixon, the queen of the ghost singers, got a frantic phone call from Fox's Ken Darby, asking if she'd drop everything and audition for the voice of the "I," Deborah Kerr, in *The King and I.*

Don't underestimate her talents. The job of a dubber, especially in a dramatic musical, isn't an easy one. In the early years, musical films were more like revues than dramatic musicals; the songs were more self-contained, often sung as part of a show within the movie. Dubbers simply sang the song in their own voice while the stars on the sound-stage moved their lips. When you see an early film musical like the *Hollywood Revue of 1929*, where Charles King dubbed Conrad Nagel, it's pretty clear that Nagel isn't actually singing. His throat muscles don't contract, he doesn't breathe as he would if actually singing. The part-silent *Show Boat* made in 1929 (Universal was late in getting into the sound game), used Eva Olivetti to dub Laura LaPlante while LaPlante pretended to play the banjo.

By the 1950s, dubbing was more of an art and could get quite involved. The most convoluted example is *Singin' in the Rain*. In the film, as you must know, Debbie Reynolds's character, Kathy Selden, is talked into dubbing for Jean Hagen's character, Lina Lamont.

The irony is that when Kathy is dubbing the song "Would You?" for Lina, in real life it's Betty Noyes singing the song for Reynolds—who is pretending to sing for Hagen. But wait, there's more. When Reynolds is supposed to be dubbing Hagen's speaking voice, it's actually Jean Hagen herself dubbing Reynolds dubbing Hagen!

Sometimes even a good singer such as Reynolds is dubbed for one reason or another. In *South Pacific*, Juanita Hall reprised Bloody Mary, the part she played on Broadway—but she was dubbed by Muriel Smith. In fact, except for the ever-too-vivacious Mitzi Gaynor, all the leads were dubbed. Giorgio Tozzi dubbed Rossano Brazzi as Emile DeBecque, much to Brazzi's dismay. (Brazzi did his own singing on "Loneliness of Evening," but the song didn't appear in the final cut.); John Kerr's Lt. Cable was dubbed by Bill Lee, Ken Clark's Stewpot was dubbed by Thurl Ravenscroft (the voice of Tony the Tiger!), and Ray Walston was dubbed by Rad Robinson.

For *The King and I*, Marni Nixon had a hard job. Not only did she have to sing well, which can be hard enough, but she had to match Deborah Kerr's voice characteristics and sense of timing. The songs required a fair amount of acting on Nixon's part as well. Luckily for her, Kerr had made an acetate demo that Nixon could refer to in preparation for her audition.

Nixon made some acetate demos of her own, which were sent east for Richard Rodgers's approval. (Although he wouldn't have the control that he and Hammerstein had had on *Oklahoma!* or *Carousel*, he did have approval on how his songs would sound in the final picture.) Once Nixon was approved, the hard work began.

It's difficult to act a song in the style of someone you haven't met, so Nixon and Kerr spent hours together, Nixon listening intently to Kerr's manner of speaking and breathing, and her inflections. The two went over and over the songs together. Remember, it wasn't just Nixon who had to capture Kerr; Kerr had the difficult job of matching Nixon when lip-synching the songs on film, even emulating Nixon's posture, stance, and breathing to make it look like she herself was singing the songs.

The recording studio actually had furniture in the places it would be used on the soundstage. If Kerr was to move around or sit down or stand up, her voice would change. Kerr ran through her blocking followed by Nixon. The singer learned Kerr's movements and handling of props. Walter Lang came by to direct both the singer and the actress.

While recording the songs with the orchestra, both Nixon and Kerr occupied the same booth. On some of the songs, Kerr had to insert dialogue or light rhythmic singing in her own voice. When Kerr was finished with these passages, Nixon took over, lowering her voice to sound as much as possible like Kerr. When filming began, it was Kerr's turn to act like Nixon.

The results were so seamless that no one suspected that Kerr was dubbed. Even when watching the film today, it's hard to find any mistakes. The fact that Nixon dubbed for Kerr was kept secret for decades from all but industry insiders. The two actresses got along together so well. Nixon dubbed Kerr again for *An Affair to Remember*. ■

"I'm sorry, I'm just not good enough."

—Deborah Kerr, after hearing a recording of her own singing

Marni Nixon

One journalist called her "the Voice of Hollywood"—get it? For most of her long career, Marni Nixon's work was secret, but when she dubbed the role of Eliza Doolittle for Audrey Hepburn in *My Fair Lady*, word got out. When VHS tapes hit the market and reissues of film soundtracks were released, Nixon was credited for many of her past roles. Although she's best known for dubbing Hepburn, as well as Deborah Kerr in *The King and I*, she also sang for Natalie Wood in *West Side Story*. In that film, Nixon also augmented Rita Moreno's singing voice along with fellow dubber Betty Wand. She even helped Marilyn Monroe reach her high notes in *Gentlemen Prefer Blondes's* "Diamonds Are a Girl's Best Friend." She finally played an on-screen role as one of the nuns in *The Sound of Music*. With the twilight of movie musicals, Nixon toured the country in a variety of live musicals, even playing Eliza Doolittle in *My Fair Lady*. We hear she sang divinely.

> "Quite satisfactory."
> —Rodgers's response to Hammerstein after receiving the lyric to "Hello, Young Lovers"

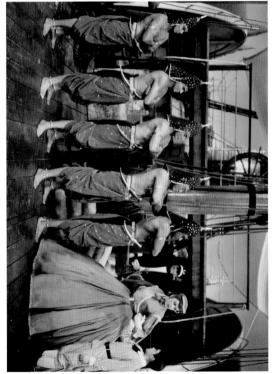

LEFT: Rita Moreno, as Tuptim, envisions her fate.

ABOVE RIGHT: The ladies of the court kneel before the King as best they can in their brand-new British hoop skirts.

BELOW RIGHT: Deborah Kerr and Rex Thompson, who plays her son, contemplate whistling a happy tune to allay their fear of the welcoming committee.

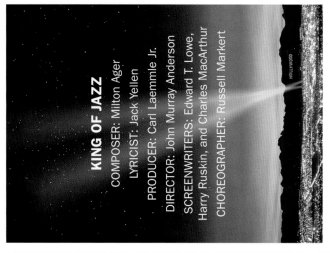

KING OF JAZZ

COMPOSER: Milton Ager
LYRICIST: Jack Yellen
PRODUCER: Carl Laemmle Jr.
DIRECTOR: John Murray Anderson
SCREENWRITERS: Edward T. Lowe,
Harry Ruskin, and Charles MacArthur
CHOREOGRAPHER: Russell Markert

Synopsis

A delirious mishmash of cartoons, jazzy music, and sketches from Paul Whiteman's scrapbook.

Cast

Paul Whiteman and His Band
John Boles
Laura La Plante
Glenn Tryon
Jeanette Loff
Merna Kennedy
Slim Summerville
Otis Harlan
William Kent
Bing Crosby
Harry Barris
Al Rinker
The Brox Sisters (Bobbe, Lorayne, and Patricia)

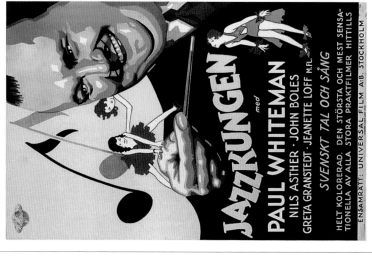

KING OF JAZZ

UNIVERSAL—APRIL 20, 1930

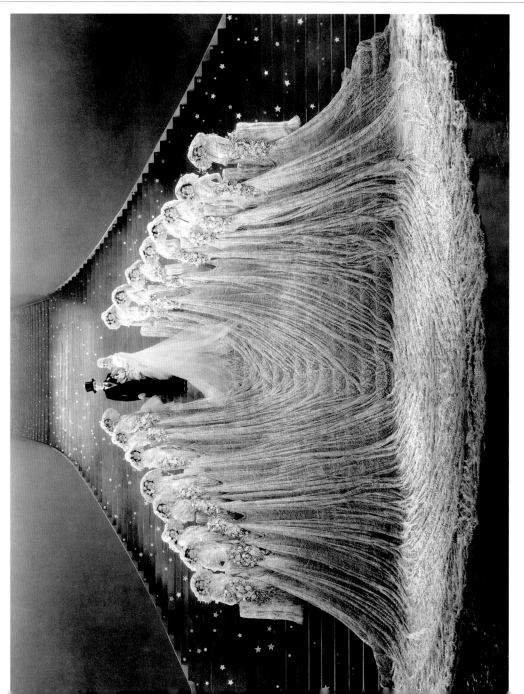

Stanley Smith with Jeanette Loff and the Russell Markert Dancers in "The Bridal Veil" number. Isn't it embarrassing when you show up at a wedding in the same dress as everyone else?

O NCE MOVIES SPOKE, IT MADE SENSE FOR THEM TO SING AND DANCE—BUT NOBODY knew exactly how to put a stage musical on the screen. As far as choreography went, most early "dance directors" simply set the camera in one spot and photographed adaptations of the original stage routines. Stage directors and choreographers were brought to Hollywood along with the Broadway's best songwriters.

These men knew how to make shows theatrical but not how to make them filmic. John Murray Anderson came from the theater and was best known as a "stager" rather than a director, what we might call an artistic supervisor today. He would think up concepts for musical numbers, leaving the teaching of the steps to others. It makes sense that he spent the latter part of his career staging the Ringling Brothers circus. In any event, he knew nothing about directing for the screen, but neither did many of his contemporaries. Where he differed from others was that he had vision and knew his limitations. "I was really at a loss to know where to begin," he wrote, "when I hit upon the idea (not very original perhaps) of interviewing all the best technical experts on the lot. . . . I asked each if he had any pet ideas and effects that he had dreamed up, but had never been given the opportunity of carrying out." Anderson thus settled on the visuals of the film, but the cutting was another thing altogether. "I was now faced with the problem of putting the picture together, for nobody but myself knew precisely what it was all about. Here again I started something new. I taught the cutters to work with a Metronome, and only changed 'angles' at the beginning of a musical phrase. In this way, although an audience was not perhaps conscious of it, the film actually kept cadence with the music."

Such cutting was revolutionary at a time when most dance sequences were shot in full figure, as if the camera were seated in one of the first few rows of a theater. Only two other dance directors of the period tried anything different: Larry Ceballos and Busby Berkeley. Others might have used some tricks of photography, but overall, the choreography was basic and the camera almost never moved.

In the 1950s, faced with the threat of television, producers began to employ elaborate effects such as 3-D and Cinemascope. In the '30s, sound itself was a novelty as was color. Anderson acknowledged that he tried to throw in as many different technical effects as possible, including cartoon sequences, elaborate lighting effects, and Technicolor. The color system had been used in a few silent films but was not widely accepted; in fact, *King of Jazz* was only the nineteenth movie shot completely in Technicolor.

If you watch MGM's *Hollywood Revue of 1929*, where even Laurel and Hardy aren't funny, you'll be reminded that comedy doesn't always do well past its sell date. Anderson may not have realized this at the time but there's blissfully little comedy in *The King of Jazz*. There is also plenty of imagination, thanks to his innovations and the Universal production staff's willingness to rise to the occasion.

In an era of star-studded studio revues such as *Paramount on Parade* and *The Broadway Melody*, Universal was severely deficient in the star category. Only Laura LaPlante was major silent star, John Boles was an excellent if stiff singer in the operetta mold, but not one person in the Universal stable really had a unique personality. So, Anderson had to bring in Paul Whiteman and his orchestra and male singing trio, the Rhythm Boys. And there, amid Al Rinker and Harry Barris, was Bing Crosby. It was his first motion picture and he was not featured, but it soon became clear that Crosby would become the greatest of the singing movie stars.

The King of Jazz is a fun film to watch today, if you allow for the limitations and musical taste of the era in which it was made. It's zippy and playful and doesn't take itself very seriously—all admirable attributes of a good movie musical. Anderson's choice of Paul Whiteman as the linchpin master of ceremonies is a felicitous one. Whiteman is completely relaxed, charmingly self-deprecating, and his energy and enthusiasm keep the party rolling. ▪

SONGS

"A Bench in the Park" (Milton Ager and Jack Yellen) ▪ "Happy Feet" (Milton Ager and Jack Yellen) ▪ "Has Anybody Seen Our Nellie" (Milton Ager and Jack Yellen) ▪ "How I'd Like to Own a Fish Store" (Billy Stone) ▪ "It Happened in Monterey" (Mabel Wayne and Billy Rose) ▪ "Music Hath Charms" (Milton Ager and Jack Yellen and James Cavanaugh) ▪ "Mississippi Mud" (Harry Barris ▪ "My Bridal Veil" (Jack Yellen and John Murray Anderson) ▪ "Oh Happy Bride" (Milton Ager and Jack Yellen) ▪ "Ragamuffin Romeo" (Mabel Wayne and Harry DeCosta) ▪ "So the Bluebirds and the Blackbirds Got Together" (Harry Barris and Billy Moll) ▪ "The Song of the Dawn" (Milton Ager and Jack Yellen)

RIGHT: The Rhythm Boys (Bing Crosby, Harry Barris, and Al Rinker) out on a date with the Brox Sisters.

BELOW: The Russell Markert Dancers atop the grand, really grand piano. The group later morphed into the Roxyettes and finally, the Rockettes.

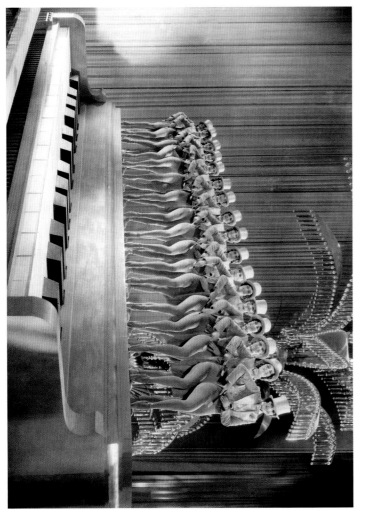

Bing Crosby

We all know about Bing Crosby's nearly sixty years in show business. He remains the most popular recording artist of all time, having sold more records than any other entertainer. Although we may not think of him as a huge movie star, the fact is, he's one of the five top-grossing film stars of all time. His role in the film *White Christmas*, and his mega-selling recording of the title song by Irving Berlin, have vaulted him permanently to the top of any "best pop artist" polls, too. Crosby's relaxed charm and superb musicianship helped make him a superstar. When we think of Crosby's movies, the Road pictures, *Going My Way*, and *White Christmas* are what come to mind. And he made many other films, including the dramatic *The Country Girl* with Grace Kelly and a Harold Arlen score, the Cole Porter *High Society* also with Kelly, and lots and lots of Paramount musicals that are memorable mainly for their plethora of popular songs, mostly by Johnny Burke and Jimmy Van Heusen. Crosby's calm, bemused demeanor hid an ambitious actor and a smart business sense. He teamed indelibly with Bob Hope, in movies, on radio and television, and in personal appearances—though in reality they weren't very friendly. There's a camp that considers Crosby the best singer of the Great American Songbook, at least until Sinatra came along. As Crosby himself said, "Sinatra's voice is the kind that comes along once in a generation. Why did it have to be mine?" Still, his devotees believe him the champion of all time and it's hard to argue against them.

Behind the Screen

▪ The failure of this film brought a temporary halt to movie musical production by the studios. It wasn't until the great success of *42nd Street*, which saved Warner Brothers from bankruptcy, that the genre was again in vogue.

▪ The film included the first Technicolor cartoon (by Walter Lantz, later of Woody Woodpecker fame, not by Walt Disney). And it was the first film to have its songs entirely prerecorded.

KISS ME KATE

COMPOSER: Cole Porter
LYRICIST: Cole Porter
PRODUCER: Jack Cummings
DIRECTOR: George Sidney
SCREENWRITER: Dorothy Kingsley
SOURCE: Based on the musical
Kiss Me, Kate by Cole Porter, Bella
Spewack, and Sam Spewack
CHOREOGRAPHER: Hermes Pan

Synopsis

It's *The Taming of the Shrew* squared—with music.

Cast

Kathryn Grayson...............*Lilli Vanessi*
Howard Keel.....................*Fred Graham*
Ann Miller.........................*Lois Lane*
Tommy Rall.......................*Bill Calhoun*
Keenan Wynn.....................*Lippy*
Bobby Van..........................*Gremio*
James Whitmore.................*Slug*
Kurt Kasznar.....................*Baptista*
Bob Fosse...........................*Hortensio*
Jeanne Coyne.....................*Specialty Dancer*
Carol Haney.......................*Specialty Dancer*

KISS ME KATE

MGM—NOVEMBER 26, 1953

Howard Keel embraces
Kathryn Grayson before
Round One.

Y
OU'VE BOUGHT THE FILM RIGHTS OF THE HIT STAGE MUSICAL. YOU WANT TO EARN
your money back as soon as possible, but you can't go into production until
the show has closed on Broadway. It keeps running and running and running—and that's a problem. *Kiss Me, Kate* obstinately refused to close on
Broadway. Finally, after over one thousand performances, the curtain rang
down and production on the film could proceed with producer Jack Cummings at the helm.

By that time, Hollywood was noticing an erosion of its audience due to the newest entertainment baby: television. What to do? The studios decided to give the public something
they couldn't see on television. Glorious Technicolor, widescreen pictures, even wider-
screen pictures, and 3-D. And so, *Kiss Me Kate* was shot in Technicolor and in Metro's
patented 3-D process, imaginatively named Metrovision Tri-Dee.

There weren't many musicals shot in 3-D. Only *The French Line* and *Top Banana*
immediately come to mind. *Kiss Me Kate* was far and away the best of the lot. The first
3-D era didn't last long (we're into the second chapter of 3-D right now). Projectors had to
be modified, the glasses were hard to keep in stock (people kept walking out with them),
keep clean, and keep in one piece (the paper would rip or the colored lenses would pop out).
But, in a test, MGM discovered that the 3-D prints attracted 40 percent more attendees

than the flat versions. Although MCM was behind 3-D all the way, the fad didn't last long enough to see *Kiss Me Kate* projected in 3-D. When Cinemascope replaced the 3-D prints, the film's first ads said, "See It Without Glasses." Even the film's debut at Radio City Music Hall was the flat version. Some film festivals have shown the film in 3-D, but generally, audiences continue to wonder why Ann Miller seems to be throwing scarves at the screen all the time and the male dancers swing out toward the audience.

In any number of dimensions, *Kiss Me Kate* is an exceptionally enjoyable film. It wasn't changed much from the Broadway version and, in fact, some of the changes—giving Ann Miller "Too Darn Hot," for example—are improvements. Another change improved the picture greatly; the inclusion of a "new" song, "From This Moment On." The number had been cut from Porter's *Out of This World* on Broadway, and Porter gave it to Saul Chaplin for *Kiss Me Kate*. It soon became a standard.

"From This Moment On" is one of the most inventive and exciting numbers in film history, as danced by Ann Miller, Carol Haney and a trio of great talents: Tommy Rall, Bobby Van, and Bob Fosse. Interestingly, Fosse choreographed his own routine. Rall in particular deserved greater fame. He could act, sing, and dance equally well. Among his other screen credits are *Seven Brides for Seven Brothers*, *Invitation to the Dance*, *My Sister Eileen*, and *Funny Girl*. On Broadway he appeared in *Milk and Honey*, *Juno*,

LEFT: Ann Miller declares it's too darn hot!

and *Cry for Us All*, and sang with opera companies in the 1960s, but for some reason he never had the success he deserved.

Everyone seems to be at his or her best in the film. Howard Keel nails the part of Fred Graham, a pompous, conceited actor. Kathryn Grayson shows real fire as his wife, Lilli, and Ann Miller gives a terrific performance with more depth than in past movie musical appearances. Perhaps it's because they all have excellent material with which to work. *Kiss Me Kate* was one of a handful of film adaptations of Broadway musicals that didn't suffer in the transition, proving that Broadway knew a thing or two about making musicals and Hollywood could do well to listen. ■

ABOVE: Keenan Wynn, Howard Keel, James Whitmore, and Kathryn Grayson as musical comedy gangsters—the funniest people there are.

Behind the Screen

■ Laurence Olivier was producer Jack Cummings's first choice to play Fred.

SONGS

"Always True to You in My Fashion" ■ "Brush Up Your Shakespeare" ■ "From This Moment On" ■ "I Hate Men" ■ "I've Come to Wive It Wealthily in Padua" ■ "So in Love" ■ "Kiss Me Kate" ■ "Tom, Dick or Harry" ■ "Too Darn Hot" ■ "We Open in Venice" ■ "Were Thine Thy Special Face" ■ "Where Is the Life That Late I Led?" ■ "Why Can't You Behave" ■ "Wunderbar"

Jack Cummings

He might have been Louis B. Mayer's nephew, but at MGM Jack Cummings rose up the ladder on his own merits to become one of the best producers on the lot. He wasn't self-promoting and dealt expediently with problems. He was put in charge of the shorts unit in 1932 and graduated to features four years later, when he produced a terrific film, Cole Porter's *Born to Dance*, with two of the studio's emerging stars, Eleanor Powell and James Stewart. He went on to be responsible for some of MGM's best musicals, including *Broadway Melody of 1938* and the 1940 edition with Eleanor Powell, Fred Astaire, and George Murphy. He was a favorite of Powell, who also appeared in Cummings's *Honolulu* and *Ship Ahoy*. He had a stint working with Esther Williams on *Bathing Beauty* and *Neptune's Daughter*, among other films. Three of his best movies are *Kiss Me Kate*, *Seven Brides for Seven Brothers*, and *Three Little Words*. His last film for MGM was the Elvis Presley hit *Viva Las Vegas* in 1964. Cummings snuck out of MGM in 1961 to serve (uncredited) as producer of the 20th Century Fox film *Can-Can*. He retired from the studio thirteen years after his uncle was fired, proving once and for all that nepotism had had nothing to do with his lasting success.

TOP LEFT: Howard Keel snags Kathryn Grayson while Ann Miller and Tommy Rall (center) look on.

TOP RIGHT: Anne Miller and the greatly underrated Tommy Rall perform on a rooftop. This one looks particularly good in 3-D.

BOTTOM LEFT: Jeanne Coyne, Carol Haney, Ann Miller, Bobby Van, Bob Fosse, and Tommy Rall in "From This Moment On," one of the most exciting dance numbers in film history. Note: Jeanne Coyne was married to both Stanley Donen and Gene Kelly. Guess she craved direction.

BOTTOM RIGHT: Ann Miller, Cole Porter, Jack Cummings, and Kathryn Grayson.

T&A, THE WOMEN

V A VA VOOM. NUMBER ONE ON ANYONE'S LIST OF THE SEXIEST women in movie musicals is Marilyn Monroe. She wasn't ever nude but some of her costumes sure made her look like she was. Have a look at her singing "I'm Through in Love" in *Some Like It Hot* in costume designer Orry-Kelly's ingenious creation. Monroe co-starred with another overtly sexual star, Jane Russell, in *Gentlemen Prefer Blondes*. Russell also never appeared nude but she did make an impression with her full-figured physique. Russell's bathing suit in *Blondes* isn't what one would call demure. Two other stars whose bathing suits clung closely were Esther Williams and Annette Funicello. Annette had two of her assets held back in her Mouseketeer days but everything was au natural on the beach. She was surrounded with other lovely ladies and some hot guys, too. Something for everyone.

TOP LEFT: Marilyn Monroe in *There's No Business Like Show Business.*
TOP RIGHT: Julie Newmar shows it all off in *Li'l Abner.*
BOTTOM LEFT: Peter Lupus has a mission possible in holding up Annette Funicello in *Muscle Beach Party.*
BOTTOM RIGHT: Esther Williams strikes a cheesecake pose in 1946.

LADY SINGS THE BLUES

PRODUCER: James S. White and Jay Weston

DIRECTOR: Sidney J. Furie

SCREENWRITER: Chris Clark, Suzanne de Pass, and Terence McCloy

Synopsis
Billie Holiday's rise and fall—and fall.

Cast
Diana Ross................Billie Holiday
Billy Dee Williams ....Louis McKay
Richard Pryor ....Piano Man
Sid Melton................Jerry
Paul Hampton..............Harry
Virginia Capers...........Mama Holiday
James T. Callahan.........Reg Hanley
Isabel Sanford............The Prostitute
Ned Glass.................The Agent
Jester Hairston...........The Butler

LADY SINGS THE BLUES

PARAMOUNT—OCTOBER 12, 1972

Diana Ross, sporting Billie Holiday's trademark gardenia.

THE FILM OPENS WITH BILLIE HOLIDAY AT HER LOWEST (UNTIL THE GRAVE, THAT IS). Under the credits, a series of Weegee-esque photos shows her drugged out and half insane, locked up in a padded cell. You've got to hand it to Diana Ross: She doesn't play the star, all prettied even while bound in a straitjacket.

In fact, the entire film is quite hard-hitting, attempting to tell it like it was (although a lot of the names were changed and incidents compressed, as in all biopics). In fact, few of the facts remain.

Spanning Holiday's life from age fourteen (Ross is almost believable) to her death at forty-four, there were bound to be a lot of Moments. Raped as a child: check. Prostitution: check. Stress of touring with a band: check. Not allowed to eat with the band in a "Whites Only" café: check. Getting hooked on drugs, standing up to the Ku Klux Klan, mini-breakdown in front of a mirror: check, check, and check. Call it one cliché after another—we won't argue with you.

So, why do we like this film? Ross's performance has a lot to do with it. It may not be completely realistic (after all, she was brand-new to acting), but she never plays the star game. She definitely carries the proceedings and makes her transitions smoothly and successfully. As might be expected, her singing is excellent and, while she's no Billie Holiday (the problem with all biopics is that no actor can equal the genius of the film's subject), she injects her own brand of magic into the onscreen performances. As in many pictures that try to evoke an earlier era, the acting and singing style of the period is never really achieved. They try hard with the orchestrations here—and there's not a hint of the Supremes in the vocals—but a heavy sheen of modernity remains. We forgive the film for the lapse: The present is part of who we are and we can never truly regain the spirit of past times.

By way of illustration, have a look at *The Jazz Singer* (the real thing) and then watch *The Jolson Story* (the re-creation). The externals may be the same—both Al Jolson and Larry Parks wear blackface and sing brashly, on one knee with arms outstretched. But the entire ambiance and feelings are different as are, of course, the technical aspects. In *Lady Sings the Blues*, we're treated to sepia-tinged freeze frames to evoke the passage of time, in a style reminiscent of *Butch Cassidy and the Sundance Kid*. An older film might have used montages to achieve the same effect—but honestly, would we want to see the Billie Holiday story filmed in black-and-white without the benefit of stereophonic sound? Of course not.

Just as Peggy Lee did in her Oscar-nominated turn in *Pete Kelly's Blues*, Ross clearly felt free to show her vulnerability. Considering that both Lee and Ross were known to be ultrasensitive about their look and image, it says a lot that they were willing to subjugate their persona to the parts they played.

Lady Sings the Blues was obviously produced with care and respect, even if it never quite captures the strength and depth of the sublime Billie Holiday. Call it a Cliff's Notes version, and admit that it doesn't make us feel as much for Holiday as we want to. There's little interest in the impact that Holiday had on jazz and, because of its episodic nature, we have to fill in some emotional blanks ourselves. But for all that, the film delivers, thanks in large part to Diana Ross's performance and the support of her producers. ■

Behind the Screen

■ Abbey Lincoln, Diahann Carroll, Dorothy Dandridge, Cicely Tyson, and Lola Falana were all considered for the role of Billie Holiday.

■ Most of Holiday's recording career is glossed over in the film.

ABOVE: Richard Pryor and Diana Ross. Surprisingly, it isn't Pryor's character who hooks Ross's Billie Holiday on drugs. Now that's acting.

FAR LEFT: Billy Dee Williams examines Diana Ross's arms for needle tracks. And finds them.

LEFT: Diana Ross as Billie Holiday at the end of the line.

SONGS

■ "All of Me" (Seymour Simons and Gerald Marks) ■ "Don't Explain" (Billie Holiday and Arthur Herzog Jr.) ■ "Fancy Passes" (William O'Malley, Ronald Miller, and Avery Vandenberg) ■ "Fine and Mellow" (Billie Holiday) ■ "Gimme a Pigsfoot and a Bottle of Beer" (Wesley Wilson) ■ "God Bless the Child" (Billie Holiday and Arthur Herzog Jr.) ■ "Good Morning Heartache" (Irene Higgenbotham, Bernard Yuffy, and Richard Jacques) ■ "Had You Been Around" (Ronald Miller, Avery Vandenberg, Bernard Yuffy, and Richard Jacques) . "Hello Broadway" (Ronald Miller and William O'Malley) ■ "I Cried for You" (Abe Lyman, Gus Arnheim, and Arthur Freed) ■ "Lady Sings the Blues" (Billie Holiday and Herbie Nichols) ■ "Lover Man" (Jimmy Davis, Jimmy Sherman, and Roger "Ram" Ramirez) ■ "The Man I Love" (George Gershwin and Ira Gershwin) ■ "Mean to Me" (Fred E. Ahlert and Roy Turk) ■ "My Man" (Maurice Yvain, A. Willemetz, Jacques Charles, and Channing Pollock) ■ "Our Love Is Here to Stay" (George Gershwin and Ira Gershwin) ■ "Strange Fruit" (Lewis Allen) ■ "Them There Eyes" (Maceo Pinkard, William Tracey, and Doris Tauber) ■ "Those Low-Down Shuffle Blues" (Gil Askey and William Robinson) ■ "Tain't Nobody's Bizness If I Do" (Porter Grainger and Everett Robbins) ■ "What a Little Moonlight Can Do" (Harry Woods) ■ "You've Changed" (Bill Carey and Carl Fischer)

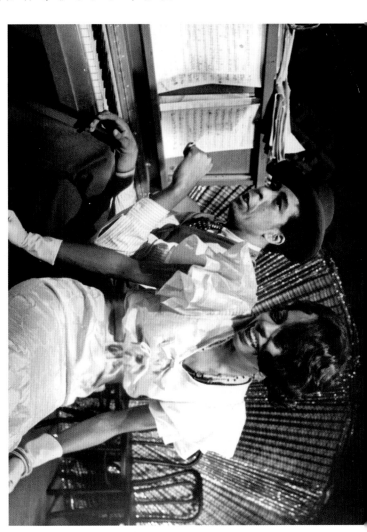

LI'L ABNER

PARAMOUNT—DECEMBER 11, 1959

LI'L ABNER

COMPOSER: Gene de Paul

LYRICIST: Johnny Mercer

PRODUCER: Norman Panama

DIRECTOR: Melvin Frank

SCREENWRITERS: Norman Panama and Melvin Frank

SOURCE: Based on the musical *Li'l Abner* by Gene de Paul, Melvin Frank, Johnny Mercer, and Norman Panama

CHOREOGRAPHER: Dee Dee Wood

Synopsis

Dogpatch, unnecessary in the first place, is about to be blown to smithereens by the government. But Mammy Yokum's home brew just might save the day.

Cast

Peter Palmer ....Li'l Abner
Leslie Parrish ....Daisy Mae
Billie Hayes ....Mammy Yokum
Joe E. Marks..................Pappy Yokum
Stubby Kaye...................Marryin' Sam
Julie Newmar..................Stupefyin' Jones
Howard St. John.............General Bullmoose
Stella Stevens.................Appassionata Von
                                    Climax
Bern Hoffman ....Earthquake McGoon
Al Nesor.........................Evil Eye Fleagle
Carmen Alvarez.............Moonbeam McSwine
Robert Strauss................Romeo Scragg
William Lanteau..............Available Jones
Ted Thurston..................Sen. Jack S.
                                    Phogbound
Alan Carney ....Mayor Daniel D.
                                    Dogmeat

SONGS

"The Country's in the Very Best of Hands" ■ "I Wish It Could Be Otherwise" ■ "I'm Past My Prime" ■ "If I Had My Druthers" ■ "It's a Typical Day" ■ "Jubiation T. Cornpone" ■ "Namely You" ■ "Put 'Em Back" ■ "Rag Off'n the Bush" ■ "There's Room Enough for Us" ■ "What's Good for General Bullmoose"

Julie Newmar stupefies Peter Palmer as Leslie Parrish looks on.

AFTER THEY HAD COMPLETED *SEVEN BRIDES FOR SEVEN BROTHERS*, JOHNNY MERCER AND composer Gene de Paul decided to try their luck on Broadway. Along with *Brides'* choreographer, Michael Kidd, they came up with the Broadway show *Li'l Abner*. It was a hit, largely due to Mercer's brilliant lyrics (and we mean brilliant) as well as Kidd's inventive choreography. This isn't to degrade the contributions of de Paul or the book writers, Melvin Frank and Norman Panama, or the creator of the original characters, Al Capp. Their contributions all added up to a hilarious and sometimes surprisingly touching musical.

Luckily for all, Panama and Frank were also constant contributors to the roster of Paramount Pictures. The team always intended to make a film version of the musical after a stop on Broadway. In fact, Paramount put up the money for the stage production. The duo wanted the show brought over virtually intact. There were a few changes made, including replacing the pregnant Edie Adams with Leslie Parrish. Charlotte Rae replaced by Billie Hayes, and a few tweaks to the score. Michael Kidd, under contract to MGM, had his dances recreated by his assistant, Dee Dee Wood, almost exactly as they had appeared on stage. Basically, *Li'l Abner* the movie is a more than satisfactory restaging of *Li'l Abner* the show.

Political satire is a hard thing to pull off, but the citizens of Dogpatch and those of Congress haven't changed much over the years and the satirical bent of *Li'l Abner* is unlikely to change in our generation or the next one. That's just one reason the film is never out-of-date. The others are the broad humor and the intelligence behind the stupidest of characters.

There is no funnier film in this book—or, in our opinion, in film history. Every aspect of the songs, story, and characters are funny. Heck, even the choreography is loaded with jokes, and how often can we say that? We can think of funny dances, such as Donald O'Connor's "Make 'Em Laugh," but there are few others, Michael Kidd's work here includes lots of effective sight gags (especially in the "Sadie Hawkins Day Ballet") as well as extremely inventive dance steps on a par with his work on the unique barn-raising dance in *Seven Brides*. And the *Abner* choreography was plenty difficult for the dancers to perform; it called for real athletes. Unlike the in-your-face gymnastic gyrations of *Seven Brides* or *Guys and Dolls*' "Luck Be a Lady," these are deceptively simple steps that define character, advance the plot, and are funny to boot.

Li'l Abner is an extremely pleasurable film to watch, one that asks no more of its audience than to go along on a journey with an open heart and mind and a finely tuned funny bone. Some films, such as the Garland-Mason *A Star Is Born* or *West Side Story*, are expertly drawn dramas; others, such as *The Road to Morocco* or Panama and Frank's *The Court Jester*, offer simple laughs. *Li'l Abner* is the one to look to for constant smiles punctuated by laugh-out-loud comedy.

The satire in *Li'l Abner* is but one component of the whole, so the show has stood up better than some satirical shows have, including *Of Thee I Sing*, which has little more than satire on its mind. In *Li'l Abner*, the characters—no matter how silly, stupid, or strange—seem real within the world of the film. Let's face it, when you start with names such as Earthquake McGoon, Evil Eye Fleagle, and Appassionata Von Climax, the humor and satire are halfway home. All the creators have to do is supply a story and songs that support the premise and keep the whole thing believable—and that they do.

The film has never really received its due and that's too bad. It's equally sad that the show has never been revived on Broadway, though, granted, it's a hard piece to revive. There can be no winking at the audience, and straightforward humor isn't something Broadway excels at these days. The film, just like the original show, can be seen as a wonderful primer on how to play it perfectly straight for laughs with no irony, commenting, or exaggeration. Trust the material, and if it's good the show or film will work. Are you listening, Broadway? ■

Johnny Mercer

Alan Jay Lerner had his "How Could You Believe Me When I Said I Love You When You Know I've Been a Liar All My Life" in *Royal Wedding* and Johnny Mercer had "The Square of the Hypoteneuse of a Right Triangle Is Equal to the Sum of the Squares of the Two Adjacent Sides" in *Merry Andrew*. As Saul Chaplin, Mercer's collaborator on that tongue-twister, wrote about Mercer, "He never chose the obvious idea to write about, and having chosen his subject matter, never wrote it in an obvious way." Mercer concentrated on lyrics but also wrote music, and some of the songs he composed became hits. Still, his words were what brought him the greatest fame. Mercer's lyrics for the ballads "Blues in the Night," "Day In—Day Out," "Skylark," "That Old Black Magic," "One for My Baby (And One More for the Road)," and "Moon River" are all standards. His comic songs are equally brilliant. "Hooray for Hollywood," "Jeepers Creepers," "Too Marvelous for Words," "Ac-cent-tchu-ate the Positive," and "On the Atchison, Topeka and the Santa Fe," as well as the entire score for *Li'l Abner*, are among the best light comic songs ever written—and comic material is a more difficult to pull off than a serious ballad. When the movie musical went into eclipse, Mercer turned to writing title songs and individual songs for films, usually with Henry Mancini—and he was equally successful it. Mercer was among the most versatile of the Hollywood lyricists, equally adept at writing for sophisticates and the denizens of Dogpatch.

LIVING IT UP

PARAMOUNT—JULY 23, 1954

Synopsis

Folks, you should never, ever lie. But sometimes lying can work in your favor and you'll not only get away with it, you'll get the key to the city—not to mention the girl.

Cast

Dean Martin.................*Dr. Steve Harris*
Jerry Lewis.................*Homer Flagg*
Janet Leigh.................*Wally Cook*
Edward Arnold.................*The Mayor*
Fred Clark.................*Oliver Stone*
Sheree North.................*Jitterbug Dancer*
Sammy White.................*Mayor*
Sig Ruman.................*Dr. Emile Egelhofer*
Sid Tomack.................*Master of Ceremonies*

The question is, was this photo of Dean Martin and Jerry Lewis taken before or after they broke up their act?

T HE 1950S BELONGED TO THE TEAM OF DEAN MARTIN AND JERRY LEWIS. NO COMEDY team before or since has risen to stardom more quickly. Dean burst on the scene in the first wave of good-looking Italian-American singers that included Perry Como, Al Martino, Vic Damone, and Jerry Vale. (The second wave came in the '60s with Bobby Rydell [born Robert Ridarelli], Fabian, Frankie Avalon, Bobby Darin, Frankie Valli, and others.) Because Dean was a terrific singer, most of the Martin and Lewis films were either full-fledged musicals or, at least, had opportunities for Dean, and sometimes Jerry, to break out in song.

Whereas Dean was the solid, good-looking, masculine figure, Jerry was the class clown seemingly almost simpleminded, a kind of Harpo Marx figure—childish and unrestrained. But while Harpo ran after women, Jerry was more the pubescent boy; he wanted a girl-friend but might have been confused as to what to do once he got one. What made the team click so well was the respect and admiration they had for each other. This resulted in their having a ball, whether on a nightclub stage or a sound stage. Their sets were rife with practical jokes and adolescent behavior, with the crew armed with squirt guns while the boys ran roughshod. A general rule of comedy is that the more fun you have making a picture, the less successful the comedy will be onscreen—but Martin and Lewis were an exception to this rule. They enjoyed themselves so much, the audience couldn't help but join in. Dean's character might have gotten frustrated at Jerry's stupidity and immaturity, but he usually acted more befuddled than angry. (Compare that to Abbott and Costello, where it often seemed that Abbott hardly liked Costello at all.)

"I find that I get the best results when I treat them like little boys."

—Norman Taurog, director of six Martin and Lewis films and two Jerry Lewis films

Over the course of their career together, some of Martin and Lewis's pictures were better than others, but they never made a flop for Paramount. They and their creative team had a strong sense of the boys' personas and audiences knew what to expect as well. The results were almost always slickly produced and well received.

You might think that giving Jerry Lewis more and more latitude would send him to new heights of insanity, but the opposite was true. When Jerry was permitted to break out of his zany persona, he calmed down and his humor was more focused. Less was definitely more. *Living It Up*, based on the Broadway musical *Hazel Flagg* and unofficially its predecessor, the film *Nothing Sacred*, had a more structured story line than the duo's earlier films, without as many digressions into comedy bits. They didn't have to push as hard for laughs as they often did, Jerry walking the edge between sanity and insanity (or just plain weirdness) and sometimes going overboard to deleterious effect; within this strong, proven plot, the boys could relax and cease to worry about carrying the whole film on their shoulders.

When Paramount adapted *Hazel Flagg* into *Living It Up*, Hazel became Homer (not the first time that Jerry took on a role originally created for a woman) and the rest of the plot was adjusted. (In *Nothing Sacred* a guy reporter falls in love with Hazel, whereas in this film the reporter, played by Janet Leigh, falls for Homer's doctor, played by Dean Martin.) There are plenty of humorous moments and Dean gets to sing some good songs—though Martin and Lewis didn't always get top-drawer material from top-drawer songwriters. The hits from *Living It Up*, "Ev'ry Street's a Boulevard in Old New York" and "How Do You Speak to an Angel?" were already well known from *Hazel Flagg*.

To understand the most interesting thing about the conversion from the show to the film, let's look back to 1943, when the musical *Oklahoma!* opened on Broadway. That show was based on the play *Green Grows the Lilacs*, a flop by Lynn Riggs that ran for under two months on Broadway. *Oklahoma!* was the biggest Broadway hit of its time, running just two days short of five years. The addition of songs by Rodgers and Hammerstein and judicious tweaking had made a flop play into a hit musical. Similarly, the musical *Hazel Flagg* was less than a success on Broadway, running only 190 performances. The changes it underwent in moving from stage to screen helped *Living It Up* to become perhaps the best of the Martin and Lewis films, a huge hit for Paramount Pictures, and a crowd-pleaser. ∎

SONGS

"Champagne and Wedding Cake" ▪ "Ev'ry Street's a Boulevard in Old New York" ▪ "How Do You Speak to An Angel?" ▪ "Money Burns a Hole in My Pocket" ▪ "That's What I Like" ▪ "You are the Bravest" ▪ "You're Gonna Dance with Me Baby"

ABOVE: Dean looks as if he's given up trying to control the little boy inside Jerry—who seems to be getting into character as the nutty professor.

LEFT: Can't a guy have any privacy? Jerry crashes Dean's bath time in *Artists and Models*.

Martin and Lewis

Dean Martin, the laid-back Italian singer, and Jerry Lewis, the manic comic, first met in 1945. Their yin and yang appeal was immediately apparent to both of them, and in 1946 they debuted as a team at Atlantic City's 500 Club, where their tightly scripted act was an immediate . . . flop. Threatened with failure, they figured they had nothing to lose by jettisoning the act entirely and concentrating on having a good time onstage. Once they let loose and stopped worrying about what the audience wanted, they were a smash hit. Jerry indulged his most infantile instincts, cracking up Dean and the audience as well. Dean's crooning gave the audience a chance to catch their breath, and his bemusement at Jerry's antics and the obvious love they shared further enthralled them. Their act felt dangerous—a roller-coaster ride full of delightfully unexpected twists and turns. In 1949, the duo moved on from nightclubs to NBC Radio and the movies, and the following year, they conquered television on the *Colgate Comedy Hour*. Reviewers who singled out Lewis for his comic zaniness and ignored or downplayed Martin's contributions to the act made the singer angry and jealous. For his part, Lewis thought he was as good a singer as Martin. Lewis continually expanded the emotional range of his characters while Martin was straitjacketed into the relatively boring straight-man role. Something had to give—and the team broke up exactly ten years after they first joined forces. Martin's later career included more ambitious film roles and great success as the soused host of a variety series. Lewis tried his hand at writing and directing and was smart enough to retain all rights to his films, making him wealthier than ever when movies such as *The Nutty Professor* were remade (badly) by succeeding generations of comics.

LOVE ME OR LEAVE ME

WARNER BROTHERS—JUNE 10, 1955

LOVE ME OR LEAVE ME

PRODUCER: Joe Pasternak
DIRECTOR: Charles Vidor
SCREENWRITERS: Daniel Fuchs and Isobel Lennart
CHOREOGRAPHER: Alex Romero

Synopsis

Dr. Phil and Oprah tell us all the time that spousal abuse is a dangerous trap. Too bad they weren't around in time to help singer Ruth Etting.

Cast

Doris Day...............Ruth Etting
James Cagney............Martin Snyder
Cameron Mitchell........Johnny Alderman
Robert Keith............Bernard V. Loomis
Tom Tully...............Frobisher
Harry Bellaver..........Georgie
Richard Gaines..........Paul Hunter
Peter Leeds.............Fred Taylor

LIFE-INSPIRED DRAMA FROM DANCE HALL TO ZIEGFELD FOLLIES!

ABOVE: Doris Day strikes a sultry pose as singer Ruth Etting.

OPPOSITE TOP: Neither Day nor Etting had luck with husbands. Here Day and James Cagney have a one-way shouting match.

OPPOSITE MIDDLE: Esther Williams underwater in Joe Pasternak's *Jupiter's Darling*. Notice the grid that helps keep Esther and the living statue firmly in place on the pool's floor.

OPPOSITE BOTTOM: The real Ruth Etting—a great singer.

P EOPLE WHO HATE MUSICALS OFTEN THINK OF THEM AS ETERNALLY SUNNY, BRIGHT, and stupid. But there's a serious, dark side to Hollywood musicals, too. And *Love Me Or Leave Me*, a hard-hitting biography of torch singer Ruth Etting, is as dramatic as any straight film. Lots of the credit goes to Doris Day's no-holds-barred performance and James Cagney's bravery in creating a real villain as sadistic and nasty as any of his Warner gangsters.

Another "and-then-I-sang" biopic with a dark, though ultimately uplifting side, is the Jane Froman story. *With a Song in My Heart*. On a USO flight in Spain, Froman had switched seats with the actress Tamara Drasin (best known as the singer who introduced "Smoke Gets in Your Eyes" in the Broadway musical *Roberta*). Tamara was killed and Froman suffered serious injuries to her legs. In her subsequent career, she was always seen either sitting down or leaning against a column or lamppost. Froman dealt with her injuries and chronic pain bravely and Susan Hayward, selected by Froman herself to play her in the picture, was the ne plus ultra of screen sufferers.

Hayward also starred in another eventually uplifting biopic, the weepy *I'll Cry Tomorrow*, which charted the descent into alcoholism of popular Broadway and film singer Lillian Roth. Hayward again tried her darnedest to be strong in the face of tragedy. In between the sobs we heard "Sing You Sinner"; Roth's theme song "When the Red, Red Robin Comes Bob, Bob Bobbin' Along"; and the ironic "I'm Sitting on Top of the World." The film was harrowing enough but Roth's true travails were watered down for moviegoers' consumption.

The next time some cynic says film musicals are all about dancing on the ceiling, singing in the rain, and painting the clouds with sunshine, suggest that they take a gander at these three dramatic musicals. And don't snicker when you pass them the Kleenex. ■

"At Sundown" (Walter Donaldson) ■ "Everybody Loves My Baby" (Jack Palmer and Spencer Williams) ■ "I Cried for You" (Gus Arnheim, Abe Lyman, and Arthur Freed) ■ "I'll Never Stop Loving You" (Nicholas Brodzky and Sammy Cahn) ■ "I'm Sitting on Top of the World" (Ray Henderson, Sam Lewis and Joe Young) ■ "It All Depends on You" (Ray Henderson, Sam Lewis and Joe Young) ■ "Love Me or Leave Me" (Walter Donaldson and Gus Kahn) ■ "Mean to Me" (Roy Turk and Fred Ahlert) ■ "My Blue Heaven" (Walter Donaldson and Richard A. Whiting) ■ "Never Look Back" (Chilton Price) ■ "Sam, the Old Accordian Man" (Walter Donaldson) ■ "Shakin' the Blues Away" (Irving Berlin) ■ "Stay on the Right Side Sister" (Rube Bloom and Ted Koehler) ■ "Ten Cents a Dance" (Richard Rodgers and Lorenz Hart) ■ "What Can I Say After I Say I'm Sorry" (Walter Donaldson and Abe Lyman) ■ "You Made Me Love You" (James V. Monaco and Joseph McCarthy)

Behind the Screen
■ Doris Day is the sixth-highest money-earning actress in film history.
■ Jack Warner dismissed band singer Doris Day as a movie star, saying she was "sexless."

"There's a separate country within MGM called Pasternakia where they make sweet, sentimental, schmaltzy pictures that critics never get very excited about but audiences flock to see."

—Dore Schary

Joe Pasternak

Joe Pasternak emigrated to the United States from his native Hungary in 1921, took a job at the Paramount commissary, and worked his way up to assistant director for Allan Dwan. He was still in his twenties when he was assigned to Berlin to oversee productions for Universal Pictures. He soon became a full-fledged producer and made a star out of Franciska Gaal, a young, virginal soprano. With the rise of the Nazis, Pasternak moved to Hollywood and Universal Studios in 1936, where he shepherded another young, virginal soprano, Deanna Durbin, through a series of hugely successful films that literally saved Universal–though her best one, *Can't Help Singing*, was produced by Felix Jackson. If Deanna was the eternally optimistic squeaky-clean virgin, then Marlene Dietrich was the exact opposite. Pasternak worked on her movies, too, revamping the star's image. In 1942, he moved to MGM and produced a series of second-string but successful musicals. Jane Powell, yet another young, virginal soprano, was a mainstay of Pasternak's productions for Leo the Lion, though her two best films, *Royal Wedding* and *Seven Brides for Seven Brothers*, were produced by others–Arthur Freed and Jack Cummings, respectively. Pasternak produced four Esther Williams movies, two films with Gene Kelly, three with Frank Sinatra, and two with Judy Garland. Doris Day appeared in three of Pasternak's films, including *Love Me or Leave Me*. He also oversaw two films for Mario Lanza, two for Connie Francis, and three for Elvis Presley. His best movies were *Destry Rides Again*, *Anchors Aweigh*, *Summer Stock*, *The Great Caruso*, *Hit the Deck*, *Love Me or Leave Me*, *Where the Boys Are*, and *Jumbo*. Given his Mittel Europa upbringing, it's no surprise that he loved operettas and produced film versions of *The Student Prince* and *The Merry Widow*. He also adored classical music and his films often featured such esteemed musicians as José Iturbi and Lauritz Melchior. (Perhaps that's why he was the perfect producer for Mario Lanza.) His long, distinguished career at MGM lasted almost twenty-five years. Esther Williams, who hated most of the MGM brass, loved Pasternak and once commented that he was "the only man I ever knew that ate spaghetti with his hands. It was such a sight to see that everybody came to the commissary to watch."

LOVE ME TONIGHT

PARAMOUNT—AUGUST 17, 1932

LOVE ME TONIGHT

COMPOSER: Richard Rodgers

LYRICIST: Lorenz Hart

PRODUCER: Rouben Mamoulian

DIRECTOR: Rouben Mamoulian

SCREENWRITERS: Samuel Hoffenstein, George Marion Jr., and Waldemar Young

SOURCE: Based on the play *Tailor in the Château* by Leopold Marchand and Paul Armont

Synopsis

The son-of-a-gun is nothing but a tailor—but he keeps the princess in stitches and sews up the plot.

Cast

Maurice Chevalier	*Maurice Coutelin*
Jeanette MacDonald	*Princess Jeanette*
Charles Ruggles	*Viscount Gilbert Varèze*
Charles Butterworth	*Count de Savignac*
Myrna Loy	*Countess Valentine*
C. Aubrey Smith	*Duke d'Artelines*
Elizabeth Patterson	*First Aunt*
Ethel Griffies	*Second Aunt*
Blanche Friderici	*Third Aunt*
Joseph Cawthorn	*Dr. Armand de Fontinac*

Behind the Screen

- George Cukor was originally slated to direct.
- Jeanette MacDonald did her own horseback riding, including the stunt in which she leaps from horseback to a moving train.

THIS IS THE MUSICAL THAT DIRECTOR ERNST LUBITSCH, THAT MASTER OF RURITANIAN romance, always aspired to make. But Rouben Mamoulian, a directing star of the Broadway stage, brought a sense of satire to the operetta form. It didn't hurt that he had the young team of Rodgers and Hart at his side, providing a delicious score and, most important, a willingness and ability to collaborate on what would become a bold experiment in film. Mamoulian couldn't have done it alone (*Applause* is a great movie but rather regular in form), nor could Rodgers and Hart have realized their ideas to such perfection. (Their previous—and first—foray into the Hollywood musical, *The Hot Heiress*, wasn't so hot.)

Right off the bat, Mamoulian expanded the possibilities of the nascent art form, setting a new standard for decades to come. As the film opens, we see Paris waking up for a new day. The montage's soundtrack is simply sounds of the city, a baby crying, workmen digging, cars honking, eventually all joining in to a symphony or sound and rhythm. The camera finally lands on Maurice Chevalier who explains to us, "That's the Song of Paree." In truth, Mamoulian borrowed the opening from his own stage production of *Porgy*, where Catfish Row comes alive through sound.

In the bravura number "Isn't It Romantic," Mamoulian, Rodgers and Hart, and screenwriters Samuel Hoffenstein, George Marion Jr., and Waldemar Young set the scene, establish the characters, and give the film its momentum. Thousands of words have been written about the "Isn't It Romantic" sequence, in which a simple song sung by the dashing Maurice Chevalier is picked up by a customer who passes it on to a taxi driver, who relays it to a musician riding in the taxi, etc., etc., until it reaches the ears of a princess in her castle, played by Jeanette MacDonald. In just a few minutes a bond is established between Chevalier and MacDonald, strangers for now, but we know not for long.

Maurice Chevalier takes the full measure of Jeanette MacDonald.

"A shameless bottom pincher."

—Jeanette MacDonald on Maurice Chevalier

"Rhythm and movement are the life of the screen." —*Lorenz Hart*

After some spicy pre-Code badinage between MacDonald and her suitor, Charles Butterworth, Mamoulian wants to change the scene. Instead of using cuts or fades, he sends the camera flying in, around, and through the castle. Tricky? Yes. Gimmicky? No. Mamoulian has other tricks up his sleeve, too. He plays with slow motion in the deer-hunting scene, matches the musical score match to Chevalier's rhythm as he walks through the castle, and sets the camera pointing down from ceilings, up from the floor, and otherwise scurries it around.

Mamoulian and his artistic compatriots knew that farce has to be played straight. As in all farces, the characters take themselves absolutely seriously, completely unaware of their foibles. Chevalier is the only one who sees himself and everyone else with a clear eye. He views the proceedings just as the audience does, and our responses are filtered through his. Yes, everyone is absurd and, as in all good farces, obsessed with sex (or the lack thereof), but they all try very hard to retain their dignity. Only when Jeanette MacDonald lands in a ditch at the end of "Lover," does she acknowledge her own absurdity.

Consider MacDonald with Maurice Chevalier in "Love Me Tonight" versus her partnership with Nelson Eddy in their string of MGM operettas. She has spunk and fortitude in both but she's too stiff and erect in the latter. Mamoulian gives her softness and a touch of whimsy. He's making a fool of her (and everyone else in the cast) but her vulnerability encourages us to root for her and relate to her, something we seldom do in the MGM operettas. Take a look at MacDonald on the train singing "Beyond the Blue Horizon" in *Monte Carlo* and compare it to her singing "Lover" as she rides in a carriage in *Love Me Tonight*. Same person, similar situation, different effect.

Love Me Tonight remains a classic movie musical in part because its sensibility seems so modern. Eighty years after its premiere, the artistry of these geniuses still speaks to us. ■

TOP RIGHT: Maurice Chevalier singing "Me and My Shadow." No, that can't be right.

BOTTOM RIGHT: Director Rouben Mamoulian helps Maurice Chevalier count his lines.

SONGS

"Isn't It Romantic?" ▪ "Love Me Tonight" ▪ "Lover" ▪ "Mimi" ▪ "The Poor Apache" ▪ "The Son-of-a-Gun Is Nothing but a Tailor" ▪ "That's the Song of Paree" ▪ "A Woman Needs Something like That"

Rouben Mamoulian

Mamoulian had a concept of filming that was almost exactly what we had in mind. Like us, he was convinced that a musical film should be created in musical terms—that dialogue, song and scoring should all be integrated as closely as possible so that the final product would have a unity of style and design." So wrote Richard Rodgers. Rouben Mamoulian was recognized as one of Broadway's most inventive directors, so it was only natural that Hollywood would call. His direction of the Helen Morgan vehicle *Applause* liberated the sound camera from the soundstage and artfully captured life in second-rate theaters, elevating a clichéd story into a piece of art. Mamoulian's version of *Dr. Jekyll and Mr. Hyde* won an Academy Award and *Becky Sharp* marked the first serious use of color as a dramatic statement—something that was common in theater. *The Mark of Zorro* transcended its genre and Mamoulian did well by Greta Garbo in *Queen Christina*. Although *Love Me Tonight* is considered his most adventurous film and the one that had the greatest impact on the art form, Mamoulian had many more successes as well as more than a few disasters. He was meant to direct the film version of *Porgy and Bess*, which he had brilliantly directed on Broadway, only to be replaced again by Otto Preminger. Shortly after beginning shooting on the infamous Elizabeth Taylor version of *Cleopatra*, Mamoulian was axed. Many of his successes are forgotten today. *The Gay Desperado* is an unsung comedy with Leo Carillo and Ida Lupino; *High, Wide and Handsome* boasts an excellent Kern and Hammerstein score; *Summer Holiday*, a musical retelling of O'Neill's *Ah! Wilderness*, is practically unknown, despite its many charms; and Fred Astaire and Cyd Charisse shine in Cole Porter's *Silk Stockings*. Perhaps it's true that Mamoulian's earliest films are his best but his later work, while not as inventive, was good solid entertainment. The fact that he didn't play well with the folks in the front office undoubtedly hurt his career, but when left to his own devices on such films as *Love Me Tonight*, which he also produced, he ranked with the greatest filmmakers.

Rodgers and Hart

When no one else was making musicals, we worked on one of the screen's most highly praised achievements (*Love Me Tonight*). When everyone else was making musicals, we had a contract, but no work," said Richard Rodgers. He and Lorenz Hart were the newest boys on the Broadway block when they opened *The Garrick Gaieties* in 1925. They went to Hollywood after the first big migration, just in time to see movie musicals go briefly out of fashion. Their first film, *The Hot Heiress*, met with indifference. Their next, *Love Me Tonight*, was hailed as an instant classic. They followed that with *The Phantom President*, starring George M. Cohan. Both that film and *Hallelujah, I'm a Bum* furthered the experiments in film musicals that the songwriting team had begun with *Love Me Tonight*. Neither of the latter films was particularly successful and, after two and a half years, it was back to Broadway and continued fame for Rodgers and Hart. Hart enjoyed life in California as long as there was booze available, but Rodgers preferred the city. He stayed in Hollywood for the money. The worst years of the Depression coincided with Rodgers and Hart's Hollywood sojourn and, though the experience wasn't consistently successful, they were pulling down a regular salary. It's sad that the team that brought so much to film with their second picture could never

replicate its success. Films would be made of Rodgers and Hart's subsequent Broadway hits but the shows were often hacked up and mistreated, as was the case with most film adaptations of Broadway shows. However, the pair did write some new songs for these screen transfers, most notably for *The Boys from Syracuse*, an altogether enjoyable film. Also, the mangling of the Rodgers and Hart canon by Hollywood convinced Rodgers to retain complete control when assigning the rights to the classic Rodgers and Hammerstein films—so, you could say that some good came out of the Rodgers and Hart's misbegotten Hollywood adventures.

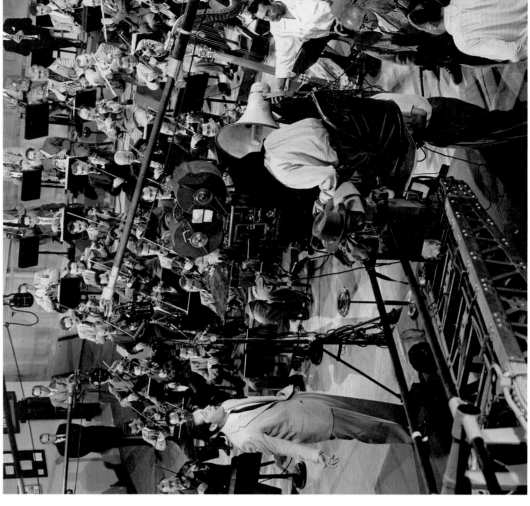

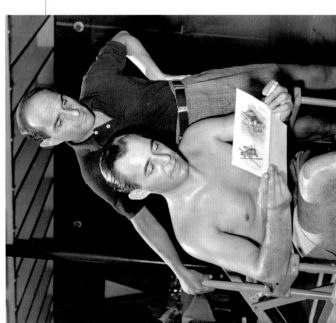

TOP LEFT: Richard Rodgers (sans clothes) and Larry Hart peruse a Christmas Card while working in Hollywood. (Hart was much shorter than Rodgers, so in their photos together, Rodgers tends to be sitting down.)

ABOVE LEFT: June Allyson and the Blackburn Twins sing "Thou Swell" in *Words and Music*.

RIGHT: Perry Como filming the Rodgers and Hart biopic, *Words and Music*.

A SALUTE TO THE CHORUS GIRL

L ET'S HEAR IT FOR THE LOVELY WOMEN WHO HAVE GRACED MANY A HOL-
lywood musical. Chorus girls were more than just living scenery.
They lent beauty and sex appeal to many a picture and pleased
the tired businessman (and the well-rested one, too).

Picture Busby Berkeley's camera panning across the array of
beauties in such pictures as *Gold Diggers of 1933, 1935, and 1937*, and you'll
recognize just how important beautiful girls were to the success of movie
musicals. Heck, Berkeley had a movie titled *Dames* and it was all about dames.
Samuel Goldwyn had the Goldwyn Girls, who decorated many a picture
whether they were integral to the plot or not. When you saw a Goldwyn picture
somehow there was a Goldwyn Girl around somewhere. Of course, chorus girls
did more than just stand around looking pretty. They were hoisted high on
pedestals, strapped to the prows of ships, and played neon violins.

A few actresses eventually escaped the chorus to become stars. Lucille Ball,
Ann Sothern, Jane Wyman, Paulette Goddard, and Betty Grable all started
out as Goldwyn Girls, and its fun trying to spot them in the chorus.

TOP LEFT: The Goldwyn Girls on break during filmin of 1934's *Kid Millions*. Lucille Ball can be spotted sixth from the left.
BOTTOM LEFT: A gam's-eye view of *Red Garters*.
RIGHT: Casting chorus girls is hard work but somebody has to do it as seen in this 1951 photo.

MAD ABOUT MUSIC
UNIVERSAL—FEBRUARY 27, 1938

MAD ABOUT MUSIC
COMPOSER: Jimmy McHugh
LYRICIST: Harold Adamson
PRODUCER: Joe Pasternak
DIRECTOR: Norman Taurog
SCREENWRITERS: Felix Jackson and Bruce Manning

Synopsis
Gloria pretends that her father is a great explorer. Her mother and a stranger go along with the lie and find themselves attracted to each other. At the finale, little Gloria is happy at last.

Cast
Deanna Durbin ....Gloria Harkinson
Herbert Marshall ....Richard Todd
Gail Patrick ....Gwen Taylor
Arthur Treacher............Tripps
William Frawley ....Dusty Turner
Marcia Mae Jones........Olga
Helen Parrish ....Felice
Jackie Moran ....Tommy
Elisabeth Risdon...........Annette Fusenot

Deanna Durbin leads her gal pals on a bike ride through the Alps. We love this photo because it was so obviously snapped on a set—a beautiful set, yes, but so . . . settish, if you know what we mean.

I
N *MAD ABOUT MUSIC*, DEANNA DURBIN PLAYS A YOUNG GIRL SENT AWAY TO A SWISS BOARDING school by her mother. She makes up a father figure to avoid the taunts of her school-mates. In one scene, she's locked in a train compartment unable to pay for a ticket. To signal to the man masquerading as her father that she's on the train, she sings, "I Love to Whistle" at the top of her lungs. Perhaps it's a precursor to Doris Day's "Que Sera Sera" in *The Man Who Knew Too Much*.

Durbin was the most popular in a long line of young sopranos including Kathryn Grayson and Jane Powell. Both of the latter had more personality than Durbin, perhaps because they went through the MGM star-making machinery, but Durbin's spunk, good looks, and voice carried her through picture after picture. Jane Powell, also under Pasternak, perpetuated the Miss-Fix-It plots of Durbin's—often playing matchmaker to single parents, etc. Powell eventually got away from the interpolated classical number routine in her films and graduated to being a real actress that could handle story songs. Durbin seldom sang songs in character; she was always peddling her bike (as in *Mad About Music*) or in a church or concert hall. In her one integrated musical, *Can't Help Singing*, she finally let go of Gounod and Arditi in favor of some excellent songs by Kern and Harburg—but even these expressed only basic primal emotions such as happiness ("Can't Help Singing") or yearning ("More and More").

RIGHT: Clockwise from left, director Norman Taurog, Herbert Marshall, Deanna Durbin, and, at the camera, cinematographer Joseph Valentine. No, the photo wasn't taken by Busby Berkeley.

BOTTOM LEFT: Herbert Marshall gives Deanna Durbin a kiss on the forehead—though it looks as if he's fallen asleep.

Universal bought the rights to the Broadway hit *Up in Central Park* for Durbin. The Broadway score by Sigmund Romberg and Dorothy Fields featured such hits as "Close as Pages in a Book" and "April Snow," but for the film, most of the score was dropped—including those two songs.

Our question is, did audiences really want to hear semi-operatic arias and art songs in pictures or was it the studios' way of classing up their reputations? Studios wanted a way to give basically uninteresting performers more oomph. Certainly, Jeanette MacDonald didn't need high falutin' music to prove she was a good actress but her career goal was to play the Metropolitan Opera in New York.

There was another reason for all this highbrow music encroaching on a populist medium. Upon closer examination, we see that MacDonald and Powell appeared together in *Three Daring Daughters* (along with Jose Iturbi). It was produced by Joe Pasternak and, surprise, many of Durbin's pictures, including *One Hundred Men and a Girl*, were also Pasternak productions. So, we have to thank/blame him for giving us such indelible musical moments/bathroom breaks in movies.

Lastly, the movie industry felt it their duty to educate and elevate audiences via culture and high art. *Fantasia* is an extreme example. Sure, not everybody liked it, but movies nurtured budding opera lovers and concertgoers.

Although the plot of *Mad about Music* is typical fluff, Deanna Durbin and her considerable vocal prowess make it a charming affair. She might never have achieved the artistic heights of her fellow sopranos, but since she retired at such a young age, we will never know what her future in motion pictures would have been. ∎

SONGS

"Chapel Bells" ▪ "I Love to Whistle" ▪ "A Serenade to the Stars"

Deanna Durbin

Deanna Durbin was Universal's answer to Judy Garland, only without the neuroses. It sort of makes sense, since Durbin and Garland costarred in the short *Every Sunday* for MGM in 1930. Metro didn't quite know what to do with either of them and by the time Louis B. Mayer decided to keep both, Durbin had signed with Universal. Soon, she was the sweetheart of the Universal lot, which must have rankled Mayer. She matured admirably, didn't make any waves whatsoever, and her movies made a bundle. In fact, along with Abbott and Costello, the Wolfman, and his horror brethren, she kept the studio in business. So, why didn't we ever see *Deanna Durbin meets Dracula*? It wouldn't have been beneath the studio to do such a thing; they did pair Abbott and Costello with Frankenstein and the rest of the bogeymen. Anyway, Durbin was pretty and polite with equal dollops of feistiness and sweetness. She could sing sweetly or jazzily and excelled in her classical warblings, clearly more comfortable with operatic arias than were her contemporaries at other studios. Durbin made it all seem easy. None other than Leopold Stowkowski costarred with her in *One Hundred Men and a Girl*. In the cast lists of such Durbin films as *Nice Girl?* and *That Certain Age*, you'll see no dancers and no other singers. She might sing one or maybe two pop songs in her films but the rest of the scores are made up of art songs or classical arias. *Can't Help Singing* (yet another film influenced by *Oklahoma!*) was a nostalgic look at the gold rush era and for it Universal hired Jerome Kern and E. Y. Harburg to write the score and featured her in glorious Technicolor. Now, isn't that more Metro than Universal? What were they thinking? Durbin is also unique in that she retired at a mere twenty-seven years old, after *For the Love of Mary* in 1948. Since then, she has never looked back or given an interview.

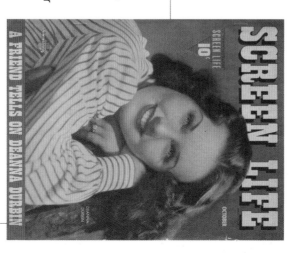

SCREEN LIFE

A FRIEND TELLS ON DEANNA DURBIN

MARY POPPINS

WALT DISNEY—AUGUST 29, 1964

Synopsis

Mary Poppins teaches her young wards a valuable lesson: when passed over for the film version of a stage play in which you starred, keep a stiff upper lip, do another project, and win the Oscar.

Cast

Julie Andrews	Mary Poppins
Dick Van Dyke	Bert and Mr. Dawes Senior
Karen Dotrice	Jane Banks
Matthew Garber	Michael Banks
David Tomlinson	Mr. Banks
Glynis Johns	Mrs. Banks
Hermione Baddeley	Ellen
Reta Shaw	Mrs. Clara Brill
Elsa Lanchester	Katie Nanna
Arthur Treacher	Constable
Reginald Owen	Admiral Boom
Ed Wynn	Uncle Albert
Jane Darwell	The Bird Lady

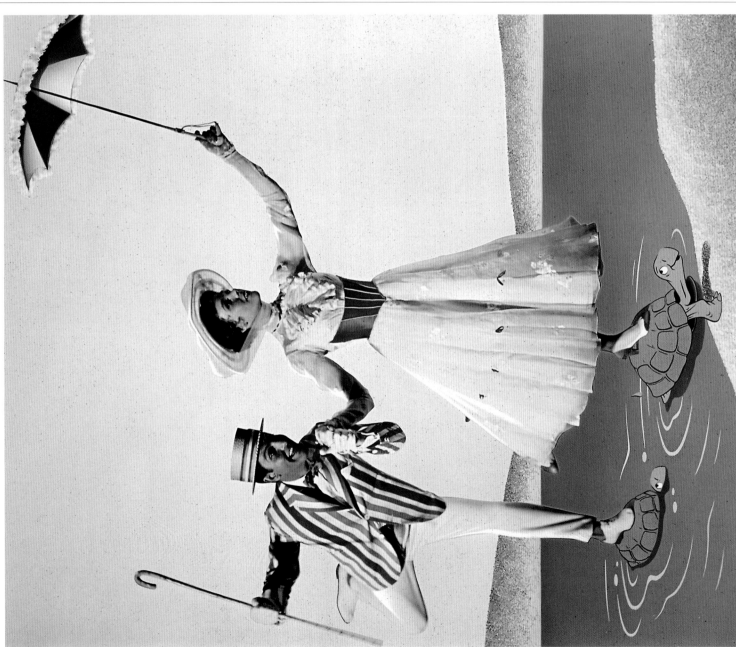

Dick Van Dyke and Julie Andrews hitch a ride on two turtles (whose names are lost to history).

JUST WHEN WALT DISNEY'S ANIMATED FEATURES WERE OPENING TO DISAPPOINTING CRITICAL and financial receptions, the old master produced the finest live action (melded with animation) feature in the studio's history.

Its artful combination of genres is but one reason for its great success. Another element that sets it apart from other films of the era, animated or not, is the score by Disney contract songwriters, Richard M. and Robert B. Sherman. The brothers had written hits for Disney before but somehow *Mary Poppins* caught their imagination in a special way. Every song fleshes out the characters perfectly while advancing the action—all without being obvious or cloying.

Casting, direction, and production design also came together in harmony with the Mary Poppins story. Even still, some Poppinsites objected to the changes from P. L. Travers's original books. Really, they had little to complain about, especially in comparison with what Disney did to Grimm's fairy tales, the legend of Robin Hood, Pinocchio, and other adapted works. Those plots were simplified considerably, scrubbed of sexuality, delivered from unhappy endings, and otherwise bowdlerized. In the case of *Mary Poppins*, the changes were all for the better.

The original books were made up of stories related only by their characters. The Disney crew drew incidents from the books and made a loose structure around them. The story of the Banks family serves the pieces well and the addition of Bert, the chimney sweep, and his relationship with Mary keeps the stories interesting for all ages.

Speaking of Bert, it's interesting to note that, despite his obvious talents, Dick Van Dyke never had a very successful film career. His portrayal of Bert shows what he could have accomplished if given the right opportunities. Bert's devil-may-care personality makes him a wonderful foil for Mary's somewhat stern, regimented view of life.

The most surprising thing about *Mary Poppins* is how it stands alone at the apex of Disney film musicals. Although members of the same production team, including the Sherman brothers, worked on other live musicals with animation elements, they were all stinkers.

The Happiest Millionaire, the last original musical produced by Walt Disney before his death, opened in 1967. Staff songwriters Richard M. and Robert B. Sherman were again on hand, and the film is a good example of the Disney style of this period: a flat, over-lit sitcom look. It included something old—Gladys Cooper and Greer Garson; something new—John Davidson and Lesley Ann Warren in their screen debuts; something borrowed—the plot about family bickering around upcoming nuptials; and nothing blue—just squeaky clean, mild humor. Oh, and it starred Fred MacMurray and Tommy Steele.

The One and Only; Genuine, Original Family Band premiered in 1968 to mediocre reviews. The Sherman brothers provided a title song and were then convinced by Disney that the film needed to be made into a full-fledged musical. Robert Sherman felt the material wasn't strong enough but perhaps that was Disney's point also. The film falls right into the Disney tradition of honoring the Midwest by proclaiming its overly sentimental and corny clichéd values, placing handsome but boring John Davidson and pretty but bland Lesley Ann Warren at the center of the action. By contrast, think about *The Music Man*,

SONGS

■ "Chim Chim Cher-ee" ■ "Feed the Birds (Tuppence a Bag)" ■ "Fidelity Fiduciary Bank" ■ "I Love to Laugh" ■ "Jolly Holiday" ■ "Let's Go Fly a Kite" ■ "The Life I Lead" ■ "The Perfect Nanny" ■ "Sister Suffragette" ■ "A Spoonful of Sugar" ■ "Stay Awake" ■ "Step in Time" ■ "Supercalifragilisticexpialidocious"

ABOVE: Julie Andrews is radiant as she waits for her setup.

TOP LEFT: Dick Van Dyke and the chimney sweeps dance over the rooftops of London.

TOP RIGHT: Dick Van Dyke as Mr. Dawes Senior with Julie Andrews's Mary Poppins. Note: They don't appear together in any scenes.

The Sherman Brothers

The Sherman Brothers, Richard M. and Robert B., were the sons of Al Sherman, a good, solid second-tier pop songwriter. They must have shocked their father when they penned hits for the likes of Annette Funicello. Disney snapped them up and put them under contract. They certainly did him proud. The Shermans won two Academy Awards for *Mary Poppins* and contributed the love-it-or-hate-it "It's a Small World" to the Pepsi Cola pavilion at the New York World's Fair in 1964. Their songs for *The Jungle Book* are right up there with the best of Disney's animation scores. The brothers' strength is in writing deceptively simple melodies and rhythms that fulfill all the roles of good theatrical songs but can be appreciated outside the score of the film. Their first non-Disney film was *Chitty Chitty Bang Bang*. Their later film scores became somewhat formulaic. *Mary Poppins* had "Supercalifragilisticexpialidocious" and "Chim Chim Cher-ee," so *The Happiest Millionaire's* score included "Fortuosity" and "Bye-Yum Pum Pum." Their other film musicals include *Bedknobs and Broomsticks*, *The Aristocats*, *The Slipper and the Rose*, and *The One and Only, Genuine Original Family Band*.

a totally satisfactory reflection of the Midwest, warts and all, that doesn't diminish its so-called values.

In 1971, the *Mary Poppins* team reunited for *Bedknobs and Broomsticks*, which emulated *Poppins's* mix of live action and animation. Angela Lansbury proved to be a tart heroine but, despite excellent production values all round, the film never really takes off.

The worst example of the genre was probably 1977's *Pete's Dragon*, starring Helen Reddy, Mickey Rooney, and Jim Dale, the last just as talented and charismatic as Dick Van Dyke and just as inexplicably lacking a substantial film career. The movie did boast the Academy Award–nominated song, "Candle in the Wind" by Al Kasha and Joel Hirschhorn, but the script and score were an energetic but charmless affair.

All of which make it the more curious that *Mary Poppins* came off so brilliantly. Julie Andrews, fresh off not being cast in *My Fair Lady*, certainly won the sympathy vote of critics and audiences and proved her movie cred. Speaking of Andrews, many critics believe that *Mary Poppins* is a superior film to Andrews's subsequent musical outing, *The Sound of Music*. In terms of imagination and spirit at least, they are absolutely correct. ■

TOP LEFT: Julie Andrews comes off the set to meet with Walt Disney.

TOP RIGHT: Richard M. Sherman, Robert B. Sherman, Irwin Kostel, Dick Van Dyke, and Julie Andrews hear the songs for the first time.

BOTTOM: Julie Andrews in her first Broadway show, *The Boy Friend*.

Julie Andrews

Pert, positive, and pretty, Julie Andrews began her American career in the winsome, gently spoofy Broadway musical *The Boy Friend*. She and the show were a hit and next up was one of the greatest roles in musical theater history, Eliza Doolittle in *My Fair Lady*. Still not a big enough name for Jack Warner to cast her in the film version, she went on to *Mary Poppins* and snagged an Academy Award, thanking Warner in her acceptance speech. Then it was on to Universal Pictures' highest grossing movie to date, *Thoroughly Modern Millie*, another '20s spoof (though shorter on satire). Andrews then outdid herself in the most successful film musical of all time, *The Sound of Music*. Realizing that hanging around on screen with animated penguins and nuns (same difference) wasn't good for her sexless image, she turned to more adult fare. She played British actress Gertrude Lawrence in *Star!* which failed to live up to its exclamation point. It was a big, bloated musical with some good production numbers—including "Berlington Bertie," the simplest number in the film—but the overall result ws as stodgy and gummy as bad treacle pudding. The *Sound of Music* team pushed too hard to prove Andrews could play a soignee bitch. The result was a joyless affair. *Victor/Victoria*, directed by husband Blake Edwards and released in 1982, was a socko farce about a woman dressing like a man, having other men fall for him/her, and generally confusing the populace. Although she made more films and had her own television variety show, musical film projects including *Say It with Music* and *She Loves Me* fell through. *Darling Lili* was an even bigger bomb than *Star!*, killing off the roadshow cycle. She never made another film musical as by then musicals had gone out of favor in Hollywood and with the public.

SINGING COWBOYS

THE GREAT TRAIN ROBBERY (FILMED WAY OUT WEST IN FORT Lee, New Jersey, in 1903) was a seminal work in the history of motion pictures, so it stands to reason that westerns were staples of the screen right from the start. But of course it took the advent of sound for the singing cowboy to become an institution. Ken Maynard was the first of the singing cowboys, warbling on horseback for the first time in the 1930 Universal picture, *Sons of the Saddle*. John Wayne incongruously appeared in the 1933 film, *Riders of Destiny* as a (dubbed) singing cowboy named Singin' Sandy Saunders. Do we have to tell you it was his only foray in the genre?

Riders of Destiny was the first film for Lone Star Productions. With movies like that, it's no surprise that the company lasted only two years. Gene Autry followed, and enjoyed a long career as perhaps the greatest singing cowboy of all. For the most part, Autry's westerns took place in contemporary times. His first picture, a serial titled *The Phantom Empire*, featured him singing on the *Radio Ranch* show. When Autry left Republic Studios in 1937, he was replaced by Roy Rogers, who surpassed Autry in his fame.

There were other singing cowboys, most notably Tex Ritter, Dick Foran, Eddie Dean, and Kirby Grant. Rex Allen came late to the game, debuting in the 1950s. Herb Jeffries was the one and only black singing cowboy. (See our chapter on black musicals for more about him.) There was even a singing cowgirl, Dorothy Page, who made three films for Grand National Pictures in 1939. Of course, later on, Dale Evans joined her husband, Roy Rogers, on the big screen and small. Sadly, when Rogers's movies were shown on television, they had to be cut down to make room for commercials. The easiest way to cut the pictures was to eliminate songs, so we were denied the pleasure of hearing the wonderful songs written and performed by such classic western songwriters as Bob Wills and the Sons of the Pioneers. It's also unfortunate that these B pictures by decidedly second-rate studios have not been remastered: on the rare occasions that they are shown, the prints tend to be horrible.

LEFT: Lynne Roberts, as Sue, gives Gene a kiss on the cheek while Sterling Holloway looks pained in *Sioux City Sue*.

BELOW: Co-stars and best friends Gene and Champion.

MEET ME IN ST. LOUIS

COMPOSER: Hugh Martin
LYRICIST: Hugh Martin
PRODUCER: Arthur Freed
DIRECTOR: Vincente Minnelli
SCREENWRITERS: Irving Brecher and Fred F. Finklehoffe
SOURCE: Based on the short story collection *5135 Kensington Avenue* by Sally Benson
CHOREOGRAPHER: Charles Walters

Synopsis

Psychologists agree that moving into a new house can be one of our most traumatic experiences. Apparently, that is especially when bells (or, rather, trolley clangs) accompany the appearance of the dreamy boy next door. Add a world's fair and you've got—a musical.

Cast

Judy Garland	Esther Smith
Margaret O'Brien	"Tootie" Smith
Mary Astor	Mrs. Anna Smith
Leon Ames	Mr. Alonzo Smith
Lucille Bremer	Rose Smith
Joan Carroll	Agnes Smith
Henry H. Daniels Jr.	Lon Smith Jr.
Tom Drake	John Truett
Marjorie Main	Katie
Harry Davenport	Grandpa
Robert Sully	Warren Sheffield

MEET ME IN ST. LOUIS

MGM—JANUARY 1945

Margaret O'Brien and Judy Garland, the two top-billed stars of *Meet Me in St. Louis.*

C ONSIDERING THAT JUDY GARLAND HAD BALKED AT APPEARING IN THE PICTURE, IT was something of a miracle that *Meet Me in St. Louis* was made at all. MGM had a hold on a Technicolor camera and needed to use it. The four existing script drafts for *Meet Me in St. Louis* weren't up to snuff, but it seemed that the story was the only thing in the MGM pipeline that could be shot in Technicolor. Arthur Freed approached screenwriters Irving Brecher and Fred Finklehoffe and ordered them to write a whole new script based on Sally Benson's "Kensington Avenue" stories. The two writers outlined a story and Finklehoffe left the project for other assignments. Brecher continued alone and, with the input of director Vincente Minnelli, came up with a workable script. But Judy Garland, under the influence of her lover Joseph Mankiewicz, was sure she would be upstaged by little Margaret O'Brien. So Freed assigned Brecher to take Garland into a room and read her the script, with the goal of convincing her to play the part.

Brecher read the script out loud to Garland and, as he described in his autobiography, *The Wicked Wit of the West*, "When I got to Margaret O'Brien's lines as Tootie the child, I kind of threw them away like they weren't there. You could barely hear them, they were in the sewer or I mumbled like it was nothing. At the same time, in every scene, I emphasized everything Judy was saying, delivered in a style that equaled the greatest line she ever heard." Brecher's performance of that script surely deserved an Academy Award; it convinced Garland that she and the script were perfectly matched.

And, of course, they were. Arthur Freed ordered the whole Halloween sequence cut from *Meet Me in St. Louis*. Luckily, he agreed to leave the scene in for one preview and the script were perfectly matched. The audience (especially Freed's guests Ira and Leonore Gershwin) convinced him to retain it.

In addition to the *Over the Rainbow* incident, Judy Garland was involved in another near-miss of a classic song in one of her films. In his autobiography, *The Boy Next Door*, Hugh Martin recalls working on "Have Yourself a Merry Little Christmas." Ralph Blane thought that the lyric "fit very naturally into the script because

Esther is very despondent at that point, so perhaps the lugubrious lyric I had written would be what they all wanted."

When Blane finished singing the song to Freed and Roger Eden, they laughed. Blane came to Martin the next day and said he had sung the song to Judy Garland who told him, "If I sing

that lyric to little Margaret O'Brien, the audience will think I'm a monster." Martin told Edens, "You tell Judy that if she wants the melody, she's gotta take the lyric—period!" Tom Drake, the actor who played the boy next door in the picture, bought Martin a cup of coffee and told the songwriter, "Hugh, this is potentially a very great and important song. I feel that in my guts. Now listen to me. Don't be a stubborn idiot. Write a lyric for that beautiful melody that Judy will sing. You'll thank me." Martin was convinced and changed the offending lyric. The song became exactly what Tom Drake promised, a very great and important song.

We assume that movies that are now classics were smooth sailing. They look so perfect, so natural, so right. But in reality, some of the greatest of films, including *Gone with the Wind*, *Casablanca*, *The Wizard of Oz*, and *Meet Me in St. Louis*, turned out as well as they did because of a strange mixture of genius and luck and opportunity. If MGM hadn't needed to use a Technicolor camera and if Hugh Martin not agreed to change his lyric, and if Irving Brecher hadn't been able to convince Judy Garland to play the part of Esther, and if the preview audience hadn't embraced the Halloween sequence, we wouldn't have one of the greatest films in motion picture history. ∎

ABOVE: Girl gets boy! Judy and Tom Drake take in the magnificence of the World's Fair.

TOP: Judy, on the famous trolley, tells her gal friends all about the boy next door. Will she get him?

"That idiot! Listening to Mankiewicz's cock . . . she's lucky she's alive! I'd like to kick her ass 'til her teeth fall out."

—*Vincente Minnelli to Irving Brecher, when Joe Mankiewicz convinced Judy Garland, with whom he was having an affair, that to do Meet Me in St. Louis would kill her career. (Minnelli ended up marrying Garland.)*

Vincente Minnelli

Vincente Minnelli was first and foremost a brilliant artistic director, his impeccable taste and artistic sensibility serving him well on Broadway and in Hollywood. Minnelli made his first impression as a costume and set designer at Radio City Music Hall and he soon directed its show utilizing his unerring eye for movement, color, and design. He was given the chance to direct on Broadway with the Dietz and Schwartz musical revue *At Home Abroad*. After stints on two more revues, Minnelli was brought by Arthur Freed to MGM, where he directed his first picture, *Cabin in the Sky*, starring Ethel Waters. Minnelli's sense of style, his perfectionism—and his kindness—took him to the top of the list of MGM's directors. Responsible for such films as *An American in Paris*, *Gigi*, *Kismet*, *Father of the Bride*, and *Meet Me in St. Louis*, Minnelli was one of the linchpins of MGM's picture factory.

Behind the Screen

■ Hugh Martin: Ralph Blane and I had dinner at the Tic-Toc, Hollywood Blvd. and Ivar Street. On our way out we passed Judy Garland and Vincente Minnelli. As we left, they said, "We'll see you at the recording." "What recording?" we said blankly. "*Meet Me in St. Louis*," they said, "the Decca recording." "Very interesting," we said. "I think we might drop in on you." No one had invited us!! I think all good songwriters hated the movies—for just that sort of reason. The one exception was Jerome Kern; he didn't seem to hate California—or find it cold and damp!

TOP RIGHT: Vincente Minnelli, safely behind the camera, films *On a Clear Day You Can See Forever* with Barbra Streisand.

CENTER: Vincente Minnelli prepares for the musical *Mata Hari* with costumer Irene Sharaff and Melissa Mell. Minnelli probably should have worried more about the show and less about the hat; it closed in D.C. and never made it to Broadway.

LEFT: Margaret O'Brien and her pals on Halloween, planning to make mischief.

RIGHT: Jane Powell and Debbie Reynolds in *Athena*.

BOTTOM LEFT: Hugh Martin, Beatrice Lillie, and Timothy Grey prepare for the Broadway musical *High Spirits*.

BOTTOM RIGHT: Judy Garland is over the moon at having won the boy next door.

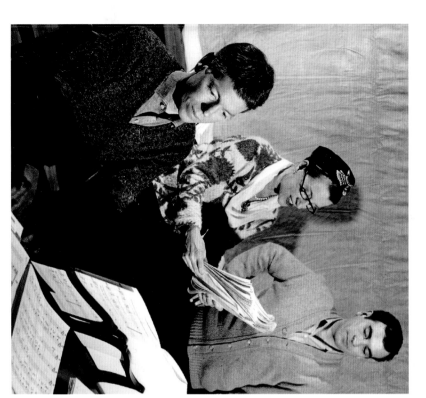

Hugh Martin

An unsung genius of Broadway and Hollywood, Hugh Martin is one of a select few songwriters who writes both music and lyrics. More than just a brilliant, sensitive songwriter, Martin is the inventor of the modern vocal arrangement. Up until Martin contacted Richard Rodgers while working on the stage show *The Boys from Syracuse*, singers were simply asked to perform in harmony and in unison. But for the song "Sing for Your Supper," Martin created an intricate vocal arrangement that literally changed the sound of Broadway and Hollywood. He worked as an arranger on shows by Cole Porter, Johnny Mercer, and Jule Styne. He usually shared songwriting credit with Ralph Blane, but the team wrote only one song as a true collaboration and, following *Best Foot Forward*, Blane never worked on any of the songs for which he was cocredited. Martin's scores for Broadway include *Best Foot Forward*, *High Spirits* (with Timothy Gray), *Make a Wish*, and *Look Ma I'm Dancin'*. His scores for films include *Athena*, *The Gold Rush*, and *The Girl Most Likely*. His vocal group, the Martins, sang in the theater and on radio and as backup for Kay Thompson. Martin also accompanied Judy Garland at her historic appearances at New York's Palace Theater. A gentle, smart, and savvy ninety-five years old, Martin is one of American music's most brilliant musicians.

THE MERRY WIDOW

MGM—NOVEMBER 2, 1934

THE MERRY WIDOW
COMPOSER: Franz Lehar
LYRICISTS: Lorenz Hart and Gus Kahn
DIRECTOR: Ernst Lubitsch
SCREENWRITERS: Samson Raphaelson and Ernest Vajda
SOURCE: Based on the operetta by Franz Lehár, Victor Leon, and Leo Stein
CHOREOGRAPHER: Albertina Rasch

Synopsis
Handsome Danilo tries his best to make the widow merry. (The title's a spoiler.)

Cast
Maurice Chevalier.........Count Danilo
Jeanette MacDonald.....Madame Sonia and Fifi
Edward Everett Horton...Ambassador Popoff
Una Merkel.....................Queen Dolores
George Barbier................King Achmet
Minna Gombell.................Marcelle
Ruth Channing...................Lulu
Sterling Holloway ....Mischa
Donald Meek.....................Valet
Herman Bing.....................Zizipoff

SONGS
"Girls, Girls, Girls!" ▪ "If Widows Are Rich"
▪ "Maxim's" ▪ "Melody of Laughter" ▪ "The Merry Widow Waltz" ▪ "Vilia"

Above: Ooh, la la. Maurice Chevalier enjoys two of the courtesans at Maxim's in Paris.

WHEN CHOOSING THE FILMS FOR INCLUSION IN THIS BOOK IT WAS HARD TO CHOOSE which Lubitsch, just as it was hard to pick which Astaire and Rogers, which Judy and Mickey, etc. In each case, all of their films contain marvelous moments. But *The Merry Widow* has the finest of all Lubitsch sequences, the scene in Maxim's. After the relative formality of life in Marshovia—lovingly spoofed by Lubitsch and his writers—Paris is the site of delightful debauchery. Chevalier is at home in Paris, and especially at Maxim's, where it seems every woman is under his spell.

It's clear to see why they are. Chevalier exudes panache. He's energetic, humorous, charming, and gay (in the old sense!). The women know they are all members of a not so exclusive club—they've all clearly slept with him and loved it. Since (like Gigi's aunt) they're all professional courtesans, they don't hold bear any ill will toward one another but celebrate their great good fortune. If you have any doubts about Chevalier's charms or why he was such a sex symbol throughout his career, have a look at this scene, which is fueled by champagne, deliriously intoxicating music, and beautiful women. It's Lubitsch's ideal of European sophistication.

In praising the film, let's not forget Lehar's melodies. The famous waltz is one of the finest musical compositions ever. It's just as mesmerizing as the dance itself; circles move

> "We had already done three pictures together. Wasn't it time for each of us to have a new partner?"
>
> —*Maurice Chevalier on Jeanette MacDonald*

Ernst Lubitsch

Yes, Ernst Lubitsch directed many successful non-musical comedies. In fact, *The Shop Around the Corner* was his own favorite film as well as that of many critics. But we especially love his musicals. Lubitsch started his film career in Germany in 1914. Eight years later, he came to Hollywood and, after one picture with Mary Pickford, soon found work with Warner Brothers. He moved to MGM in 1927 where he directed a silent version of *The Student Prince in Heidelberg*. His first three sound films, all made at Paramount, were musicals: *The Love Parade* with Jeanette MacDonald and Maurice Chevalier, *Paramount on Parade*, and *Monte Carlo*. Lubitsch's movies were risqué, sophisticated, and amused by the human condition—especially where sex was concerned. Mitteleuropa, with its juxtaposition of old ways and new ideas, was the setting for many of his farces, perhaps because he felt that Americans wouldn't feel threatened by the sexy antics of Europeans. Lubitsch pushed the envelope with 1932's *Trouble in Paradise*, an early victim of the Production Code. *Design for Living* translated Noel Coward's comedy of manners to the screen. *Ninotchka* made a comedian of Greta Garbo, and *To Be or Not to Be* was a controversial anti-Nazi comedy. They all had that indefinable lightness, wry worldview, and elegance that can be summed up by the phrase, "The Lubitsch Touch." Perhaps Lubitsch's films were so successful because he was so beloved by his collaborators. His assistant director on *The Merry Widow*, Joseph M. Newman, put it this way: "He had the greatest sense of humor of any individual I've ever met. The actors all loved him. He had a very . . . human quality about him. He was the type of man that became your friend after you met him once."

TOP RIGHT: Ernst Lubitsch, with his favorite cigar, directs Jeanette MacDonald and Maurice Chevalier. Jeanette seems perturbed while Maurice is only slightly shocked.

BOTTOM RIGHT: Jeanette MacDonald, as the eponymous widow, thinks about her options while her ladies-in-waiting . . . wait.

Behind the Screen

- Although Richard Rodgers and Lorenz Hart are both credited with additional lyrics, only Hart actually worked on them.
- Grace Moore was originally set to star in the movie.
- There was a real-life Prince Danilo who sued MGM after the 1925 version.
- In the 1970s, Ingmar Bergman announced a remake starring Barbra Streisand!

---

within circles in an almost feverish way. Never mind the lyrics; you probably can't catch them anyway. MacDonald's soprano (she does most of the singing in the film) sometimes obscures the words, but no matter, the tunes are good enough to stand on their own. The choreography of the famous waltz by the brilliant Albertina Rasch (a specialist in patterned dances) takes us round and round the dance floor and through mirrored hallways where we seem to see thousands of dancers. The black-and-white cinematography works to advantage here, with Rasch parlaying the white gowns of the women and the black formalwear of the men into interesting groupings that break up the rigidity of the waltz. And, hey, MacDonald and Chevalier make a heck of a dance team. Now *that's* dancing with the stars!

A master of the Ruritanian operettas, Lubitsch lets us in on the fact that while he does take all this fluff seriously, the lives of the people on screen are quite farcical. At the very top of the film, when Chevalier is marching through the charming streets leading his soldiers, he's singing "Girls, Girls, Girls." Every female hanging out the window has either slept with him or wishes she has. Just to make sure that we don't take any of the ensuing events too seriously, Lubitsch has two errant oxen wander into the scene, blocking the soldiers; so much for "Stouthearted Men." Throughout, it seems that Eros controls the fates with a sense of humor: There are liaisons behind closed doors, on the dance floor, and in private dining rooms. What to do when your kingdom is threatened with bankruptcy? Why, send in your most handsome soldier to woo the woman who owns more than half of every cow along with everything else.

In Lubitsch movies, there are no casualties in the battle of the sexes. On the contrary, misunderstandings actually lead to bliss. The path to true love is never easy but a few bumps along the way only make for a more delicious denouement. In the world that Lubitsch creates, men and women overcome their differences to form a more perfect union in the end.

By the way, a cliché started here. A man (it's always a man) is paid to woo a woman. Unexpectedly, they fall in love for real, but when she finds out he was paid, she doubts his sincerity. They break up and the man has to prove his love all over again. Haven't we seen that in a host of teen movies? ∎

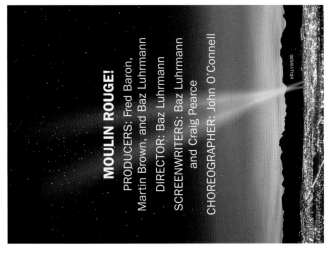

MOULIN ROUGE!

PRODUCERS: Fred Baron,
Martin Brown, and Baz Luhrmann
DIRECTOR: Baz Luhrmann
SCREENWRITERS: Baz Luhrmann
and Craig Pearce
CHOREOGRAPHER: John O'Connell

Synopsis

Poor Christian falls in love with the beautiful actress-courtesan, Satine, but a rich duke wants her all to himself. Or is it just the absinthe talking (and singing and dancing)?

Cast

Nicole Kidman	Satine
Ewan McGregor	Christian
John Leguizamo	Toulouse-Lautrec
Jim Broadbent	Harold Zidler
Richard Roxburgh	The Duke
Garry McDonald	The Doctor
Caroline O'Connor	Nini Legs in the Air
Kylie Minogue	The Green Fairy
Ozzy Osbourne	Voice of the Green Fairy

MOULIN ROUGE!

20TH CENTURY FOX—JUNE 1, 2001

Nicole Kidman and Ewan McGregor whip off a Bollywood number on the stage of the Moulin Rouge.

John Huston's 1952 film about the Moulin Rouge was one of the first to show close-ups of dancers' legs, hands, face, and torsos, along with the full-body shots popularized by Fred Astaire. Huston knew that the notorious nightclub broke all the rules and he wanted to do the same with his picture.

Likewise, director Baz Luhrmann wanted to break some rules—by taking everything over the top. Compare this lavish production with the films of Fred Astaire for a second: whereas he employed minimal camera movement, classic orchestrations, and straightforward interpretations of lyric and music, Luhrmann's film possesses a kind of overexcited, ADHD quality. It's the ultimate music video drawn out to movie length, purposely daring the audience not to be overwhelmed by its abundance of everything. In an effort to force the audience to pay attention, Luhrmann purposely refrains from explaining anything that happens in the first twenty minutes of the film. By forcing viewers to ground themselves and figure out what is going on, he enlists their active participation in the film experience.

Luhrmann had logical reasons for his frenetic editing and plotting, but Moulin Rouge seems to have provided license to a number of his contemporaries for the use of excess for its own sake. In any case, there is historical precedent for the kind of delightful excess that has inspired today's music videos. Check out Busby Berkeley's imaginative extravaganzas, including "Pettin' in the Park" and "Lullaby of Broadway." Flash forward to Elvis's pelvis thrusts in Jailhouse Rock, whose style owed more to Vegas than Broadway. Moulin Rouge! exploded all the prior ways of staging musical numbers. In its wake, the music video, which had become a bit passé, regained steam by employing Luhrmann's techniques. Perhaps he felt that his use of popular recordings would act as a shortcut to the emotions he was trying to elicit with each number.

ABOVE: Nicole Kidman surrounded by her fans.

BELOW: Nicole Kidman swinging over the proceedings.

BELOW LEFT: John Leguizamo, Garry MacDonald, Matthew Wittet, Jim Broadbent, Nicole Kidman, and Jacek Koman could not be happier with themselves. You'll notice Ewan McGregor's absence. Smart move, Ewan.

Moulin Rouge!'s absolute commitment to detail is reflected in its brilliant art direction and wealth of unified ideas. What might have been a bewildering hodge podge in the hands of another director feels harmonious here, as Luhrmann and company find ways to bring together the film's design, direction, and performance styles. Speaking of which, the lead actors are a revelation. Ewan McGregor and Nicole Kidman, both stunning to look at, have real chemistry and an intensity that cuts through the spectacle. And—who knew?—they can really sing! McGregor's somewhat soft persona and Kidman's ice-maiden tendencies somehow work beautifully together in their romantic scenes. They perfectly complement each other's strengths.

The cunning use of contemporary songs selected to comment upon the action makes the film more than a lavish period piece. The point Luhrmann seems to be making is that the highs and lows of relationships were no different in nineteenth-century Paris than they are here and now. The juxtaposition of a remote time and place with contemporary musical idioms gives this remarkable film a timelessness that is unusual in historical romances. Is there really much difference between the couple in *Moulin Rouge!* and the characters played by Jeanette MacDonald and Nelson Eddy? Not really; but *Moulin Rouge!*'s use of music, and its directorial style, lend emotional weight and believability to its melodramatic plot—and the honesty of the performances seal the deal. It's no wonder *Moulin Rouge!* scored a hit when it came out and remains a Netflix favorite. ∎

SONGS

"Children of the Revolution" (Mark Bolan) ∎ "Come What May" (David Baerwald) ∎ "Coup d'État" (various) ∎ "Elephant Love Medley" (various) ∎ "Fool to Believe" (Baz Luhrmann, Craig Pearce, Marius DeVries, and Craig Armstrong) ∎ "Górecki" (Andrew Barlow and Louise Rose) ∎ "Hindi Sad Diamonds Medley" (various) ∎ "Like a Virgin" (Billy Steinberg and Tom Kelly) ∎ "Nature Boy" (eden ahbez) ∎ "One Day I'll Fly Away" (Joe Sample and Will Jennings) ∎ "The Pitch Medley (Spectacular Spectacular)" (various) ∎ "Rhythm of the Night" (Diane Warren) ∎ "The Show Must Go On" (Brian May) ∎ "The Sound of Music" (Richard Rodgers and Oscar Hammerstein II) ∎ "Sparkling Diamonds Medley" (various) ∎ "El Tango de Roxanne Medley" (various) ∎ "Your Song" (Elton John) ∎ "Zidler's Rap (The Can-Can)" (Baz Luhrmann, Craig Pearce, and Marius DeVries)

THE MUPPET MOVIE

AFD—JUNE 22, 1979

THE MUPPET MOVIE

COMPOSERS: Paul Williams and Kenny Ascher

LYRICISTS: Paul Williams and Kenny Ascher

PRODUCER: Jim Henson

DIRECTOR: James Frawley

SCREENWRITERS: Jack Burns and Jerry Juhl

Synopsis

Call it *The Road to Hollywood* with Kermit in the Bing Crosby role and Fozzie Bear as Bob Hope. Throw in Charles Durning as Colonel Sanders.

Cast

Jim Henson..............*Kermit the Frog, Rowlf, Dr. Teeth, Waldorf, Link Hogthrob, and Swedish Chef (voice)*

Frank Oz ....*Miss Piggy, Fozzie Bear, Animal, Sam the Eagle, Marvin Suggs, and Swedish Chef*

Jerry Nelson..............*Floyd Pepper, Robin the Frog, Crazy Harry, Lew Zealand, and Camilla*

Richard Hunt..............*Scooter, Statler, Janice, Sweetums, and Beaker*

Dave Goelz..............*The Great Gonzo, Dr. Bunsen Honeydew, Zoot, Doglion*

Charles Durning............*Doc Hopper*

Miss Piggy conquers Hollywood.

THE MUPPETS OCCUPY THEIR OWN WORLD, A PLACE DEVOID OF ANXIETY AND STRESS and filled with whimsy, optimism, and childlike appreciation for the simple things in life. It's a world in which evil (which isn't really all that evil in the end) exists simply to propel the plot along. We say elsewhere in this book that animated villains have to have real teeth or there isn't any true suspense. The Muppet films are the exception to this rule. On the most basic level, these movies are directed to the youngest members of the audience. The true art is in the way successive layers of sophistication are applied so there's something for every age group—including adults.

The kind of simplicity these films represent is far from simple. For example, early in the film Kermit sits on a log in the swamp singing "The Rainbow Connection" while accompanying himself on the banjo. For everyone in the audience, it's a charming moment. Little kids like the setting, the colors, the ambience, the song, and Kermit. Older kids are additionally entranced by the lyric. Adults appreciate all of the above but also wonder (a) how the heck the filmmakers got Kermit to strum a banjo and (b) how he is being operated in what is obviously a pool of water. Well, we'll tell you. Jim Henson, the creator, voice, and manipulator of Kermit, had to endure five days of sitting in a modified oil drum, breathing through a tube, and watching a monitor to coordinate Kermit's movements.

Another mystery is how Fozzie drives a Studebaker (and why a Studebaker?). We know, but we won't tell. Why risk ruining the magic? After watching the Muppets for a while, we adults turn into children and accept the impossible as normal. Thanks to the gifts of the Muppeteers (hey, we made that up!), we begin to believe that Kermit, Miss Piggy, and the rest of the Muppets are real beings with distinctive personalities. Of course we also

SONGS

"Can You Picture That" ■ "I Hope That Somethin' Better Comes Along" ■ "I'm Going to Back There Someday" ■ "Movin' Right Along" ■ "Never Before Never Again" ■ "Rainbow Connection"

believe that Homer, Bart, Lisa, Maggie, and Marge Simpson are real—unless we think about it. And most of the time, we prefer not to think about it.

It's not like that for most of the Disney fairy tales, during which we are constantly aware that we're watching animated characters. Perhaps that's because they're not like us in the same way the Muppets are. Sure, the Muppets can be sophomoric and the plot turns a bit wacky, but they are so sweetly human, right down to their foibles, character flaws (think about Miss Piggy's insufferable vanity), and heartfelt goofiness.

And in the best tradition of musical comedy, the songs are genuinely expressive of the characters singing them. The tunes have a sense of longing and romantic appeal and the lyrics express a devotion to the simple life. "Rainbow Connection" could turn sappy, but it never does because it never trades on clichés nor pushes its point of view. (By contrast, think of the horrible "Living Together, Growing Together" in *Lost Horizon*. Never mind that the movie is horrendous; the song is preachy and trite.) Rodgers and Hammerstein's noble ballads "You'll Never Walk Alone" and "Climb Ev'ry Mountain" could easily be parodied (and they have been)—but they have sincerity and true poetry on their side, along with the magnificent arrangements and powerful contexts. Their integrity can make even the most curmudgeonly among us a believer. So it is with the Muppets' songs. Joe Raposo, who wrote "It's Not Easy Being

Green" for Kermit, and *The Muppet Movie*'s songwriters, Paul Williams and Kenny Ascher, understand the value of understatement and honesty.

Yes, *The Muppet Movie* follows the conventions of a corny old movie genre, the road picture. But it comes to life because the characters are delightful, the events are surprising, and the feelings are so warm that we're happy to turn off our minds and go along with Kermit and Fozzie wherever they may take us—including right back to our childhood. ■

Behind the Screen

■ This would be the last film appearance by Edgar Bergen and Charlie McCarthy. Their first one was in 1930.

■ Stars making cameo appearances include Bob Hope, Carol Kane, Cloris Leachman, Orson Welles, Steve Martin, Paul Williams, Telly Savalas, Elliott Gould, Madeline Kahn, Milton Berle, Dom DeLuise, Richard Pryor, Austin Pendleton, and James Coburn.

ABOVE LEFT: Fozzie Bear and Kermit hit the road to Hollywood. Guess they couldn't get the Partridge Family bus.

ABOVE RIGHT: Kermit sings "The Rainbow Connection."

THE MUSIC MAN

WARNER BROTHERS—JUNE 19, 1962

THE MUSIC MAN

COMPOSER: Meredith Willson
LYRICIST: Meredith Willson
PRODUCER: Morton DaCosta
DIRECTOR: Morton DaCosta
SCREENWRITER: Marion Hargrove
SOURCE: From the musical *The Music Man* by Meredith Willson and Franklin Lacey
CHOREOGRAPHER: Onna White

Synopsis

They got trouble in River City, Iowa, and it's not the new pool table. It's grifter Harold Hill—but love will tame him.

Cast

Robert Preston.............Harold Hill
Shirley Jones...............Marian Paroo
Ronny Howard..............Winthrop Paroo
Buddy Hackett..............Marcellus Washburn
Pert Kelton.................Mrs. Paroo
Paul Ford...................Mayor Shinn
Hermione Gingold........Eulalie Mackechnie Shinn
Timmy Everett.............Tommy Djilas
Susan Luckey...............Zaneeta Shinn
Harry Hickox...............Charlie Cowell
Charles Lane...............Constable Locke
Mary Wickes................Mrs. Squires

SONGS

"Being in Love" • "Gary Indiana" • "Goodnight My Someone" • "If You Don't Mind My Saying So" • "Iowa Stubborn" • "It's You" • "Lida Rose" • "Marian the Librarian" • "Pick-a-Little, Talk-a-Little" • "Rock Island" • "The Sadder but Wiser Girl" • "Seventy-Six Trombones" • "Shipoopi" • "Sincere" • "Till There Was You" • "Wah-Tan-Ee" • "Wells Fargo" • "Will I Ever Tell You?" • "Ya Got Trouble"

Ssssh. Robert Preston, as Professor Harold Hill, causes a stir while romancing Shirley Jones as Marian the librarian.

O N BROADWAY, *THE MUSIC MAN* WAS A SLEEPER, AN UNANTICIPATED SMASH HIT. WHEN it came time to make the inevitable film version, Robert Preston, Pert Kelton, and the Buffalo Bills reprised their roles. Onna White again choreographed and the score was exactly as presented on Broadway, with the exception of one new song that replaced, "My White Knight" (perhaps because it was rumored that Frank Loesser had actually written the song). Morton DaCosta, director of the stage show, was brought on board to direct as well as produce.

Warner Brothers built River City (a stand-in for Meredith Willson's hometown of Mason City) on the backlot, and it rivaled Fox's set for *Hello, Dolly!* The cast rehearsed and rehearsed. The orchestra is spot on and the lip-synching is matchless. Everything is perfect.

And that's the problem. While the movie is completely enjoyable, beautifully acted, sung, and produced, there's something missing. It's too reverent, not cinematic enough, and a tad boring. DaCosta simply sets up the camera and lets it linger. There are cuts here and there but nothing particularly imaginative. The camera sometimes travels along as characters walk or march down the street, but it's almost as it you're watching a filmed version of the stage show. Compare the marching band camera setups and editing to those in Fox's *Stars and Stripes Forever*. Watch the "Marian the Librarian" number and then the barn-raising dance in *Seven Brides for Seven Brothers*. There's nothing wrong with Onna White's wonderfully athletic choreography, but the camera placement and cuts are mostly straight on, and numbers often culminate in a blackout with the characters in a spotlight. Pretty stagey.

There are a couple of other musicals in which the stage version was transferred to film virtually intact: *Damn Yankees* and *The Pajama Game*. George Abbott directed the stage shows of both and codirected the film versions. That "co" is key. Unlike DaCosta, knowing he was a film neophyte Abbott got veteran Stanley Donen to codirect. It was a film and the difference is striking. Although *The Music Man* has more opportunities for exciting numbers than either *Damn Yankees* or *Pajama Game* (what with the marching band, the "Trouble" number, and the scenes in the gym), there's a discernible lack of cinematic energy in the film, whereas the Abbott-Donen movies fairly leap off the screen.

So, Broadway purists, when it comes to transferring Broadway shows to film what you really want, beyond authenticity, is the presence of a strong, experienced director at the helm. *The Music Man* is an entirely watchable, professional, well-made movie musical—but it could have been so much more. ∎

> "Bob Preston never knew anything about his vocal chords—never knew he had any, as far as his ever having heard from them was concerned."
>
> —*Meredith Willson*

ABOVE: Robert Preston demonstrates the "thinkology" method of learning a musical instrument. That's Mary Wickes sitting on the left, in the purple hat.

BELOW RIGHT: Marian the librarian has an "Aha" moment when she realizes she loves Professor Harold Hill.

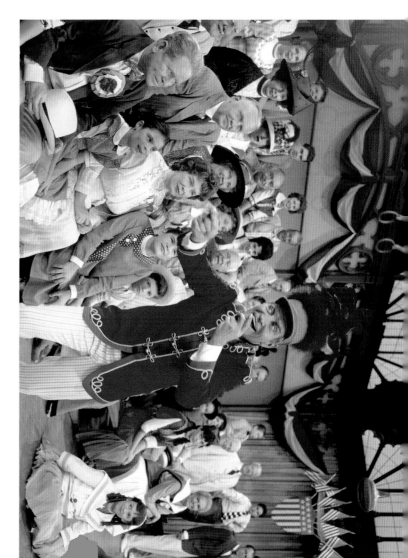

Shirley Jones

Beautiful, fresh-faced, feminine, but with a spine, Shirley Jones was the epitome of the all-American ingenue. None other than all-American songwriters Rodgers and Hammerstein discovered Jones and cast her as a replacement in the national tour of *Me and Juliet*. When it came time to cast the film versions of their *Oklahoma!* and *Carousel*, the songwriting team cast Jones (if only they'd have chosen her for *South Pacific*'s screen transfer, but that was not to be). She played a more stereotypical part against that big, handsome hunk of white bread, Pat Boone, in *April Love*. Then came the widow who needs a not-so-bad-man to bring her out of her shell, Marian the librarian, in *The Music Man*. Like Barbara Cook, who made several successful forays into nonmusicals, Jones proved she could act between warbles. She won an Oscar for her portrayal of a prostitute with an agenda in the fire and brimstone drama, *Elmer Gantry*. Jones was married to Broadway star Jack Cassidy and together they gave the world mini-heartthrob Shaun and Broadway performer Patrick (with whom she was pregnant during the filming of *The Music Man*). Cassidy's son from a previous marriage, David, was brought up by Jones and together they became the only mother-and-son team to have a hit song on the *Billboard* chart. Jones and Jack Cassidy appeared on Broadway in the best forgotten (don't worry, it is) musical, *Maggie Flinn*. With son David and some other semi-appealing moppets, she even had a hit sitcom, *The Partridge Family*.

ABOVE LEFT, TOP: Buddy Hackett tries on the latest Idaho fashions, courtesy of Robert Preston.

ABOVE LEFT, BOTTOM: Shirley Jones and Robert Preston inform Ron Howard that he has a bright future in the film business.

MY FAIR LADY

WARNER BROTHERS—DECEMBER 25, 1964

MY FAIR LADY

COMPOSER: Frederick Loewe

LYRICIST: Alan Jay Lerner

PRODUCER: Jack L. Warner

DIRECTOR: George Cukor

SCREENWRITER: Alan Jay Lerner

SOURCE: Based on the musical *My Fair Lady* by Alan Jay Lerner and Frederick Loewe

CHOREOGRAPHER: Hermes Pan

Synopsis

Drab to fab—Eliza Doolittle gets a makeover and then the bachelor. It's like two reality series in one!

Cast

Audrey Hepburn..........Eliza Doolittle

Rex Harrison..........Professor Henry Higgins

Wilfred Hyde-White.....Colonel Hugh Pickering

Stanley Holloway..........Alfred P. Doolittle

Gladys Cooper..........Mrs. Higgins

Jeremy Brett..........Freddy Eynsford-Hill

Mona Washbourne......Mrs. Pearce

Theodore Bikel..........Zoltan Karpathy

Isobel Elsom..........Mrs. Eynsford-Hil

Rex Harrison admires Audrey Hepburn, all dressed up in her Cecil Beaton finery.

P EOPLE RAIL ABOUT MUSICALS ADAPTED FROM BROADWAY HITS. "THEY HAD NO RESPECT for the material. None at all!" These folks yearn for literal translations from stage to screen. To which I say, be careful what you wish for. George Cukor's *My Fair Lady* is quite faithful but missing a couple of essential things—spontaneity and spirit. Although the script hews closely to the play (and to the spirit of Shaw's original), it's all treated with kid gloves. This is a movie with manners and decorum and good posture to a fault.

My Fair Lady was and is rightly considered the apex of musical theater: bright, witty, and intelligent. When you begin with such a great, towering property, what is there to do but respect it at all costs?

Audrey Hepburn is fine in the scenes at Ascot, when she's putting on airs, but as the guttersnipe she's a bit out of place with her perfect complexion, long beautiful neck, and charm-school bearing. Her performance is more plausible in the film *Funny Face*, where she plays an uptight, naïve intellectual transformed into a beautiful fashion model by Rex Harrison. Er, make that Fred Astaire. Since *Funny Face* was written for the screen, its creators didn't have to worry about being faithful to a stage masterpiece. Hepburn could play within her comfort zone, growing from a shy, immature girl into a beautiful woman without losing her sense of fun. The proof that she's mature? She takes romance very, very seriously.

Hepburn had made a splash onstage in *Gigi*, yet another tale of girlhood giving way to womanhood. Unlike Julie Andrews, who played the role of Eliza Doolittle on Broadway,

"I'm rich and famous. I don't have to be around." —Frederick Loewe on why he was absent during the making of the film

Hepburn was a star—but the property was the biggest star of all. Nothing less than total respect and admiration would do. So, George Cukor, et al., created a stolid, respectful piece. "Get Me to the Church on Time" was the most dynamic number in the film.

Nothing was left to chance. No freewheeling fun was permitted. In an interview with Gavin Lambert, Cukor told how he researched the sets and backgrounds. "In England, Beaton, Gene Allen and I looked at actual houses to get the architectural feel. We'd go through book after book of the period and suddenly something would hit us. 'Here's a significant detail,' we'd say. 'They'd have a gong in the hall.' Little details like that bring places and habits to life, like the stuffed animals on the second floor of Professor Higgins' house and the art nouveau in his mother's house. In the same way, we checked on all the techniques of phonetics. We discovered a man who'd been a pupil of Jones', the original of Shaw's Higgins. We made all the instruments he actually used, so all of that was correct."

Actually, all of that was incorrect. The viewer doesn't know or care about the rightness of the instruments or a gong in the hall. My Fair Lady's sets are like museum pieces and the show itself is treated as a very important artifact that must be admired but not touched. Contrast that with the experience of watching On the Town. Those sets capture the essence and spirit of New York City without one nod to the realities of Manhattan street life.

Perhaps My Fair Lady would have been a more enjoyable movie if the whole affair had been treated like a movie rather than a precious objet d'art. Its individual elements are a testament to the craftsmen of Hollywood, but the film as a whole feels impersonal, save the fire of Rex Harrison's performance. One wishes Cukor was allowed the boldness he exercised on A Star Is Born. However, for its many fans, My Fair Lady represents a very glamorous finale to classical Hollywood moviemaking. At the time, audiences and critics oohed and aahed over the movie and it won many awards, including Best Picture. Are we wrong or is the case that Best Picture musicals are never the ones we love? ■

SONGS

"Ascot Gavotte" ■ "Get Me to the Church on Time" ■ "A Hymn to Him" ■ "I Could Have Danced All Night" ■ "I'm an Ordinary Man" ■ "I've Grown Accustomed to Her Face" ■ "Just You Wait" ■ "On the Street Where You Live" ■ "The Rain in Spain" ■ "The Servants' Chorus" ■ "Show Me" ■ "Why Can't the English?" ■ "With a Little Bit of Luck" ■ "Without You" ■ "Wouldn't It Be Loverly" ■ "You Did It"

ABOVE: Audrey exhorts her horse to "move his bloomin' arse" at the Ascot races.

"He was the single most conceited man I ever knew. Well, I don't know whether that is the right word. Perhaps vain is a better word."

—André Previn, about Frederick Loewe

ABOVE LEFT: Cecil Beaton's original costume sketch for the Ascot dress.

ABOVE RIGHT: Audrey is cowed by Rex Harrison.

LEFT: Alan Jay Lerner and Frederick Loewe (at piano) play the score of Gigi for Audrey Hepburn.

Lerner and Loewe

Alan Jay Lerner and Frederick Loewe were men of the theater. Most of their work as a team was first produced on Broadway, and their musicals, including *Paint Your Wagon*, *Brigadoon*, *My Fair Lady*, and *Camelot*, were transferred to the screen with varying degrees of success. But in a couple of instances, they tackled Hollywood directly. Their first direct-to-screen musical was the smash hit *Gigi*, written just after the Broadway premiere of *My Fair Lady*. The partners went back to Broadway and the grueling experience of getting *Camelot* to opening night on Broadway in 1960. That experience was so exhausting that Loewe vowed to retire from composing. Fifteen years would pass before Lerner could convince him to return to the piano to write the score for the film *The Little Prince*. That score is underappreciated, probably because the movie was a critical disaster. And that was it for Frederick Loewe. Lerner had always liked to work more than Loewe did, and he had more debts, so when not working with Loewe Lerner turned to other collaborators, teaming with Burton Lane in 1951. The result was MGM's *Royal Wedding* with Fred Astaire and Jane Powell. "Too Late Now" was the hit song from that score. Lerner also contributed the screenplay for *An American in Paris*. Lerner and Lane later collaborated on the Broadway musical *On a Clear Day You Can See Forever*, which transferred to the screen in 1970 with Barbra Streisand in the lead role.

Behind the Screen

- Rex Harrison sang live during filming, which aided his performance immeasurably.

- James Cagney wouldn't come out of retirement to play Alfred P. Doolittle.

- Cockney-accented Cary Grant turned down the role of Higgins.

- George Cukor, actors' director par excellence, was second choice. The first choice, Vincente Minnelli, outpriced himself.

- *My Fair Lady's* high fidelity to its stage model extended to the familiar overture. Maintaining its full length necessitated stretching the opening credits with a montage of massed flowers.

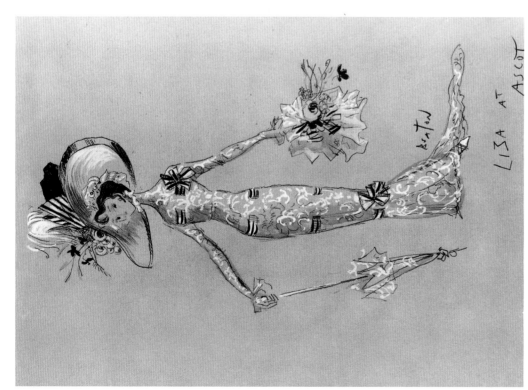

LISA AT ASCOT

BEATON

FOREIGN MUSICALS

AMERICA WASN'T ALONE IN CREATING MOVIE MUSICALS. ENGLAND AND France have a long tradition in the American style. But the advent of the Second World War stopped production of European films for the most part. After the war, the domination of American movies in the foreign market further hampered the attempts of local studios to make films.

In Britain, Gracie Fields and Jessie Matthews were the leading stars of musicals. Fields, in particular, made a series of hugely successful musical films though it was hard to tell one from another. Matthews was wooed by Hollywood but she never caught on there, despite being dubbed the female Fred Astaire. In the 1960s and '70s, the line between British and American film musicals blurred as many of the films were produced in Britain with British talent but financed by American studios. There were some wholly British film musicals made during this period, mainly rock-and-roll movies starring the likes of Cliff Richards and Herman's Hermits. You might have heard of the Beatles?

Over in France, René Clair directed one of the greatest of all musicals, *Le Million*, (1931), which, luckily for us, is available on DVD through Criterion. Clair also directed the 1930 hit, *Sous les toits de Paris*. After the war, France produced a series of operetta films starring heartthrob Luis Mariano with scores by Francis Lopez. Some French stage musicals, including Maurice Yvain's *Toi C'est Moi*, were transferred to the screen, but most of the French musicals of the 1940s and '50s featured bands as musical relief. In the 1960s, Jacques Demy achieved international success with two musical films featuring

scores by Michel Legrand: *Les Parapluies de Cherbourg* and *Les Demoiselles de Rochefort*. American musical performers Gene Kelly, George Chakiris, and Grover Dale were featured in the latter, along with a French cast. In recent years, French musicals have tended to relegate their musical numbers to the soundtrack rather than allowing the actors to perform. An exception is 2007's totally captivating *Les Chansons d'Amour*, which you can rent under the more prosaic-sounding *Love Songs*.

The 2006 Irish musical *Once*... (which would have been included among our 101 if it were an American film, along with *Le Million* and *Les Chansons d'Amour*), found success in the United States, even winning the Academy Award for Best Song. Oh, and in 2000 Bjork starred in and wrote the score for Lars Von Trier's *Dancer in the Dark*—but the less about that the better.

TOP LEFT: Jessie Matthews in the Rodgers and Hart musical, *Evergreen*.

BOTTOM: Nino Castelnuovo tells Catherine Deneuve that if it takes forever he will wait for her. But he doesn't in The Umbrellas of Cherbourg.

NASHVILLE

COMPOSER: Richard Baskin
PRODUCER: Robert Altman
DIRECTOR: Robert Altman
SCREENWRITER: Joan Tewkesbury

Synopsis

If you thought *Crash* was the first of its kind, think again. This is the quintessential film in which a bunch of unrelated people spend the whole picture pursuing separate paths, only to come together momentously at the end.

Cast

Keith Carradine	Tom Frank
Karen Black	Connie White
Lily Tomlin	Linnea Reese
Ronee Blakley	Barbara Jean
Henry Gibson	Haven Hamilton
Geraldine Chaplin	Opal
Timothy Brown	Tommy Brown
Ned Beatty	Delbert Reese
Shelley Duvall	L.A. Joan
Allen Garfield	Bennett
Barbara Harris	Albuquerque
Richard Baskin	Frog
Jeff Goldblum	Tricycle Man
Scott Glenn	Pfc. Glenn Kelly
Keenan Wynn	Mr. Green

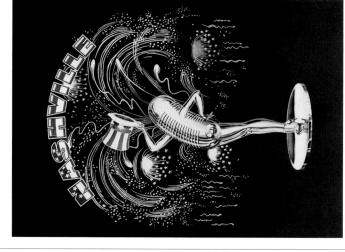

NASHVILLE

PARAMOUNT—JUNE 11, 1975

Henry Gibson and Barbara Baxley. His Replacement Party is hell bent on getting rid of those Commie Pinko liberals in Congress. They want to rewrite the Constitution and the national anthem. Sound familiar?

HEY KIDS, LET'S PUT ON A MOVIE MUSICAL! THAT CERTAINLY SEEMS TO BE THE Altman credo. Although screenwriter Joan Tewkesbury wrote a screenplay, Altman encouraged the performers to improvise their lines whenever they felt like it, and even write their own songs.

There's a certain percentage of the population that doesn't give much credit to country music—but many of them accepted the songs in *Nashville*. Keith Carradine's "I'm Easy," performed to quietly sexy perfection, even nabbed an Oscar and a Golden Globe. Conversely, the country music establishment didn't much care for the songs, or the movie itself for that matter. To them, the script seemed condescending, reducing their lives to clichés.

Did the Academy voters really separate Carradine's come-hither performance from the song itself? By the 1975 Oscars, the quality of songwriting for musicals had begun to deteriorate rapidly. "I'm Easy" was up against Kander and Ebb's song "How Lucky Can You Get" from *Funny Lady*; "Now that We're in Love" from *Whiffs*, by George Barrie and Sammy Cahn; Charles Fox and Norman Gimbel's "Richard's Window," written for *The Other Side of the Mountain*; and "Theme from *Mahogany* (Do You Know Where You're Going To)" by Michael Masser and Gerry Goffin. At least two of the songs are practically unknown today as, frankly, is "I'm Easy." (Of course, longevity isn't the only criterion, but it can be an indication of a song's quality.) "How Lucky Can You Get" is known because of Streisand's recording on the soundtrack album. The best-known song of the bunch is the "Theme from *Mahogany*," sung by Diana Ross. Still, none of these holds a candle to the great songs of Oscars past.

We used to think the "Theme from *Shaft*" was the worst song ever to win an Oscar, but that mantle has been passed to "It's Hard out Here for a Pimp," a song written by hip-hop band Three 6 Mafia and Cedric Coleman for the film *Hustle and Flow*. It's really not that we're old fuddy-duddies who can't keep up with the new music; it's that most of the newer songs don't have the emotion or craft that mark a great song.

Beginning in the '70s, most of the Best Songs have been self-contained, written to be played over the titles or end credits. (After all, there haven't been many musicals from which contextual songs could be drawn.) For better or worse, these songs serve the pop market, not the musical theater market. That's not to say that there haven't been any good songs written for pictures in the past three or four decades—but the standards are certainly lower.

Musical film and theater lovers have had to lower their musical expectations or hole up with their iPods. Even the flop stage and film musicals of the past don't sound so bad when compared to today's movie songs. By current standards, "I'm Easy" is a great song. It may not follow the rules of classic American popular songs, but at least it is evocative, well thought out and serves the dramatic needs of the character and plot.

And if *Nashville* has anything, it's characters and plots. A ragtag group of performers without a movie star among them, they're the quirkiest bunch of character actors that one could hope to find. That offbeat ensemble, sharing the dramatic burden of a rangy, unconventional story, is one of the reasons *Nashville* is so successful. Everyone is equal and their fates intertwine in surprising ways. We're constantly kept off balance because we expect Hollywood conventions and there are none to be found. We have no idea where the story is heading or where it will end up.

Because the acting is so natural and lines so conversational, *Nashville* feels like a documentary. The songs, written by the performers themselves for the most part, add to the sense of reality and give the film a unique flavor. They come across as real country songs, not ultrapolished Hollywood versions of the same. In arguably his best film, Altman hit upon a uniquely exciting way to construct a film. It's been imitated (even by Altman), but never improved upon. ∎

SONGS

"Bluebird" (Ronee Blakley) ∎ "The Day I Looked Jesus in the Eye" (Richard Baskin and Robert Altman) ∎ "Down to the River" (Ronee Blakley) ∎ "Dues" (Ronee Blakley) ∎ "For the Sake of the Children" (Richard Baskin and Richard Reicheg) ∎ "Honey" (Keith Carradine) ∎ "I Never Get Enough" (Richard Baskin and Ben Raleigh) ∎ "I Don't Know If I Found It in You" (Karen Black) ∎ "It Don't Worry Me" (Keith Carradine) ∎ "I'm Easy" (Keith Carradine) ∎ "Keep a 'Goin'" (Richard Baskin and Henry Gibson) ∎ "Let Me Be the One" (Richard Baskin) ∎ "Memphis" (Karen Black) ∎ "My Baby's Cookin' in Another Man's Pan" (Jonnie Barnett) ∎ "My Idaho Home" (C/L: Ronee Blakley) ∎ "Old Man Mississippi" (Juan Grizzle) ∎ "One, I Love You" (Richard Baskin) ∎ "Rolling Stone" (Karen Black) ∎ "Rose's Café" (Allan Nicholls) ∎ "Since You've Gone" (Gary Busey) ∎ "Sing (Sing a Song)" (Joseph Raposo) ∎ "Tapedeck in His Tractor" (Ronee Blakley) ∎ "(There's) Trouble in the U.S.A." (Arleight Barnett) ∎ "200 Years" (Richard Baskin and Henry Gibson) ∎ "Yes, I Do" (Richard Baskin and Lily Tomlin)

Behind the Screen

∎ Are you surprised that Gary Busey wrote a song for the film? It's because he was originally going to play the role of Tom. He was jettisoned but the song stayed in the film.

∎ Elliott Gould, Julie Christie, and newsman Howard K. Smith all had cameos in the film playing themselves.

CLOCKWISE FROM TOP: Henry Gibson as a Nashville country star with political ambitions; Lily Tomlin sings the gospel; Barbara Harris as a songwriter who's not as dumb as she acts and Karen Black as a singer who probably is; Geraldine Chaplin as the BBC reporter who acts more like a groupie; Keith Carradine's mantra is "I'm easy." Shelley Duvall wants him to prove it.

A NIGHT AT THE OPERA

MGM—NOVEMBER 15, 1935

A NIGHT AT THE OPERA

DIRECTOR: Sam Katz

SCREENWRITERS: George S. Kaufman
and Morrie Ryskind

CHOREOGRAPHER: Chester Hale

Synopsis

Illegal immigration has always been a huge problem in America. Right up there with slightly stiff, opera-singing ingénues.

Cast

Groucho Marx ....Otis B. Driftwood
Chico Marx......................Fiorello
Harpo Marx....................Tomasso
Kitty Carlisle...............Rosa Castaldi
Allan Jones ....Ricardo Baroni
Walter Woolf King.......Rodolfo Lassparri
Sig Ruman...................Herman Gottlieb
Margaret Dumont.........Mrs. Claypool

Behind the Screen

- The Marx Brothers wanted "Alone" cut from the film, but Allan Jones appealed to Irving Thalberg, who acknowledged that the comics might be experts in what was funny but Jones might be the better judge of a good song.

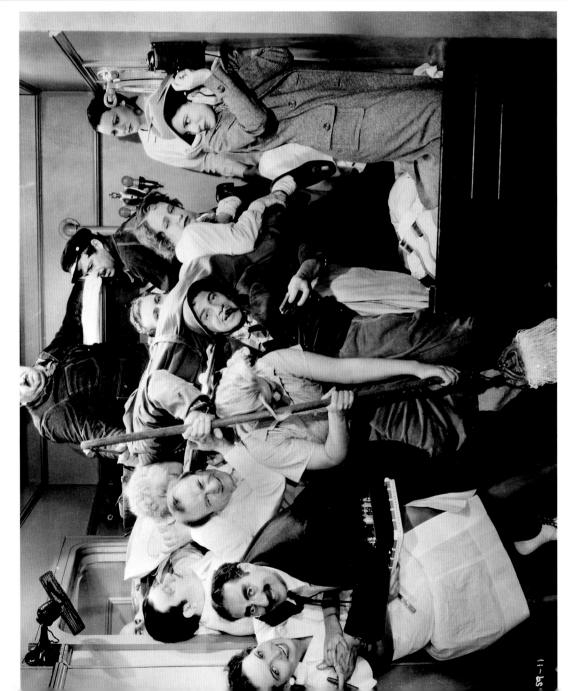

ABOVE: Is my Aunt Minnie in here? One of the greatest comic scenes in film history.

OPPOSITE TOP LEFT: Groucho wants to know how Walter Woolf King, as Rodolfo Lassparri, sleeps on his stomach with those big buttons on his pajamas. But just as Rodolfo is about to answer he gets a big headache.

OPPOSITE TOP RIGHT: Allan Jones gives the eye to Walter Woolf King, who's too busy flirting with Kitty Carlisle to notice.

A FTER YEARS AT PARAMOUNT, THE MARX BROTHERS WERE IN A SLUMP. WOMEN JUST didn't want to see their pictures. *Horse Feathers* and *Duck Soup* would find favor long after their original bookings but immediately after they came out. Paramount didn't want anything else to do with the quartet. When the brothers were summoned by MGM's producer extraordinaire, Irving Thalberg, Zeppo packed it in and became an agent, leaving Groucho, Harpo, and Chico to make MGM magic. At every meeting, the brothers insulted Thalberg, but instead of firing them on the spot, Thalberg, nicknamed "the Boy Wonder," was amused by their insolence. It dawned on him that the brothers' onscreen humor should arise from upending convention, skewering pretension, and flouting authority. He also figured out that they needed to have a solid plot underpinning their antics. Yes, they could still be zany and madcap, but their craziness had to exist within a quasi-serious context or audiences wouldn't care what happened. Thalberg also believed that the obligatory love story at the heart of each film needed to be taken seriously. No more boring, sappy ingenues: the Marxes needed to help a couple that deserved their ministrations.

All of this made sense to the trio, too—and a succession of script writers was assigned to what would be titled, *A Night at the Opera.* (What's more pretentious to middle American audiences than opera, after all?) It's worth pointing out that the third stab at a screenplay, by George Seaton and Robert Pirosh, made Groucho a Broadway producer determined to stage the worst opera in history. If he succeeded in producing a show that would close

quickly, no one would ever know that he sold the backers more than 900 percent of the show. Surprise, surprise, the opera is a smash hit. (Does that plot sound familiar? . . . Mel Brooks would of course use the same notion, but about a play, for *The Producers*.)

Obviously, that script wasn't made. Ultimately, George S. Kaufman and Morrie Ryskind were hired to write the final treatment. Gag man and script doctor Al Boasberg joined the mix to pump up the proceedings. Boasberg, all 300 pounds of him, was as much an iconoclast as the brothers. He told them and Thalberg that the script would be in his office one evening. They entered to find the office completely cleared of personnel, desks, lamps, telephones, everything. Groucho finally found the script, torn into pieces and glued to the ceiling. Once it was taken down and reconstructed, it turned out to be the famous stateroom scene.

To test the final script for laughs (and because the Marx Brothers started out as stage performers), it was decided to send the entire cast on the road to vaudeville theaters. As Kaufman once said, "We learned that when an audience does not laugh at a line at which they're supposed to laugh, then the thing to do was to take out that line and get a funnier line. So help me, we didn't know that before. I always thought it was the audience's fault."

Have you noticed that we've gotten this far but never mentioned the songs? It's not because they are beneath mention. There are some who consider *A Night at the Opera* to be a comedy with songs as opposed to a musical—but we disagree. For one thing, the film had a big hit song in Arthur Freed and Nacio Herb Brown's tune "Alone." And the numbers performed by Chico on the piano and Harpo on the harp perfectly communicate all that we need to know about their true personalities. Harpo reveals a depth to his psyche that isn't readily apparent from his lascivious man-child film persona. When playing the harp, Harpo reveals his soul. So, too, does Chico with his whimsical pianism. He invariably shows his happiness when entertaining children and, in this film, his democratic embrace of the steerage passengers and their spirit,

which is in clear contrast to the likes of Margaret Dumont's grande dame upstairs in first class.

Other Marx films might be more typical musical comedies—both *Cocoanuts* and *Animal Crackers* started as full-fledged Broadway musical vehicles for the brothers. But *A Night at the Opera* represents the Marxes at their apex. Unfortunately, it would be their last film under Thalberg. The great producer died before filming began on *A Day at the Races*. ■

> "Mr. Thalberg, do you want it Wednesday or good?"
> —*George S. Kaufman to Irving Thalberg, who was pushing him for a final script*

The Marx Brothers

The five Marx Brothers, Groucho (Julius), Chico (Leonard), Harpo (Adolph/Arthur), Zeppo (Herbert), and Gummo (Milton), began as a musical act in vaudeville, pushed and prodded by their stage mother, Minnie. When Groucho began ad-libbing during the act, it became clear that comedy might be his forte. The five eventually worked their way up to Broadway and Gummo left the act. The remaining four brothers appeared in a series of extremely successful musicals, summoned to Paramount Pictures where they would recreate their stage hits *Cocoanuts* and *Animal Crackers* for the screen. The Marxes' Paramount films fit the studio's mold exactly—they were loosely plotted, quickly shot, and their stars would do anything for a laugh. But in spite of (or perhaps because of) their slapdashery, they remain among the team's funniest. The team's first picture at Metro, *A Night at the Opera*, was a huge hit, but each succeeding film was a little less successful than the one before. Like many movie comedy teams, including Laurel and Hardy and Abbott and Costello, the Marx Brothers never knew when to quit. Eventually, the movies petered out. Chico led his orchestra and Harpo devoted most of his time to his family. Never a success as a family man, Groucho kept going on television and in concerts.

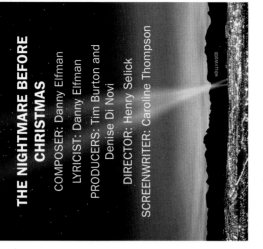

THE NIGHTMARE BEFORE CHRISTMAS

COMPOSER: Danny Elfman
LYRICIST: Danny Elfman
PRODUCERS: Tim Burton and Denise Di Novi
DIRECTOR: Henry Selick
SCREENWRITER: Caroline Thompson

Synopsis

Jack Skellington tries to bring Christmas to Halloween Town. Which is sort of like bringing Easter to Shaker Heights.

Cast

Danny Elfman	Jack Skellington (singing)
Chris Sarandon	Jack Skellington
Catherine O'Hara	Sally
William Hickey	Dr. Finkelstein
Glenn Shadix	Mayor
Paul Reubens	Lock
Ken Page	Oogie Boogie
Edward Ivory	Santa

THE NIGHTMARE BEFORE CHRISTMAS

TOUCHSTONE PICTURES—OCTOBER 29, 1993

Jack Skellington and his main squeeze (but not too hard), Sally.

Nerds rule and shy people have a lot more depth than anyone imagines. That's the story of Tim Burton growing up in Burbank, California, close to the Disney Studios—and that's the story of the main characters in his offbeat films. As a kid, Burton, living largely inside his head, had lots of time to imagine things. He was good at art but not at academics and he loved B pictures, especially the Corman horror films that starred Vincent Price. That particular form of the macabre fascinated him, as did stop-motion animation, especially that of the master in the field, Ray Harryhausen. No special effects snob, Burton also loved Godzilla, who was just a guy in a big rubber dinosaur costume. Perhaps it was the sense of the ridiculously false meant to be real that captivated him.

All these influences were bubbling around inside of him when Burton graduated from the Disney-supported California Institute of the Arts and found work as an animator on the Disney film, *The Fox and the Hound*. To say the least, that rather tedious affair did not prove a good fit. He next made a couple of short films: *Vincent*, which was animated, and *Frankenweenie* a live-action short. Each was a true expression of Burton's artistry. And which one starred Burton's idol, Vincent Price? Not the eponymous one, but *Frankenweenie*.

That film led indirectly to Burton's first feature directing gig. Stephen King, who has a similarly skewed view of reality (though his vision is darker than Burton's), saw the short and recommended the young artist as director of *Pee-wee's Big Adventure*. If you thought Paul Rubens's Pee-wee character was a stranger in an unstrange land, the title character in Burton's next project, *Beetlejuice*, upped the ante. Burton went on to helm the big-budget *Batman*, which was a box-office success if not as true to Burton's vision as his smaller, more personal films are.

Then came *Edward Scissorhands*, which Burton wrote, directed, and produced. It's an extreme example of the odd man in—misunderstood, trying to fit in normally without the skill set, and profoundly lonely. Audiences and Hollywood execs finally got it. Burton went on to direct the Batman sequel, *Batman Forever*, and then came his most personal film, *The Nightmare Before Christmas*.

> **"I don't want to take away from Tim, but he was not in San Francisco when we made it. He came up five times over two years, and spent no more than eight or ten days total."** —Henry Selick

If *Edward Scissorhands* explored an uber-suburban world and *Batman Forever* the uber-urban city, *Nightmare Before Christmas* was simply uber. Its world has little to do with anything on this planet. Take the drawings of Dr. Seuss and mix in a generous portion of German Expressionism and you might have an inkling of the oddity of design of Halloween Town, the stomping ground of our hero Jack Skellington and his girlfriend Sally.

Burton didn't direct the picture but it certainly sprang from his fertile mind. He produced it, his sketches served as the template for the film's unique look, the story was all his, and the overall artistic direction was definitely Burtonian. The great thing about *The Nightmare Before Christmas* is that it immerses us completely in a strange, alternative world. Visual surprises abound, but there is total consistency of style and conceit. That the filmmakers never waver in their tone or art direction is a testament to the impressive preproduction work as well as the professionalism of the entire team. If anyone was tempted to go for an easy joke or an out-of-character gesture, it doesn't show.

There are few films that so fully immerse us in a "realistic" fantasy world. The German silent film *Metropolis*, *The Wizard of Oz*, and *The 5,000 Fingers of Dr. T* (designed by none other than Dr. Seuss) immediately come to mind.

Of course, superlative art direction and consistency of tone are not enough to make a successful film. Although Disney felt that the film might be too dark for children, the good nature of Jack, his girlfriend Sally, and his ghostly dog Zero imbue it with a sweetness that offsets the darker actions of its characters. Everything Jack does, no matter how misbegotten, is done with the best intentions and naïveté.

The songs by Danny Elfman, quite a surprise to those who know him from his power scores for action pictures, help set a whimsical tone with a touch of the macabre. In all, *The Nightmare Before Christmas* is a unique work of art that refuses to behave like a conventional film musical. It's a stunning achievement, both technically and artistically. ■

LEFT: Christmas bounty, or one thing to do with your old tree and unwanted presents.

BELOW: The mayor seems to be having a bad day with werewolves.

SONGS

"Jack's Lament" ■ "Jack's Obsession" ■ "Kidnap the Sandy Claws" ■ "Making Christmas" ■ "Oogie Boogie's Song" ■ "Opening" ■ "Poor Jack" ■ "Sally's Song" ■ "This Is Halloween" ■ "Town Meeting Song" ■ "What's This?"

Behind the Screen

- The Jack Skellington puppet had over four hundred heads the animators could swap in so he could express a wide variety of emotions.
- Vincent Price originally voiced the part of Santa Claus but his health was so bad his tracks were unusable.

OKLAHOMA!

20TH CENTURY FOX—OCTOBER 11, 1955

OKLAHOMA!

COMPOSER: Richard Rodgers

LYRICIST: Oscar Hammerstein II

PRODUCER: Arthur Hornblow Jr.

DIRECTOR: Fred Zinnemann

SCREENWRITERS: Sonya Levien and William Ludwig

SOURCE: Based on the musical *Oklahoma!* by Richard Rodgers and Oscar Hammerstein II

CHOREOGRAPHER: Agnes de Mille

Synopsis

Will Curley manage to take Laurey on a date? Will the farmer and the cowman ever make friends? Oklahoma Territory is about to get its statehood—and an exclamation point!

Cast

Gordon MacRae...........*Curly*
Shirley Jones..............*Laurey Williams*
Gloria Grahame...........*Ado Annie Carnes*
Gene Nelson................*Will Parker*
Charlotte Greenwood .....*Aunt Eller*
Eddie Albert.................*Ali Hakim*
James Whitmore...........*Andrew Carnes*
Rod Steiger..................*Jud Fry*
Jay C. Flippin...............*Ike Skidmore*
James Mitchell.............*Dream Curly*
Bambi Linn..................*Dream Laurie*

Gordon MacRae proves to Shirley Jones that there really is a surrey with fringe on top.

F
OR THEIR FIRST BROADWAY SHOW TRANSFER TO FILM, *OKLAHOMA!*, RODGERS AND HAM-
merstein decided to sign on as executive producers. After the film came out,
Rodgers stated, "The wide-screen process was not always ideal for the more
intimate scenes, and I don't think the casting was totally satisfactory." Of
course, he failed to mention that he and Hammerstein received a large amount
of money for the privilege of shooting the film in the brand-new and previously untested
Todd-AO widescreen process. What he also failed to disclose was that he and Hammerstein
had final approval over casting. The director, Fred Zinnemann, had preferred James Dean
for the lead but Rodgers and Hammerstein's priority was the songs and, although Gordon
MacRae was a limited actor, he had a terrific voice and a nice Midwestern openness. Sexy
and wholesome like Pat Boone but with more humor, he was their pick.

With only a handful of directors who specialized in musicals around, Rodger and
Hammerstein cast against type, choosing ultra-serious Fred Zinnemann, trading quick
pacing for spectacular vistas. A frequent problem in adapting stage hits is trying to retain
complete scores. In retaining all but two songs, *Oklahoma!* feels way too long. Still, the
film is a perfect example of a glorious movie musical. The huge orchestra, conducted by
Adolph Deutsch and Jay Blackton, enrich not only the songs but provide sensitive underscoring as well.

Rodgers may have had his quibbles with the intimate scenes, but critic William K. Zinsser of the *New York Herald Tribune* opined that "Todd-AO is best in close-ups." Others called the film alternately "lumbering and somewhat tedious," and a "match in vitality, eloquence and melody for any musical this reviewer has ever seen." Hmmmm. Yet another critic wrote that the film "bears about as much relation to the Broadway *Oklahoma!* as a 1956 Cadillac does to the surrey with the fringe on top," while one more called it "a handsome piece of entertainment." You get the point. You can't please all of the people any of the time.

Watching *Oklahoma!* today, we tend not to be as critical as viewers were at the time of its release. It's taken on the mantle of an acknowledged classic and our role is to sit back and have a good time watching it. Some people say that the state of musicals now is so dismal that even Grade B examples of the past

seem brilliant by comparison. Even the ones we might've thought clunkers in their day are eminently sit-throughable now. (I'd say not all them.) Keep in mind that in their day, audiences grew tired of Astaire and Rogers, Maurice Chevalier, Jeanette MacDonald, and the Warner Brothers Dubin and Warren pictures. Today they all seem like minor masterpieces.

Oklahoma! may not be flawless but from where we're sitting, it's a damned fine reflection of the Broadway original. Looking forward, that "bright golden haze" is bound to remain undimmed. ■

ABOVE: It's hard to see the bright golden haze from this angle, but just wait.

RIGHT: Right: Oscar Hammerstein II and director Fred Zinnemann.

BELOW: Gene Nelson tells his friends that everything's up-to-date in Kansas City.

Oscar Hammerstein II

Have you noticed that sons and daughters of famous artists seldom live up to their parents' talents? It's almost like the gene pool becomes more and more watered down as the generations progress. There are exceptions, of course, and preeminent among them is the Hammerstein family. Oscar's uncles were exceptionally important producers and his father was a theater manager, so the theater was definitely in his blood. He wrote an amazing number of great shows and songs in the early decades of the twentieth century. Jerome Kern and Hammerstein's historic collaboration on *Show Boat* changed the direction of musical theater forever. After a dry period in the late 1930s, Hammerstein teamed with Richard Rodgers and together they continued to expand the art form. With *Oklahoma!*, *Carousel*, *Me and Juliet*, *Allegro*, *Pipe Dream*, *The Flower Drum Song*, and *The Sound of Music*, they established themselves as the greatest songwriting team in musical theatre history. Hammerstein was a humanist and his libretti and lyrics reflected an understanding of all his characters, good or bad, and a soft spot for the human condition. His lyrics were expansive and poetic without the show-off qualities of other lyricists. Stephen Sondheim said of his mentor, "What few people understand is that Oscar's big contribution to the theatre was as a theoretician, as a Peter Brook, as an innovator. People don't understand how experimental *Show Boat* and *Oklahoma!* felt at the time they were done. Oscar is not about the 'lark that is learning to pray'—that's easy to make fun of."

"Do you know what Oscar used to do? He would go to his farm in Bucks County and sometimes it would be three weeks before he would appear with a lyric. I never knew what he was doing down there. You know a lyric couldn't possibly take three weeks."

—*Richard Rodgers, spoiled after working with Larry Hart, one of the fastest lyric writers ever, to Alan Jay Lerner, another lyricist whose words gestated for weeks*

Gordon MacRae

Gordon MacRae was an amiable guy with an open smile and a wonderfully masculine voice. Straight ahead, unthreatening, with a twinkle in his eye, he certainly filled the requirements when a role called for a good-natured, American male. He was a man of his time, the 1950s, when singers sang bland pop songs without a hint of jazz or drama in their interpretations. Hollywood saw him as ideal for nostalgia films set in the '20s, musicals such as *Look for the Silver Lining* (1949), *The Daughter of Rosie O'Grady* (1950), *Tea for Two* (1950), *The West Point Story* (1950), *On Moonlight Bay* (1951), *By the Light of the Silvery Moon* (1952), *The Desert Song* (1953), *Three Sailors and a Girl* (1953), and *The Best Things in Life Are Free* (1956). The titles tell you all you need to know about these; four of them are named for old Tin Pan Alley songs, two have military references, and one is an operetta. In a sense, Rodgers and Hammerstein's *Oklahoma!* and *Carousel* brought MacRae into the present, giving him current-sounding songs to sing—both are set around the turn of the twentieth century.

Behind the Screen

- The film was shot in Nogales, Arizona, and environs.
- Betty Hutton was offered the roll of Ado Annie, and might've been a smarter choice than Gloria Grahame, who couldn't really sing.

ABOVE: Shooting outside of Aunt Eller's house.

CENTER: Isn't it clear that Jones and MacRae adore each other?

BELOW: Gordon MacRae meets the Starkeeper in *Carousel*.

"You're just like a father to me."
—*Shirley Jones to Richard Rodgers, after he made a pass at her*

OLIVER!

COLUMBIA—DECEMBER 10, 1968

COMPOSER: Lionel Bart
LYRICIST: Lionel Bart
PRODUCER: John Woolf
DIRECTOR: Carol Reed
SCREENWRITER: Vernon Harris
SOURCE: Based on the musical *Oliver!* by Lionel Bart
CHOREOGRAPHER: Onna White

Synopsis

Annie in drag—or is it the other way around?

Cast

Mark Lester	Oliver Twist
Ron Moody	Fagin
Oliver Reed	Bill Sikes
Shani Wallis	Nancy
Jack Wild	The Artful Dodger
Harry Secombe	Mr. Bumble
Hugh Griffith	Magistrate
Leonard Rossiter	Sowerberry
Joseph O'Conor	Mr. Brownlow
Peggy Mount	Mrs. Bumble
Hylda Baker	Mrs. Sowerberry

Ron Moody, as Fagin, explains to the kids that he'd do anything, anything, for your smile, anything. Shani Wallis, at rear in the red dress, will soon have her turn to tell us what she'd do for love.

T HE ONLY G-RATED FILM TO WIN THE BEST PICTURE OSCAR, *OLIVER!* IS ALSO THE ONLY Best Picture winner in which townsfolk dance while holding giant hams over their heads. We like the film a lot but it's an odd amalgam, juxtaposing musical comedy whimsy with the murder of a leading character. Carol Reed had never directed a musical—and never directed another one—but he certainly knew his stuff when it came to actors: the dramatic scenes are beautifully acted.

The dramatic scenes are intimate affairs, taking place in dank attics or basements and involving intense conversations about all manner of skullduggery. By contrast, there are the outdoor scenes, everything bright and, if not exactly cheery, certainly full of life and activity. They represent late 1960s musical filmmaking at its most boisterous and generous. "Who Will Buy" is a case in point. It starts off as Oliver looks out the window of his grandfather's house. A few women and men come by offering their wares, and are soon joined by a few more. The music picks up as a line of carriages come down the street. More and more people join the song. Maids, nannies with prams, milk sellers, window washers. . . a teacher and her pupils dance by like a mother duck and her ducklings, soldiers parade in. Then, all goes quiet as the camera picks up Bill Sikes and the Artful Dodger peering from behind a tree. This is delightfully stylized, grand-scale filmmaking at its best.

The production numbers in *Oliver!* are surpassed in grandiosity only by those in *Hello, Dolly!*, particularly "Before the Parade Passes By"—a moment of spectacle that exists

168 HOLLYWOOD MUSICALS

simply to wow the audience. And it does. But in *Oliver!* Onna White's choreography has a deeper meaning. There aren't really hundreds of people dancing joyously down the street but in Oliver's boyish imagination, there are. We're seeing the world through his eyes. When Gillian Lynne tried to do the same in *Half a Sixpence* in 1967, she failed. There was no character work, no payoff, just dancing till the music stopped—and it seemed it would never stop. (Of course, British musicals, with the exception of *Ever Green* and maybe a Gracie Fields movie, have never been so hot.)

Onna White brought theatrical choreography to film. The "I'd Do Anything" number tells a story; defines character; and has a beginning, middle, and end. It even has a final lift, when Fagin, curmudgeonly throughout the number, jumps from his alcove, feather sticking up from his head and umbrella aloft, his long coat swinging around like a dress. It's a brilliant piece of choreography without calling attention to just how smart it is.

Leaving Oliver! for a moment, we suggest you look at the film version of *The Music Man*, specifically the "Marian the Librarian," also choreographed by Onna White (repeating her Broadway assignment). As did Michael Kidd, White used gymnastic moves—but she used them for a purpose: to add color to the dance. In one number, Marian's entire story unfolds; we watch as she slowly but steadily sheds her inhibitions. For *Oliver!* White received a special Oscar for choreography, one of the few times that award has been bestowed.

Upon watching *Oliver!* recently, we were struck by the intimacies and small details of acting and production that stand out amid the spectacle and general hubbub. It is that specificity, as well as the movie's heart, that make it great—not the spectacle or even the great score. The enduring legacy of *Oliver!* is the way it touches viewers' emotions. That's what's missing from most musicals of the period. ∎

TOP: Jack Wild, as the Artful Dodger, joins the beautifully costumed and meticulously art-directed throngs of London.

BOTTOM: Ron Moody offers advice to the lovelorn Shani Wallis while Oliver Reed looks on from the shadows.

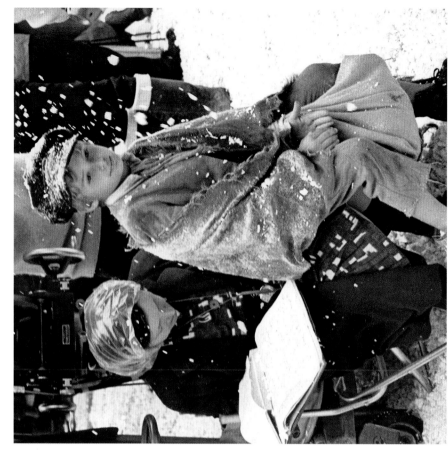

Behind the Screen

- For the "Boy for Sale" number, the snowballs were made of polystyrene, salt, Crazy Foam, and mashed potatoes—realistic, if not delicious.

- Apparently, Dick Van Dyke was considered for the role of Fagin, probably because of his incomparable Cockney accent in *Mary Poppins*.

- Elizabeth Taylor wanted to play Nancy and actually locked Lionel Bart in his own bathroom while she sang "As Long As He Needs Me" through the door.

ABOVE: Shani Wallis gives "As Long as He Needs Me" all she's got. And that's a lot.

LEFT: Mark Lester gets some direction from Carol Reed.

BELOW LEFT: Jack Wild has a look at things from the other side of the camera.

BELOW RIGHT: Mark Lester waits for his call.

ON THE TOWN

MGM—DECEMBER 30, 1949

Frank Sinatra, Jules Munshin, and Gene Kelly enjoy Rockefeller Plaza.

ON THE TOWN

COMPOSER: Roger Edens.
LYRICIST: Roger Edens
and Gene Kelly
PRODUCER: Arthur Freed
DIRECTORS: Stanley Donen
and Gene Kelly
SCREENWRITERS: Betty Comden
and Adolph Green
SOURCE: Based on the musical
On the Town by Leonard Bernstein,
Betty Comden, and Adolph Green
CHOREOGRAPHERS: Stanley Donen
and Gene Kelly

Synopsis

Three sailors on leave have twenty-four hours to make sure that the Bronx is up, the Battery's down, and Coney Island is the last refuge of a pretty girl.

Cast

Gene Kelly	Gabey
Frank Sinatra	Chip
Jules Munshin	Ozzie
Betty Garrett	Brunhilde Esterhazy
Ann Miller	Claire Huddesen
Vera-Ellen	Ivy Smith
Alice Pearce	Lucy Shmeeler
Florence Bates	Mme. Dilyovska

NEW YORK IS A PLAYGROUND IN *ON THE TOWN*, A LIGHTHEARTED YET SURPRISINGLY emotional lark by first-rate larksters Betty Comden and Adolph Green along with longhair composer Leonard Bernstein. Oh, and composer Roger Edens, too. In fact, more Roger Edens than Leonard Bernstein. It didn't seem to matter to Comden and Green, who wrote the script and additional songs with Edens, but it sure bothered Lenny Bernstein (though he had given his approval). And it sure bothered fans of the original show.

Here was a successful Broadway show with an admired score, but practically nothing was left of it when it made the transition to Hollywood. This seems strange, as MCM had been so eager to acquire the rights. In fact, they'd put up $250,000 toward the show's Broadway production, marking the first ever Broadway/Hollywood preproduction deal. Why did MCM spend so much and then eliminate most of the score?

Bernstein was known as a snobbish musician who wrote highbrow music. For that reason, perhaps, MGM was nervous about how the songs would be received. Sure, they admired the score—but they didn't trust that the moviegoing public would agree with them. And in fact, Broadway reviewers had declared the show not tuneful enough, not

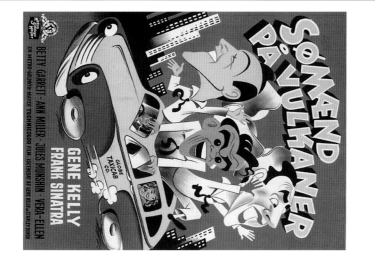

Betty Garrett gets Frank Sinatra, Ann Miller grabs Jules Munshin, and Vera-Ellen nabs Gene Kelly. What could be neater?

"I've been asked for years how one 'co-directs' . . . ? If you substitute the word 'fight' for 'codirect,' then you have it."

—Stanley Donen on working with Gene Kelly

SONGS

"Count on Me" ■ "Main Street"; "New York, New York" (Leonard Bernstein, Betty Comden, and Adolph Green) ■ "On the Town" ■ "Pearl of the Persian Sea" ■ "Prehistoric Man" ■ "That's All There Is Folks" ■ "You're Awful"

Tin Pan Alley enough—too Carnegie Hall. Hollywood was especially wary of melancholy songs like Bernstein's "Lonely Town" and "Some Other Time."

Composer Jule Styne worked with Comden and Green right after *On the Town* opened on Broadway. His response to their collaborations with Bernstein is perhaps the best reflection of how people felt about the show's songs: "Lenny's songs prevailed over the lyrics. Melodically he prevailed. I said [to Comden and Green], 'Look, you've never written with anyone who gave you songs that people sing on the streets. That's what we like to do. Don't be afraid to write songs—not *ungepachke*, special material—you've written a show but I call that writing special material. Because, no one can get up in the café and sing those songs because people don't know what you're talking about.' "

Movie studios also owned music publishing houses. MGM owned Robbins Music and they wanted to publish any popular songs that came out of their movies—so there had to be popular songs. Besides, they had composers and lyricists on staff. Why not put them to work for their money? Let's be honest, Roger Edens's music and the lyrics by Comden and Green aren't bad; in fact they're fun. But purists still resent that Bernstein's score, save two songs, was jettisoned.

The thrilling, rhythmically edited opening, "New York, New York," was a rare early example of location shooting, a jolt to audiences used to a musical's studio-bound fantasy world. *On the Town* has a particular kind of charm, and it resonated with audiences sensitive to the sacrifices of soldiers and sailors during the war. In another age, those sailors on the prowl might have seemed sleazy—but in the 1940s, they were viewed as lonely guys with only one day to grab for some gusto. Even now, the movie is an infectious romp through Manhattan with lots of love and mischief thrown into the mix. ■

ABOVE: Top of the world, Ma! Frank Sinatra, Stanley Donen, and Gene Kelly atop the Loew's State Theatre at Times Square.

LEFT: The three couples play leap-frog.

Behind the Screen

■ Leonard Bernstein was so angry at the way his score was treated in *On the Town*, he refused to let Columbia Pictures have the rights to *Wonderful Town*, also written with Comden and Green. The move backfired when Columbia discovered that they owned the underlying rights to the short stories upon which *Wonderful Town* was based and hired Jule Styne and Sammy Cahn to write the score for *My Sister Eileen*.

Saul Chaplin

One of Hollywood's most beloved arrangers, musical directors, and producers, Saul Chaplin oversaw production on a host of great musical movies. The list of films on which he worked is nothing less than phenomenal: *The Sound of Music*, *An American in Paris*, *On the Town*, *West Side Story*, *Seven Brides for Seven Brothers*, *Kiss Me, Kate*, and *Star!* In addition, with collaborator Sammy Cahn, Chaplin wrote songs for Columbia Pictures' B movies. Although no hits emerged from those scores, the duo's English lyric to the Yiddish song "Bei Mir Bist du Schön" was a million-seller for the Andrews Sisters. Another million-seller was Chaplin's adaptation of Ion Ivanovici's "Waves of the Danube," "The Anniversary Waltz." The lyric to that one is credited to Al Jolson, who also recorded the song. Cahn and Chaplin also had great success with "Please Be Kind" and "Until the Real Thing Comes Along."

Chaplin contributed arrangements to the films *Cover Girl* with Gene Kelly, the Rita Hayworth vehicle *Tonight and Every Night*, and *Summer Stock, Les Girls*, and *Can-Can*.

ONE HOUR WITH YOU

PARAMOUNT—MARCH 23, 1932

ONE HOUR WITH YOU

COMPOSER: Oscar Straus
LYRICIST: Leo Robin
PRODUCER: Ernst Lubitsch
DIRECTORS: Ernst Lubitsch and George Cukor
SCREENWRITER: Samson Raphaelson
SOURCE: Based on the play *Only a Dream* by Lothar Schmidt

Synopsis

Maurice Chevalier has an affair with his wife's best friend; his wife retaliates by pursuing another man. All of the others, married or not, are doing their darnedest to enjoy one another's company.

Cast

Jeanette MacDonald	Colette Bertier
Maurice Chevalier	Dr. Andre Bertier
Genevieve Tobin	Mitzi Olivier
Charles Ruggles	Adolph
Roland Young	Professor Olivier
Josephine Dunn	Mademoiselle Martel
Richard Carle	Henri Dornier
Barbara Leonard	Maid
George Barbier	Police Commissioner

"I didn't like Chevalier and he didn't like me." —*George Cukor*

I N 1915, THE SUPREME COURT RULED THAT MOTION PICTURES WERE NOT AN ART FORM, merely a business, and so were not covered by the First Amendment. That ruling set the stage for increased calls for censorship of motion pictures. Beginning in 1930, the Hays Code charged studios with keeping Americans' morals from being sullied. Before the repeal of Prohibition, Americans were in the mood to control the lives of others. The Code was bolstered with the help of the Catholic Church that put pressure on the studios, but in the early years, nothing much changed under the Code.

While the administrators of the Code set themselves the task of fighting for the morals of Americans they felt were too naïve to make decisions on their own, they were also, coincidentally, keeping a tight rein on what children saw in films. Up until in 1950s, movies weren't produced specifically for a children's audience. Even cartoons, serials, and Westerns, while attracting many children, weren't made specifically for the youth market. Children were expected to go to adult films and "get" whatever they could.

The early Code lacked bite until 1934, when the Production Code went into enforcement and every film had to earn a certificate before being released. Between 1930 and 1934, studios were still relatively unconcerned with the Hays Code and the films they made are referred to as "pre-Code"—which brings us to *One Hour with You.*

This film, one of Lubitsch's best, has sex on its mind from the first frame to the last. It's all about infidelities—in fact, the title song is a roundelay in which the entire cast hooks up for a good time after a dance. Even the score accents the naughty goings-on. Audiences were shocked to find the married couple played by Jeanette MacDonald and Maurice Chevalier sharing the same bed, an arrangement that was seldom illustrated in films up until the 1960s. The specific bed in question, we might add, is almost a featured character in the film. At the end of the song, "What a Little Thing like a Wedding Ring Can Do," the camera dwells on that bed, which seems to wink at us.

ABOVE: Maurice Chevalier is surprised to have met his match in Jeanette MacDonald.

OPPOSITE: Busby Berkeley it's not—but Maurice Chevalier and friends look up at the camera or is it a mirrored ceiling?

In addition to the circular nature of the relationships, Lubitsch's dialogue kept up the froth of the piece. Roland Young allows that, "When I married her, she was a brunette. Now you can't believe anything she says." He further elucidates, "In Switzerland they have a very peculiar law. When a husband shoots his wife, they put him in jail." Charles Ruggles's butler confesses that he misled his master into wearing a Romeo costume, adding, "Oh, Monsieur, I did so want to see you in tights." At one point, Ruggles avers, "You have a right to be wrong. You're a woman. Women are born to be wrong. I like my women wrong." On the stand, MacDonald testifies to punishing her husband by having a flirtation with Ruggles's character, Adolph, unashamedly explaining, "An eye for an eye. An Adolph for an Adolph." All slightly risqué but with a sense of humor that takes the sting and tawdriness away.

As if to emphasize the vicarious thrill we get by eavesdropping on the sexual machinations, the characters address us directly, as if unembarrassed to find voyeurs peeping at them through a keyhole. Paramount actors such as the Marx Brothers, W. C. Fields, and Hope and Crosby often broke the fourth wall to speak to the audience, but in *One Hour with You*, the convention adds to the naughtiness as we become the characters' confidants. In song, Chevalier asks us what would we would do if confronted by such a tempting dish as Mitzi? He pauses and agrees with our unspoken response, "That's what I did, too!" Of course, all of Lubitsch's romantic musical comedies take place in Europe, not Des Moines or Lompoc. As staunch, reserved, upright Americans, we knew that those things went on in Europe but could never, never happen in our backyards or bedrooms.

All this folderol, harmless teasing, and mild flirtation would disappear within a few years of *One Hour with You's* premiere. Directors and screenwriters might sneak in naughty bits here and there—but it was a whole new, squeaky-clean ballgame. In the 1960s, Universal released a lot of so-called sex comedies, usually starring Doris Day and Rock Hudson, but they were missing one thing—sex! For the most part, sex farces, long a staple of the dramatic tradition, were scarce on American screens until *Bob and Carol and Ted and Alice* shared a bed and celebrated the sexual revolution of the late 1960s. Ultimately, the Production Code morphed into our current, far-from-perfect ratings system. ■

Maurice Chevalier

His mischievous, twinkling eyes and Gallic charm caught the imagination of women. In the silent era, Latin lovers were the sex objects of choice in American films but Chevalier turned the tide in favor of the French when sound came in, his joyful sexiness thrillingly attractive to staid American audiences. Alas, they grew tired of him just as musicals were going out of favor and he returned to Paris, where he remained a hugely popular star. From the midthirties through the forties, he spent his screen time in French and English pictures. In 1957, he returned to American film with *Love in the Afternoon*, which was made in France. A year later he again became a huge star in American movies after his role in *Gigi*. Chevalier continued in films until *Monkey's, Go Home!* in 1967. Not an auspicious finale but his body of work is impressive and nothing can equal his early sound musicals, especially those with Jeannette MacDonald.

SONGS

"It was Only a Dream Kiss" ■ "Oh, That Mitzi" ■ "One Hour with You" (Richard A. Whiting, Leo Robin) ■ "Three Times a Day" (Richard A. Whiting, Leo Robin) ■ "We Will Always Be Sweethearts" ■ "What a Little Thing like a Wedding Ring Can Do" ■ "What Would You Do?" (Richard A. Whiting, Leo Robin)

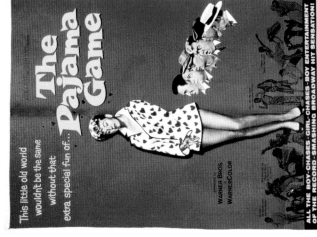
THE PAJAMA GAME

COMPOSERS: Richard Adler
and Jerry Ross

LYRICISTS: Richard Adler
and Jerry Ross

PRODUCERS: George Abbott
and Stanley Donen

DIRECTORS: George Abbott
and Stanley Donen

SCREENWRITERS: George Abbott
and Richard Bissell

SOURCE: Based on the musical *The
Pajama Game* by George Abbott,
Richard Bissell, Richard Adler, and
Jerry Ross

CHOREOGRAPHER: Bob Fosse

Synopsis

The new foreman comes to the pajama factory,
where he immediately butts heads with the
comely union representative. Can you guess
where this ends? Sparks fly both professionally
and personally before they get together to share a
single pair of pajamas.

Cast

Doris Day	Babe Williams
John Raitt	Sid Sorokin
Carol Haney	Gladys Hotchkiss
Eddie Foy Jr.	Hinesie
Reta Shaw	Mabel
Barbara Nichols	Poopsie
Thelma Pelish	Mae
Jack Straw	Prez

THE PAJAMA GAME

WARNER BROTHERS—AUGUST 29, 1957

When times get tough,
why not share a pair
of pajamas with your
mate? John Raitt and
Doris Day give it a try—
and it works!

A FAITHFUL TRANSFER OF THE BROADWAY PRODUCTION TO HOLLYWOOD, *THE PAJAMA GAME* included the original director, writers, and cast members John Raitt, Eddie Foy Jr., Carol Haney, and Reta Shaw. In fact, though Stanley Donen was brought in to help George Abbott with the specifics of film directing, the show proceeded almost as on the stage. With one exception: Doris Day replaced Janis Paige in the lead role. Poor Janis. She was star on Broadway but the movies viewed her as a secondary character from her turns in such films as *Silk Stockings*. True, she had a little pitch problem, but that hadn't stopped Hollywood in other cases; on film that kind of flaw can be corrected. Initially, Paige was in and Raitt was out, in favor of Frank Sinatra. But when Sinatra turned down the role, Paige was dumped and Raitt got to reprise his role. Day was a contract player at Warner and a real star who could bring in audiences, whereas Raitt had no recognition among filmgoers (even on Broadway he was known mostly for playing Billy Bigelow in *Carousel*). But once Day was signed, he was in.

Nobody made much of a fuss when Paige didn't get the role, but other choices made by Hollywood when adapting Broadway properties were more controversial. Where to start? The most egregious slight (to quote Julie Andrews, but we'll get to her later) was the replacement of Ethel Merman with Rosalind Russell in *Gypsy* (and after Jack Warner, himself, promised Merman the part). Can you imagine two more disparate performers? Merman was all brass and balls, and the part and score were written for her strengths. Russell was more sophisticated, lacking the powerhouse personality of Merman. Really, Russell ended up doing a fine job (though she was dubbed for most of it)—but she was no Merman.

"He'd play tennis, come watch on the set for an hour, then watch the rushes, then go home."

—*Stanley Donen on George Abbott's codirection.*

Strangely, Merman never had a huge film career. She did recreate her original performances in both *Anything Goes* and *Call Me Madam* and she was a success in *There's No Business Like Show Business*, but somehow the movies never embraced her. Nor did they take to her co-greatest Broadway musical queen, Mary Martin. But it was understandable when Julie Andrews took over in the film version of *The Sound of Music*. If Martin was too old (though wonderful) in the Broadway original, close-ups would have revealed her to be old enough to be Maria's mother or even grandmother.

Aficionados think Julie Andrews's losing the part of Eliza Doolittle to Audrey Hepburn in *My Fair Lady* was another crime against the natural laws of musical theater. Her Oscar win for *Mary Poppins* provided slight recompense for her snub. But what the fans don't realise is that except for the TV musical *Cinderella*, most of American had never seen Julie Andrews perform. Jack Warner couldn't trust as important and expensive production to an unknown. Warner Brothers is the studio that was the most devoted to bringing Broadway musicals o the screen.

Speaking of Warner, nobody made noise when Andrews and Richard Burton were overlooked for the film version of *Camelot*, but maybe that was because the movie turned out to be a real dog. Remember when Angela Lansbury was replaced by Lucille Ball (Lucy to you) in *Mame* (another Warner production), and Bea Arthur was dragged along? Broadway star Gwen Verdon appeared in several films as a member of Jack Cole's company of dancers, but only starred in one: *Damn Yankees*. She wasn't considered pretty enough for the screen. Carol Channing lost out on *Hello, Dolly!* but she never had much of a film career anyway (*The First Travelling Saleslady*, anyone?). She was just too "big" for the screen. Norman

Jewison thought the same of Zero Mostel when casting *Fiddler on the Roof*. Which brings us to the B side of the subject . . .

Some Broadway performers might have been better off being replaced. Take the film version of *Half a Sixpence* . . . please. It was a typical movie musical of the late 1960s, namely, overlong and bloated. (The following year's *Oliver!* was another overlong, bloated musical—but that one actually worked.) Starring in *Half a Sixpence* was the original West End and Broadway star of the show, Tommy Steele. One hears all the time about actors and actresses performing for the camera and appearing to do nothing, but when the rushes are viewed it's all there in its subtle beauty. Not so with Steele. He overdid everything. He was not only playing to the back row of the mezzanine, he was aiming at audiences miles away. And with those chompers, in close-ups he looked like he could bite your head off! Thank God it wasn't a 3-D film. Steele gave essentially the same performance in *The Happiest Millionaire* and *Finian's Rainbow*, and there you have his entire Hollywood oeuvre. He had shown himself to be so charismatic and talented onstage in *Half a Sixpence*. But blown up to sixty feet across, the screen still wasn't large enough to hold his performance.

To Hollywood's credit, many worthy Broadway performers have recreated their original roles well. Helen Morgan, Eddie Cantor, Rex Harrison, Yul Brynner, Robert Preston, Desi Arnaz, Ethel Waters, Miyoshi Umeki, Gwen Verdon, Zero Mostel, Jack Gilford, Barbra Streisand, Judy Holliday, Marilyn Miller, Joel Grey, Dick Van Dyke, Sherree North, Nathan Lane, Matthew Broderick, Ray Bolger, Vivian Blaine, Robert Morse, Rudy Vallee, Fannie Brice, and Bert Lahr, to name a few. But we seem to remember and still rue (talk about holding a grudge!) the ones who were passed over for established movie stars. ■

ABOVE LEFT: George Abbott and Barbara Nichols on the set.

ABOVE RIGHT: John Raitt and Doris Day are on the road to love, but they don't know it. The employees listening in do, though.

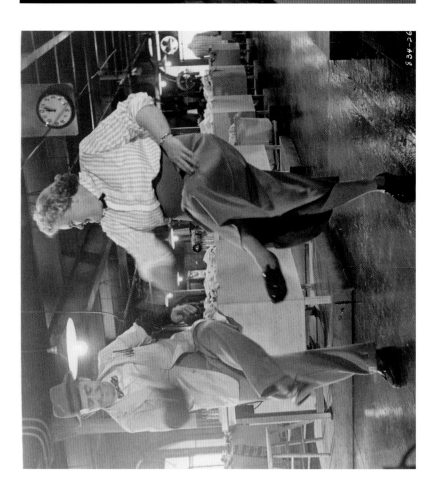

Behind the Screen

■ Carol Haney was extremely ill during the making of *The Pajama Game*. She wanted to soldier on, and those behind the camera didn't seem to care—but Doris Day called a halt to shooting and announced that she wouldn't work unless Haney was taken to the doctor.

SONGS

"Hernando's Hideaway" ■ "Hey There" ■ "I'll Never Be Jealous Again" ■ "I'm Not at All in Love" ■ "Once a Year Day" ■ "The Pajama Game" ■ "Racing with the Clock" ■ "Seven and a Half Cents" ■ "Small Talk" ■ "Steam Heat" ■ "There Once Was a Man"

Doris Day

Doris Day has been stereotyped as the sunny virgin-for-life, but her wide-ranging film career marked her as one of the greatest film actresses of all time. Day could be sunny and bright and virginal, but she also had a toughness that she could draw upon when required. She was equally successful in musicals, comedies, and dramas. Her private life might have been messy but her career had very few lows. She began as a band singer with the Barney Rapp, Bob Crosby, and Les Brown congregations. Her recording of "Sentimental Journey" with Brown was one of the top songs during World War II and attracted Day attention from Hollywood. Composer Jule Styne heard Day sing at the Little Club in New York City and immediately thought of her as the lead for his and Sammy Cahn's new movie, *Romance on the High Seas*. Cahn arranged for Day to test for the film and she beat out Marion Hutton and Janis Paige for the part. Her Hollywood career was launched when Styne and Cahn gave her the song "It's Magic" to sing in the film. Warner put her in a bunch of okay but not always special films until *Calamity Jane*, Warner's answer to *Annie Get Your Gun*. Her recording of "Secret Love" capped her time at Warner and she left the studio. She worked as a freelancer in a variety of dramas and comedies in which she'd sing the title song or one song woven into the plot of the film. She returned to musicals with *The Pajama Game*, again at Warner. *Jumbo* would be her last musical film. The Doris Day–Rock Hudson era followed, and then came her retirement from the screen (or perhaps it was the screen's retirement from her). She turned to television, starring in *The Doris Day Show*, in which she appeared foggily, through a Vaseline-covered lens. Optometrists across the country were besieged by puzzled viewers whose eyesight seemed to grow blurry whenever Day was in the shot. The success of the series allowed her to pay off her crooked husbands' debts. Since then, she has devoted her life to animal rights causes. It might be noted that Day's sunny screen disposition was a true reflection of her personality.

O NE OF THE FIRST AND BEST MOVIE MUSICALS, *THE KING OF JAZZ* (1930), centered on the talents of Paul White- man and his Orchestra. But big bands really became staples of the musicals in the 1940s, at the peak of the big band era. It's hard to think of any popular band of the time that wasn't featured in a movie. Swing bands, sweet bands, Latin bands, all received exposure through motion pictures. Kay Kyser and his band headlined seven pictures and appeared in many more—no band was more successful on the screen.

Because of underlying racism in the south, the black bands of Cab Calloway, Duke Ellington, Count Basie, and others made only rare appearances in white films, and were mainly represented in the occasional black musical. Because of the happy collision of the rise of swing orchestras, the heyday of nightclubs, and the proliferation of new movies (nearly 100 a week at one point), the best bands appeared often on film and their performances are immortalized for us to appreciate today.

TOP RIGHT: Harry James and His Music Makers in *Do You Love Me?*.

CENTER RIGHT: Charlie Barnet, Tommy Dorsey, Benny Goodman, Louis Armstrong, and Lionel Hampton jamming in *A Song is Born*.

BOTTOM RIGHT: Benny Goodman and His Orchestra on the air in *The Big Broadcast of 1937*.

BOTTOM LEFT: Peggy Lee records a message for members of the Academy thanking them for her Oscar nomination as Best Supporting Actress in *Pete Kelly's Blues*.

BIG BAND MUSICALS

PINOCCHIO

WALT DISNEY—FEBRUARY 9, 1940

PINOCCHIO

COMPOSER: Leigh Harline
LYRICIST: Ned Washington
PRODUCER: Walt Disney
DIRECTORS: Hamilton Luske and Ben Sharpsteen
SCREENWRITERS: Aurelius Battaglia, William Cottrell, Otto Englander, Erdman Penner, Joseph Sabo, Ted Sears, and Webb Smith
Based on the story "Pinocchio" by Collodi

Synopsis

All play and no work makes a jackass out of Pinocchio, but what he wants is to be a real boy. He'll have to let his conscience be his guide.

Cast

Christian Rub...............*Gepetto*
Dickie Jones................*Pinocchio*
Cliff Edwards..............*Jiminy Cricket*
Evelyn Venable............*The Blue Fairy*
Charles Judels.............*Stromboli*
Mel Blanc ....*Gideon*
Walter Catlett..............*J. Worthington Foulfellow*
Frankie Darro..............*Lampwick*

Either Pinocchio has told a whopper of a lie or the Blue Fairy is celebrating Arbor Day.

K IDS TODAY WATCH THE ANTIC ADVENTURES OF WOODY AND BUZZ IN *TOY STORY*, LAUGH at the crude humor of Shrek, and are thrilled by Alvin and the Chipmunks. Those are all nice, bland children's entertainments. Nothing for parents to get upset about.

It wasn't always thus. There was a time when moviemakers weren't afraid to scare the piss out of the little tykes. Literally. Many a theater had to clean the upholstery after a children's matinee. And who was the sadist who would inflict such trauma on the whippersnappers? None other than dear, kindly Uncle Walt. Disney, that is.

Take *Pinocchio*. Mommy brings you to the movies and buys you some popcorn and Jujubes. The film starts and everything's going swimmingly. Gepetto makes a little wooden puppet and wishes that he could be a real boy. That is so sweet. His prayers are heard by the Blue Fairy who gives life to Pinocchio, on condition that he behave himself. Cleo the goldfish and Figaro the cat have a jolly time with the little fellow, and just in case he strays, there's the happy little cricket, Jiminy, to act as his conscience. Funny fellow that he is, Jiminy tells Pinocchio that if he ever needs him, all he has to do is whistle. This is heartwarming stuff. And isn't that popcorn good?

On his way to school one day, Pinocchio runs into two scalawags who convince the little fellow that he belongs on the stage. They sell Pinocchio to Stromboli, a puppeteer. Hmmm. He's a big, mean-looking guy . . . but then Pinocchio sings a charming song, "I've Got No Strings," and dances with two charming girl puppets. Maybe we were wrong about Stromboli after all. And the candy is yummy.

Wait—what's happening? Stromboli locks Pinocchio in a birdcage! We were right about him! But then the Blue Fairy comes and forgives Pinocchio for his bad behavior (even though his nose grows as a result of some naughty lies). She sets him free. Whew!

Have a sip of soda. It's only a cartoon. Why would Mommy take us to a scary movie? But she did! Pinocchio is kidnapped and sent to Pleasure Island amusement park, where he learns to smoke fat cigars and drink beer! That can't be good for him. What's even worse, in Pinocchio's world, when boys act like jackasses, they actually become jackasses! Yikes!

Pinocchio escapes but Gepetto isn't at home. Abandoned by his father, he doesn't know what to do—until the Blue Fairy sends a carrier pigeon (all right, a dove) with a note for the young boy, telling him that his father went looking for him and got eaten by a whale! The little puppet and the cricket find Monstro the whale and somehow get inside his stomach (now, that's a jolly image), where they find Gepetto. So, of course they set a fire in the whale's belly and are sneezed out. Monstro is understandably peeved and tries to catch the merry band who are swimming for their lives. This is really, really scary stuff, boys and girls. Time to pee your pants. By the time Pinocchio saves Gepetto from drowning and the Blue Fairy makes him a real boy, we can't wait to get out of there and into Mom's nice, safe car.

Uncle Walt, how could you?

As you know, he didn't stop there. Snow White was poisoned by a witch. Dumbo's mother was imprisoned and had to rock him by sticking her trunk through the bars of her cell. Bambi's mother was shot, for God's sake! Cinderella had a lot of housework (and if you don't think that was scary for the little princesses in the audience, you're wrong).

But . . . you know what? We all lived through it, enjoyed it, and went back to the movies again and again. Our point is, children don't mind being scared as long as everything comes out all right in the end. Generations of children saw these films and turned out just fine. Today's children's entertainment is, for the most part—meaning everything but Pixar—sappy, crude and manic, or self-referential. *Pinocchio* and the other Disney films are true classics. They don't pull punches and they don't condescend to their audience. Their scores were written by great songwriters, their animation is exquisite (damn you, Hanna-Barbera, for ruining animation—until computers came along, anyway), and the art direction is rich and lustrous.

This is classic children's entertainment that treats kids like humans, and we are better off for it. *Pinocchio* can't be beat. Is it really better than any of the other Disney classics? We wouldn't go to the mats for it, though many consider it Disney's best animated film. What we do know is that it is exceptional moviemaking that stands the test of time. ∎

SONGS

"Give a Little Whistle" ▪ "Hi-Diddle-Dee-Dee (An Actor's Life for Me)" ▪ "I've Got No Strings" ▪ "When You Wish Upon a Star"

Behind the Screen

▪ Walt Disney was disappointed in the score for *Pinocchio* and let everyone on his staff know it, especially the songwriters. When Ned Washington and Leigh Harline won the Oscar for "When You Wish Upon a Star" and Harline won another for best score, Disney loved all the music very, very much—but Harline held a grudge and left the studio.

▪ The record album of *Pinocchio* was the first to use the word soundtrack.

▪ *Pinocchio* cost over $200,000 to make—more than *The Wizard of Oz*.

TOP: In a beautiful example of Disney's artistry, Gepetto's workshop is filled with a wondrous array of toys.

BOTTOM: Jiminy Cricket tries vainly to convince Pinocchio to follow his advice.

POOR LITTLE RICH GIRL

20TH CENTURY FOX—JULY 24, 1936

POOR LITTLE RICH GIRL

COMPOSER: Harry Revel

LYRICIST: Mack Gordon

PRODUCER: Darryl F. Zanuck

DIRECTOR: Irving Cummings

SCREENWRITER: Sam Hellman, Gladys Lehman, and Harry Tugend

SOURCE: Based on the story "Poor Little Rich Girl" by Eleanor Gates

CHOREOGRAPHER: Ralph Cooper and Jack Haskell

Synopsis

A rich widower's daughter spontaneously decides to take a vacation, during which she wins the heart of an old curmudgeon, joins a vaudeville act, is almost kidnapped, gets the vaudevillians arrested, and arranges the merger of two competing companies. Some vacation!

Cast

Shirley Temple............Barbara Barry
Gloria Stuart..............Margaret Allen
Jack Haley ....Jimmy Dolan
Michael Whalen ....Richard Barry
Sara Haden ....Collins
Jane Darwell ....Woodward
Claude Gillingwater......Simon Peck
Paul Stanton................George Hathaway
Henry Armetta.................Tony

Shirley Temple helps Jack Haley with his terpsichore.

WAS SHIRLEY TEMPLE REALLY AS TALENTED AS SHE SEEMED ON SCREEN? Wouldn't it thrill us to hear that she was a cute and perky fraud? That it was all camera tricks and editing? Alas, dear cynics, Shirley was every bit as remarkable a performer as any that ever was captured on the silver screen. Her sometime dance partner, Bill Robinson, was asked by Gene Kelly's talented dancing brother, Fred, if Shirley was really as terrific as people thought. He replied, "Aw, Fred, that girl was so perfect it was embarrassing. I'd show her a step and the next day I come down and start to do the step and she'd say: 'Uncle Bill, yesterday you started on the other foot.'"

Through the mists of time, we misremember Shirley Temple's films, recalling only the conventions. That doesn't make her any different from Jeanette and Nelson, Fred and Ginger, or Mickey and Judy, all of whose performances are thought of by the unknowing as a series of clichés. We can't blame anyone but the studios for that. All of those performers were typecast time after time and their films, despite their individual successes, were nearly interchangeable. Who can say whether those stars were limited by their own talents or by the studios' typecasting? In Shirley Temple's case, as in Mary Pickford's before her, our memory of the performances is that they were rather cloying.

Alice Faye

Mmmm. We love smoky-voiced singers in the vein of Francis Langford and Alice Faye. We're not sure that Langford could really act but Faye was as good an actress as any singer. She was hired to sing a number in Fox's *George White's 1935 Scandals* but was elevated to the leading role when Lillian Harvey bowed out. She followed it up with three Shirley Temple films, beginning with *Poor Little Rich Girl.* Then it was on to the Fox nostalgia series starting with 1937's *In Old Chicago.* Faye was featured in a number of these films, interspersed with modern-day musicals. Almost all of them were backstagers in which she played performers who sang on stage rather than in character. Faye's roles tended to be good-natured strivers who wanted to make it big, ladies with a sense of forgiveness and a sense of humor. Faye's films are almost interchangeable but she was given the opportunity to introduce lots of great numbers, most important, "You'll Never Know." In 1942, she took a year off to raise her newborn daughter and then returned to Fox for two more musicals, *Hello, Frisco, Hello;* and, the apex of the Fox musical, *The Gang's All Here.* Insecure and unhappy, Faye preferred radio where she didn't have to memorize a script and where she didn't have to worry about her weight. Faye drove off the lot, handing in her dressing room keys to the security guard at the front gate, and never looked back. She did return to Fox seventeen years later for the remake of *State Fair,* but then made only a few cameo appearances.

SONGS

"But Definitely" ■ "Buy a Bar of Barry's" ■ "Here Comes Cookie" (C/L: Mack Gordon) ■ "Military Man" ■ "Oh My Goodness" ■ "Peck's Theme Song" ■ "When I'm with You" ■ "You Gotta Eat Your Spinach, Baby"

ABOVE LEFT: Jack Haley, Shirley Temple, and Alice Faye hit the airwaves in *Poor Little Rich Girl.*

Behind the Screen

■ German censors refused to approve the film because several of the creators were non-Aryan. Fox proved to the Germans that the offending names—Gordon, Cummings, Hellman, Armetta, and Haden—were not Jewish, and the film was cleared.

■ The "Military Man" number was so difficult that Shirley Temple's taps had to be dubbed.

"Why don't you talk to me? I'm the star." —*Shirley Temple to a reporter interviewing her mother on the set*

Although her films were often nearly remakes of one another, Temple's screen personality was seldom sappy. Yes, she could be affectionate but she was also feisty, standing up to those who got in her way, strong-willed in her belief in herself, and steadfast about those she loved. Above all, she enjoyed herself while singing and that enjoyment was contagious. Temple had an almost magical way of softening the curmudgeons and downright nasty men she met on screen.

The importance of Temple's ability to melt hearts and bring cheer during the Depression cannot be overestimated. President Franklin D. Roosevelt acknowledged this when he said, "It is a splendid thing that for just a fifteen cents an American can go to a movie and look at the smiling face of a baby and forget his troubles."

The title itself—*Poor Little Rich Girl*—was a nod to the Depression, and in it, Shirley makes everyone she meets whole (with the exception of a kidnapper, that is). Her innocence and good cheer are just the thing that grown-ups need to be able to see the light. The lovers find each other, two companies see the value in a merger, she's reunited with her father, and all is right in Shirley's world. The numbers, as usual for a Temple film, are sprightly, tuneful, and optimistic. Alice Faye (a favorite in Temple films) and Jack Haley exhibit a wonderful rapport with each other and with Temple that adds to the enjoyment.

If you haven't seen one of Temple's films because you fear you'll gag on the treacle, we suggest you watch one. You'll be pleasantly surprised at the top-drawer entertainment and astounded by the talent that moppet possesses. She blows everyone else off the screen. ■

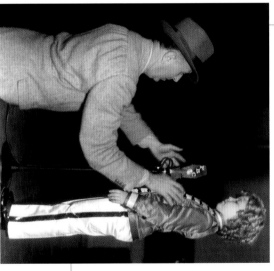

LEFT: *Poor Little Rich Girl's* director, Irving Cummings, puts little Shirley in her place.

Shirley Temple

Shirley Temple was unique in the history of the movie musical, mainly because of her age. Where adult stars had their doppelgangers at other studios, young Shirley was the biggest pipsqueak musical comedy star. Why was this? The studios resolutely copied one another's successes. Shirley Temple could sing, dance, and act with aplomb. After a series of shorts for Educational Pictures, she signed with Fox Films and the studio gave her bit roles and loaned her to Warner Brothers while they figured out what to do with the youngster. Temple's first feature at Fox, 1934's *Stand Up and Cheer,* became an immediate sensation. A loanout to Paramount for *Little Miss Marker* further enhanced her standing. She finished the year with *Bright Eyes,* a tremendous hit that introduced Temple's greatest screen song, "On the Good Ship Lollipop." By then, Darryl F. Zanuck had merged his Twentieth Century Pictures with Fox and the Temple machine was churning out hit after hit. It's said that the cheery Temple saved the studio from bankruptcy during the Depression. She was often cast as an orphan or practically abandoned by her parents. Sadly, all children must grow up. After a series of huge hits, the magic seemed to wear off. By 1940, Fox didn't quite know what to do with her and she left the studio. She made one film for MGM, *Kathleen,* which was not a success, and then went on to United Artists and Selznick, which loaned her out to a variety of other studios. *The Bachelor and the Bobby-Soxer* in 1947 was her best picture of this period. In 1950, she retired from the screen once and for all.

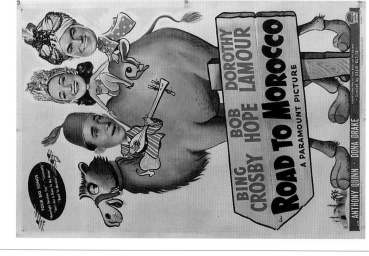

ROAD TO MOROCCO

PARAMOUNT—APRIL 22, 1943

ROAD TO MOROCCO

COMPOSER: James Van Heusen

LYRICIST: Johnny Burke

PRODUCER: Paul Jones

DIRECTOR: David Butler

SCREENWRITERS: Frank Butler and Don Hartman

CHOREOGRAPHER: Paul Oscard

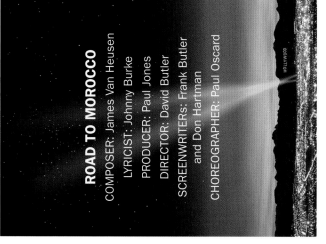

Synopsis

After blowing up a ship, Bob and Bing find themselves washed up in the desert, where, with the help of their writers, they ad lib for the next eighty-three minutes.

Cast

Bob Hope ....Orville "Turkey" Jackson
Bing Crosby ....Jeff Peters
Dorothy Lamour ....Princess Shalmar
Anthony Quinn ....Mullay Kasim
Dona Drake..................Mirirmah
Vladimir Sokoloff........Hyder Khan
Mikhail Rasumny..........Ahmed Fey
George Givot................Neb Jolla

A hand-tinted color photo of Dorothy Lamour, Bing Crosby (not looking very happy), Bob Hope, and Dona Drake.

YOU KNOW HOW BOB HOPE AND BING CROSBY WOULD ACKNOWLEDGE THE CAMERA AND speak right to the audience in their films? Remember how Groucho would throw a look at the camera when Chico or Harpo would do something particularly absurd? How about those W. C. Fields films, completely devoid of plot beyond the torments suffered by Fields at the hands of his family and various other inane bumpkins and situations? Then there was Mae West, who vamped through acres of men with only a slight nod to the action around her. George Burns and Gracie Allen mined comic gold from a series of dizzy routines, never offering the slightest nod toward logic or reality. All these characters were in full comic bloom at Paramount, the studio that took the best comics and comical personalities from vaudeville and the Broadway stage and gave them free rein to do what they did best while they learned to tailor their talents for the screen. Unlike Fox or MGM or Universal, Paramount tolerated a little anarchy and looseness of plot, often letting the stories make left turns or stop completely for the benefit of a good bit. In *The Road to Morocco*, even a camel admits, "This is the screwiest picture I've ever been in."

You'll note that none of the Paramount comics conformed to the expectations of society. The Marx Brothers thumbed their Jewish noses at bluenoses; Mae West's entendres could be so blatant they were barely double; W. C. Fields just wanted to be left alone to take a nip before his nap; and, in a later era, Dean Martin and Jerry Lewis played it as fast and loose as it gets.

Paramount let their stars go wild. Perhaps Irving Thalberg was right in reining in the Marx Brothers with a solid structure and a dose of heart in *A Night at the Opera*, but when we watch it, we can't help missing the anything-goes, slapdash qualities of *Animal Crackers* and *Duck Soup*. The studio made lots of musicals but they weren't considered as good as MGM's. Between the excellence of Lubitsch's sophisticated musicals of the 1930s and

SONGS

"Ain't Got a Dime to My Name (Ho Ho Hum)"
■ "Constantly" ■ "Moonlight Becomes You"
■ "The Road to Morocco"

Bob Hope

What accounts for longevity in show business? Talent has a lot to do with it, of course, as do luck and smarts. But there's another component, difficult to characterize, that separates the famous from the legendary. Bob Hope is legendary. From the early days of vaudeville, through radio, Broadway, movies, and many wars, Hope was at the top of his game. Only at the end of his career, during the Vietnam War era when his right-wing views were out of favor, did Hope alienate audiences. (And even then, his staunch support of the troops seemed admirable to most.) In his early films, Hope played the smart-aleck fool, full of braggadocio and bravado, covering cowardice with an almost feminine softness. He seldom got the girl and when he did, it was as surprising to him as it was to the audience. In the 1960s, he teamed up with other no-longer-as-hot stars for a string of mildly amusing, somewhat sexist farces. Older audiences probably remember the series of Christmas television specials Hope filmed at the front of whatever war was taking place. He'd share the stage with Jerry Colonna, Frances Langford, the current Miss America, and some busty young women, swinging his golf club and cracking wise while the troops went wild. Throughout his career, Hope relied on several running gags that were always sure to get a laugh, including his imaginary feud with Bing Crosby and his futile hope of being nominated for an Academy Award. (In reality, he received four honorary Oscars plus the Jean Hersholt Humanitarian Award, and hosted the Oscars eighteen times.) Hope's theme song (remember when performers had theme songs?) was "Thanks for the Memory," and he surely racked up plenty of great ones over the course of his eighty-eight years in show business.

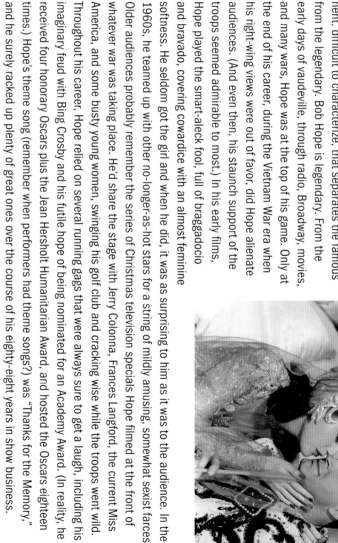

Burke and Van Heusen

Johnny Burke's lyrics were playful, humorous, and romantic. He wrote like the man on the street would talk—if the man was an exceptional lyricist, that is. But his plain-speaking lyrics made him a favorite of all classes of music lovers. Burke made a stab at the movies during the Great Song Rush of 1929, but Fox dropped him after only six months—a decision he endorsed wholeheartedly. He went back to writing popular song lyrics and had a few hits. In 1935, he returned to Hollywood and was signed by Paramount Pictures the following year. At the studio, he and his partner, James V. Monaco, replaced the team of Robin and Rainger as Bing Crosby's writers of choice. What was good enough for Bing was good enough for Bob, and so the songwriting team joined the pair for the first of the Road pictures, The Road to Singapore. Monaco soon left Paramount for Fox, leaving and Burke without a partner. Luckily, he stumbled upon the gambling, drinking, hard-living playboy around town, James Van Heusen. Their first assignment was on the Road to Zanzibar—and a new songwriting team was born. In 1953, as the era of the movie musical waned, the two split up. (They would subsequently work together again twice, but only briefly.) Burke went to Broadway and Van Heusen joined the court of Sinatra and provided the singer with many of his biggest hits. But it's the team of Burke and Van Heusen that we particularly love. Their songs are often jaunty, optimistic, and funny. And the Paramount arrangements were unique, featuring ocarinas, percussion, and harps—making them a far cry from MGM's usual string-heavy arrangements. Burke wrote for forty-one films and of those, twenty-five, including six Road pictures, starred Bing Crosby. Burke and Van Heusen's songs can be creamy, like "Moonlight Becomes You," "Imagination," "But Beautiful," "Like Someone in Love," and "It's Always You." Or they can be jaunty, like "Swinging on a Star," "Aren't You Glad You're You?" "My Heart is a Hobo," "Personality," and "Road to Morocco."

the last great Paramount musical, Funny Face (which was really an MGM musical in every way), there was a lot of mostly easygoing, sometimes manic and always unconventional fun. You could relax during a Paramount musical and not feel slightly intimidated or awed, as you might by MGM's prowess. Paramount's stars may have been a bit unorthodox but the studio's biggest musical star, Bing Crosby, was an everyman—a great singer but with the pleasing, relaxed style of the guy next door—if that guy hung out with the likes of Bob Hope, that is.

We've noted that Fox's nostalgia musicals and RKO's Astaire-Rogers cat-and-mouse jaunts were basically the same pictures made over and over again. So it was with the Road pictures, in which Bob and Bing were on the lam for some reason and found themselves in some exotic studio back lot. In pursuit of the extremely underrated Dorothy Lamour, they fought and bickered but remained pals to the end or rather, "The End." Along the way, Bob played the fool, Bing "buh-buh-ba-boo'd" some catchy tunes, Lamour found herself draped (or undraped) in something that accentuated the positive, and Bing and Bob played pattycake. Unlike other studios' variations on a single theme, the Road pictures constantly acknowledged their debt to the likeminded films that had come before—in fact, they even parodied themselves.

For all the fooling around, the songs were topnotch, the production values of equal quality, and the direction clear and concise. The roadtrips to Morocco, Zanzibar, Bali, Rio, and Utopia were of equal value, more or less. It wasn't until much later that the boys went on their last outing, to Hong Kong, that the magic wore off. Lamour had only a cameo in that one. ■

ABOVE LEFT: Der Bingle seems ready to punch his partner in hijinks in his infamous ski nose.

RIGHT: Jimmy Van Heusen (at piano), Johnny Burke (looking dreamy), and Mary Martin (with the gams) go through the score of Love Thy Neighbor.

THE ROCKY HORROR PICTURE SHOW

20TH CENTURY FOX—SEPTEMBER 26, 1975

THE ROCKY HORROR PICTURE SHOW

COMPOSER: Richard O'Brien
LYRICIST: Richard O'Brien
PRODUCERS: Michael White and Lou Adler
DIRECTOR: Jim Sharman
SCREENWRITERS: Jim Sharman and Richard O'Brien
SOURCE: Based on the musical *The Rocky Horror Show* by Richard O'Brien

Synopsis

Innocent newlyweds Brad and Janet stumble upon a wild party at the castle of the mad, transvestite Dr. Frank-N-Furter. The honeymooners spend the rest of the film trying to uphold "Don't Ask–Don't Tell" while everyone surrounding them is asking and telling . . . and doing.

Cast

Tim Curry ....*Dr. Frank-N-Furter*
Susan Sarandon ....*Janet Weiss*
Barry Bostwick............*Brad Majors*
Richard O'Brien...........*Riff Raff*
Patricia Quinn ....*Magenta*
Nell Campbell.............*Columbia*
Jonathan Adams ....*Dr. Everett V. Scott*
Peter Hinwood.............*Rocky Horror*
Meat Loaf ....*Eddie*
Charles Gray ....*A Criminologist*
Jeremy Newson...........*Ralph Hapschatt*
Hilary Labow ....*Betty Monroe Hapschatt*

Tim Curry relaxes as his minions (including author Richard O'Brien, at right) fawn over him.

F OLKS, A LITTLE LEATHER AND LIPSTICK ON A MAN DOES NOT A ROCK-AND-ROLL MUSI-cal make. *The Rocky Horror Picture Show*, based on the stage musical *The Rocky Horror Show*, was a flop when originally exhibited, but it became a phenomenal cult hit with the advent of long-running midnight screenings in college towns. Audiences would come dressed as their favorite characters—how naughty—and throw toast and rice at the screen at appropriate moments in the story, repeat the lines with the cast, sing the songs, dance the dances, and generally create a party of their own. The line between the entertainers and the entertained was blurred, and everybody had a gay old time.

Rocky Horror wasn't the first film to get this kind of treatment—or the last. It all started, albeit in a small way, with *Grease*, where oft-returning audiences performed the hand jive with the characters on the screen. But *Rocky Horror* took the tomfoolery to the nth degree. Heck, the film might have broken in the projector and the audience could have kept the show going. In recent years, happy audiences have gathered at "sing-along" screenings of *The Sound of Music*—complete with karaoke-style onscreen lyrics.

Rock and roll has had a hard time in musicals. Sometimes the rock is cleaned up so much it barely rocks—as evidenced in the aforementioned *Grease*, which could only be called pop rock. True rock and roll, especially the harder variety, has never been a success with movie audiences. Even Elvis the Pelvis toned down his dangerous sexuality in his films. Heck, by the end of Elvis's career, there was little difference between him and Pat Boone, save Boone's piety.

The most successful rock films have been concert documentaries such as *Woodstock* and *The Last Waltz*—but those aren't narrative films. Film biographies such as *The Buddy Holly Story* and *Walk the Line* have worked at remaining musically faithful to their subjects (all the while playing it loose with the facts, in the best tradition of the Hollywood biopic). The song stylings of Joaquin Phoenix and Reese Witherspoon couldn't hold a candle to those of the real superstars Johnny Cash and June Carter. Keefe Braselle in *The Eddie Cantor Story* and Larry Parks in *The Jolson Story* went the lip-synch route, to better effect.

Eminem played himself in *8 Mile* so we have to assume he was telling it as it was. Prince played himself (sort of) in *Purple Rain* and proved what a truly radical and ahead-of-his-time musician he is (with an ego to match, by all accounts). The same can't be said for his costar Morris Day, who has hardly been heard from again. (Okay, he did appear in *The Adventures of Ford Fairlane* with Andrew Dice Clay and Priscilla Presley—we rest our case.) Anyway, *8 Mile* and *Purple Rain* are probably as real as we can ever hope a rock pic to be.

Just as Hollywood and independents alike have watered down rock to make it palatable to middle-class, middle school audiences, *The Rocky Horror Picture Show* took hard rock and S&M imagery and made them palatable for the mall movieplex audience. Throw in a little titillation, a bucketful of homoeroticism, and a script made up almost entirely of quotable lines, and you've got the recipe for decade upon decade of college shenanigans. For it's longevity and ability to please audiences, we've got to admit that *The Rocky Horror Picture Show* is one of the greatest Hollywood musicals—even if we can't quite bring ourselves to throw toast. ∎

Behind the Screen

- Mick Jagger was interested in playing Dr. Frank-N-Furter, which we think would have given the film some cred.
- Steve Martin wanted to play Brad. That wouldn't have hurt, either.
- Vincent Price wanted to play the Criminologist and was offered the part, but his schedule didn't permit it.

ABOVE: Susan Sarandon seems upset to be found nude next to Peter Hinwood (as Rocky). Many in the audience would react otherwise.

RIGHT: Sue Blane's stunning costume design for Tim Curry's character, Dr. Frank-N-Furter.

SONGS

"Charles Atlas" ∎ "Dammit Janet" ∎ "Don't Dream It, Do It" ∎ "Eddie's Teddy". "Floor Show" ∎ "Frankenstein's Place" ∎ "Gunfight Music" ∎ "Hot Dog". "Hot Patootie" ∎ "I Can Make You a Man" ∎ "I'm Going Home". "Science Fiction" ∎ "Sweet Hero" ∎ "Sweet Transsexual" ∎ "Sweet Transvestite" ∎ "Sword of Damocles" ∎ "Time Warp" ∎ "Touch Touch Me" ∎ "Wild and Untamed Thing" ∎ "Wise Up, Janet Weiss"

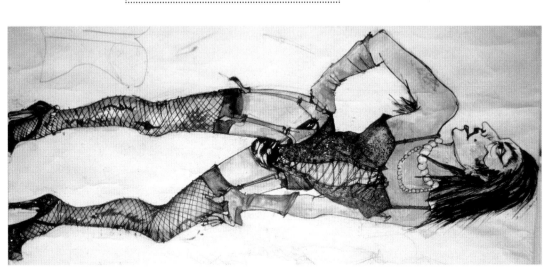

THE ROSE

20TH CENTURY FOX—NOVEMBER 7, 1979

THE ROSE

PRODUCERS: Aaron Russo and Marvin Worth

DIRECTOR: Mark Rydell

SCREENWRITERS: Michael Cimino, Bo Goldman, and William Kerby

CHOREOGRAPHER: Toni Basil

Synopsis

Whatever this movie is about, we know it is definitely not inspired by the life of Janis Joplin. Absolutely not. Positively.

Cast

Bette Midler.............Mary Rose Foster
Alan Bates..............Rudge Campbell
Frederic Forrest.........Huston Dyer
Harry Dean Stanton......Billy Ray
Barry Primus............Dennis
David Keith.............Pfc. Mal
Sandra McCabe..........Sarah Willingham
Will Hare...............Mr. Leonard
Rudy Bond.............Monty

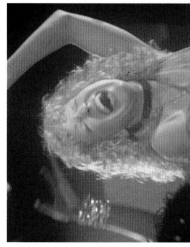

The many faces of Bette Midler.

SEX AND GUTS—ALONG WITH TALENT, BRAINS, AND A WICKED SENSE OF HUMOR—MADE Bette Midler into a star. It's too bad that her only other film musical to date has been the heartfelt but soggy *For the Boys*, a tale about entertaining the troops during World War II that was probably inspired by Midler's successful recording of "Boogie Woogie Bugle Boy." Mark Rydell directed both pictures. Who'd have thought that the director of the uncompromising *The Rose* would later helm the sentimental *On Golden Pond?*

> "[The producers] thought it was dull and a hymn and NOT rock and roll and totally wrong. They put it in the reject box."
>
> —*Amanda McBroom, on her title song*

Like Diana Ross in the Billie Holliday biopic *Lady Sings the Blues* (and like countless other singers, as well), Midler wanted to chomp onto a real dramatic role, one that would show her range. This tale of a woman on her way down would have pathos, drama, tears, and depressing makeup. In short, it would all but guarantee her an Oscar nomination. Like Ross before her, Midler did not prettify her subject. She didn't die beautifully, as Ali MacGraw had in *Love Story*; rather, she opted to show the ravages of a life cut short by drugs and alcohol.

Audiences go into both *Lady Sings the Blues* and *The Rose* knowing how they will turn out, so the filmmakers have their work cut out for them when it comes to holding our interest while avoiding clichés. *The Rose* is a bit more successful than *Lady Sings the Blues* in that department, perhaps because Midler's own success wasn't built on glamour or looks, as Ross's was. Whereas Ross tends to hold her emotions in check behind a blank slate of mechanized Motown delivery, Midler lets it all hang out. And whereas Ross descends into a drug induced stupor, Midler's fire continues to burn red hot until the moment of her death.

Much of the success of *The Rose* can be attributed to the title song by Amanda McBroom. As a song, "The Rose" is an impassioned piece of writing, imbued with a kind of optimism and romanticism that contrast starkly with the tragic aspects of the film's story. With the song resonating in our mind, instead of thinking of Midler's character as a car crash waiting to happen we view her as a tortured soul who can only achieve emotional release through her music. Although the song was a little too non–Tin Pan Alley for the older-skewing Academy of Motion Picture Arts and Sciences, who didn't even nominate it, McBroom did win a Golden Globe and Midler picked up a Grammy for her performance of the song.

Most important, the song, like the film, is a love story—the story of an insecure young singer longing for a safe haven but choosing an emotionally abusive father figure who enables her addictions. The need to be controlled and the need for escape are the warring forces within Mary Rose Foster. And, just like those other film clichés, the racecar driver whose dream is to win one last Grand Prix and the cop who's up for retirement after one last case, Mary Rose's dream of a triumphant comeback concert in her hometown simply can't end well. We don't see the cliché because we are so invested in the character. That's thanks to Midler's performance—and that song. ∎

SONGS

■ "Fire Down Below" (Bob Seger) ■ "I've Written a Letter to Daddy (If I Had My Life to Live Over)" (Larry Vincent, Henry Tobias, and Moe Jaffe) ■ "Keep on Rockin'" (John Carter and Sammy Hagar) ■ "Love Her with a Feeling" (Jon Hendricks and Tampa Red) ■ "Midnight in Memphis" (Tony Johnson) ■ "The Rose" (Amanda McBroom) ■ "Sold My Soul to Rock and Roll" (Gene Pistilli) ■ "Stay with Me" (Jerry Ragovoy and George David Weiss) ■ "When a Man Loves a Woman" (Calvin Lewis and Andrew Wright) ■ "Whose Side Are You On?" (Kenny Hopkins and Charley Williams)

Behind the Screen

■ The picture was supposed to be titled *The Pearl* but the Janis Joplin estate refused to let producers use her well-known nickname.

ROSE-MARIE

MGM—FEBRUARY 1, 1936

ROSE-MARIE

COMPOSERS: Rudolf Friml and Herbert Stothart

LYRICISTS: Oscar Hammerstein II and Otto Harbach

PRODUCER: Hunt Stromberg

DIRECTOR: W. S. Van Dyke

SCREENWRITERS: Frances Goodrich, Albert Hackett, and Alice Duer Miller

SOURCE: Based on the musical *Rose Marie* by Rudolf Friml, Oscar Hammerstein II, Otto Harbach, and Herbert Stothart

CHOREOGRAPHER: Chester Hale

Synopsis

The Mounties always get their man. And they always get their girl, too, even if she's strong enough to beat up her brother the nerd.

Cast

Jeanette MacDonald .....*Marie de Flor*
Nelson Eddy................*Myerson*
Allan Jones ....*Tenor*
James Stewart ....*Rose's brother*
Alan Mowbray ....*Premier*
Gilda Gray................*Bella*
George Regas............*Boniface*

Nelson Eddy: "I don't know how to act."

Director W. S. Van Dyke: "You're telling me!"

ABOVE RIGHT: Nelson Eddy embraces Jeanette MacDonald as a totem pole graciously looks the other way.

BELOW RIGHT: Jimmy Stewart, in an unusual turn as the villainous brother of Rose-Marie. Yes, he's the man that Mountie Nelson Eddy must get.

OLKS, THE LAUGH'S NOT ON MACDONALD AND EDDY, IT'S ON THE PEOPLE WHO NAIVELY think the couple's on-screen high jinks were schmaltzy, clichéd operettas. We bet those folk haven't actually seen one of the team's pictures they've only seen decades of parodies. If they have seen the films, they laugh because they're embarrassed by the expression of emotion without irony or cynicism. It's true that most of the MacDonald-Eddy films were a bit over the top—as most good operettas are—but the MGM writers acknowledged the artifice and the pictures were surprisingly sophisticated, with absolutely no winking at the camera or expressions of regret or embarrassment.

One thing that all the movie studios had in common was their absolute belief in the projects they undertook, whether they were shorts, B-pictures, or first-class features. Each project received the same consideration. Each was created to entertain audiences in the best way possible.

MacDonald and Eddy operettas have top-drawer production values. The cinematography, for instance, in such movies as *Maytime, Bitter Sweet,* and *Rose-Marie* is as good as in any film from any studio at the time.

Though the film hewed less closely to the plot of the original Broadway production than either the 1928 silent version (there were also silent versions of *The Red Mill, The Student*

BACK...BY POPULAR DEMAND/

JEANETTE MACDONALD • NELSON EDDY

ROSE-MARIE

Directed by W·S·VAN DYKE
Produced by Hunt Stromberg

Prince and *Maytime* as well as a mostly silent *Show Boat*) or the 1954 color extravaganza, the version of *Rose-Marie* that sticks most in the public's mind is the MacDonald-Eddy incarnation. It's almost impossible to picture Nelson Eddy in anything other than his Mountie uniform from *Rose-Marie*, warbling that damned "When I'm calling you-oo-oo-oo-oo-oo-oo" with his costar. Sadly, that brief refrain from the "Indian Love Call" has defined not only *Rose-Marie* and not only the MacDonald-Eddy films, but all operettas, which have consequently come to be thought of as twee and sappy. But one look at the scene in *Rose-Marie*—the intent gaze of the two lovers, the beauty of the mountains and lake beyond, and the utter commitment of the entire movie—should erase all giggles from all but the most stubbornly snide viewers. ■

SONGS

"Indian Love Call" ■ "Just for You" (music by Rudolf Friml and Herbert Stothart, lyrics by Gus Kahn) ■ "The Mounties (music by Rudolf Friml and Herbert Stothart)" ■ "Oh, Rose-Marie" ■ "Pardon Me Madame" (music by Herbert Stothart, lyrics by Gus Kahn) ■ "Totem Tom-Tom" (music by Rudolf Friml and Herbert Stothart)

"The ice between them was thick, cold, and scary."

—Cinematographer Charles Schoenbaum, on MacDonald and Eddy's relationship

---

Jeanette MacDonald and Nelson Eddy

During the filming of *Maytime*, director Robert Z. Leonard asked Jeanette MacDonald to make a sweeping entrance. She did just as requested—pushing a janitor's broom. MacDonald could have a good time on a movie set, but she could also be a diva. For her hot temper, Leonard nicknamed her "the Red Volcano." Nelson Eddy, on the other hand, was certainly conscious of the disparity between his salary and that of MacDonald. He kept track of the amount of fan mail she received as well as the lengths to which the studio brass would go to cater to her. In fact, song-writer Robert Wright opined that "Nelson was the team's real prima donna." MacDonald got her start on the Broadway stage, appearing in many musical comedies. She was offered a part in a Hollywood film but her stage producers, the Shubert Brothers, refused to let her out of her contract. Later, Ernst Lubitsch was going through some old screen tests and came across MacDonald's. He offered her a part in *The Love Parade* and she became an immediate star. Eddy and MacDonald left MGM and spent most of their time working in radio. MacDonald returned to MGM after five years for two more films before she left the movies for good. Eddy's musical background was opera: he'd performed with many companies before hitting the movies. MacDonald's one regret was that she was never allowed to sing on the stage of the Metropolitan Opera. Certainly, she possessed the requisite acting talent and voice; she'd appeared in several operas in Canada and the United States to excellent reviews. But the Met's snobbery toward Hollywood kept her dream unfulfilled. Although the pair had their temperamental periods, they were devoted to each other.

ABOVE LEFT: House Peters and Joan Crawford (as Rose-Marie) in the 1928 silent version of the operetta.

ABOVE RIGHT: Ann Blyth (as Rose Marie—sans hyphen) and Howard Keel in the 1954 MGM version.

RIGHT: Nelson and Jeanette go for a stroll on the MGM lot.

SATURDAY NIGHT FEVER

PARAMOUNT—DECEMBER 16, 1977

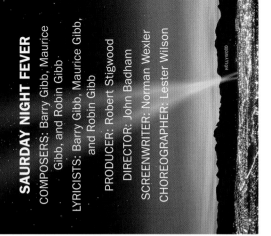

SAURDAY NIGHT FEVER

COMPOSERS: Barry Gibb, Maurice Gibb, and Robin Gibb

LYRICISTS: Barry Gibb, Maurice Gibb, and Robin Gibb

PRODUCER: Robert Stigwood
DIRECTOR: John Badham
SCREENWRITER: Norman Wexler
CHOREOGRAPHER: Lester Wilson

Synopsis

A young boy from an outer borough of New York wants to make it big, figuring if he can make it there he can make it anywhere. So, he puts on his white suit, hits the dance floor, and that's what killed rock-and-roll.

Cast

John Travolta..............Tony Manero
Karen Lynn Gorney.......Stephanie
Barry Miller..................Bobby C.
Joseph Cali...................Joey
Paul Pape.....................Double J.
Donna Pescow...............Annette
Bruce Ornstein...............Gus
Julie Bovasso.................Flo
Monti Rock III...............DJ

Donna Pescow and John Travolta catch the fever every Saturday night.

ORGET ABOUT HIS *DISCO* MOVES. EVEN JOHN TRAVOLTA'S STRUT DOWN A BROOKLYN street is choreography. Think of Fred Astaire on the Champs-Élysées in *Funny Face* during "Bonjour Paree" and it's the same thing: a joyous, everything-is-all-right swagger that perfectly defines the personality.

Saturday Night Fever gave John Travolta plenty of opportunity to show off his moves and it is his performance that makes it a terrific movie. Subsequent attempts to exploit the genre, such as *Roller Boogie*, *Skatetown, U.S.A.*, and *Can't Stop the Music*, could never touch it.

The film's genesis was a story by Nik Cohn in *New York* magazine titled "The Return of Saturday Night." Clay Felker, the founder and editor of the magazine, changed the title to "Tribal Rights of the New Saturday Night." It turned out that Cohn had made up the entire article, but it was based on a very real phenomenon: disco was sweeping the country. At the time he wrote it, Cohn was crashing on the couch of Bill Oakes, the president of RSO Records, owned by Robert Stigwood.

Stigwood was also the manager of the Bee Gees and he immediately optioned the story and put the brothers Gibb to work writing a score for the film. They wrote the songs in one week and added an update of one of their existing songs, "You Should Be Dancing." As Barry Gibb explained in 1983, "When we wrote the music, the only songs we thought were disco were 'You Should Be Dancing' and maybe 'Jive Talkin'.' We never thought of 'Stayin' Alive' as disco." But the public sure did—and that song and "How Deep Is Your Love?" each hit the number one spot on the *Billboard* chart before the film had even opened.

> "After *Saturday Night Fever*, we wanted to do a poster, with the three of us in Rambo's bodies, with machine guns, and in the background there'd be a body in a white suit, bullet-ridden, and the mirror ball all shot to pieces."
>
> —*Maurice Gibb*

Although Travolta had done a fair amount of dancing on Broadway, he wasn't anywhere near a professional disco dancer, so he spent all the preproduction time polishing his moves with the help of an uncredited Deney Terrio, later of *Dance Fever* fame. Months later, it all paid off. Travolta had always been a fan of film musicals and adored Fred Astaire. Taking a page from the Astaire playbook, he recognized that the audience needed to see his feet while he was dancing. But director John Badham had shot the centerpiece dance solo from the waist up. Travolta insisted that Badham reshoot and add footage of his whole body (and that marvelous dance floor). Good move, John—the dance is the best thing in the movie.

Sadly, as happens all too often, the mainstreaming of disco—helped along enormously by *Saturday Night Fever*—hastened the backlash against it. Soon, everyone was tired of the sound and for better or worse (and like swing, bop, and Latin dance before it), disco fell out of fashion. But we'll always have Bay Ridge. ■

ABOVE: John Travolta on the dance floor with authentic outer-borough girl, Fran Drescher.

CENTER: Director John Badham gives John Travolta some pointers.

BOTTOM LEFT: John Travolta dips Karen Lynn Gorney.

BELOW RIGHT: John Travolta's Tony considers becoming a man of the cloth, but in the end he picks polyester as the fabric of his life.

SONGS

"How Deep Is Your Love" ■ "If I Can't Have You" ■ "More than a Woman" ■ "Night Fever" ■ "Stayin' Alive" ■ "You Should Be Dancing"

John Travolta

After appearances in the Broadway musicals *Grease* (as a replacement) and *Over Here!* John Travolta made the trip west to make it big. And he did. After he found fame in the TV show *Welcome Back, Kotter*, his Broadway experiences as a dancer came in handy for *Saturday Night Fever*. He played a similar character in the film of *Grease* but managed to escape typecasting by also undertaking a variety of comedic and dramatic parts that didn't demand strutting around in black leather. He even survived the *Saturday Night Fever* sequel, *Staying Alive*. Interestingly, he continued to play the charismatic lug Vinnie Barbarino on *Kotter* even as he appeared in his first two musical films. He's had his career ups and downs,

perhaps more than many, but the recently came back to great acclaim in drag in the musical film version of *Hairspray*. Be honest. Having seen him in *Saturday Night Fever* and *Pulp Fiction*, could you ever have imagined he'd play such an affecting Edna Turnblad? Even his association with Scientology and the persistent tabloid rumors about his sexuality have never managed to dim his well-deserved popularity with audiences.

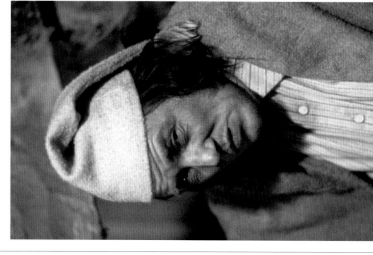

SCROOGE

CINEMA CENTER—NOVEMBER 5, 1970

SCROOGE

COMPOSER: Leslie Bricusse
LYRICIST: Leslie Bricusse
PRODUCER: Robert H. Solo
DIRECTOR: Ronald Neame
SCREENWRITER: Leslie Bricusse
SOURCE: *A Christmas Carol* by Charles Dickens
CHOREOGRAPHER: Paddy Stone

Synopsis

Ebenezer Scrooge travels through time, meets himself coming and going, and doesn't like much what he finds.

Cast

Albert Finney................*Ebenezer Scrooge*
Edith Evans...................*Ghost of Christmas Past*
Kenneth More................*Ghost of Christmas Present*
Paddy Stone ....*Ghost of Christmas Yet to Come*
Alec Guinness...............*Jacob Marley's Ghost*
Laurence Naismith........*Mr. Fezziwig*
David Collings..............*Bob Cratchit*
Michael Medwin............*Nephew Harry*

A reformed man, Scrooge leads the crowd as Father Christmas.

DID WE NEED ANOTHER RETELLING OF CHARLES DICKENS'S IMMORTAL *A CHRISTMAS CAROL?* The story was filmed as early as 1908 with Charles Ogle, a member of Thomas Edison's film company, as the first film Scrooge. Ogle returned in the 1910 version of the story, this time as Bob Cratchit. An English version of the tale premiered in 1914. Alistair Sim, thought by many to have been the best *Scrooge* ever, starred in the 1951 version, titled Scrooge. Walt Disney's studio got into the act in 1983 with the animated *Mickey's Christmas Carol.* In 1988, Bill Murray appeared in an updated variation of the story titled *Scrooged.* Additional animated versions came along in 1994-1997 (featuring the voices of Tim Curry and Whoopi Goldberg), and 2001. That last one, overexplicitly titled *A Christmas Carol,* was excellent; the cast of voices included Simon Callow, Michael Gambon, and Kate Winslet. In 1992, Kermit the Frog costarred with Michael Caine in *The Muppet Christmas Carol,* the first (and to date only) human-puppet version of the story.

There have been other *Christmas Carols,* including versions starring dogs and the Flintstones. But for our money, the Albert Finney musical version, *Scrooge,* is at the top of the heap. In its native England, it was titled *A Christmas Carol,* but in the United States, the title became *Scrooge* (no doubt the idea of some marketing genius). As in *Oliver!* the production values are top notch, creating a wonderful sense of place and time. But the things that really set this version apart are the excellent score by Leslie Bricusse, the orchestrations by Herbert Spencer, and the musical direction and arrangements by Ian Fraser. (Fraser had previously worked with Bricusse on *Doctor Doolittle* and *Goodbye Mr. Chips.*)

Paddy Stone, who devised the film's dances, was a noted West End choreographer, and as Onna White did in the film version of *Oliver!* Stone brought great imagination and character work to his routines. His staging of "December the 25th" captures the joy and humor of the *Fezziwig's* Christmas celebrations, injecting real warmth into the humor rather than relying on easy slapstick jokes. In the Oscar-nominated song "Thank You Very Much" (as well as its reprises) Stone made great use of Ian Fraser's imaginative arrangements. The numbers build to a conclusion both choreographically and musically, unlike many movie musical dances that seem simply to take up time until the music stops.

The reprises that make up your typical megamix. They begin with "I Like Life," then move into "Father Christmas" and ultimately into the finale, which blends "Thank You Very Much" with a reprise of "A Christmas Carol." As White did, Stone made dances with a beginning, middle, and end; they were true to the story as well as the characters. For example, in one sequence he began a dance with Scrooge and a passing woman. They then met a quartet of street musicians and joined forces. The group in turn met eight bell ringers. More and more people joined the procession and then—in one moment—the dance steps of all of the various groups melded into one routine. This sequence also reintroduced the characters and each plot line was neatly resolved.

In composing an inherently cinematic score, Bricusse was continuing the work he had done on *Doctor Dolittle* and *Goodbye Mr. Chips.* Listen to "I'll Begin Again" and the sequence that blends "You . . . You . . ." with "Happiness." They both transform

what would be a stage soliloquy into a voiceover that provides a cinematic transition. As in "Goodbye Mr. Chips," the score opens with a boys' choir, this time singing "A Christmas Carol" in an especially sumptuous arrangement by Fraser. The songs have real dramatic punch, unlike many film (and show) songs that rely on a series of modulations and an increase in volume to indicate emotional build.

A Christmas Carol is a surprisingly resilient novella, and the hundreds of interpretations of it in a variety of forms are a testament to its timeless qualities. Some adaptations have been less than respectful, many less than successful. Scrooge remains one of the best retellings of the classic story. ■

LEFT: Michael Medwin, as Scrooge's nephew Fred, hopes to get a Christmas bonus from his uncle. ABOVE: Flashback! Suzanne Neve and Albert Finney in happier times.

Behind the Screen

■ Albert Finney was only thirty-four years old when he made the film.

SONGS

"The Beautiful Day" ■ "A Christmas Carol!" ■ "Christmas Children" ■ "December the 25th" ■ "Father Chris'mas" ■ "I Like Life" ■ "Happiness" ■ "I Hate People" ■ "I'll Begin Again" ■ "See the Phantoms" ■ "Thank You Very Much" ■ "You . . . You . . ."

Synopsis

Kidnapping may be a federal offense—but if the good-looking kidnappers (seven brothers) and the comely kidnappees (seven sisters) happen to get snowed in for the winter, it can also lead to love. And that's no crime.

Cast

Howard Keel ....Adam Pontipee
Jane Powell ....Milly Pontipee
Jeff Richards ....Benjamin Pontipee
Russ Tamblyn ....Gideon Pontipee
Tommy Rall ....Frank Pontipee
Marc Platt ....Dan Pontipee
Matt Mattox ....Caleb Pontipee
Jacques d'Amboise ....Ephraim Pontipee
Julie Newmar ....Dorcas Gailen
Nancy Kilgas ....Alice Elcott
Betty Carr ....Sarah Kine
Virginia Gibson...........Liza
Ruta Lee ....Ruth Jebson
Norma Doggett...........Martha

SEVEN BRIDES FOR SEVEN BROTHERS

MGM—JULY 22, 1954

Howard Keel and Jane Powell stare lovingly into each other's eyes.

I N THIS AGE OF CABLE TELEVISION, NETFLIX, IPHONES, AND STREAMING VIDEO, IT'S HARD TO believe that there was a time (not so long ago) when you were out of luck if you didn't catch a movie in its first run. We have a friend who was too young to see *Seven Brides for Seven Brothers* on its first release, much to his continuing chagrin. Sure, he could listen to the soundtrack recording and imagine what was going on in the picture, but it is unlikely that what he imagined during the dance sequence was as fresh and exciting as what Michael Kidd created. It wasn't until the film hit television and then videotape that he understood just how excellent the film is.

Kidd's gymnastic barn-raising number for *Seven Brides* is amazing in its versatility. Look closer and you'll see that the dance has a beginning, middle, and end. It's not just a bunch of guys taking swings at each other and showing off their mettle. Every section of the dance has its reason for being and expands upon plot points as well as character. Young Russ Tamblyn, who actually was a gymnast, not a trained dancer, reveals himself to be the most naive of the brothers through the dance. Never mind, he'll step up to the plate when his time comes. And so it goes with each brother and each bride.

And though the guys are dancers, real dancers from ballet and such, they are real men, too. Kidd recalled the studio bosses' reactions to his casting ideas: "They kept saying to me in words of one syllable, 'You can't have a bunch of guys jumping around; the audience will think you've got some pansy backwoodsmen.'" But, as in *West Side Story*, the dancers' conviction and demeanor carries the audience along. We understand that the dance isn't real, but rather an expression of the interior thoughts and feelings of the characters.

LEFT: One bride and six brothers.

"Jack Cummings' only contribution to the film "was to make it more difficult."

—Stanley Donen

SONGS

"Bless Your Beautiful Hide" ■ "Goin' Courtin'" ■ "June Bride" ■ "Lonesome Polecat" ■ "Sobbin' Women" ■ "Spring, Spring, Spring" ■ "When You're in Love" ■ "Wonderful, Wonderful Day"

Michael Kidd

■ n a dyspeptic mood, Jerome Robbins once said, "Dance hasn't been very successful on the screen. . . . What the audience does get, most of the time, is sex, charm, and daring, but not the genuine energy that dance should have. I'd make an exception in behalf of Michael Kidd's ballets in *Seven Brides for Seven Brothers*." Kidd, best known for his athletic, masculine choreography, was also capable of making wonderfully romantic dances, as exemplified by the "Dancing in the Dark" sequence in *The Band Wagon* (which he cochoreographed with Fred Astaire). Kidd built upon the accomplishments of Gene Kelly and Stanley Donen in his utilization of the widescreen format for dance. He once remarked, "I have found that the camera's ability to see more than the human eye allows an emphasis on close-ups at important moments and at the same time gives varying angles to the dance that stage audiences could not catch from their static positions." Kidd was a noted Broadway choreographer of such shows as *Finian's Rainbow*, *Guys and Dolls*, *Can Can*, and *Li'l Abner*. But it is his film choreography, especially that of *Seven Brides for Seven Brothers*, that best showcases his greatness.

Most important, the *Seven Brides* dance has a conclusion, a kind of "button" that surprises and delights the audience even while it advances the plot. Kidd composed this dance as a great songwriter conceives a song—to advance the action, express character, and entertain. This isn't to denigrate the other numbers. There's just as much invention in "Spring, Spring, Spring," but not the fireworks. Again, the choreography is just right for the scene. It's a simple dance but it pinpoints the exact moment when the girls finally get it: being holed up for the winter with a bunch of hunky (if dirty and ill-mannered) boys may not be so bad after all.

We don't even mind that, with the exception of a couple of second-unit shots, the film is completely studio bound. Rather than making it feel hokey or unrealistic, this turns it into a kind of fairy tale. And that's why we don't mind the sexism of the script or its incredible premise, either. If the film was more naturalistic, we might not be as charmed. That artifice is part of the beauty of film.

No matter who you are or what your background, you can probably enjoy spending some fantasy time in the company of beautiful brides and handsome brothers, marveling at their sense of fun and romance and musicality. So, thank your lucky stars that you are alive at a time when you can watch thousands of films via video, DVDs, cable television, and Internet downloads, *Seven Brides for Seven Brothers* ain't a bad place to start. ■

RIGHT: Michael Kidd teaches Lucille Ball and Don Tomkins a new step for the 1961 Broadway musical, *Wildcat*.

Jane Powell

Jane Powell, she of the high soprano, seemed a sweet little talented girl when she first started in pictures, but she matured into a woman who could hold her own with Fred Astaire in *Royal Wedding*—and that's no small accomplishment. She began her career strictly in the Deanna Durbin mode, spunky but polite. Then she found herself assigned to the Joe Pasternak unit and a bunch of drippy, colloquial films even less exciting than the Andy Hardy movies—including *A Date with Judy* and *Nancy Goes to Rio*. (Strangely, MGM didn't quite know what to do with their ingenues—look at Judy Garland, for example. Both Garland and Powell were lent out to other studios for their first films.) After her stint with Astaire, Powell proved her mettle as a fully formed leading lady. It's only too bad that she never really got to exploit her sense of humor and wit. After *Royal Wedding* and *Seven Brides for Seven Brothers*, it was back to B musicals such as *Rich, Young and Pretty*; *Small Town Girl*; and *Three Sailors and a Girl*. *Athena* was a better-than-average Powell vehicle, though not really top drawer in spite of a terrific Hugh Martin score. *Hit the Deck* was nothing to write home about but it had some nice moments. Ah, well. By the end of the 1950s the studio system was dead and, like all MGM stars, she had to look for other employment. Powell made some television musicals and appeared on a few series, including that elephant's graveyard of stars, *Murder, She Wrote*. She did some summer stock and appeared on Broadway in *Irene*, taking over for Debbie Reynolds. More recently, she appeared in *Chicago* and in the Stephen Sondheim musical *Bounce* and was excellent in the part. She's always kept her sunny disposition and charm—and her voice, too.

ABOVE: Peter Lawford, Jane Powell, Fred Astaire, and Sarah Churchill in *Royal Wedding*.

BELOW: It's tough to film in the dead of winter—unless you are in a studio, that is.

GREAT NUMBERS FROM MUSICALS

THERE ARE SOME GREAT MOVIES IN OUR LIST BELOW. SOME ALMOST MADE it into our 101 list. In fact, you probably think a few or more than a few of them definitely should have been in our list. In any case, the movies below all have terrific numbers. Some are simple and some are elaborate but all are special in some way. Though many are great songs, not all of them are but the accoutrements, shall we say, are great. So, here's a partial list of our favorite musical numbers from musicals and non-musicals alike. Most of these films are terrific but some, well, not so much (are you listening, *Star?*). The great thing about DVDs is you can skip right to the numbers without having to watch ridiculous plots and bad acting. Still, as we said before, most of these pictures are well worth watching on every level.

Ali Baba Goes to Town, "Swing Is Here to Stay" • *Applause,* "What Wouldn't I Do for That Man" • *Artists and Models,* "Public Melody No. 1" • *Athena,* "I Never Felt Better" • *Babes on Broadway,* "Anything Can Happen in New York" • *Bandwagon,* "Seeing's Believing" • *Bye Bye Birdie,* "I Wanna Be a Dancin' Man," "Oops," "Seeing's Believing" • *Bye Bye Birdie,* "Bye Bye Birdie," "Gotta Lot of Livin' to Do," "The Telephone Hour" (the choreography by Onna White was iconic and copied by hundreds of choreographers) • *Call Me Madam,* "The International Rag," "It's a Lovely Day Today," "What Chance Have I with Love?" • *Centennial Summer,* "Up with the Lark" • *Cover Girl,* "I've Turned the Corner" (which is Gene Kelly's fantastic dance with his alter ego), "Make Way for Tomorrow" • *Dames,* "I Only Have Eyes for You" • *A Day at the Races,* "All God's Chillun' Got Rhythm" • *Deep in My Heart,* "It," "One Alone," "Leg o' Mutton" • *Down to Earth,* "This Can't Be Legal" • *DuBarry Was a Lady,* "Madam, I Love Your Crepes Suzettes" • *The Farmer Takes a Wife,* "Today I Love Everybody" • *Flower Drum Song,* "Sunday" • *Gilda,* "Put the Blame on Mame" (is simplicity itself) • *Give a Girl a Break,* "Applause, Applause" (and its really clever staging) • *Go Into Your Dance,* "About a Quarter to Nine" • *Going Places,* "Mutiny in the Nursery" • *Gold Diggers of 1935,* "Lullaby of Broadway" • *High Society,* "Who wants to Be a Millionaire," "You're Sensational," "Hit

the Deck," "Lady from the Bayou" • *It's a Great Feeling,* "There's Nothin' Rougher than Love," *It's Always Fair Weather,* "Baby You Knock Me Out," "I Like Myself," "Late night dance sequence," "Thanks a Lot but No Thanks" (which was filmed in one take!) • *The Joy of Living,* "You Couldn't Be Cuter" • *Jupiter's Darling* • *Kid from Brooklyn, The,* "Hey, What's Your Name?" (Jule Styne used the music again in the Broadway show *Fade Out-Fade In* as "A Girl to Remember") • *Kid Millions,* "When My Ship Comes In" • *Les Girls,* "Ca C'est L'Amour," "Les Girls," "You're Just Too Too!" • *Let's Make Love,* "My Heart Belongs to Daddy" • *The Life of an Elephant" • Jumbo,* "Little Girl Blue," "Over and Over Again" • *Mother Wore Tights,* "Kokomo, Indiana" • *My Sister Eileen,* "Competition Dance" for Bob Fosse and Tommy Rall • *The Night They Raided Minsky's,* "Take Ten Terrific Girls" • *On a Clear Day You Can See Forever,* "Love with All the Trimmings" • *101 Dalmations,* "Cruella DeVille" • *Orchestra Wives,* "(I've Got a Gal in) Kalamazoo" • *Pennies from Heaven,* 1981 "Let's Misbehave," "Love Is Good for What Ails You" • *The Pirate,* "Be a Clown" not to be confused with "Make 'Em Laugh" from *Singin' in the Rain* (which uses the exact same music as the Cole Porter original, "Nina"), "Love of My Life" • *The Producers,* "Springtime for Hitler" • *Ready, Willing, and Able,* "Too Marvelous for Words" • *Royal Wedding,* "Every Night at Seven," "How Could You Believe Me when I Said I Loved You when You Know I've Been a Liar All My Life," "I Left My Heart in Haiti," "You're All the World to Me" • *1776,* "He Plays the Violin" • *The Sky's the Limit,* "My Shining Hour," "One for My Baby" • *Small Town Girl—"I Gotta Hear that Beat," "Some Like It Hot," "I Wanna Be Loved By You," "Runnin' Wild" • Star!,* "Burlington Bertie," "Has Anybody Seen Our Ship?" • *Summer Holiday;* "The Stanley Steamer" • *Sweet Adeline,* "Don't Ever Leave Me," "Why Was I Born?" • *Sweet Charity,* "Big Spender," "I'm a Brass Band" • *Thank Your Lucky Stars,* "Love Isn't Born," "There's Gotta Be Something Better Than This" • *There's No Business Like Show Business,* "Alexander's Ragtime Band," "Sailor's Not a Sailor," "Heat Wave," "Too Many Girls," "You're Nearer" • *Whatever Happened to Baby Jane,* "I've Written a Letter to Daddy" (as sung by the grown-up Jane is good and grotesque) • *Ziegfeld Follies,* "Limehouse Blues," "Love," "This Heart of Mine"

SHOW BOAT

SHOW BOAT

COMPOSER: Jerome Kern
LYRICIST: Oscar Hammerstein II
PRODUCER: Carl Laemmle Jr.
DIRECTOR: James Whale
SCREENWRITER: Oscar Hammerstein II
SOURCE: Based on the musical
Show Boat by Jerome Kern and
Oscar Hammerstein II
CHOREOGRAPHER: LeRoy Prinz

Synopsis

Girl gets boy, girl loses boy, girl gets fame, girl gets boy. The blacks get nothin' but sweat and strain and some great songs.

Cast

Irene Dunne	Magnolia Hawks
Allan Jones	Gaylord Ravenal
Charles Winninger	Cap'n Andy Hawks
Paul Robeson	Joe
Helen Morgan	Julie LaVerne
Helen Westley	Parthy Hawks
Queenie Smith	Ellie May Chipley
Hattie McDaniel	Queenie
Donald Cook	Steve Baker

SHOW BOAT
UNIVERSAL—MAY 14, 1936

Allan Jones, in the real world, woos Irene Dunne on the deck of her beloved show boat.

J UST LIKE OL' MAN RIVER, *SHOW BOAT* JUST KEEPS ROLLIN' ALONG. ALTHOUGH IT HAD A rocky tryout prior to Broadway, when it opened in New York it was immediately celebrated as one of the greatest of all stage musicals. Now, more than eighty years since its premiere, *Show Boat* is still revived frequently throughout the world.

Hollywood was hot to get its hands on *Show Boat*, even though sound hadn't taken hold of the screen, at least as far Universal Pictures was concerned. Other musicals and operas had been adapted to the silent screen so, after leasing the rights to the novel from author Edna Ferber, Universal went ahead with a silent version. By the time the film was about to open in 1929, two years after the Broadway smash hit had premiered, it was clear that sound was the wave of the future.

So, Universal inserted several sound set pieces into the film. Since they had obtained rights to the novel but not the famed Jerome Kern–Oscar Hammerstein show, new songs were added and none of them was particularly effective. Universal saw the error of its ways and contacted the show's producer, Florenz Ziegfeld, who licensed them two songs: "Ol' Man River" and "Can't Help Lovin' Dat Man." These were inserted into the story as sung by Laura La Plante—or, rather, singer Eva Olivetti dubbing for La Plante. In addition, a two-reel prologue was filmed that featured Ziegfeld and producer Carl Laemmle as well as original Broadway cast members Helen Morgan, Jules Bledsoe, Tess Gardella, and the Jubilee Singers. For all of Universal's efforts at doctoring it, the film was a failure—and deservedly so. It wasn't quite a talkie, wasn't quite the famous stage version, and wasn't quite the story originally told by Ferber. What's more, La Plante and Joseph Schildkraut just didn't make a very convincing romantic couple.

Universal's inability to make a satisfactory musical out of *Show Boat* was a portent of future musical attempts by the studio. Because owner Carl Laemmle was indifferent to sound films, Universal produced few musicals except for the Deanna Durbin series (and her horrible successors like Gloria Jean) and the weird hybrid musicals like *The Phantom of the Opera* that mixed horror and operetta. So, they never really developed a style—but that didn't keep them from trying. When the studio's rights to *Show Boat* were about to lapse, Universal execs went to Kern and Hammerstein and asked them to oversee a new film version of the musical.

The second film version featured the stage original and never-to-be-equaled Helen Morgan as Julie; Paul Robeson, Kern and Hammerstein's first pick to play Joe in the original Broadway cast; Irene Dunne, who had played the role of Magnolia on the road; Charles Winninger, the original Captain Andy; and popular tenor Allan Jones. This is the definitive version of *Show Boat*, and how

could it be anything but that, with the hand-picked cast, three new songs, and—most important—supervision by the creators, Hammerstein and Kern dropped some of the score and scenes,

This isn't merely a slavish recreation of the property. In fact, opting for a faster-moving, modern version of the operetta. Hattie McDaniel's lead turn is worth mentioning. She's especially good in her scenes with Paul Robeson—they have a chemistry that's rare in films. Like Mickey and Judy, Paul and Hattie clearly adore each other and are having fun sparring. McDaniel also shows great sensitivity in her scenes with Irene Dunne as the young Magnolia. In a way, it's a softer take on how she'd treat Vivien Leigh in *Gone with the Wind*. Hers is a well-rounded character (in all ways) and she never stoops to stereotype. Perhaps Paul Robeson's strength of character showed her the way. In any event, her performance is understated but impressive.

Strangely enough, Universal, whose only previous success in the genre was *King of Jazz*, pulled out a winner. Out of nowhere, they made one of the best movie musicals of all time, albeit from one

ABOVE LEFT: Paul Robeson confers with director James Whale.

ABOVE RIGHT: Paul Robeson lifts dat bale.

BELOW LEFT: Robeson, Dunne, Hattie McDaniel, and Helen Morgan join in the chorus of "Can't Help Lovin' Dat Man."

ABOVE LEFT: Laura LaPlante strums her banjo in a sound portion of the silent 1929 *Show Boat*.

BELOW: Ava Gardner just has to look beautiful in the 1951 MGM remake.

Behind the Screen

- Pulitzer Prize-winning playwright Zoe Akins made three attempts at continuity before Oscar Hammerstein II was called in.
- When Helen Morgan leaves Magnolia, she's also bidding farewell to her screen career. *Show Boat* was her last film.
- It would also be the last film of Carl Laemmle, *père* and *fils*. They were bought out of their company by a corporation.
- Virtually all of the principals had been in stage productions of *Show Boat*—nationally, regionally, in London, or on Broadway.
- The original Broadway conductor, Victor Baravalle, repeated the assignment for the picture; Robert Russell Bennett re-created his original orchestrations; John Harkrider, costumer of the original production, provided the paper cutouts for the credit sequence.

although they are far too talented for the Cotton Blossom. The best sequence is the close of the film, directed by Roger Edens with real sensitivity. MGM would routinely rewrite the plots of Broadway musicals they produced and the MGM *Show Boat* was no exception, though reuniting the principals with the aid of Julie as a smart and gratifying adjustment.

The lesson of the three cinematic mountings of *Show Boat* is that if you've got a great property that still feels relevant, stick to the original intent of the piece. Slavish reproduction isn't necessary, but let the strengths come through without ladling on the "good ideas." *Show* some respect—just not too much. ∎

SONGS

"Ah Still Suits Me" ∎ "Bill" (lyric by Oscar Hammerstein II and P. G. Wodehouse) ∎ "Can't Help Lovin' Dat Man" ∎ "Cotton Blossom" ∎ "Gallavantin' Around" ∎ "I Have the Room above Her" ∎ "Make Believe" ∎ "Ol' Man River" ∎ "Where's the Mate for Me?" ∎ "You Are Love"

of the greatest stage musicals. James Whale might not have had the confidence of Irene Dunne and Allan Jones (they thought his English background prevented him from understanding Southern mores) but he proved a sensitive director. In collaboration with cinematographer John Mescall, Whale gave the proceedings a naturalistic feel, quite different from the overly slick MGM version to follow. Whale let the actors alone for the most part, stepping in only to tone down the histrionics (see MGM) and made an exquisitely emotional film.

The studio would make more musicals, some with Abbott and Costello (who didn't even sing), a bunch with a youthful Donald O'Connor (sometimes paired with Gloria Jean—ugh!), and many with classical/pop soprano Deanna Durbin, the biggest musical star at the studio. And they also came back to Jerome Kern, in association with lyricist E. Y. Harburg, for the Durbin vehicle *Can't Help Singing*, a totally enjoyable film.

Once Universal had lost the rights to *Show Boat*, it seemed natural that the Hollywood operetta leader, MGM, would pick up the project. They did so in 1951, mounting a huge production that threw stars and money at the vehicle without much sensitivity or real panache. In a way, the MGM *Show Boat* is like the Warner Brothers *My Fair Lady*—so much respect, so much attention to production values. In MGM's too capable hands, Captain Andy's Cotton Blossom is a Disneyfied "Carnival Cruise Line" version of what is meant to be a respectable but somewhat down-on-its-luck floating theater. Universal's film version, by contrast, was a dime-store knockoff—but one that proved less can be more.

The power of *Show Boat* rests upon the relationships of the characters. So, who did MGM cast? Joe E. Brown played the clown as Captain Andy, threatening to swallow the camera with his gaping maw. Ava Gardner was far too beautiful and strong as Julie. (And let's put the Lena Horne issue to rest. She spent the rest of her life complaining that she could've played and sung the role better than Gardner—who didn't even sing her part. But Horne didn't have an ounce of the necessary delicacy or insecurity the role of Julie requires. She was far too cool.) Howard Keel and Kathryn Grayson teamed up two years later in the infinitely more successful *Kiss Me, Kate*, but Grayson, in particular, is miscast in *Show Boat*. She just doesn't have the strength to play Magnolia or the acting chops to make the transition from child to grown woman. She and Keel are far too operatic in style. Marge and Gower Champion come across the best in the MGM version,

Irene Dunne

The beautiful Irene Dunne was adept at comedy, tragedy, and musical films. She had a special affinity for the music of Jerome Kern. In addition to *Show Boat*, she sang Kern's music in *Sweet Adeline*; *Roberta*; *Joy of Living*; and *High, Wide and Handsome*. Dunne was that rare soprano whose high notes never turned shrill. Her musicality extended to her speaking voice, creating a lilt that made listening to even the worst dialogue interesting. Her spirit also shone through such nonmusicals as *I Remember Mama*, *Penny Serenade*, *Theodora Goes Wild*, and *Love Affair*. Irene Dunne left acting in 1952, stating, "I drifted into acting and drifted out. Acting is not everything. Living is."

ABOVE: Irene Dunne is radiant in *High Wide and Handsome*.
LEFT: Douglas Fairbanks and Irene Dunne illustrate *The Joy of Living*.
RIGHT: Mervyn LeRoy, Irene Dunne, and Donald Woods in the charming *Sweet Adeline*.

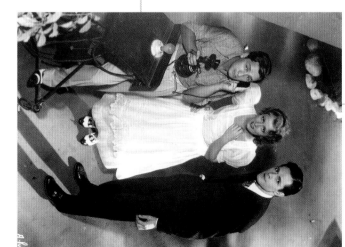

SINGIN' IN THE RAIN

COMPOSER: Nacio Herb Brown
LYRICIST: Arthur Freed
PRODUCER: Arthur Freed
DIRECTORS: Stanley Donen and Gene Kelly
SCREENWRITERS: Betty Comden and Adolph Green
CHOREOGRAPHERS: Stanley Donen and Gene Kelly

Synopsis
Boy gets girl, films get sound, boy gets wet.

Cast
Gene Kelly..............Don Lockwood
Debbie Reynolds...........Kathy Selden
Donald O'Connor ....Cosmo Brown
Jean Hagen................Lina Lamont
Millard Mitchell.........R. F. Simpson
Rita Moreno...............Zelda Zanders
Douglas Fowley.............Roscoe Dexter
Cyd Charisse..........Principle Dancer

SINGIN' IN THE RAIN

MGM—APRIL 11, 1952

ABOVE: Gene Kelly in a publicity shot for *Singin' in the Rain*.

OPPOSITE: Gene Kelly's gotta dance 'cause Broadway rhythm's got him!

L ET'S TALK ABOUT BROADWAY TODAY. WE KNOW YOU'RE DYING TO. IF YOU GO UP AND down the Street of Dreams, you'll find such hit shows as *Jersey Boys*, *Mamma Mia*, *Rock of Ages*, and *Million Dollar Quartet* (or their up-to-the-moment equivalents). These shows represent an increasingly popular form of musical theater, the catalog show or "jukebox musical."

Well, young whippersnappers, we hate to burst your bubble, but the jukebox musical has been around at least since the turn of the twentieth century, when Johann Strauss's music was crammed into *The Great Waltz*. Robert Wright and George Forrest took public-domain classical melodies, added lyrics and a new book, and out came such shows as *Kismet*, *Song of Norway*, and *Kean*.

That, dear hearts, brings us to the movies. A great theater writer, Alan Jay Lerner, took the Gershwins' songbook as the basis of the MGM musical, *An American in Paris*. Irving Berlin stuck his back catalog into a series of musicals that included *Alexander's Ragtime Band*, *There's No Business Like Show Business*, *Easter Parade*, and *White Christmas*, among others. Of course, Berlin's songs were usually put into movies that were set in the theater or vaudeville, so the songs could be sung as part of stage performances. They weren't expected to express the emotions of the films' characters or advance the plot.

With *Singin' in the Rain*, Betty Comden and Adolph Green became the instant masters of the catalog movie musical. Taking the songs of Arthur Freed and Nacio Herb Brown, they constructed a story of early-era sound movies and the result is merely the most popular movie musical of all time. Arguably. They did it again by concocting *The Band Wagon* out of some Arthur Schwartz and Howard Dietz ditties.

When it's Comden and Green doing the concocting, it looks easy. Just take some old, nondramatic songs and create a plot around them. But take a good look at *Singin' in the Rain*. Although some songs, including "Fit as a Fiddle,"

"I didn't like him because he would make me dance a scene 40 times. My feet would be bleeding." —*Debbie Reynolds on Gene Kelly*

are performed on a stage, it still serves the purpose of revealing the schlocky vaudeville backgrounds of the male leads. A generic love song like "All I Do Is Dream of You" becomes stronger than its words or music might suggest when placed in context: in Comden and Green's hands, it becomes a fervent, romantic turning point in the relationship between Don Lockwood and Kathy Selden. "Singin' in the Rain" itself, previously a production number in a variety of films, becomes a joyous celebration of life as Gene Kelly discovers he's in love with a great girl and nothing, not even a downpour, can spoil his elation.

Still think it's easy? Give it a try yourself. Take some songs from any Tin Pan Alley catalog and see if you can come up with a believable plot that will turn the pop songs into show songs, advancing the plot or revealing the characters' inner thoughts and emotions. Not so easy.

Singin' in the Rain has terrific performances, a script full of humor and romance that never seems to take itself too seriously, and a brilliant sense of fun. These are all trademarks of Comden and Green. Plus, the film has real momentum, both in the plot line and the journeys of the lead characters from the first frames to the finale. The production values are the best—no surprise since it's an MGM film, but lots of others of the studios had brilliant art direc-

tors, cinematographers, and designers and never managed to come up with a film that could touch *Singin' in the Rain.*

Maybe it's because none of those elements, separately or together, could make a brilliantly entertaining film on its level. It's the show's score and its integration into the plot that made old, clichéd songs of the '20s and '30s sound current in the mid-'50s, even though the film takes place in the late '20s.

So, here's a toast to the masters of the catalog musical, Betty Comden and Adolph Green. We'll never see their like again. *Singin' in the Rain* will still be here, though, and is bound to remain a favorite of film fans for another fifty years or more. ∎

ABOVE: Sitting around waiting for Donald O'Connor to do his star turn in "Make 'Em Laugh."

LEFT: Donald O'Connor having his tie adjusted by Debbie Reynolds between shots for *I Love Melvin.*

BELOW: Donald O'Connor and Gene Kelly welcome Fred Astaire to the set.

Behind the Screen

■ Debbie Reynolds' singing was dubbed by Betty Royce for the song "Would You."

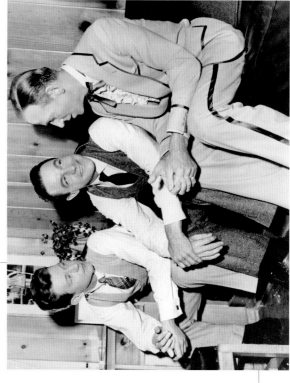

Donald O'Connor

Ever youthful, Donald O'Connor spent his entire life performing. His parents were vaudevillians and Donald kept up the family business. In 1937, at age twelve, he began his film career at Paramount Studios. Three years later, his voice began changing so he again trod the boards in variety. In 1942, he joined the Universal Pictures roster, starring alongside Gloria Jean (a lesser Deanna Durbin) and Francis the talking mule. Although he starred mainly in B musicals (really,

the only kind Universal made, with the exception of *Can't Help Singing*) his musical numbers were exquisitely performed. His slim frame would bounce around in almost gymnastic routines. O'Connor's stardom was assured when he played his greatest role, Cosmo Brown in *Singin' in the Rain.* That film provided such a spectacular showcase for his artistry that he could never top it. In any case, the role came late in his career, when the movie studios had begun shedding their contract players and movie musicals were on the wane. O'Connor toured in summer stock, appeared on a variety of television shows, and occasionally returned to the stage or film. In 1981, he made an appearance in the movie *Ragtime* and opened on Broadway in the unfortunate sequel to *Bye, Bye Birdie* titled *Bring Back Birdie.* O'Connor's happy-go-lucky screen characters mirrored his attitude toward his life. Seldom has an actor had such profound impact on pop culture on the basis of one remarkable performance.

"I was a young pisher. I was 26. I was worried as hell about what I was going to do and how I was going to do it. And at the same time I felt I knew better than everybody else."

—*Stanley Donen*

Comden and Green

Betty Comden and Adolph Green seemed eternally youthful. Their screenplays, lyrics, and Broadway musicals all had an infectious energy, a humorous worldview, and a strong sense of goodwill. After nightclub, radio, and Broadway successes and failures, Comden and Green went to Hollywood, where their first assignment was adapting the 1920s musical *Good News* for the filmgoers of 1947. Two years later, still at MGM, they wrote lyrics for *Take Me Out to the Ball Game*, adapted their Broadway hit *On the Town*, and penned the show (with help on the songs from Roger Edens) that would be the last pairing of Astaire and Rogers, *The Barkleys of Broadway*. After returning briefly to Broadway, the team came back to Hollywood, where they provided the screenplay for what is considered by many to be the greatest movie musical of all time, *Singin' in the Rain*. It was followed a year later by another of the best movie musicals, called *It's Always Fair Weather*, for which they also supplied lyrics to André Previn's melodies. They adapted their stage musical *Bells Are Ringing* for film and, in 1964, wrote an original screen musical, *What a Way to Go*, their last film project. Comden and Green wrote about the middle class, the common man, and their moments of joy and sadness, but mainly the former. Comden once referred to their seamless writing style as "mental radar." Whatever it was, it resulted in two of the greatest film musicals and an impressive catalog of Broadway shows and hit songs.

BELOW: The Revuers, where Comden and Green got their start. Adolph Green, John Frank, Betty Comden, Alvin Hammer, and Judy Holliday.

SONGS

"All I Do Is Dream of You" ▪ "Beautiful Girl" ▪ "Fit as a Fiddle" (Al Goodhart, Al Hoffman, and Arthur Freed) ▪ "Broadway Melody" ▪ "Broadway Rhythm" ▪ "Good Morning" ▪ "I've Got a Feelin' You're Foolin'" ▪ "Make 'Em Laugh" ▪ "Moses (Roger Edens, Betty Comden, and Adolph Green)" ▪ "Should I?" ▪ "Singin' in the Rain" ▪ "Wedding of the Painted Doll" ▪ "Would You" ▪ "You Are My Lucky Star" ▪ "You Were Meant for Me"

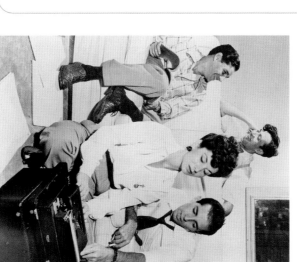

ABOVE: Writing the Broadway production of *On the Town* in 1944, (clockwise from right) Leonard Bernstein, Adolph Green, Jerome Robbins, and Betty Comden.

TOP: Betty Comden playfully strangles Adolph Green."

SNOW WHITE AND THE SEVEN DWARFS

WALT DISNEY—DECEMBER 21, 1937

ABOVE: With a smile and a song, Snow White confides in the woodland creatures that someday her prince will come.

BELOW RIGHT: Adriana Caselotti, the voice of Snow White.

SNOW WHITE AND THE SEVEN DWARFS

COMPOSER: Frank E. Churchill.

LYRICIST: Larry Morey.

PRODUCER: Walt Disney.

DIRECTOR: David D. Hand.

SCREENWRITERS: Otto Englander, Ted Sears, Earl Hurd, Dorothy Ann Blank, Richard Creedon, Dick Rickard, Merrill De Maris, and Webb Smith

SOURCE: Based on the fairy tale "Snow White and the Seven Dwarfs" by the Brothers Grimm

Synopsis

Girl gets poison apple, girl gets nice beauty sleep, girl gets dwarfs, girl gets kissed, girl gets prince and castle and Austrian Express Platinum card.

Cast

Adriana Caselotti........Snow White
Roy Atwell........Doc
Eddie Collins........Dopey
Zeke Clements........Bashful
Pinto Colvig........Sleepy, Grumpy
Billy Gilbert........Sneezy
Otis Harlan........Happy
Lucille LaVerne........Queen
Moroni Olsen........Magic Mirror
Harry Stockwell........Prince
Stuart Buchanan........Huntsman

TODAY WE TAKE FOR GRANTED THE ANIMATED FEATURE. EVERY YEAR WE'RE INUNDATED with them and some even get nominated for big awards. But, back in 1938, cartoons were exclusively short subjects. Winsor McCay, a noted comic strip artist, made the first animated film, based on his strip "Little Nemo in Slumberland." It premiered in 1911 as part of McCay's vaudeville appearances. Three years later, McCay created his most important film, *Gertie the Dinosaur*, the first character animation. We mention this because it launched the entire animation industry, including Walt Disney's first attempts at short subjects.

In the two-dozen years between that ground-breaker and *Snow White and the Seven Dwarfs*, only two full-length animated features came out: Quirino Cristiani's *The Apostle*, an Argentinian film released in 1917, and Lotte Reiniger's *The Adventures of Prince Achmed*, a 1926 German film. The first of these was understandably crude and the latter was a silhouette film featuring animated cutouts.

It's strange that no one thought to attempt an animated feature with the scope and artistry of *Snow White*. After all, live-action movies started as shorts and one-reelers but soon evolved into features, some quite long. Perhaps it is because animation has always been thought of as a poor stepchild to "real" movies that it took a visionary like Disney to glimpse the possibilities. Today, animated films are finally coming into their own.

Fourteen years after *Gertie* charmed audiences, when sound film was emerging, Disney unveiled *Steamboat Willie*, the world's first animated sound short. It proved to be a huge success and Disney grew ever more confident in his radical ideas. As early as 1934, he was thinking about producing a full-length feature. He began been beefing up his animation

"Nelson Rockefeller told my wife a long time ago that they had to reupholster the seats in Radio City Music Hall because they were wet so often by frightened children."

—*Childcare expert Dr. Benjamin Spock*

staff and putting money aside, figuring that the project would take eighteen months and a quarter of a million dollars. He started the publicity machine moving before the first drawing was made. He told reporters, "We've got to be sure of it before we start, because if it isn't good we will destroy it. If it is good, we shall make at least a million."

Disney crammed additional staff into the small Hyperion Studios and created an atmosphere conducive to creativity. There were no time clocks, everyone called him Walt, and animators were expected to trash any work they didn't deem acceptable. When it came to story meetings, Disney was the genius but anyone could pitch an idea, and if it was good, it was accepted. He bought top-of-the-line equipment so his staff could work at peak efficiency. Disney knew that he needed all the help he could get to make his dream of a full-length animated movie a reality.

Gertie the Dinosaur had evoked real emotions in audiences but in the intervening years, animated cartoons expressed only one goal: to make people laugh. Disney believed that animated films could do much more. "Our most important aim," he stated, "is to develop definite personalities in our cartoon characters. We don't want them to be just shadows, for merely as moving figures they would provoke no emotional response from the public."

Imbuing each character in *Snow White* with a distinctive personality was certainly a challenge. There were seven dwarfs, after

TOP: Seven, count 'em, seven dwarfs go hi-hoing off to work.
BOTTOM: Kids, never take presents from strangers. Snow White didn't have a mother to warn her about that, and look what happened to her.

Behind the Screen

■ Walt Disney asked a well-known singing teacher in L.A. if he could recommend a girl to voice the role of Snow White. The teacher's daughter was listening in on another phone and asked, "What about me?" The eighteen-year-old Adriana Caselotti got the job.

"There's something so nasty about them."

—Lillian Disney's response to her husband's plan to make a film featuring dwarfs

WALT DISNEY'S **Snow White** and the Seven Dwarfs in the Marvelous MULTIPLANE TECHNICOLOR

HIS FIRST FULL LENGTH FEATURE PRODUCTION

all. (The dwarfs were entirely a Disney Studio conceit, added to lighten the traditional tale.) Once the creators had conquered the dwarfs' characters, animating and writing for them was easy. But animating naturalistic humans is a tougher nut to crack. Disney filmed Marge Belcher as Snow White and Lewis Hightower, Belcher's dance partner, as the Prince to capture exactly how humans move.

Problems remained in the groundbreaking enterprise. The first six months of footage was scrapped. Later, when the filming was almost completed, Disney (ever the consummate storyteller) threw out two whole sequences, feeling that they held up the narrative flow. Advance word going around rival studios was dire. Word was, the film would be a tremendous failure and close down the studio for good. (This isn't unlike the chatter on the Internet today: check out the buzz on *Avatar*, just prior to its release.) Need we tell you that the prognosticators were wrong? The final film cost Disney around 2 million dollars—eight times his original estimate. And it took almost five years to complete. The first release earned the studio 8 million dollars—and that was in the midst of the Depression. (Keep in mind that back then, tickets cost as little as a nickel. That's a lot of nickels!)

We might be stating the obvious but we want to remind you that *Snow White* is a full-blown musial with a perfect blend of pop and operetta syles. And the songs are just as well written as those in any Broadway musical.

Although critics lauded the film, they didn't quite understand what a remarkable achievement it was or how great a film of any kind. But one group did understand the impact it would have: the Academy of Motion Picture Arts and Sciences, who awarded Disney a special Oscar with seven smaller Oscars trailing behind. Despite the whimsy, the Academy knew what was coming. The award was inscribed: "To Walt Disney for 'Snow White and the Seven Dwarfs,' recognized as a significant screen innovation which has charmed millions and pioneered a great new entertainment field from the motion picture cartoon." ∎

Behind the Screen

■ Marge Belcher was photographed as Snow White so the animators could mimic human movement. She later got married and took her husband's surname—Champion.

BELOW LEFT: Marge Belcher was filmed to help the animators with Snow White's movements. Later she'd grow up to be a star in her own right, Marge Champion.

BELOW CENTER: Lucille La Verne, seen here in *A Tale of Two Cities*, is the voice of the Witch. She looks a little witchy herself.

BELOW RIGHT: Come to think of it, Harry Stockwell, the voice of the Prince, looks a little princey himself.

Walt Disney

Walt Disney's career, spanning the decades from the '20s to the '60s, was a series of firsts. He was responsible for the first cartoon with sound (*Steamboat Willie*), the first color cartoon (*Flowers and Trees*), the first American animated feature (ditto), the first Technicolor cartoon (*Snow White*), the first cartoon to win an Oscar (ditto), the first themed amusement park (*Disneyland*)—and probably more. As with all the greatest artists, Disney didn't believe in catering to the masses. "I don't make films exclusively for children," he commented. "I make them to suit myself, hoping they will also suit the audience." Some have criticized him for pandering, for whitewashing the more violent sides of fairy tales, and for depending on cute little animals to tell his stories—but he was always true to himself. "I don't like depressing pictures," he told a reporter. "I don't like pestholes. I don't like pictures that are dirty. I don't ever go out and pay money for studies in abnormality. I don't have depressed moods and I don't want to have any. I'm happy, just very, very happy." "Edge" was a concept that did not appeal to him. At the beginning of his career he was a benevolent boss, but he became increasingly rigid and conservative in his taste. Still, his artistic vision never faltered and he continued to produce what is now known as "family fare," minus the pejorative implication. His art pleased millions and his single-mindedness ensured that the company would grow artistically and financially. By keeping his standards high and hiring the best artists and writers, he popularized cartoons, expanded the audience for them, and redefined the art form. When he won the Medal of Freedom from President Johnson, the citation read, "Artist and impresario, in the course of entertaining an age, he has created an American folklore."

> "We considered changing the name of the picture from *Snow White* to *Frankenstein*."
>
> —*Walt Disney, commenting on the film's soaring budget*

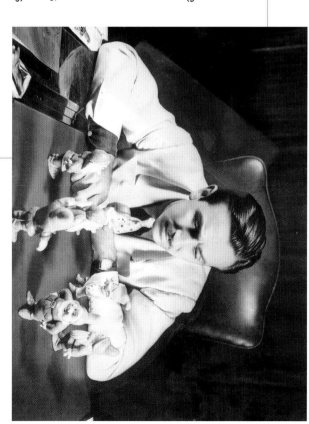

ABOVE: Boys will be boys. Walt Disney plays with his toys.

BELOW RIGHT: She was right! One day her prince did come!

SONGS

"Bluddle-Uddle-Um-Dum (Washing Song)" ■ "Heigh-Ho" ■ "I'm Wishing" ■ "One Song" ■ "The Silly Song (Dwarf's Yodel Song)" ■ "Some Day My Prince Will Come" ■ "Whistle While You Work" ■ "With a Smile and a Song"

SONS OF THE PIONEERS

REPUBLIC—JULY 2, 1942

SONS OF THE PIONEERS

PRODUCER: Joseph Kane
DIRECTOR: Joseph Kane
SCREENWRITERS: Webster M. Coates,
Mauri Grashin, and Robert T. Shannon

Synopsis

Roy and Trigger to go after bad guys and clean up the West.

Cast

Roy Rogers.............Roy Rogers
George "Gabby" Hayes...Gabby Whittaker
Bob Nolan..............Bob Nolan, Sons of the
                       Pioneers
Pat Brady..............Pat, Sons of the
                       Pioneers
Hugh Farr..............Sons of the Pioneers
Karl Farr..............Sons of the Pioneers
Tim Spencer............Sons of the Pioneers
Lloyd Perryman.........Sons of the Pioneers
Maris Wrixon...........Louise Harper
Minerva Urecal.........Ellie Bixby
Chester Conklin........Old Timer

Behind the Screen

■ Director Joseph Kane (once a cello virtuoso) directed Roy Rogers, Gene Autry, and John Wayne westerns for Republic Studios.

■ Roy and the rest of the Sons of the Pioneers had been performing under the names the Gold Star Rangers and the Pioneer Trio, when, much to their surprise, announcer Harry Hall introduced them as the Sons of the Pioneers. Hall explained that they were all too young to be pioneers. The new name stuck.

■ Under his real name, Golden Cloud, Trigger appeared with (under?) Olivia De Havilland in *The Adventures of Robin Hood*. Roy Rogers

Roy Rogers (with guitar) and the Sons of the Pioneers. Leader Bob Nolan is at right.

WE PICKED *SONS OF THE PIONEERS* AS OUR REPRESENTATIVE ROY ROGERS MOVIE but, honestly, we don't know if it's better or worse than many of his other pictures. What we do know is that Rogers made some of the most important movie musicals—and perhaps movies in general—of all time. Really? To understand this, you have to know how pervasive Roy Rogers's movies were in their day, and understand their impact on the culture.

From the 1903 debut of *The Great Train Robbery* (filmed in the wilds of Fort Lee, New Jersey) until recently, the cowboy film represented our most important genre. Once the movies had settled out west in California, it seemed only natural that they explore western lore. And the history of the west is the history of the cowboy. We might add that the cowboy was a staple of the stage also. Owen Wister's play *The Virginian*, starring Dustin Farnum, premiered in 1904 and was an immediate success. The next year saw the Broadway premiere of *The Squaw Man*, featuring future Hollywood cowboy star William S. Hart. Cecil B. DeMille, hoping to escape the Edison Company's patent suits, traveled to Hollywood and filmed his own version of *The Squaw Man* in 1914. Scenes were filmed at the corner of Sunset and Vine. That same year, DeMille brought the film version of *The Virginian* to the screen with its stage star Farnum.

The title character of *The Virginian* was a noble, good man and that characterization became the role model for all western heroes. Cowboy films were all action and no nonsense, and William S. Hart, Tom Mix, and later, William Boyd, Charles Starrett, Tex Ritter, and Ken Maynard let the action do the talking. There weren't any gray areas in the fight of good versus evil. The lines were clearly drawn and audiences knew exactly who to root for and who to emulate.

"My God, you can't even ride a horse."

—Hubert Voight, publicity director of Republic Pictures

"I can learn, can't I?" *—Roy Rogers*

Gene Autry introduced the singing cowboy as a cameo of sorts in Ken Maynard's *In Old Santa Fe*, a modern-day cowboy film. Soon, the singing-cowboy film was an established subgenre and an up-to-date setting was the norm. Most Roy Rogers films took place in the present-day West.

The legend of the cowboy wasn't only for kids. *The Outlaw*, *Shane*, and John Ford's John Wayne movies were all A films and contained psychological and sexual themes not present in the Saturday morning offerings. Still, the films of Rogers and his ilk had an important impact on the lives of the thousands of kids who enjoyed the shoot-'em-up action while learning the value of goodness over evil and the right way to lead their lives. These films, along with comic books featuring the likes of Superman (who fought for "truth, justice, and the American way"), had an overwhelming and lasting cultural impact.

As musicals, the films of Rogers and his singing-cowboy brethren were completely satisfying, although most of the musical numbers were presented as performances rather than elaborations on plot and character through song. The films featured plenty of songs (*Sons of the Pioneers* has six), especially considering that they ran under ninety minutes. The Sons of the Pioneers was a top-notch singing group that enjoyed (and continues to enjoy) a solid fan base through its recordings. And Roy and Dale, too, were no slouches in the singing department. Dale wrote the duo's theme song, "Happy Trails to You," as well as "The Bible Tells Me So."

Roy Rogers's westerns, including *Sons of the Pioneers*, are all pretty much the same. You'll always find Roy standing up for the good person, fighting evil, racing through the sagebrush with his horse Trigger, shooting only when necessary, and singing songs that honor the west and its history. Call these things clichés, if you will, but they are just as entertaining today as they were when the films were made—and all of that repetition can be downright comforting . . . pardner. ∎

SONGS

- "Come and Get It" (Tim Spencer) ∎ "He's Gone Up the Trail" (Tim Spencer)
- "Lily of Hillbilly Valley" (Tim Spencer) ∎ "Things Are Never What They Seem" (Bob Nolan) ∎ "Trail Herdin' Cowboy" ∎ (Bob Nolan) ∎ "The West Is in My Soul" (Bob Nolan)

Roy Rogers

Growing up in Duck Run, Ohio, little Leonard Slye wanted to be a dentist when he grew up. Sadly, he never achieved his dream. Instead, he had to settle for becoming the most popular cowboy of all time. A star of the movies, radio, and television, he made hundreds of live appearances throughout the world. At his peak, over half the population of the United States, over 80 million people, saw his movies annually. "The King of the Cowboys" was married to Dale Evans, "the Queen of the West." He rode Trigger, "the Smartest Horse in the Movies," while Dale rode Buttermilk, who was . . . just Buttermilk. Growing up during the Depression, Leonard worked in a shoe factory and picked fruit in California. In 1931, he teamed up with his cousin Stanley to try his luck singing. He worked for the next few years with only sporadic success but in 1934 he formed the Sons of the Pioneers with Tim Spencer and Bob Nolan. They were an immense success with such songs as "Tumbling Tumbleweeds" and "Cool Water." In 1935, he sang in the Republic Picture *The Phantom Empire*, which starred Gene Autry. In 1938, Autry argued with Republic head Herbert Yates and was fired. Guess who replaced him? Yup. Leonard Slye became Roy Rogers and his career took off. Rogers appeared in noncowboy pictures, including the Kurt Weill–Ira Gershwin musical film *Where Do We Go from Here* (though his sequence was deleted from the final print). He did better in 1944, singing Cole Porter and Robert Fletcher's "Don't Fence Me In" in *Hollywood Canteen*. From 1951 to 1957, he and Dale Evans appeared in one hundred television shows. Rogers and Evans were devout Christians and deeply involved in children's issues. Perhaps more important to him than his professional accomplishments was his embodiment of American values and his moral influence on millions of baby boomers.

TOP RIGHT: Roy and his trusty guitar.

RIGHT: It looks like Jack O'Shea and Bradley Page have the drop on Roy Rogers, but we bet it's not for long.

THE SOUND OF MUSIC

20TH CENTURY FOX—MARCH 2, 1965

Charmian Carr, Julie Andrews, Angela Cartwright, Duane Chase, Nicholas Hammond, and Heather Menzies have a ball telling the story of the lonely goatherd, with help of the Bil Baird Marionettes.

Synopsis

The Lord works in mysterious ways. Cavort in the hills, come late for prayers, and be rewarded with a ready-made family and a new life in America.

Cast

Julie Andrews.................*Maria*
Christopher Plummer....*Captain Von Trapp*
Eleanor Parker.................*The Baroness*
Richard Haydn................*Max Detweiler*
Peggy Wood....................*Mother Abbess*
Charmian Carr.................*Liesl*
Heather Menzies.............*Louisa*
Nicholas Hammond ....*Friedrich*
Duane Chase...................*Kurt*
Angela Cartwright..........*Brigitta*
Debbie Turner................*Marta*
Kym Karath......................*Gretl*
Daniel Truhitte................*Rolfe*
Anna Lee ....*Sister Margaretta*
Portia Nelson..............*Sister Berthe*
Marni Nixon ....*Sister Sophia*

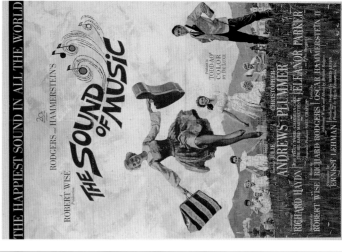

T HE SOUND OF MUCAS." "LIKE BEING BEATEN TO DEATH BY A HALLMARK CARD." "Everything so icky sticky purely ever-lovin' that even Constant Andrews Admirer will get a wittle woozy long before intermission." "I felt myself slowly drowning in a pit of sticky-sweet whipped cream not of the first freshness."

Really? That bad? Well . . . critics do love the extravagant pan, and their readers enjoy the vitriol. No matter, the film was a gigantic hit, the greatest moneymaker in movie history up to that time.

In making *The Sound of Music*, Fox decided to pull out all the stops. They didn't have a lot of choice: after holding out on granting film rights for years, Richard Rodgers finally relented on condition that the production be first class all the way. Except for Universal's film of *Flower Drum Song*, all of Rodgers and Hammerstein's film musicals—including the only one that went straight to film, *State Fair*—were released by Fox and both the studio and the authors benefited handsomely. (Fox actually filmed the Rodgers and Hammerstein musical version of *State Fair* twice, the second time not so felicitously.)

Ernest Lehman, a well-regarded screenwriter who had spiffed up *The King and I* and *West Side Story* for the screen (to excellent effect), was hired to write the screenplay. Lehman did his usual good job, using his innate sense of what to retain, what to cut, and what to restructure. While *The Sound of Music* retained its treacle factor, it was

Julie Andrews proves to the kids that the hills really are alive with the sound of music.

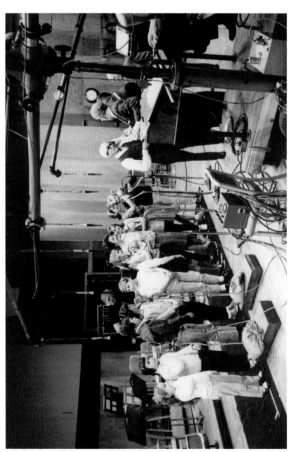

TOP LEFT: Julie Andrews runs a gantlet of nuns, all of whom wonder how to solve a problem like her.

BOTTOM LEFT: Saul Chaplin (with arm on podium) oversees the recording of the children (including additional kids brought in to sweeten the sound).

TOP RIGHT: Christopher Plummer finally loosens up and serenades the kids.

BOTTOM RIGHT: The real, honest to god, Maria Von Trapp visits Robert Wise and Christopher Plummer on the set.

diminished greatly by Lehman and his fellow *West Side Story* toiler, director Robert Wise. (Lehman would go on to write Fox's *Hello, Dolly!* but we don't blame him.)

Another *West Side Story* alum, associate producer and de facto musical supervisor Saul Chaplin, is also due a heap of credit for the film's success. He hadn't liked the original stage production for the same reasons as everyone else—too darned sweet. But he read Lehman's screenplay and loved it, and advised Robert Wise (who hadn't been a fan of the stage show, either) to direct it. Chaplin scouted all the locations, helped cast the movie, oversaw the location filming, and even wrote one of the songs with Richard Rodgers. You could say that, given the revolving door on the Fox executive offices, he was the producer of the film.

We know now that *The Sound of Music* is the most financially successful movie musical of all time, right up there with the largest-grossing movies of any genre, pulling in almost $80 million on its initial run having cost Fox only a little over $8 million. Upon its release, *Sound of Music* fever seemed to grip the nation and the world. Myra Franklin of Wales (of all places) claimed that she saw the film almost one thousand times; things are slow in Wales, so why should we doubt her? In the film's first nineteen months of release, Salt Lake City—with a population just shy of 200,000 people, posted sales of more than 500,000 tickets!

Unfortunately for Fox—and for us—*The Sound of Music* was the last of the great Rodgers and Hammerstein movies. *Sound of Music* fever can still be contracted today, thanks to DVD sales and the international phenomenon of the *Sing-a-long Sound of Music*, which blends the audience theatrics of *The Rocky Horror Picture Show* and karaoke.

And, while amateur and professional mountings of the stage version had been plentiful and done well, after the film came out the number of international productions skyrocketed. Of course, audiences expect to see something akin to the film version, not the original play, so, while the original stage show opens with Maria literally up a tree, revivals tend to come upon her cavorting in the hills, arms spread wide in Julie Andrews fashion. And in most productions, the songs "No Way to Stop It," "An Ordinary Couple" and "How Can Love Survive?" are cut in favor of the film's additions, "I Have Confidence" and "Something Good." For what it's worth, the estates of the original librettists, Howard Lindsay and Russel Crouse, are none too happy with the tampering.

Call it "The Sound of Mucas" or "The Sound of Money," if you will. *The Sound of Music* will probably never be surpassed by any film musical, financially or artistically. With the exception of *The Wizard of Oz*, it is the most fervently beloved musical. ∎

"The most that could be said for his singing was that he could carry a tune in a moderately pleasant manner."

—*Saul Chaplin on Christopher Plummer*

"My behavior was unconscionable."

—*Christopher Plummer*

SONGS

- "Alleluia" (traditional lyrics) ■ "Do-Re-Mi" ■
"Climb Every Mountain" ■ "I Have Confidence
in Me" (Saul Chaplin and Richard Rodgers)
■ "Edelweiss" ■ "The Lonely Goatherd"
"Maria" ■ "Morning Hymn" (traditional lyrics)
■ "My Favorite Things" ■ "Sixteen Going
on Seventeen" ■ "So Long, Farewell"
"Something Good" (Richard Rodgers) ■ "The
Sound of Music"

Richard Rodgers

After the death of Oscar Hammerstein II in 1960, Richard Rodgers kept up the legacy of the partnership. In 1962, he approved a new film version of *State Fair* for Fox and wrote some inconsequential new songs for it. He also continued his own Broadway work with *No Strings*, tackling both music and lyrics. A few other shows followed, with lyrics by Stephen Sondheim and Martin Charnin, but none were successes. Although Rodgers didn't have much to do with the film of *The Sound of Music*, it was the triumph of his later years. Long after his death, one of his daughters decided to spill the proverbial beans about what a horrible, unemotional father he had been. Be that as it may, on the basis of his collaborations with Hammerstein and Lorenz Hart, enumerated elsewhere in this volume, he remains a giant of the musical theater—one of the few artists who genuinely deserve that description.

Behind the Screen

■ The real Maria Von Trapp appears briefly during the song "I Have Confidence in Me."

ABOVE: Even in a formal portrait, Richard Rodgers looks wary.

LEFT: Oscar Hammerstein and Richard Rodgers work on their last score together.

TOP RIGHT: Whistle while you work. Christopher Plummer calls for the children.

ABOVE: Richard Rodgers, Gertrude Lawrence, and Oscar Hammerstein II on *The Ed Sullivan Show*. Rodgers and Lawrence are about to perform "Getting to Know You," from *The King and I*.

THE WORST MOVIE MUSICALS

THERE ARE HUNDREDS OF LOUSY MOVIE MUSICALS, BUT THE ones on the list below started out with a good pedigree and much potential. That makes them worse than musicals written and directed by hacks. For example, the remake of The Great Waltz didn't stand a chance of being a good film and so isn't on our list. The films listed here had the benefit of talented stars and filmmakers but it somewhere along the line, it all turned rotten.

- *Annie*, 1982: Directed by noted musical movie director John Huston, this film has the feeling of a made-for-television movie.

- *At Long Last Love*, 1975: What did Cole Porter do to have such bad karma? Burt Reynolds and Cybill Shepherd! Singing. And dancing. Brrrr.

- *Can't Stop the Music*, 1980: Well somebody should have. It's a camp classic now.

- *A Chorus Line*, 1985: One of the greatest stage musicals ever gets all it's emotion drained out.

- *Copacabana*, 1947: Two great talents, Groucho Marx and Carmen Miranda, reach the absolute nadir of their careers.

- *De-lovely*, 2004: This movie makes the previous Cole Porter biopic, *Night and Day*, look like a documentary. Yes, it tells more of the truth of Porter's life—but the music treatments make it . . . (can't resist) it's De-lovely.

- *The French Line*, 1953: Even in 3-D this film falls flat—and that's saying something what with Jane Russell starring and all.

- *Funny Lady*, 1975: A downer of a plot with shorthand emotions, the film never answers the biggest question of all for any artistic endeavor—why? (Most of the films on this list can't answer that one.)

- *Grease 2*, 1982: Hollywood just can't leave well enough alone.

- *Half a Sixpence*, 1967: It's pretty hard to get past Tommy Steele and his gigantic chompers. They hoped it would be another *Oliver!* but no dice. And it's soooo loooong.

- *The Happiest Millionaire*, 1967: This one is tied with *The One and Only Genuine Original Family Band* (1968) for embodying the most ersatz middle-American values musicals.

- *A Little Night Music*, 1977: Moving it from Sweden to Austria (where the sun does set) was just one of a series of mistakes. The Like ponderous editing was another.

- *Lost Horizon*, 1973: We never miss a Liv Ullman musical. Just try to get through the score without experiencing a spike in your blood sugar levels.

- *Mame*, 1974: Desi told her not to do the movie but Lucy wanted to be a real movie star, something she never really was, and so she accepted the role. The problem with casting Lucy is that Mame is a lady who clowns not a clown trying to be a lady. When the film opened at Radio City Music Hall, the crowd turned from loving Auntie Mame to anti-Mame. Lucy took a curtain call and the crowd actually hissed her. Then Bea Arthur took a bow and the crowd cheered. Then back came Lucy and there were more boos. Whenever Lucy's on the screen it's like the fog mysteriously rolls in. Critics didn't really review the

film, they reviewed Lucy's face. The one who suffered the most wa the great Jerry Herman who, like Coleman and Sondheim, can't get a break in Hollywood.

- *Moonlight and Pretzels*, 1933: This horror was shot in something like five days, and it shows. Roger Pryor is a most unlikely leading man and the score and plot stink. "Dusty Shoes" is Jay Gorney and E.Y. Harburg's sequel to the immensely superior, "Brother Can You Spare a Dime." Ray of light: Leo Carillo is always wonderful, as always.

- *Nine*, 2009: Nein.

- *One Touch of Venus*, 1948: Should have been titled The Bad and the Beautiful—the movie is bad and Ginger Rogers is beautiful (but stolid). The Kurt Weill/Ogden Nash score was eviscerated with only two songs making the cut.

- *Paint Your Wagon*, 1969: In one of the many classic episodes of the *The Simpsons*, Bart and Homer Simpson rent this one expecting a great action movie. Who can blame them with bad boys Lee Marvin and Clint Eastwood starring? Are they disappointed! Alan Jay Lerner's script is basically *Design for Living* transposed to the Wild West. In its favor, the film does have powerfully good vocal arrangements.

- *The Phantom of the Opera*, 2004: This Broadway show is coming up on its twenty-fifth anniversary. The movie doesn't have twenty-five good minutes in it.

- *Mr. Quilp*, 1975: Anthony Newley and Charles Dickens sounds like a great team but Newley without Bricusse just couldn't cut it.

- *Rent*, 2005: Most of the original Broadway cast showed up for this inexusably juiceless version of an impassioned musical.

- *Song of Norway*, 1970: Florence Henderson, like her contemporary Shirley Jones, stretched her career and broadened her fame thanks to television motherhood. But Henderson was never a movie star thanks to this misbegotten film. It's ironic as she was the bigger success in Broadway musicals than Shirley Jones.

- *Star!*, 1968: The Sound of Music team reconvened and came up with this!

- *Staying Alive*, 1983: Was there ever a title that tempted the critics more?

- *Sweeney Todd: The Demon Barber of Fleet Street*, 2007: Poor Mr. Sondheim. Has any composer/genius had worse luck in the movies?

- *Xanadu*, 1980: Xanadon't (actually the name of an off-Broadway musical).

- *Yentl*, 1983: Barbra Streisand and Mandy Patinkin go nose to nose and make no sense whatsoever.

ABOVE LEFT: Marc Platt, it's no use hiding your face. We see you there with Rita Hayworth in *Down to Earth*.

ABOVE RIGHT: John Travolta shows us what Tony Manero was wearing under that white suit! Did you know that Sylvester Stalone wrote and directed *Staying Alive*? He made Travolta into the Rambo of musical stars.

BELOW: Clint Eastwood uses his injury as an excuse for his guitar playing in *Paint Your Wagon*. So, what's your excuse for your singing, Clint?

A STAR IS BORN

A STAR IS BORN

COMPOSER: Harold Arlen
LYRICIST: Ira Gershwin
PRODUCER: Sidney Luft
DIRECTOR: George Cukor
SCREENWRITER: Moss Hart
SOURCE: Based on the motion picture
A Star Is Born.
CHOREOGRAPHER: Richard Barstow

Synopsis

California's crumbling economy forces layoffs at beaches. Damn you! Norman Maine would be alive today.

Cast

Judy Garland..............	*Esther Blodgett/Vicki Lester*
James Mason..............	*Norman Maine*
Jack Carson	*Matt Libby*
Charles Bickford..............	*Oliver Niles*
Tommy Noonan..............	*Danny McGuire*

Behind the Screen

■ The "Lose That Long Face" number was shot on old sets from *A Streetcar Named Desire*.

■ The insertion of "Born in a Trunk" was opposed both by Cukor and lyricist Ira Gershwin but it was filmed with Richard Barstow directing and Roger Edens putting the sequence together. Since Edens was under contract to MGM, his boyfriend, Leonard Gershe, got his name on the piece.

A STAR IS BORN

WARNER BROTHERS—OCTOBER 16, 1954

ABOVE: Members of the Academy of Motion Picture Arts and Sciences applaud Mrs. Norman Maine.

RIGHT: A rare photo from the deleted "When My Sugar Walks Down the Street" sequence within "Born In A Trunk."

G arland's performance in *A Star Is Born* is exceptional, perhaps the best film musical performance ever. The film allowed Garland to display the gamut of her maturation process from tremulous wannabe star to stoic wife. She's one of the rare actresses who doesn't drop character when singing (some even drop their accents). Others play up their personas and call it acting. Helen Morgan came closest to the real thing in the slightly pathetic vulnerability department. Irene Dunne, an excellent actress, tended to depend on her voice to carry the emotion in a song. Mae West really sang a lyric, not just the music, but she was ultimately a one-note singer, excellent though she was. Even Lena Horne was more a song stylist than a dramatic singer. By contrast, take a look at "Lose That Long Face" in *A Star Is Born*. Judy puts everything into that song: her optimism, her doubts, her strengths and weaknesses. Someone like Mitzi Gaynor would simply have sung it as an upbeat Vegas number.

Garland seemed to know the perfect way to play every scene and song. Screenwriter Moss Hart was in awe of her abilities. "Give her a scene and instinctively she'll play it right. Watching her, you get the almost weird impression that she's—I don't know quite how to explain it—but it's something like a great musician plucking strings on a harp." Judy might have been a wreck before going on stage or in front of the camera, but once in place, her instincts took over and she couldn't be topped. It was as if she could access and express her true self only in front of an audience.

Were the powers at MGM second-guessing their decision to suspend her after the debacle of *Annie Get Your Gun*? Judy and her husband, Sid Luft, were in charge of the picture through their company, Transcona. At the beginning of shooting, she was the perfect professional and her abilities shocked even Cukor. He was amazed by her depth and the way she could do take after take equally brilliantly. Soon, though, she began to slip and then slip more. Even Cukor lost patience. He wrote, "This is the behavior of someone unhinged but there is an arrogance and a ruthless selfishness that eventually alienates one's sympathy."

A Star Is Born was not a new property. In 1937, Janet Gaynor and Fredric March starred in the first Hollywood telling of this tale of an up-and-coming star married to a famous actor on the downslide due to his alcoholism. The story was perfect for Garland, who might have related more to the star than the starlet. If you want to appreciate just how truthful these first two incarnations were, have a gander at the 1976 version with Barbra Streisand and Kris Kristofferson. Whatever their relative merits, all three versions were hits. Something about the themes of fame and loyalty transcend generational differences. But there's no doubt whatsoever that the Garland version of the story is the most successful artistically.

In spite of all the problems on the set—and a running time of over three hours—the reviews were glorious and the box office boomed. But the theaters weren't happy with the long running time, which caused them to lose out on one valuable screening each evening. So Warner cut the film, eliminating a lot of important material but keeping "Born in a Trunk."

Film historians and fans had longed to see a complete print of the film. In 1981, Ronald Haver, head of the film division of the LA County Museum of Art, went through the Warner Brothers vaults and private collections looking for footage. He found "Here's What I'm Here For" and "Lose That Long Face," both excised from the master print. Some missing scene footage was also saved, but not all of it. Haver also discovered a complete stereo soundtrack. In 1983, a restored version of the film was shown in theaters across the country to great acclaim, after a premiere at Radio City Music Hall.

> "Every time the camera rolls, I think to myself, 'Maybe this is the time they're gonna catch me.'"
>
> —*Judy Garland to George Cukor*

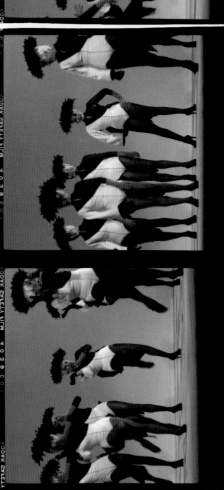

Rumor has long had it that more than one complete print is in the hands of private collectors, and there seems to be truth to the rumor. Sometimes, when a new administration took over a studio, they tossed older films to save money on storage. This practice took a particular toll on silent films that seemingly had no value. (Remember, there was no television up until the 1950s. It would be several decades more before there was a large market for videotapes and DVDs.)

When lengthy musicals needed to be cut down, the easiest thing to do was snip out musical numbers. Many of today's DVD bonuses of hitherto unseen numbers come from private collectors. In the 1950s, studios often cut down films after their initial big-city releases, to allow for more showings in neighborhood theaters. Widescreen, stereo prints were thrown away and stereo soundtracks were reduced to mono versions. Studio employees, theater projectionists and managers, and collectors took the discarded footage home with them and a bustling collectors market grew. Cut numbers tossed in the studio trash were saved and complete prints rescued.

Even an incomplete *Star Is Born* is better than none and Warner continues to update and improve the surviving material using increasingly sophisticated technology. There is no more worthy film for preservation than this masterpiece. It is the culmination of Judy Garland's career and a superb film in its own right with brilliant direction, acting, art direction, and cinematography—not to mention the brilliant Arlen and Gershwin score. ■

RIGHT: Judy Garland and James Mason in happy times.

BELOW: Filming the "Born in a Trunk" sequence.

ABOVE: Four sequences from "Born in a Trunk."

SONGS

"Born in a Trunk" (Leonard Gershe and Roger Edens) ■ "Gotta Have Me Go with You" ■ "Here's What I'm Here For" ■ "It's a New World" ■ "Lose That Long Face" ■ "The Man That Got Away" ■ "Someone at Last" ■ "TV Commercial"

"I found myself wishing that dear, enchanting Judy was at the bottom of the sea."

"They didn't cut the picture, Harry [Warner] gummed it to pieces."

—*Judy Garland*

Judy Garland

Call them the bookends of Judy Garland's legend: *The Wizard of Oz* and *A Star Is Born*. Both films capitalize on the vulnerability that set her apart from other great song-and-dance performers. It is that catch in the throat, that furtive, lost glance that tear at the heart of audiences even now. She was a lost little girl throughout her life—acting out, trying to find happiness by going down the yellow brick road or chasing after a happy Hollywood marriage and fame. From her first film appearance at age thirteen, in the short *Every Sunday*, through *The Wizard of Oz* and the Mickey Rooney musicals, and up to her finest hour (or hours) in *A Star Is Born*, Judy Garland's performances were never less than spectacular. None of it made her happy or secure. Of course, the real Garland was more complicated than what we could see, but we chose to disregard the messiness of her personal life. We were (and are) protective above all—more caring toward our Judy than that monster Louis B. Mayer was—or at least that's what we believed. Of course, as fans, we never had to put up with the late arrivals—or no arrival at all, the misplaced trust, the bad choices. For us, none of it was Judy's fault. And make no mistake about it, she was always "Judy," our hurt little girl, never "Garland"—any more than Garbo was ever "Greta." She was the most instinctual of performers. There wasn't a role or song that she couldn't interpret while letting the audience in to see a little bit of herself. It's that give and take, that peek-a-boo game she played with us, that made her so

unique and so appealing. The strength of her performances masked the insecure woman behind them, and that only served to give her acting more depth and emotion. Naturally, audiences responded. In our imagination, her films became her own home movies.

Perhaps it was Garland's ability to rise after every fall that gave people hope for their own lives. In 1950, her contract with MGM was cut short and a year later she made a triumphant appearance at New York's Palace Theatre that played a sold-out run of nineteen weeks. In 1955, following the disappointment of being denied the Oscar for *A Star Is Born*, she signed with Capitol Records and created a series of classic albums. In 1959, she was the first pop star to play New York's Metropolitan Opera House. Two years later she lent her voice to the animated cartoon, *Gay Purr-ee*, won rave reviews for her performance in the dramatic movie *Judgement at Nuremberg*, and appeared in the legendary Carnegie Hall concert. She was unable to complete a concert engagement in Melbourne but gathered strength and wowed 'em at the London Palladium, soon beginning her CBS weekly variety show series—all in 1963. She was undisputedly the greatest musical film star of all time. Her death at age of forty-seven was a tragedy, though her star remains undimmed.

ABOVE: Judy Garland sits on the edge of the stage—and film history is made.

LEFT: Judy Garland films a scene from *I Could Go on Singing*.

STAR SPANGLED RHYTHM

COMPOSER: Harold Arlen
LYRICIST: Johnny Mercer
PRODUCER: Joseph Sistrom
DIRECTOR: George Marshall
SCREENWRITER: Harry Tugend
CHOREOGRAPHERS: George Balanchine and Danny Dare

Synopsis

USA! USA!

Cast

Betty Hutton	Polly Judson
Eddie Bracken	Johnny Webster
Victor Moore	William "Bronco Billy" Webster
Walter Abel	B. G. DeSoto
Cass Daley	Mimi
Gil Lamb	High Pockets

Bing Crosby, Bob Hope, Susan Hayward, Marjorie Reynolds, Fred MacMurray, Franchot Tone, Ray Milland, Eddie "Rochester" Anderson, William Bendix, Jerry Colonna, MacDonald Carey, Dorothy Lamour, Paulette Goddard, Vera Zorina, Mary Martin, Dick Powell, Veronica Lake, Alan Ladd, Betty Jane Rhodes, Dona Drake, Lynne Overman, Johnny Johnston, Arthur Treacher, Walter Catlett, Sterling Holloway, the Golden Gate Quartet, Cecil B. DeMille, Ernest Truex, Katherine Dunham .....As Themselves

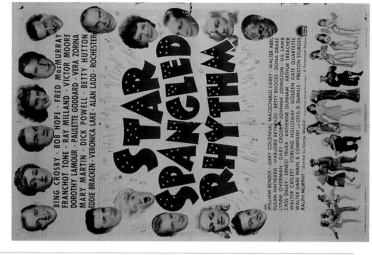

STAR SPANGLED RHYTHM

PARAMOUNT—DECEMBER 2, 1942

Victor Moore listens in on Betty Hutton's phone call.

FILM PRODUCTION SLOWED WHEN THE UNITED STATES ENTERED THE SECOND WORLD War and studios were puzzled as to what to do with all the talent under contract. After all, they were paying the stars a fortune, whether they worked or not. Soon, someone at Paramount came up with the bright idea of all-star movie revues—films with flimsy plots and lots of opportunities for star turns. The best of these uncontrollable behemoths might be Warner's *Thank Your Lucky Stars* but the best score, and one of the best scores ever written for the screen, is the one Harold Arlen and Johnny Mercer wrote for *Star Spangled Rhythm*, the first of these patriotic extravaganzas.

"On the Swing Shift" celebrated all those "Rosie the Riveters" working in factories around the country. Betty Hutton bounced around in a jeep declaring that she was "Doing It for Defense." (What "doing it" implied was never overtly stated, but audiences got the point.) Less subtle was "A Sweater, a Sarong, and a Peek-a-boo Bang," wherein three Paramount stars, Paulette Goddard, Dorothy Lamour, and Veronica Lake, extolled their unique looks while showing off their memorable physiques. Eddie "Rochester" Anderson danced with the brilliant modern dancer Katherine Dunham—as unlikely a pairing as you're likely ever to see. Anderson sang "Sharp as a Tack," a paean to his zoot suit and how fine he looked in it—but the payoff of the number reveals that an army uniform is what the well-dressed man of 1942 looks best in.

In "Old Glory," inspired by "Ballad for Americans," Bing Crosby was backed by images of the presidents on Mount Rushmore, a huge chorus proclaiming the freedoms, blah, blah, blah of America, and the evil facing us overseas. It's laid on pretty thick but presumably viewers of the time found the propaganda stirring enough. (Composer Harold Arlen said he didn't much care for it.)

Songwriters say that they are inspired by the people who sing their songs. The singers were entirely fine in the picture (with the exception of the exceptional Bing Crosby); they clearly weren't inspired. Arlen and Mercer just went through the motions with their numbers, except when they wrote the songs for Dick Powell, Mary Martin, and the dancer Vera Zorina. Powell and Martin sing "Hit the Road to Dreamland," one of the all-time best gently swinging numbers. The song gets even better when the Golden Gate Quartet, a black gospel group that also sang secular numbers, joins in with a rhythmic counterpoint. It's a terrific moment.

Johnny Johnston sings the big hit song from the score, "That Old Black Magic," while Zorina does an interpretive dance. Arlen had written a melody for the song, along with a rhythmic bass figure. Mercer suggested that if Arlen expanded the song and made it longer, it could be a narrative song rather than a typical 32-bar pop song. Arlen complied and, three days later Mercer came in with his lyric. Arlen credited the lyric with the great success of the song: "The words sustain your interest, make sense, contain memorable phrases, and tell a story. Without the lyric, the song would be just another long song." We have to state that Arlen's music is pretty darned good, too, with its almost circular melody.

Mercer took the song to his newly established Capitol Records, and had eighteen-year-old Margaret Whiting record it. The success of the recording started off Capitol Records with a bang.

As for the musical revue format, the other studios jumped on the bandwagon: Warner with *Thank Your Lucky Stars*, United Artists offered up *Stage Door Canteen* (to be followed by Warner's *Hollywood Canteen*), Universal gave America *Follow the Boys*, and MGM brought forth *Thousands Cheer*. ∎

SONGS

"Hit the Road to Dreamland" ∎ "I'm Doing It for Defense" ∎ "Old Glory" ∎ "On the Swing Shift" ∎ "Sharp As a Tack" ∎ "A Sweater, a Sarong, and a Peekaboo Bang" ∎ "That Old Black Magic"

Betty Hutton

A five-foot-two (or so) barrel of dynamite, Betty Hutton burst upon the scene as a member of Vincent Lopez's band. Not content to sit demurely, hands crossed on lap, spine erect, grin slapped on, she flew onto the stage with manic energy. Betty graduated from the Lopez organization, with whom she made some notable short subjects, to perform on Broadway in Cole Porter's *Panama Hattie*. It was there that she met producer/lyricist B. G. DeSylva, who took her to Hollywood. Her boundless energy suited Paramount's musicals perfectly, but she wasn't just a powerhouse. She also had her tender side and a vulnerability that touched moviegoers. As Hutton's fragile mental condition worsened she broke her Paramount contract, probably to the relief of the suits. In 1950, Hutton replaced another "difficult" performer, Judy Garland, in MGM's eagerly awaited film version of *Annie Get Your Gun*. Her typically rough-and-ready turn (the kind that had suited Paramount films to a T) was simply out of step with the beautifully managed and constricting MGM musical. Nevertheless, the film and star received terrific reviews. After three more films, she fled Hollywood and tried nightclubs, Broadway again (*Fade Out–Fade In*), and television (*The Betty Hutton Show*), but her career careered wildly and, after bouts with alcohol and drugs, a suicide attempt, and a nervous breakdown, she was saved by religion. Following rehab she found Father Peter Maguire, who basically adopted her and gave her work in his rectory. She returned to Broadway in 1980 in *Annie*, where she would break character after a fellow cast member's songs and ask the audience, "Wasn't that wonderful?"

Behind the Screen

∎ Johnny Mercer's lyric to "That Old Black Magic" was written about Judy Garland, with whom Mercer had a longtime affair.

TOP LEFT: Bing Crosby sings "Old Glory."

TOP RIGHT: Paulette Goddard, Dorothy Lamour, and Veronica Lake sing that durable classic, "A Sweater, a Sarong, and a Peak-a-boo Bang."

MIDDLE RIGHT: Arthur Treacher, Walter Catlett, and Sterling Holloway parody Misses Goddard, Lamour, and Lake.

STATE FAIR

COMPOSER: Richard Rodgers
LYRICIST: Oscar Hammerstein II
PRODUCER: William Perlberg
DIRECTOR: Walter Lang
SCREENWRITER: Oscar Hammerstein II
SOURCE: Based on the novel *State Fair* by Philip Strong

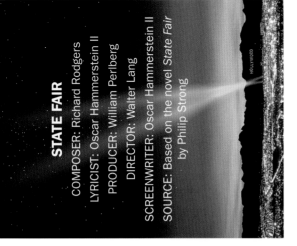

Synopsis

Mom and Dad get blue ribbons, Sis gets a handsome beau, brother gets a girlfriend. Vivian Blaine gets a bad, bad cold . . . no . . . wait. That's another show.

Cast

Jeanne Crain.................*Margy Frake*
Dana Andrews................*Pat Gilbert*
Dick Haymes..................*Wayne Frake*
Vivian Blaine.................*Emily Edwards*
Charles Winninger.........*Abel Frake*
Fay Bainter.....................*Melissa Frake*
Donald Meek...................*Hippenstahl*
Frank McHugh.................*McGee*
Percy Kilbride..................*Dave Miller*

STATE FAIR

20TH CENTURY FOX—AUGUST 30, 1945

Jeanne Crain is vaguely discontented while sitting on the porch.

IT'S NO *OKLAHOMA!* OR *CAROUSEL*, BUT *STATE FAIR* IS A NICE LITTLE MOVIE WITH A MORE THAN adequate score. The film has a sweet quality and a lesson, that even salt-of-the-earth farmers need a little excitement once in a while. While nothing much goes on and there are happy endings all around, the cast is amiable, the color (especially in the original nitrate print) is stunning—and then there's that score.

You might know that "It Might As Well Be Spring," won the Academy Award as the best song of that year. Nowadays, in a whole year of films, it's hard to find even one song that's worth listening to. And most of today's film songs occur over the credit sequences, not in the body of the films. But back in 1945, movie musicals were alive and well and some of America's greatest songwriters were writing for the screen.

Here's the list of song nominees for the 18th Annual Academy Awards in 1945. "It Might As Well Be Spring" had to contend with these:

"Ac-cen-tchu-ate the Positive" by Harold Arlen and Johnny Mercer, from *Here Come the Waves*

"Anywhere" by Jule Styne and Sammy Cahn, from *Tonight and Every Night*

"Aren't You Glad You're You" by James Van Heusen and Johnny Burke, from *The Bells of St. Mary's*

"The Cat and the Canary" by Jay Livingston and Ray Evans, from *Why Girls Leave Home*

"Endlessly" by Walter Kent and Kim Gannon, from *Earl Carroll Vanities*

"I Fall in Love Too Easily" by Jule Styne and Sammy Cahn, from *Anchors Aweigh*

"I'll Buy That Dream" by Allie Wrubel and Herb Magidson, from *Sing Your Way Home*

"Linda" by Ann Ronell, from *G.I. Joe*

"Love Letters" by Victor Young and Edward Heyman, from *Love Letters*

"More and More" by Jerome Kern and E. Y. Harburg, from *Can't Help Singing*

"I don't know where the hell I'm going."

—Oscar Hammerstein II, while writing the screenplay for State Fair

"Sleighride in July" by James Van Heusen and Johnny Burke, from *Belle of the Yukon*

"So in Love" by David Rose and Leo Robin, from *Wonder Man*

"Some Sunday Morning" by Ray Heindorf, M. K. Jerome, and Ted Koehler, from *San Antonio*

Stiff competition.

Nowadays, the Academy is hard pressed to nominate five songs each year. Even excluding the seven songs above that are completely unknown today (more if you're not an aficionado), it's an impressive list. Two teams of songwriters have two nominations each. There are at least four songs that are still recorded today, more than sixty years later.

Can you name even one of the songs nominated in 2009? Do you think there might be a reason that none were performed at the Oscar ceremony? The fact is, the Academy of Motion Picture Arts and Sciences keeps threatening to delete the category altogether.

The score to *State Fair* had only six songs but three or four of them are still sung and recorded. That's a pretty high average. So, for those who say nothing happens in *State Fair*, or that it's corny, we say it's still enjoyable, professional entertainment with an exceptional score. ■

SONGS

"All I Owe Ioway" ■ "Isn't It Kinda Fun" ■ "It Might As Well Be Spring" ■ "It's a Grand Night for Singing" ■ "Our State Fair" ■ "That's for Me"

TOP RIGHT: Vivian Blaine and Dick Haymes strike up a romance at the annual shindig that gives the film its name.

MIDDLE LEFT: The family at the fair: Dick Haymes, Fay Bainter, Jeanne Crain, and Charles Winninger. Spoiler alert: All will come back winners in one way or another.

MIDDLE RIGHT: The family at the fair: Norman Foster, Louise Dresser, Janet Gaynor, and Will Rogers in the 1933 non-musical version of *State Fair*.

RIGHT: Walter Lang gives some pointers to a couple of kids while Ethel Merman patiently stands by, during the shooting of *There's No Business Like Show Business*.

Walter Lang

In the '70s when French film critics came up with the auteur theory, lots of terrific directors got left by the wayside directors who were equally adept at different styles of film but didn't parade their egos in the press and so were overlooked by the film cognoscenti. Walter Lang is one of those artists who never got his due. Most books that purport to cover Hollywood film history don't even mention him. Like many studio pioneers, he worked at a variety of jobs before becoming an assistant director at Cosmopolitan Productions. He matriculated to full directorship in 1925, for Mrs. Wallace Reid's film company, then bopped around from studio to studio. When sound came in he briefly left the business, traveling to Paris to be an artist. Returning to Hollywood, he eventually landed at Fox (before the merger with Zanuck's 20th Century company), where he remained for the rest of his career. For the most part, Lang was handed comedies and musicals and his work was utterly dependable if not inspired. He made eminently enjoyable films, sometimes out of what might be called claptrap upon examination of the material. Lang's musicals included three with Shirley Temple—one excellent, *The Little Princess* (1939); one pretty good, *Susannah of the Mounties* (1939); and one execrable, *The Blue Bird* (1940). He was a favorite of Alice Faye and Betty Grable and handled Fox's nostalgia musicals, including *Tin Pan Alley* (1940), *Coney Island* (1943), *Mother Wore Tights* (1947), and *When My Baby Smiles at Me* (1948). Lang also directed two Fox stalwarts, *Week-End in Havana* (1941) and *Moon Over Miami* (1941). In the 1950s, he undertook *With a Song in My Heart* (1952), *Call Me Madam* (1953)—Fox's last non-Cinemascope musical—and then Fox's first Cinemascope musical, *There's No Business Like Show Business* (1954). He also helmed the blockbusters *The King and I* (1956) and *Can-Can* (1960). His last film was the epic *Snow White and the Three Stooges*. With typical professionalism, Lang took this job as seriously as he did any of his other films.

STORMY WEATHER

20TH CENTURY FOX—JULY 21, 1943

STORMY WEATHER

PRODUCER: William LeBaron

DIRECTOR: Andrew L. Stone

SCREENWRITERS: Ted Koehler and Frederick Jackson

CHOREOGRAPHER: Charles Robinson

Synopsis

Bill Robinson and Lena Horne have a September-May romance—but who cares, when the music and performances are so magnificent?

Cast

Lena Horne................Selina Rogers
Bill Robinson ....Bill Williamson
Dooley Wilson ....Gabe Tucker
Cab Calloway
Katherine Dunham
Thomas "Fats" Waller
Ada Brown
The Nicholas Brothers

Behind the Screen

- The army screened *Stormy Weather* for black units only.
- The film's working title was *Thanks, Pal.*

Lena Horne pretends to like Bill Robinson. What an actress!

I T WAS NOT A HAPPY SET, BUT GOOD THINGS CAN HAPPEN EVEN WHEN THERE'S DISCORD IN the ranks. Besides, *Stormy Weather* was one of the few first-class all-black films of the 1940s. Watching the film now, with its great panoply of stars, is a delight and sad at the same time because, no matter how great their talents, none of these performers really made it in Hollywood.

Take Lena Horne. Although she's considered a movie star, she was given featured roles in just a handful of movies. Otherwise, MGM stuck her in individual numbers that could easily be cut for markets hostile to integrated films. The Nicholas Brothers, certainly among the greatest singers and dancers of all time, likewise had spots in films here and there but never were given their due. It's to both Horne's and the Nicholas Brothers' credit that their few appearances struck such an emotional chord in viewers that their meager output is thought to be greater than the sum of its parts.

Likewise, Bill Robinson, perhaps the greatest tap dancer of all time, is now best remembered for partnering with little Shirley Temple. Fats Waller, a terrific performer and one of the great American composers, made some shorts and appeared in a few movies but the writer of "Ain't Misbehavin'" and "Honeysuckle Rose" was never asked to write a film score. And Katherine Dunham, an important choreographer with her own company . . . well, you get the point. It is our good fortune that all of these performers could successfully showcase their talents on Broadway, on recordings, and in live appearances. Still, we're lucky to have all these talents in one film.

In 1943, the Fox studio didn't treat all of its stars well—the black ones, we mean. The studio maintained a whites-only commissary and black artists' dressing rooms were segregated from the others on the lot. In just a year, Darryl Zanuck would take over the company and become a champion of race relations, producing such movies as *Pinky*; but until that point, Fox's behavior toward minorities was worse than the other studios.

As we mentioned, the set wasn't a happy one. Lena Horne resented Bill Robinson, thinking him an Uncle Tom. Robinson didn't exactly ingratiate himself with the rest of the cast, either, coming on to all the women and supposedly drawing a gun on Benny Carter.

Horne was unhappy with director Andrew Stone, as well, who didn't seem to know how to treat his black cast. He never earned their respect and that caused unnecessary stress on the set. (Stone had a long, undistinguished career, topped off by two musical bombs, *Song of Norway* and *The Great Waltz*.)

Horne also had a difficult time letting her emotions out during the big title song. Stone cajoled her to no avail. Even Cab Calloway chewed her out, but Horne wasn't used to letting her feelings show, even when performing, thus earning a reputation among her peers as "uppity." Finally, Calloway whispered two words to her and Horne came to life, making the song her own. Those two words were "Ethel Waters," the performer who had originated the song at the famed Cotton Club in Harlem. Once the film opened, the song became Horne's signature tune for all time.

Despite the problems surrounding the production, *Stormy Weather* broke important barriers and a lot of good came out of it. Yes, it bears traces of condescension and stereotyping, but the talents assembled do their work brilliantly. ∎

"Twentieth Century-Fox . . . would have found a way to star us if we had been two little white guys. They did it with the Ritz Brothers. But I say I'm not *too* bitter."

—*Fayard Nicholas*

"For God's sake! Talk to this girl, see if you can get her to show some emotion."

—Director Andrew Stone to Cab Calloway about Lena Horne's rendition of "Stormy Weather"

Lena Horne

Lena Horne never knew where or even how she fit into Hollywood, and Hollywood didn't know, either. She had appeared in one feature prior to her employment with MGM, 1938's *The Duke Is Tops*. When MGM signed her, she was the first black performer to be offered a seven-year contract by one of the major studios. In 1942, they put her in the Ann Sothern film *Panama Hattie*. She starred alongside Ethel Waters and Eddie Anderson in *Cabin in the Sky*, considered by historians and Horne, herself, to be her greatest role. Still, MGM didn't quite know what to do with a black performer who refused to play maids or stereotypical roles. Not that she would have been convincing, given her beauty, carriage, and class. Thanks in part to interference from state censorship boards, black performers were hot potatoes in Hollywood for a long time. Their scenes were often cut, they couldn't appear in roles perceived to be equal to those of their white counterparts, and there just wasn't a big or vocal enough audience who would accept them as stars. For the majority of her career, Horne made cameo appearances in films, mainly in revues where she sang a number or two. These include *Thousands Cheer, Ziegfeld Follies* (where she sang Hugh Martin's song "Love" and made it a semistandard), *Till the Clouds Roll By* (a Jerome Kern biopic where Horne sang "Can't Help Lovin' Dat Man" from *Show Boat* and "Why Was I Born?"), and *Words and Music* (where she sang "The Lady Is a Tramp" and "Where or When"). Having successfully committed a song from *Show Boat* to the screen, and being a light-skinned black woman who exactly fit the part's description, Horne believed she should play the part of Julie LaVerne in MGM's 1951 filming of *Show Boat*. But the studio chose Horne's friend Ava Gardner instead. Horne never got over it. She made only two more films at MGM: *The Duchess of Idaho*, a flop; and 1956's *Meet Me in Las Vegas*. Along the way, she was blacklisted from pictures, and she and the film business seemed to give up on each other. She returned to Hollywood in 1969's *Death of a Gunfighter*, appeared in *The Wiz* as Glinda, and finally, as a host in *That's Entertainment III*. When her movie career went into hibernation, Horne turned to Broadway, nightclubs, and recordings, but she is considered a great movie star by the public and critics alike.

SONGS

"African Dance" (Clarence Muse and Connie Bemis) ■ "Ain't Misbehavin'" (Thomas "Fats" Waller and Harry Brooks) ■ "Dah, Dat, Dah" (Cyril J. Mockridge and Bill Robinson) ■ "Diga Diga Do" (Jimmy McHugh and Dorothy Fields) ■ "Geechy Joe" (Cab Calloway, Jack Palmer, and Andy Gibson) ■ "I Can't Give You Anything but Love" (Jimmy McHugh and Dorothy Fields) ■ "I Lost My Sugar in Salt Lake City" (Leon Rene) ■ "The Jumpin' Jive" (Cab Calloway, Jack Palmer, and Frank Froeba) ■ "Linda Brown" (Al Cowans) ■ "My, My, Ain't That Something" (Pinky Tomlin) ■ "Patter" (Lionel Newman and Ted Koehler) ■ "Rang Tang Tang" (Cyril J. Mockridge and Bill Robinson) ■ "Rhythm Cocktail" (Cab Calloway, Illinois Jacquet, and Buster Harding) ■ "Stormy Weather" (Harold Arlen and Ted Koehler) ■ "That's Not Right" (Nat "King" Cole) ■ "There's No Two Ways about Love" (James P. Johnson and Irving Mills)

LEFT: Thomas "Fats" Waller really does like Ada Brown's singing. And the feeling is mutual.

BLACK MUSICALS

W HITE-RUN STUDIOS MADE THE OCCASIONAL ALL-BLACK MUSICAL for their mainly white audiences. Several of these, *Hallelujah*, *Stormy Weather*, and *Cabin in the Sky*, were successful with all audiences. But in both Hollywood and New York City, several black producers and directors put out a series of musicals targeted exclusively to the black audience. Working in the same successful genres as the major studios did, they produced melodramas, backstage musicals, and even black cowboy musicals. More than 500 "race movies" were made, but fewer than a third of them still exist. Here, we present a gallery of posters from these all-black musicals, many of which starred terrific performers.

HERB JEFFRIES

H erb Jeffries grew up on a farm in Michigan, where he rode horses, milked cows, and did sundry other chores. On weekends, he watched Buck Jones and Tom Mix ride across the screen in Detroit's segregated movie houses. When he was older, he saw the all-little-people western *The Terror of Tiny Town's* and wondered why it didn't include any black cowboys. He contacted Tiny Town's producer, Jed Buell, in Hollywood and offered to star in an all-black cowboy picture. Jeffries later recalled, "I felt that dark-skinned children could identify with me and, in the Bronze Buckaroo, they could have a hero. Many people don't realize (to this very day) that in the old West, was a black... and there were many Mexican cowboys, too." Jeffries' first film was *Harlem on the Prairie* in 1937. After four more oaters, in 1939 he gave up pictures and joined Duke Ellington's orchestra. In 1940, he recorded in one take with the song "Flamingo," which he recorded in one take with no rehearsal. It has sold over 15 million recordings. Jeffries may be best remembered as a singer, but many still think of him as the Bronze Buckaroo, one of the first positive role models for young blacks.

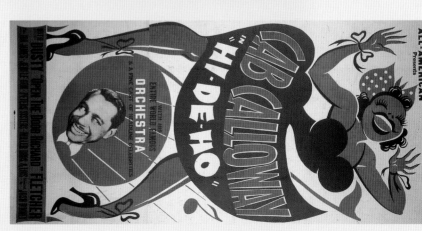

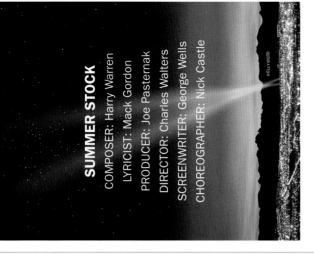

SUMMER STOCK

COMPOSER: Harry Warren
LYRICIST: Mack Gordon
PRODUCER: Joe Pasternak
DIRECTOR: Charles Walters
SCREENWRITER: George Wells
CHOREOGRAPHER: Nick Castle

Synopsis

Hey kids, let's put on a show in a barn! Only this time it's Judy Garland who's against the idea—until Gene Kelly woos her, that is.

Cast

Judy Garland..............Jane Falbury
Gene Kelly..................Joe D. Ross
Eddie Bracken..............Orville Wingait
Phil Silvers..................Herb Blake
Gloria DeHaven............Abigail Falbury
Marjorie Main...............Esme
Ray Collins...................Jasper G. Wingait
Nita Bieber...................Sara Higgins
Carleton Carpenter.......Artie
Hans Conreid...............Harrison I. Keath

Behind the Screen

■ When Mack Gordon disappeared during the filming, Saul Chaplin was forced to step in and write additional songs.

SUMMER STOCK

MGM—AUGUST 31, 1950

ABOVE: Judy Garland is back in the barn, putting on another show and keeping up nicely with Gene Kelly.

BOTTOM RIGHT: A svelte Judy performs the brilliant "Get Happy" number.

Producing pictures under the aegis of a great and powerful studio like MGM (the greatest and most powerful) had its advantages. No film in the history of movies has had completely fair sailing, but some movies hit more rocks than most. *Summer Stock* had a rough crossing from page to screen but audiences viewing the finished film had no idea that there had been anything but bluebirds and flowers on the set.

We all know that due to mental and physical problems, Judy Garland could be a pain in the neck. She didn't prove otherwise on *Summer Stock*. Having just been replaced by Betty Hutton in *Annie Get Your Gun*, she viewed *Summer Stock* as her chance to redeem herself and regain her standing in the MGM pantheon of stars. Unfortunately, her problems were nearly insurmountable. We don't want to dwell on the oft-told stories of Garland's problems, but a couple of first-person accounts provide a window into life on the set and indicate that Garland's troubles ran deep.

Kelly, director Charles Walters, and costumer Walter Plunkett tried to protect Garland. "Gene took her left arm," Walters remembered, "and I took her right one, and between us, we literally tried to keep her on her feet. But it wasn't easy. Emotionally she was at her lowest ebb. Physically she was pretty unsure of herself as well. There were even times when we had to nail the scenery down and provide her with supports so she wouldn't fall over. Once, I remember, she had to walk up a few steps, and she couldn't do it. So I had to cheat the shot, and shoot the scene from a different angle. The whole experience was a ghastly, hideous nightmare which, happily, is a blur in my memory."

Walter Plunkett told author Clive Hirschhorn that he did his best to hide Garland's burgeoning figure. "We tried to make her look as thin as possible, but we weren't miracle workers, and we didn't succeed. She was paranoid about her inability to work and felt herself together, the more hysterical she became. It was heart-breaking to see." Producer Joe Pasternak wanted to shut down the production but, surprisingly, studio head Louis B. Mayer refused. He told Pasternak, "Judy Garland has made this studio a fortune in the good days, and the least we can do is to give her one more chance. If you stop production now, it'll finish her."

What's important here is that MGM did everything it could to make Garland look great on the screen and create an entertaining work of art. Luckily, they succeeded and *Summer Stock* is a breezy, artifice-free entertainment. It doesn't have any of that striving-for-art feeling of some other Gene Kelly vehicles. Perhaps that's because Joe Pasternak didn't feel he needed to create art for the ages, so avoided that reach for perfection that can squeeze the life out of a musical film.

In *Summer Stock*, Kelly has a marvelous solo, more in the style of Fred Astaire than the usual athletic dancing or tortured-by-love posturing exemplified by the *American in Paris* ballet. Kelly simply dances with a newspaper, employing a series of inventive moves. It's a joy to watch.

Kelly has another stellar moment, and in our opinion, one of the great moments in movie musical history. He and Phil Silvers, dressed in hillbilly garb, are singing "Heavenly Music" when a pack of wild dogs decides to get in on the act. The dogs are let loose on the set to do what they will. And what they will is to run and jump and bark and cause general mayhem while Kelly and Silvers are trying to get through their ridiculous number with a straight face. Sometimes, a bit of spontaneity is refreshing—and they are really, really rare in studio productions.

Comedy is difficult, especially when it doesn't have any room to breathe. Unfortunately, many studio productions are rehearsed within an inch of their lives. There are lots of examples of supposedly funny songs landing like lead balloons—for example, the whole show-within-a-show disaster sequence in *The Band Wagon*. On the other side of the equation is the Bob Hope–Martha Raye "How'dja Like to Love Me" number in *College Swing*, a brilliantly under rehearsed comedy number.

As for *Summer Stock*, we have to point out that Judy Garland comes across wonderfully, even in the midst of her personal torments. Riding on a tractor singing "Happy Harvest," she's relaxed and in complete control. A hallmark of Garland's talent is her ability to give her all to the audience, and she really does that here, as well as in "If You Feel Like Singing Sing." And we want to repeat that sometimes the most famous songs from a film aren't the best. "Friendly Star" is a beautiful ballad and Judy Garland renders it with all of her vulnerability and optimism. It's a terrific song that deserves to have a life of its own.

Surprising everyone, Garland had one last brilliant moment in her MGM history. After shooting was completed, it was decided that one more number was needed for the end of the film, so she was called in to talk to Saul Chaplin, the co–musical director. In the six weeks that had passed between the end of shooting and her meeting, Garland had lost around fifteen pounds and changed back into the wonderfully cooperative performer that everyone loved. She wanted to sing the Harold Arlen and Ted Koehler song "Get Happy." Chaplin came up with an arrangement and taught it to her. The set was still standing but the original choreographer, Nick Castle, wasn't around, so Charles Walters stepped in and directed. The results were magical, an iconic moment in the history of MGM and in Garland's career. She's got it all: a sense of fun, sexuality, and sensuality all in one number. She showed us once and for all how instinctual and smart she could be at her best. Sadly, it was to be her last turn on the MGM lot.

Summer Stock isn't one of the greatest of MGM musicals but it's one of the most enjoyable and beats the pants off of most other studios' A-list gems. ■

"We loved her and we understood what she was going through, and I had every reason to be grateful for all the help she had given me." —*Gene Kelly on Judy Garland*

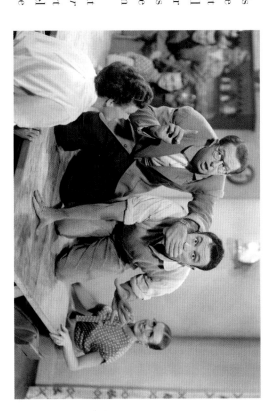

SONGS

"All for You" (Saul Chaplin) ■ "Dig-Dig-Dig for Your Dinner" ■ "Friendly Star" ■ "Happy Harvest Howdy Neighbor" ■ "Heavenly Music" (Saul Chaplin) ■ "If You Feel Like Singing, Sing" ■ "Mem'ry Island" ■ "You, Wonderful You" (Harry Warren, Jack Brooks, and Saul Chaplin)

TOP: Phil Silvers and Gene Kelly make a wonderful team—even when Phil doesn't let Gene get a word in edgewise.

MIDDLE: Phil and Gene again, in one of the all-time funniest film numbers, "Heavenly Music."

BOTTOM: Judy "gets happy"—for the moment, anyway.

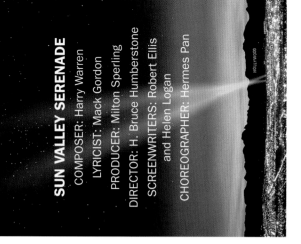

SUN VALLEY SERENADE

COMPOSER: Harry Warren
LYRICIST: Mack Gordon
PRODUCER: Milton Sperling
DIRECTOR: H. Bruce Humberstone
SCREENWRITERS: Robert Ellis
and Helen Logan
CHOREOGRAPHER: Hermes Pan

Synopsis

Sonja and John's romance is chilly but Glenn
Miller's music warms up the proceedings nicely.

Cast

Sonja Henie .... *Karen Benson*
John Payne .... *Ted Scott*
Glenn Miller .... *Phil Corey*
Milton Berle .... *Jerome K. "Nifty" Allen*
Lynn Bari .... *Vivian Dawn*
Joan Davis .... *Miss Carstairs*
Dorothy Dandridge .... *Specialty Act*
The Modernaires .... *Themselves*
The Nicholas Brothers ... *Themselves*

SUN VALLEY SERENADE

20TH CENTURY FOX—AUGUST 20, 1941

Sonja Henie gets all limbered up (that's what they called it in the 1940s) with the help of John Payne.

YOU COULD CALL *SUN VALLEY SERENADE* A GENEROUS SHOT OF SCHMALTZ ON THE ROCKS with a twist. The schmaltz is the plot, the rocks are the ice on which Sonja Henie spins, and the twist is what really provides the excitement—Glenn Miller's bouncy, hard-driving, and creamy orchestra.

MGM wasn't the only studio to employ Olympic stars as movie actors. Metro's Johnny Weissmuller and Esther Williams were champs *in the water*; Fox's Sonja Henie was a goddess *on* it—when it was hard and cold, that is. But Henie wasn't the real draw of *Sun Valley Serenade*; the true star was Glenn Miller.

This was by no means the first time that an established band or orchestra was featured in a movie musical. Ted Lewis appeared in the films *The Show of Shows* and *Is Everybody Happy?* in 1929. (The latter title was taken from Lewis's famous catchphrase, and was used again for a short subject based on cut numbers from the Universal feature *Hold That Ghost* [1941] and a Columbia biopic of Lewis [1943].) The estimable Paul Whiteman was the star of Universal's *King of Jazz* in 1930. Throughout that decade, a who's who of bandleaders found their way to the screen.

Not surprisingly, black bandleaders didn't fare as well as their Caucasian counterparts. Their appearances tended to be segregated from the plots so that their scenes could be cut from prints in the South. Duke Ellington, perhaps the greatest of the big band leaders, was featured in Mae West's *Belle of the Nineties*, and Thomas "Fats" Waller's oversize personality graced a couple of motion pictures beginning with 1935's *Hooray for Love*. Waller's next feature appearance was in Fox's all-black musical *Stormy Weather*, alongside Cab Calloway and his band. Darryl Zanuck, then head of Fox, was a fervent believer in racial equality and put his movies where his mouth was.

SONGS

"At Last" ■ "Chattanooga Choo Choo" ■ "I Know Why (And So-Do-You)" ■ "In the Mood" ■ "It Happened in Sun Valley" ■ "The Kiss Polka"

TOP RIGHT: Sonja Henie in the 1943 Broadway extravaganza, *Stars on Ice.*

BELOW LEFT: Lynn Bari "singing" (she was dubbed by Pat Friday) "At Last" with the Glenn Miller Orchestra in a deleted sequence.

BOTTOM RIGHT: The Nicholas Brothers, great singers as well as inspired dancers, perform the "Chattanooga Choo Choo" number.

Sonja Henie

Sonja Henie's character in this film was named Karen Benson—what's up with that? Somehow it doesn't seem grand enough for a Norwegian Olympic skater turned musical theater star. The most successful figure skater in Olympics history, Henie was pretty enough and could skate the pants off all her costars. Consequently, she didn't get to play it like Fred Astaire wooing the ladies by squiring them through Terpsichore and making love on the dance floor. Henie's love interests mostly stood at the edge of the rink and waited for the spectacle to conclude. Yes, there were lots of skaters and sometimes even flaming torches, but the cameras seldom soared across the ice, so we were stuck on the edges of the rink with John Payne and all the others. Henie controlled all the skating in her films. Throughout her film career, she and producer Arthur Wirtz created a series of ice shows titled the "Hollywood Ice Revue." These were the first big ice entertainments and their huge success paved the way for Holiday on Ice and the Ice Capades. After she retired from the screen, Henie continued to perform in ice shows. Although she was cute and petite, while watching the movies we always get the impression that Henie wasn't a nice person off screen. Oh, and did we mention she was a Nazi sympathizer? True.

SONJA HENIE

But with Sonja Henie's skating extravaganzas, we're glad to have a little respite. Even as great a choreographer as Astaire's frequent collaborative partner, Hermes Pan, couldn't enliven the proceedings. But Pan's specialty was expressing emotion through dance. Neither the dance nor the emotion was really possible with ice skating, especially when the leading man couldn't skate well, leaving that task entirely to Henie. What the picture probably needed was a Busby Berkeley, who specialized in group numbers rather than steps.

Think about what Berkeley did with Esther Williams's aquatic forays. Of course there was a little more room there for variation: he could have her swimming through the water, aquadancing (we made that word up!) underneath, even diving in. Henie was stuck with the icy surface, making things a bit monotonous no matter how many patterns she made, how high her jumps, or how fast her spins.

Still, the score makes this a great musical and the Miller Orchestra becomes its star, relegating Henie and Payne to a subplot. We continually look forward to the next appearance of the band, the Modernaires, and those great songs. In the end, *Sun Valley Serenade* provides a lot of entertainment along with a bonus: Dorothy Dandridge in "Chattanooga-Choo-Choo," one of those memorable (easily curable) numbers featuring black performers that were

As far as *Sun Valley Serenade* goes, Glenn Miller and his band were cast to punch up the proceedings, along with vaudevillian Milton Berle, whom producers hoped would inject some personality into the picture. They were just facing facts: the leads were as bland as bland can be. Sonja Henie was a terrific skater and sort of cute but without any sex appeal. Plus, she was a triple threat—with an emphasis on the word *threat.* She could neither sing, dance, nor act, although she was a cutup on the ice. John Payne, her leading man, was quite handsome, sexy, and easy to watch but he had no heat with Henie, a child-woman. So, the Warren and Gordon tunes, Bill Finnegan's powerful musical arrangements for Miller's band, and Milton Berle were pressed into service and provide the real dynamics of the picture.

The fact is, except for Alice Faye, Betty Grable, and Carmen Miranda, Fox had few musical stars. On the male side, Don Ameche and John Payne were the only Fox players who could sing. Tyrone Power played leads in musicals without being very musical himself.

Except for Fred Astaire's dances, most numbers set in nightclubs or on stages have cutaways where characters in the seats have little conversations while the music goes on in the background or provide reactions with their faces. When a star is strutting his or her stuff on the stage and we're into the performance and song, there's nothing more annoying than these cutaways.

SUNNY SIDE UP

20TH CENTURY FOX—DECEMBER 25, 1929

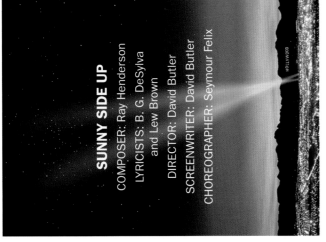

SUNNY SIDE UP

COMPOSER: Ray Henderson
LYRICISTS: B. G. DeSylva
and Lew Brown

DIRECTOR: David Butler
SCREENWRITER: David Butler
CHOREOGRAPHER: Seymour Felix

Synopsis

Rich boy Jack hires poor little Molly to make his fiancée jealous. It works—but Molly goes back to her little flat in love with Jack. Wouldn't you know it—once she's gone, he realizes he loves her, too! Cue happy ending.

Cast

Janet Gaynor................*Molly Carr*
Charles Farrell...............*Jack Cromwell*
Marjorie White................*Bea Nichols*
El Brendel.......................*Eric Swenson*
Mary Forbes................*Mrs. Cromwell*

SONGS

"If I Had a Talking Picture of You" ▪ "I'm a Dreamer, Aren't We All?" ▪ "It's Great to Be Necked" ▪ "Sunny Side Up" ▪ "Turn on the Heat" ▪ "You Find the Time and I'll Find the Place" ▪ "You've Got Me Pickin' Petals Off o' Daisies"

Behind the Screen

▪ In 1934, Janet Gaynor was the movies' top box-office star.

ABOVE: Charles Farrell and Janet Gaynor were a popular film team in the early days of sound musicals. Here, they get to know each other while Marjorie White, El Brendel, and Frank Richardson eavesdrop.

OPPOSITE: Never mind trying to figure out what it is doing in the musical; "Turn on the Heat" is one of the most jaw-dropping numbers in film history. Top right, the girls are Eskimos in the frozen north. Then the heat comes on and presto, they're on a volcanic island in the Pacific. Pure bliss.

THAT THE COMING OF SOUND PROVIDED NEW CHALLENGES TO THE FILM INDUSTRY IS an understatement. At first, the potential of sound film was underestimated by studio heads, directors, and producers alike. Some felt it unnecessary, that sound could never improve the telling of stories. Then there was the foreign market to consider. Silent films could play all over the world with only the substitution of title cards—but how to export talkies?

Warner Brothers had a smallish studio on Sunset Boulevard and nothing to lose by investing in new sound technology. Sam Warner thought of sound as a means to replace the individual accompanists in theaters large and small across America. Large theaters would save money by replacing their symphony orchestras rather than live pianos, string quartets, or organs. He was right—all that happened—but the unintended side effect that wouldn't have bothered Sam Warner even if he'd thought of it was that thousands of musicians were put out of work.

Warner put its feet in the water with a series of Vitaphone shorts featuring stars of vaudeville and the Broadway stage. When the sound-on-disc format was perfected (sort of), they put soundtracks on feature films. But there was a hesitation to have music in a film unless the source of the music was apparent. As Max Steiner recalled, "A constant fear prevailed among producers, directors, and musicians that they would be asked, where does the music come from? Therefore, they never used music unless it could be explained by the presence of a source like an orchestra, piano player, phonograph, or radio, which was specified in the script."

The first musical film to have a soundtrack was *The Jazz Singer* (but since you're reading this book, you probably knew that). With Broadway superstar Jolson an immense success on film, too, studios raided the Broadway roster of stars and songwriters. Soon, Broadway conductors were brought in to oversee the music for films. The studios knew how little they knew about musicals, so stage directors and choreographers made the trek westward. The Broadway shows first adapted into musical films were pretty faithful to the source material (after all, there weren't really music departments in place for arranging, scoring, and adapting songs, nor were there many composers under contract). As with all musical films at the time, the orchestra played live on the soundstage while the cast sang along.

Since the studios didn't have their own orchestras, musicians were drawn from the Los Angeles area. Warner was the first studio to hire a permanent orchestra that could play any style, the core of which were six members of Jimmie Grier's dance band, then playing at the Cocoanut Grove and the Biltmore Hotel. Sam Warner died on the eve of the opening of *The Jazz Singer* but brother Jack took over the mantle of musical proponent.

Fox also invested in newfangled sound technology—in their case, sound on film. William Fox joined in importing talent from Broadway. The songwriting team of B. G. "Buddy" DeSylva, Lew Brown, and Ray Henderson had achieved fame with such shows as *Good News* and *Follow Thru*. For *Sunny Side Up*, the team supplied three standards: the title song, "If I Had a Talking Picture of You," and "I'm a Dreamer, Aren't We All?"

Sweet, sensitive, and somewhat naïve Janet Gaynor was Fox Studio's great silent star. To her credit, she never became cloying in her roles. Her first great film was *Seventh Heaven*, opposite boyishly handsome Charles Farrell. They would eventually make twelve films together. No less a talent that the great director F. W. Murnau cast Gaynor in his masterpiece, *Sunrise*. Her performance in that film and in *Street Angel* would win her the first Academy Award for Best Actress. (It was the last time any artist was permitted to win for more than one picture.) Gaynor made a successful transition to sound, along with Farrell. She starred in the Gershwins' first film musical, *Delicious*, but when Darryl Zanuck took over the studio he didn't cotton to her talents, preferring a more contemporary heroine with more sex appeal and less of a Mary Pickford quality. Gaynor got out of her contract and went on to log more excellent performances, including in the original film version of *A Star Is Born*. She retired from films in 1938, returning only to make an appearance in the film *Bernadine* in 1957, working back where it all began, at Fox.

If at all, *Sunny Side Up* is known today for "Turn on the Heat," one of the most jaw-dropping musical numbers of all time. The scene is the frozen north and the chorus girls are bundled in parkas and surrounded by ice and igloos. It's darned cold up there on the stage (yes, this is supposed to take place on a stage!) so they naturally ask for the heat to be turned on. Voilà! Their wish is granted and they doff their parkas as the igloos and ice melt (where is that water going, exactly—into the orchestra pit?) and huge palm trees and ferns grow out of the floor. But be careful of what you wish for. The stage is soon engulfed in smoke and flames. It's too darned hot! The whole remarkable and ridiculous number seems to have been shot in one continuous take, with multiple cameras. ∎

BOTTOM RIGHT: Lionel Barrymore, Shirley Temple, and director David Butler on the set of *The Little Colonel*.

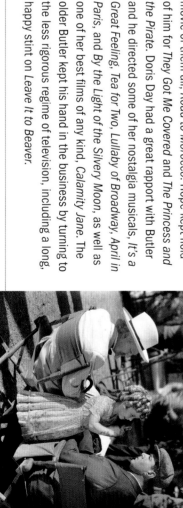

David Butler

Here's an unsung director. Look in the reference books and you are unlikely to find an mention of David Butler–though he directed some important pictures. He may not have had a discernible style, but the hard-working craftsman shouldn't be ignored.

After a few appearances in silent films, Butler found himself at William Fox's studio in Rancho Park. In 1927, just as sound was just about to dawn in Hollywood, he directed his first film, *High School Hero*. He soon graduated to sound films and a series of early Fox musicals including *Sunny Side Up*, the futuristic *Just Imagine*–also with a score by DeSylva, Brown, and Henderson–and the Gershwins' *Delicious*, a totally pleasing romp. Then it was on to a series of films starring Fox's most bankable star, Shirley Temple. Butler directed the moppet in *Bright Eyes*, *The Little Colonel*, *The Littlest Rebel*, *Captain January*, and *Dimples*. He then shepherded Judy Garland through her first feature, *Pigskin Parade*, along with future Tin Woodsman, Jack Haley. This was followed by one of Eddie Cantor's best films, *Ali Baba Goes to Town* (featuring the totally swinging Peters Sisters). Butler did a yeoman's work on the Kay Kyser vehicle *That's Right–You're Wrong* and ushered Bing Crosby through *If I Had My Way*. Der Bingle liked him so much that he tapped Butler to direct the best Road movie of them all, *Road to Morocco*. Hope kept hold of him for *They Got Me Covered* and *The Princess and the Pirate*. Doris Day had a great rapport with Butler and he directed some of her nostalgia musicals, *It's a Great Feeling*, *Tea for Two*, *Lullaby of Broadway*, *April in Paris*, and *By the Light of the Silvery Moon*, as well as one of her best films of any kind, *Calamity Jane*. The older Butler kept his hand in the business by turning to the less rigorous regime of television, including a long, happy stint on *Leave It to Beaver*.

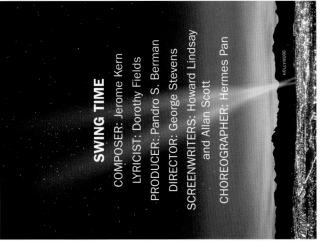

SWING TIME

COMPOSER: Jerome Kern
LYRICIST: Dorothy Fields
PRODUCER: Pandro S. Berman
DIRECTOR: George Stevens
SCREENWRITERS: Howard Lindsay and Allan Scott
CHOREOGRAPHER: Hermes Pan

Synopsis

Fred's too busy gambling to make it to his wedding, so the bride's father tells him he's got to earn $25,000 or forget about his daughter's hand—or any other parts. His luck changes when he runs into Ginger. (Fred's character's name is "Lucky"—is there any doubt how this will turn out?)

Cast

Fred Astaire.................Lucky Garnett
Ginger Rogers.............Penny Carroll
Victor Moore..............Pop Cardetti
Helen Broderick..........Mabel Anderson
Eric Blore...................Gordon
Betty Furness.............Margaret Watson
George Metaxa...........Ricky Romero

SWING TIME

RKO—AUGUST 27, 1936

Fred Astaire and Ginger Rogers.

H EY, IF IT WORKS, WHY FIX IT—UNTIL AUDIENCES LOSE INTEREST, ANYWAY. THE team of Fred Astaire and Ginger Rogers was boffo at the B.O. through a series of similar musicals at RKO. Astaire was already well known as a star on Broadway teamed with his sister Adele. In fact, when Adele chose to retire, some people, including Fred himself, doubted he could continue. It wasn't that Fred was untalented, but would he be able to succeed without his sister's support? Astaire's appearance in Broadway's *Gay Divorce* was a success but Brooks Atkinson wrote in the *New York Times*, "Some of us cannot help feeling the joyousness of the Astaire team is missing now that the team has parted."

When Fred came to Hollywood, there weren't any comparisons to Adele as the majority of the public had never seen the duo perform. But history would repeat itself as the Astaire-and-Rogers team wound down in the public's estimation. As early as 1935, when *Follow the Fleet* was in production, Astaire began to worry about being linked exclusively with Rogers. His contract was under negotiation the following year and he insisted that Rogers could appear in only three of his next five pictures. Still, the team was riding high with critics and the public. They were in fourth place in the 1935 *Motion Picture Herald*'s top ten moneymakers, right below Shirley Temple, Will Rogers, and Clark Gable.

Cracks in the partnership began to appear when the excellent *Shall We Dance* didn't do as well as previous Astaire-Rogers pictures. Even the critic for Cork, Ireland's *Examiner* wrote, "One begins to wonder how many more of that type of film the public is prepared to enjoy. I know of at least one member of it who had reached the limit."

Swing Time did very well in the initial weeks of its release but the box office took a tumble sooner than the studio expected. Rogers had emulated Astaire's agreement with RKO and insisted that she would appear with Astaire in only two of her next four pictures. She starred in the straight film *Stage Door* while Astaire moved on to the musical *A Damsel in Distress*, teamed with Joan Fontaine, of all people.

As when he'd ended his partnership with sister Adele, Astaire was scrutinized by the critics. Each of his dance partners was compared with Rogers and, needless to say, Fontaine didn't measure up; the box office was not the best. Despite Astaire's reunion with Rogers and an Irving Berlin score, *Carefree* was also not a success at the wickets. Around that time, the Independent Theater Owners of America released a list of stars who were box-office poison. Although Astaire's name wasn't on the list it was included, along with his photo, when *Time* magazine covered the story. In just three years Astaire and Rogers had gone from the top of the heap precipitously downward.

There would be one more Astaire-Rogers pairing at RKO, *The Story of Vernon and Irene Castle*. The box office for that one was good but not when measured against their past hits. Critics saluted the team in their reviews, but the team was in fact split up. Fred moved to MGM.

> "I never even kissed Ginger Rogers in most of our pictures, not only because I didn't want to, but my wife didn't want me to."
>
> —*Fred Astaire*

His next picture was *Broadway Melody of 1940*, in which he was paired with Eleanor Powell. True to form, the critics compared her to Rogers. Powell was obviously no Joan Fontaine—they couldn't criticize her dancing skills—so they declared her . . . too good! The critic from London's *Daily Express* commented, "Powell is . . . a nice, good-tempered girl from out of town who keeps superb time. But she looks so strong and confident on her own, you just don't care whether Fred gets her or not."

A guy just couldn't win. After more criticism (perhaps justified) when Astaire teamed with Paulette Goddard in the second-rate *Second Chorus*, he redeemed himself with Rita Hayworth as a partner in *You'll Never Get Rich*. Finally, the critics took notice and approved. So, did audiences. Perhaps because he was tired of the constant comparison of his leading ladies to Ginger, for *Holiday*

Inn Astaire chose as his partner none other than Bing Crosby. That shut the critics up. Though Astaire also danced with Marjorie Reynolds and Virginia Dale in the movie, it was his Crosby moments that excited audiences. The same could be said of their work together in *Blue Skies*.

Finally, in 1949, Astaire was paired with a partner no critic could disapprove of—Ginger Rogers. The team was back together for one final time in *The Barkleys of Broadway*. And what was the plot? A husband-and-wife dance team break up when the wife decides to pursue a dramatic career.

When we look at the best of the Astaire-Rogers pairings, we can't help but be amazed that audiences could ever tire of such well-made concoctions. *Swing Time* is as fresh today as ever: there is a lightness in the relationships, an easygoing acting style, and of course the blissfully wonderful songs. Fred and Ginger (it's always "Fred and Ginger" never "Ginger and Fred") are so comfortable with their personas that we can relax and know we're in good hands. There's a playful quality to all of the performances and true wit in the dialogue. In fact, wielding their pointed barbs, Victor Moore, Helen Broderick, and the rest of the supporting cast are like softer versions of Warner Brothers musical characters of the early '30s. Thinking of those musicals, we can see that she became an adult when she moved to RKO. And with her pairing with Fred, she got class and a soupçon of savoir faire. Both Astaire and Rogers play real adults who know their love and happiness are on the line despite the lighthearted goings-on—and that's why we're willing to go along for the ride. They remind us that love really does matter. ■

ABOVE: Ginger and Fred pick themselves up and dust themselves off.

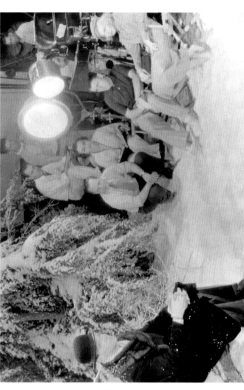

TOP LEFT: Helen Broderick with Victor Moore, her secondary love interest. Can you imagine this happening in a film today?

TOP RIGHT: A gaggle of gorgeous gamines.

BOTTOM RIGHT: Fred sits in the studio snow while director George Stevens and Ginger Rogers look on.

BOTTOM LEFT: Composer Jerome Kern and lyricist Dorothy Fields work on the score for *Swing Time*.

ABOVE: Fred Astaire and Hermes Pan work out a complicated dance sequence for the 1935 musical *Roberta*.

Behind the Screen

■ Fred starred on Broadway in *The Band Wagon* with his *Swing Time* costars Helen Broderick and Victor Moore.

SONGS

"Bojangles of Harlem" ■ "A Fine Romance" ■ "Never Gonna Dance" ■ "Pick Yourself Up" ■ "Waltz in Swing Time" (instrumental) ■ "The Way You Look Tonight"

"The amount of singing one can stand of these two is quite limited."

—George Gershwin on Fred and Ginger

Hermes Pan

Hermes Pan's long collaboration with Fred Astaire began on *Flying Down to Rio*, Astaire's second picture and his first with Ginger Rogers. Pan was the assistant to choreographer Dave Gould. He had already worked with Rogers as a chorus boy in the Broadway show *Top Speed*, and when Astaire asked him for help with a step, their friendship was sealed. Astaire and Pan (and Ginger) teamed up again on *The Gay Divorcee*, and this time Pan was elevated to choreographer. They worked in true collaboration on the dances. Pan, who resembled Astaire physically, would dance Rogers's parts in rehearsal and record her taps on the soundtrack. Then Pan would teach Rogers the steps he had worked out with Astaire. Since Astaire had problems watching himself during the rushes (he thought his hands were too big, among other things), Pan would act as his eyes, letting Astaire know how things looked. Once, Pan told Astaire that a number looked "great", always a perfectionist and a worrier, Astaire replied, "There's something in the way you said 'great.' What's wrong?" Pan's work with Astaire on the non-Ginger *A Damsel in Distress* at RKO won him an Academy Award. When the Astaire-Rogers reign was over, Pan went on to other projects. In 1940, he cochoreographed Astaire in *Second Chorus*. In 1946, he reunited with the dancer on *Blue Skies* at Paramount. In between times, Pan worked at a number of studios on such films as *Springtime in the Rockies* and *State Fair* at Fox, and *Lovely to Look At* and *Kiss Me Kate* at MGM. Pan worked on the last Astaire-Rogers film, *The Barkleys of Broadway* (1949) and on *Finian's Rainbow*. Pan appeared on screen a few times, most importantly squiring Betty Grable in *Moon over Miami* and Rita Hayworth in the number "On the Gay White Way" in *My Gal Sal*.

T&A, THE MEN

B EEFCAKE IS SURPRISINGLY RARE IN MOVIE MUSICALS. THERE are a few exceptions of course, mainly with Esther Williams's swimming partners. Somehow she always snagged the most handsome and fit of Hollywood's male corps. Fernando Lamas, Peter Lawford, and Ricardo Montalban all took dips with Williams, Red Skelton and Van Johnson also appeared with Williams in a few films each but they hardly put a toe in the water. Gene Kelly, in the ballet of *The Pirate* is one of the sexiest moments in movie history. The athletes backing up Jane Russell while she sings *"Ain't There Anyone Here for Love"* wear flesh-colored, skimpy bathing suites. Body builder parades were featured in at least two musicals, *Athena* (with muscleman Steve Reeves) and *Li'l Abner* wherein the females asked that scientists "put 'em back the way they was," namely scrawny hillbillies. Ah well, to each his own.

RIGHT: Jane Russell asks, *"Ain't there anyone here for love?,"* but receives no answers in *Gentlemen Prefer Blondes.*
BELOW RIGHT: Pat Boone always found an excuse to take his shirt off in every film.
BELOW CENTER: John Kerr and France Nuyen in *South Pacific.*
BELOW LEFT: Steve Reeves gives a lift to Jane Powell and Debbie Reynolds in *Athena.*

THIS IS SPINAL TAP

EMBASSY—MARCH 2, 1984

THIS IS SPINAL TAP

COMPOSERS: Christopher Guest, Michael McKean, Harry Shearer, and Rob Reiner

LYRICISTS: Christopher Guest, Michael McKean, Harry Shearer, and Rob Reiner

PRODUCER: Karen Murphy

DIRECTOR: Rob Reiner

SCREENWRITERS: Christopher Guest, Michael McKean, Harry Shearer, and Rob Reiner

CHOREOGRAPHER: Carol Kravetz

Synopsis

On a one-to-ten scale, this mockumentary (the one that started it all) about a heavy-metal rock group goes up to eleven.

Cast

Rob Reiner.............................Marti DiBergi
Tony Hendra............................Ian Faith
Michael McKean...........David St. Hubbins
Christopher Guest..............Nigel Tufnel
Harry Hearer......................Derek Smalls
June Chadwick.......................Jeanine
Bruno Kirby.................Tommy Pischedda
R. J. Parnell.....................Mick Shrimpton
Ed Begley Jr..............John "Stumpy" Pepys
Paul Shaffer.......................Artie Fufkin

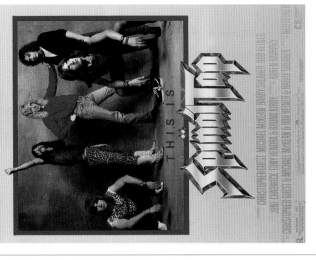

Harry Shearer, Christopher Guest, and Michael McKean do the rock-star pout.

This is the only heavy-metal musical included in our 101 greatest, but there's no question it belongs here. *This Is Spinal Tap* is a revelatory journey into the life of what we imagine is the greatest of the metal bands. Our insight into their obvious dedication to their music and their fans is a tribute to the talent of documentarian Marty DiBergi, about whom there is scant information in the usual databases and books. As for the members of Spinal Tap, it's heartening to know that we could find no reference to the usual rock band antics, such as trashing hotel rooms, knocking up their groupies, or rehearsing late into the night. In fact, David St. Hubbins, Derek Smalls, and Nigel Tufnel are a bit of a mystery, given their absence from the tabloids or even mainstream rock publications such as *Rolling Stone* or *Billboard*. We admit we don't know much about their music genre but you'd think they would rate at least passing mentions in the aforementioned periodicals.

Given the group's evolution from the Originals to the New Originals to the Thames-men, before becoming the band known affectionately as Tap, they are tantamount to rock royalty. If more evidence of their musicianship is necessary, just have a listen to Tufnel's classical piano solo, "Lick My Love Pump." It's not a long piece but once heard, it can never be forgotten. From their pop, R&B, and metal backgrounds to their classical music virtuosity, Tap is, in the words of today's youngsters, "bitchin'."

The band made a rare television appearance on the prestigious *Joe Franklin Show* as well as on such lesser showcases as *The Tonight Show*. They released an album, *Break Like the Wind*, in 1992, and another, *Back from the Dead*, in 2009.

"Everything in that movie happened to me." —*Eddie Van Halen*

Speaking (a bit more seriously) about this, the greatest of all "mockumentaries," none other than Roger Ebert honored it with an upraised thumb, designating it one of the ten best of the year. We were personally upset he didn't give it an eleven. It was selected by the National Film Registry of the Library of Congress as "culturally, historically, or aesthetically significant" and guaranteed for preservation forever—just like the Snail Darter, Spotted Owl, and Elizabeth Taylor.

Whether showcasing the band's performances at an air force base, an amusement park, or for crowds of extremely short Japanese citizens, *This Is Spinal Tap* reveals the extreme dedication of a band on its way up—and down. We feel the closeness among the band's members, and the tensions, too. Tribute is even paid to former members who made the ultimate sacrifice, spontaneously exploding during a drum solo or choking to death on someone else's vomit. The camera unflinchingly shows what happens when a musician falls under the spell of his interfering girlfriend (you know who you are, David St. Hubbins)—but when all is said and done, we come away feeling that Spinal Tap is just a group of guys who have been through a lot together and will continue to do their best, with or without an audience to hear them.

If none of this makes sense to you, for heaven's sake watch this film! You'll never view a documentary or listen to rock and roll in quite the same way again. ■

Behind the Screen

- Most of this film was improvised by the cast but, against the wishes of the four credited screenwriters, the Writers Guild refused to credit the entire company.
- The members of Spinal Tap are actually playing their instruments throughout the film.

SONGS

- "All the Way Home" (Michael McKean and Christopher Guest) ■ "America" ■ "Big Bottom" ■ "Cups and Cakes" ■ "(Listen to the) Flower People" ■ "Gimme Some Money" ■ "A Grateful Nation" (Michael McKean, Christopher Guest, and Harry Shearer) ■ "Heavy Duty" ■ "Hell Hole" ■ "Jazz Odyssey" (Michael McKean and Harry Shearer) ■ "Lick My Love Pump" (Christopher Guest) ■ "The Mule Died" (Christopher Guest) ■ "Rock 'n' Roll Creation" ■ "Sex Farm" ■ "Stonehenge" ■ "Tonight I'm Gonna Rock You Tonight"

TOP: Christopher Guest and Michael McKean rock out, dude.
BOTTOM: Christopher Guest really gets down--or gets electrocuted

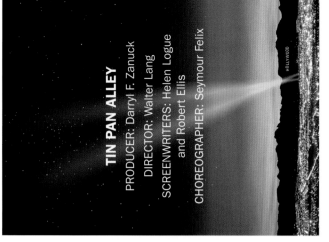

TIN PAN ALLEY

PRODUCER: Darryl F. Zanuck
DIRECTOR: Walter Lang
SCREENWRITERS: Helen Logue
and Robert Ellis
CHOREOGRAPHER: Seymour Felix

Synopsis

Two songwriters meet a sister act. One of the girls leaves the picture for a long time, while the other falls in an out of love with one of the songwriters. Then a tumble into the British Channel results in the hit song "K-K-K Katy."

Cast

Alice Faye	Katie Blane
Betty Grable	Lily Blane
John Payne	Francis Aloysius
	"Skeets" Harrigan
Jack Oakie	Harry Aloysius Calhoun
Allen Jenkins	Casey
Esther Ralston	Nora Bayes
The Nicholas Brothers	Themselves

TIN PAN ALLEY

20TH CENTURY FOX—NOVEMBER 29, 1940

Betty Grable consoles Alice Faye, who's just found out that Grable has been added to the film at the last minute. Perhaps she has somehow sensed that when she leaves the studio she'll be replaced by Grable?

ALL THE STUDIOS CAPITALIZED ON NOSTALGIA, BUT THE CHAMPION WAS TWENTIETH Century Fox. They loved to turn back the clock to a time when ladies performed in saloons and mustachioed men had a touch of larceny in their hearts. Then there were the upper crust that looked down on the lower classes when, in truth, the lower classes had more class than the uppers. Throw in a bunch of old classic tunes that audiences could sing along with, then sprinkle in a few new numbers that could sell sheet music and maybe nab an Oscar, and you had a real crowd-pleaser no matter how many times you repeated the same formula.

Starting in the forties, the Fox nostalgia mill ground out a large number of extremely similar pictures whose names tell you everything you need to know. Following *Tin Pan Alley*, there was *Coney Island, Sweet Rosie O'Grady, The Dolly Sisters, Mother Wore Tights, When My Baby Smiles at Me, Wabash Avenue, My Blue Heaven,* and *Meet Me after the Show*. All of them starred Betty Grable, sometimes with Alice Faye as costar. Speaking of Faye, she had her share of Fox nostalgiathons, too, in addition to those with Grable. Faye was featured in *Alexander's Ragtime Band, In Old Chicago, Rose of Washington Square, Little Old New York, Lillian Russell,* and *Hello, Frisco, Hello*. But wait, there's more: *There's No Business Like Show Business, Swanee River, Nob Hill, Greenwich Village,* and on and on. You get the idea.

What we love about *Tin Pan Alley* is its affection for the early music business and its songs. Even before the credits start, we are treated to a brief montage featuring the song pluggers and songwriters of *Tin Pan Alley*. The film is also well cast. Originally, Fox had wanted to reunite the *Alexander's Ragtime Band* team of Faye, Tyrone Power, and Don Ameche, but the men had other projects in development. Betty Grable wasn't supposed to be in the film at all, but the success of *Down Argentine Way* convinced Fox to give her a leading role—though it's clear that her inclusion was something of an afterthought. Grable's figure echoes the hourglass of such turn-of-the-century lovelies as Lillian Russell and, while she's no Mae West in the curves department, she parades her assets well. Grable's costar, Alice Faye, has a bit of the Tin Pan Alley era in her voice, a slightly smoky richness that reminds us of Helen Morgan, Libbie Holman, and Ruth Etting. John Payne looks swell in a nicely starched collar. Jack Oakie, Payne's songwriting partner, has a good rapport with Payne and together they're almost Warner Brotherish in their ability to speak the snappy dialogue and show off a slightly cynical view of life.

Remember that in 1940, the "good old days" of Tin Pan Alley were only thirty to forty years old. Think about it. That would be like writing a musical today about 1970! Depressing, isn't it? For the authors and production staff, it wasn't like they were writing about a period they knew nothing about—and that lends an air of authenticity and respect for the era. Amazingly, before the final cast credits, the film lists the old-time songs sung in the film and their songwriters and music publishers! We can't think of another film of the era that gives that kind of prominence to interpolated songs.

Later, Fox catalog musicals turned a little overproduced and stiff. Don't get us wrong: they're great entertainment, but films such as *There's No Business Like Show Business* try too hard in the production department and don't have a real feeling of the era. *Tin Pan Alley*'s plot consists of the usual hooey—song publisher gets girl, loses girl, gets girl, loses girl, and finally gets girl—but the humor and respect for the songs and era makes it one of the top Fox nostalgia musicals. ∎

Behind the Screen

■ *Tin Pan Alley* was remade in 1951 as the June Haver vehicle *I'll Get By.*

TOP: Alice Faye and John Payne fall in and out and in and out of love...seemingly interminably.

BOTTOM: Two great songwriters...are not pictured in this photo. Meet John Payne and Jack Oakie.

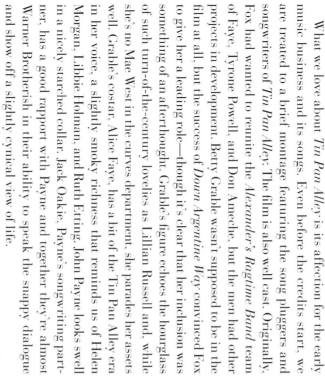

SONGS

"America I Love You" (Archie Gottler and Edgar Leslie) ■ "Goodbye Broadway Hello France" (Billy Baskette, C. Francis Resiner, and Benny Davis) ■ "Harem Days" (Ralph Rainger) ■ "K-k-k-Katy" (Geoffrey O'Hara with additional lyrics by Mack Gordon) ■ "Honeysuckle Rose" (Thomas 'Fats' Waller and Andy Razaf) ■ "I Want a Girl-Just Like the Girl That Married Dear Old Dad" (William Dillon and Harry Von Tilzer) ■ "Moonlight and Roses" (Edwin Lemare, Ben Black, and Neil Moret) ■ "Moonlight Bay" (Percy Wenrich and Edward Madden) ■ "Old Folks at Home" (Stephen Foster with additional lyrics by Mack Gordon) ■ "The Sheik of Araby" (Ted Snyder, Harry B. Smith, and Francis Wheeler with additional lyrics by Leo Robin and Charles Henderson) ■ "You Say the Sweetest Things Baby" (Harry Warren and Mack Gordon)

TOP LEFT: Betty Grable leads the troops in 1944's *Pin Up Girl*.

TOP RIGHT: Alice and Betty in the costumes that gave the censors fits.

BOTTOM RIGHT: John Payne and Alice Faye go over their lines.

LEFT: Betty Grable in a dress cut up to here and down to there.

Betty Grable

By her own admission, Betty Grable didn't have the greatest voice, wasn't the greatest actress, didn't have the greatest dancing skills, but she did have the greatest gams. Those two pins plus her particularly likeable personality earned her stardom. Her mother had pushed her into performing and she played chorus roles in her first pictures. It's fun to put one of her early films into the DVD player and try to spot her among the other lovelies. Her first film appearance was in the forgotten feature *Let's Go Places* (1930) when she was just fourteen years old. In Eddie Cantor's *The Kid from Spain*, Grable shows up in the opening number along with future luminaries Paulette Goddard, Toby Wing, and Jane Wyman. After a stint at Goldwyn, she got her break at RKO, where she signed a five-year contract and was assigned small parts. During a slow period, she joined the cast of the live musical revue, *Tattle Tales*, but left the tour to go back to pictures. After an appearance in the Astaire-Rogers movie *The Gay Divorcee*, her career picked up. She went to Paramount for a time, then to Broadway, receiving good reviews opposite Ethel Merman and Bert Lahr in Cole Porter's *DuBarry Was a Lady*, which helped her standing in Hollywood. We might mention that her pinup photo, a favorite of servicemen overseas, didn't hurt her, either. After almost thirty films and at least a decade as one of the top ten stars in pictures, she made her last film in 1955. She saw the studio system faltering and felt she needed a break from pictures to devote more time to family, so she retired at thirty-nine.

Fred Astaire and Ginger Rogers dance "The Piccolino."

TOP HAT

RKO—SEPTEMBER 6, 1935

I F THERE'S ONE THING HOLLYWOOD LIKES MORE THAN SEQUELS, IT'S THE PAIRING OF TWO performers over a series of films. Sequels are comforting; audiences go in knowing what kind of a film they'll be seeing, stylistically and in terms of content. Films starring established teams provide the same kind of comfort. Dramatic features have had their share of couples, most prominently Katharine Hepburn and Spencer Tracy, William Powell and Myrna Loy in the Thin Man films, and Johnny Weissmuller and Maureen O'Sullivan in the Tarzan series. There were lots of comedy teams, too, starting way back in the medium's earliest decades. The most successful and long lasting of these were Stan Laurel and Oliver Hardy, who went from silent shorts to feature films during their long-lasting partnership. Although Hardy sang in some of their films, *Babes in Toyland* was their only full-fledged musical. In the 1930s, Olsen and Johnson starred in the musical *Hellz-a-poppin'* and in the '40s, Abbott and Costello appeared in lots of musical films, though they never sang. Wheeler and Woolsey were the top draws

TOP HAT

COMPOSER: Irving Berlin
LYRICIST: Irving Berlin
PRODUCER: Pandro S. Berman
DIRECTOR: Mark Sandrich
SCREENWRITERS: Allan Scott and Dwight Taylor
CHOREOGRAPHER: Hermes Pan

Synopsis

The top hat pursues the feathered gown. Class wins out in the end.

Cast

Fred Astaire........................*Jerry Travers*
Ginger Rogers....................*Dale Tremont*
Edward Everett Horton....*Horace Hardwick*
Erik Rhodes......................*Alberto Beddini*
Eric Blore...............................*Bates*
Helen Broderick.............*Madge Hardwick*

"Dancing for the screen is approximately 80 percent brain work. Only about 20 percent of the strain is on the feet."

—Fred Astaire

for RKO until another team, Fred Astaire and Ginger Rogers, supplanted them. Astaire and Rogers and MGM's Nelson Eddy and Jeanette MacDonald were the top teams when it came to musical films.

Top Hat was the first of the Astaire-Rogers films to have been written especially for the screen. With their elaborate (if extremely similar) plots, these movies were smart, sophisticated entertainments, employing the best screenwriters, producers, actors, directors, and songwriters. Everyone wanted to write for Astaire and Rogers, especially Astaire, and the team debuted songs by George and Ira Gershwin, Jerome Kern and Dorothy Fields, and Irving Berlin, among others. Berlin wrote, "I'd rather have Fred Astaire introduce one of my songs than any singer I know—not because he has a great voice, but because his delivery and diction are so good that he can put over a song like nobody else."

Ginger was a good singer in her own right and a good dancer and partner for Astaire. She had that magic that was missing from Fred's other dancing ladies. Cyd Charisse was technical but cool; Rita Hayworth was beautiful and a terrific dancer; and never mind Joan Fontaine, who was sweet but not a dancer. Ginger and Fred clicked in that special way—they had that something that comes, perhaps, from mutual admiration with a soupçon of tension. They weren't the best of buddies off screen and probably wouldn't have picked each other as partners—but some indefinable thing worked when the camera was on them, and the two clicked with audiences.

And now a word about their films and audiences. Whereas some musical teams played to the balcony and others played to the orchestra, Astaire and Rogers pleased everyone, high brow and low. The silliness of their plots, the eccentric supporting troupe that followed them from film to film, and Ginger's exquisite costumes pleased the gallery gods. The songs; the intelligent, complex choreography; and the brilliant execution made the upper crust take note. And that's what makes an immortal team—one that pleases everyone, even if in different ways. ■

Ginger Rogers

Best known for the ten films she made opposite Fred Astaire, Ginger Rogers also played a wide range of other roles with sexiness and aplomb. She could act comedy or drama equally well in addition to her skills as a dancer and singer. But somehow she's never mentioned in the top rank of Hollywood actors. Rogers made a few films in 1929 to little effect and then turned her sights on Broadway. After an appearance in the show *Top Speed*, she appeared in the Gershwins' *Girl Crazy*. Unfortunately for Ginger, making her Broadway debut in that show was Ethel Merman, who blew the roof off the theater and stole the reviews. Still, Rogers became a bona fide star and Hollywood soon called. After an inconsequential stint at Pathe, she wound up at Warner's, where her smart-aleck performances in backstage musicals brought her more and more attention. When she sang a chorus of "We're in the Money" in pig latin in the film *Gold Diggers of 1933*, she achieved real fame. She moved across the mountains to RKO, where she reunited with Fred Astaire, who had come into *Girl Crazy* to spiff up the choreography. They danced together in her second RKO outing, *Flying Down to Rio*, and a team was instantly born. Rogers was a serious, tough performer who depended on her mother to do the dirty work. Astaire, a noted taskmaster and rehearsal junkie, commented, "All the girls I ever danced with thought they couldn't do it, but of course they could. So they always cried. All except Ginger. No no, Ginger never cried." Rogers undertook a variety of characters in dramatic movies between dancing stints with Astaire and won the Academy Award for *Kitty Foyle*. In the 1950s, things slowed up for her, though she continued to make films until the '60s. Then it was off to summer stock, touring shows, and an appearance on Broadway in *Hello, Dolly!* She continued to perform in nightclubs, at Radio City, and at other venues, usually wearing a powder blue dress with a feathered collar.

> "I don't mind making another picture with her but as for this team idea it's out! I've just managed to live down one partnership and I don't want to be bothered with any more."
> —*Fred Astaire to his agent, about teaming up with Ginger Rogers*

Fred Astaire

Thank heavens for stage mothers. It was Fred and his older sister Adele's mother who dreamed of a life on the stage for her children as a means of escape from Omaha, Nebraska. Are you surprised that Mr. Top Hat, White Tie and Tails came from such an uncool location? Luckily for Mrs. Austerlitz (Fred and Adele's real surname), her children had talent. When Papa Austerlitz lost his job, the family moved to New York City so the kids could pursue their mother's dream. In 1905, the siblings picked the name "Astaire" for billing purposes. Never mind Vernon and Irene Castle or even Fred and Ginger, Fred and Adele were the best. They hit small-time vaudeville in an act that featured Fred in top hat, white tie, and tails . . . and a lobster costume in the second act, but never mind. Their father wheedled them a chance at the prestigious Orpheum Circuit and they were soon stars of vaudeville. After conquering that world, the next logical step was Broadway, and in 1917, they made their Broadway debut. Fred had had a chance meeting with George Gershwin the year before and, for as long as the composer lived, they would be linked personally and professionally. Gershwin and his brother Ira wrote the scores to *Lady Be Good!* and *Funny Face*, two of the team's biggest hits. It was after the highpoint of the great musical revue *The Band Wagon*, in 1931, that Adele decided to retire and marry an English lord. Critics handicapped Fred's chances on his own, with several naysayers in the bunch—but he opened to great acclaim in Cole Porter's *Gay Divorce*, his last stage show. Then it was on to Hollywood for Fred, where his first film was *Dancing Lady*. In his next one, *Flying Down to Rio*, Fred was the secondary male lead and his partner was Ginger Rogers. Also on the film was choreographer Hermes Pan, assistant to choreographer Dave Gould. With these three members of the team in place—Astaire, Rogers, and Pan—the movie musical would be changed forever. Astaire famously said, "Either the camera will dance or I will." Not for him the Busby Berkeley-inspired sweeping cameras. Astaire believed in the full-figure, single-shot take for his dances. (Take that, *Moulin Rouge!*) He also integrated dance into the script much in the way that songs were utilized in the best Broadway musicals, to establish character and move the plot along. Astaire continued in movies without Ginger though he could never quite escape the inevitable comparisons of his later dancing partners with Ginger. In films like *Broadway Melody of 1940* (Eleanor Powell), *You Were Never Lovelier* (Rita Hayworth), *The Sky's the Limit* (Joan Leslie), *Easter Parade* (Judy Garland), *Royal Wedding* (Jane Powell), *The Belle of New York* (Vera-Ellen), and *Silk Stockings* (Cyd Charisse), Fred proved himself the greatest of all film dancers. . .

Behind the Screen

■ Irving Berlin had a smart deal on this picture. If the film earned more than one and a quarter million dollars, Berlin would get 10 percent of the gross. In its initial release, *Top Hat* earned three million dollars, making it the decade's most profitable film for RKO.

SONGS

"Cheek to Cheek" ■ "Isn't This a Lovely Day" ■ "No Strings" ■ "The Piccolino" ■ "Top Hat, White Tie and Tails"

JEWISH MUSICALS

J UST AS THERE WERE SPECIALIZED MUSICALS FOR BLACK THEATER-goers, the Yiddish-speaking Jewish population had musical movies made especially for them. Would *The Jazz Singer* be made today? We doubt it. A good number of Yiddish films were made in the United States and, before the Second World War, in Eastern Europe. Except for the two Molly Picon films, all the movies described below were made in America for an international market.

In the 1931 film *His Wife's Lover*, an older man bets a younger one that women don't care about love, only money. To prove the old man wrong, the young man disguises himself as rich, old Herman Weingarten. The girl spurns Weingarten since she's fallen in love with the young man (who's playing Weingarten). The twist is that because of her poverty, she agrees to marry Weingarten. But the young man has fallen in love with the woman and... well, it's a big mess, worthy of a Hollywood farce of the '40s.

Actress Molly Picon, a star of the Yiddish stage and later Broadway, television, and motion pictures, made such classics as *Yiddle with His Fiddle (Yidl Mitn Fidl)* (1936) in which a young girl joins a band of travelling musicians. To avoid troubles on the road, she dresses up as a man. (Hmmm. She dresses up like a man and her name is Yidl. Where've we heard that one before?) The music was by Abraham Ellstein, an American composer for the Yiddish Theatre in New York. The film was directed by Joseph Green who wrote the piece and directed other Yiddish films for the American market. Picon also starred in the musical *Mamele* (1938), a classic of the Yiddish theatre.

In 1937, the celebrated Cantor Moyshe Oysher starred in what has been called the "anti-*Jazz Singer*," *The Cantor's Son*. As in the earlier film, a young man has to decide between a life in show biz or a life of religion. He decides on the latter. Along the way, we get a fascinating glimpse of New York's Second Avenue and its thriving Yiddish theatres. If Al Jolson could have hit recordings of "My Mammy" and "Sonny Boy," leave it to the Yiddish film industry to come up with the 1939 musical comedy, *My Sonny* (aka *The Living Orphan*), in which a wife leaves her infant and husband to pursue a life upon the stage. It's a melodramatic musical mess but lots of fun.

Edgar G. Ulmer, who began his career at Universal, made several Yiddish films. Among them are another Moyshe Oysher film, 1938's *The Singing Blacksmith*, and the musical. *American Matchmaker* (1940) starring Leo Fuchs, the "Yiddish Fred Astaire." *Catskills Honeymoon* (1949) provides an astonishing glimpse of life at a Catskills resort, including a real Borscht Belt show. Luckily, these films and many more have been preserved on DVD for future generations.

TOP: Molly Picon and Simche Fostel in *Yiddle with His Fiddle*.

LEFT: We have no idea why someone is singing Pagliacci in the film *Mazel Tov Yidden (Mazel Tov Jews)*.

VIVA LAS VEGAS

MGM—MAY 20, 1964

No, it's not *Spinout*, it's Elvis and Ann-Margret enjoying themselves in Las Vegas.

CAN IT BE THAT THE SAME WOMAN WHO WROTE THE STORIES UPON WHICH *MEET ME IN ST. LOUIS* was based also wrote the screenplay for this film? Actually most Elvis films are remarkably chaste. There's not even implied sex. This film has him chasing after Ann-Margret, his own female doppelganger. She's a kittenish tease who really enjoys being chased—chastely.

The most surprising thing about *Viva Las Vegas* is how un-Vegas the whole thing is. Sure, Elvis and Cesare Danova spend a good portion of the beginning of the film roaming around a series of casinos, looking for Ann-Margret. In the process, we get a glimpse of Las Vegas as it was in the good old, bad old days. The skimpy, feathered costumes on the nonskimpy girls on the skimpy stages . . . it's almost a documentary. Ultimately, the two men end up in some down-and-out dive where Elvis becomes the Pied Piper, leading a bunch of redneck drunks out of the room by singing a soft rock version of "The Yellow Rose of Texas." It's downright bewildering.

But neither that sequence nor any other bizarre scene would come as a surprise to fans of Elvis movies. After his early recording successes and shocking (we tell you, shocking) TV appearances in the late 1950s, Elvis's manager, Colonel Tom Parker, signed him to Paramount Pictures. But the studio couldn't quite figure out what to do with him so they lent him to Twentieth Century Fox for his first film, 1956's *Love Me Tender.* Yes, the title was changed to echo one of Elvis's current hits—though he didn't get top billing and (spoiler alert) he actually died at the end. No one considered it anything but an Elvis vehicle, and its success convinced Paramount that there was gold in them thar hips.

VIVA LAS VEGAS

PRODUCER: Jack Cummings
DIRECTOR: George Sidney
SCREENWRITER: Sally Benson
CHOREOGRAPHER: David Winters

Synopsis

In Reel One, Elvis is a racecar driver who wants to win. In the last reel he wins. In between, all racing is forgotten and Elvis wins Ann-Margret.

Cast

Elvis Presley	Lucky Jackson
Ann-Margret	Rusty Martin
Cesare Danova	Count Elmo Mancini
William Demarest	Mr. Martin
Nicky Blair	Shorty Farnsworth

Behind the Screen

- Apparently, Elvis and Ann-Margret had a hot and heavy affair while making this picture, which led to reports that the wedding scene filmed for the movie was real.

- Early in her career, Ann-Margret was billed as the female Elvis Presley.

LEFT: Ann-Margret and Elvis try their best to avoid soiling their white costumes.

BELOW: Still enjoying themselves in Las Vegas, Ann-Margret and Elvis take a spin on two motorbikes and do their own driving!

"As a straight actor, the guy has great potentialities."

—Producer Joe Hazen, upon viewing Elvis's first screen test

SONGS

"Appreciation" (Bernie Wayne and Marvin Moore) ▪ "The Climb" (Jerry Leiber and Mike Stoller) ▪ "C'mon Everybody" (Joy Byers) ▪ "The Eyes of Texas" (John Lang Sinclair) ▪ "I Need Somebody to Lean On" (Doc Pomus and Mort Shuman) ▪ "If You Think I Don't Need You" (Bob "Red" West and Joe Cooper) ▪ "The Lady Loves Me" (Sid Tepper and Roy C. Bennett) ▪ "My Rival" (Bernie Wayne and Marvin Moore) ▪ "Santa Lucia" (Traditional) ▪ "Today, Tomorrow and Forever" (Bill Giant, Bernie Baum, and Florence Kaye) ▪ "Viva Las Vegas" (Doc Pomus and Mort Shuman) ▪ "The Yellow Rose of Texas" (J.K. and Don George) ▪ "What'd I Say" (Ray Charles)

Presley's career stalled when he was drafted into the army in 1958, though the publicity didn't hurt. When he got out, Paramount cast him in *G.I. Blues*. Presley then began his tour of other studios. Fox was next and cast him in the Don Siegel western *Flaming Star*. It wasn't really a musical: Elvis sang only over the title sequence and had a brief little dance number. (His other number was cut.) Elvis was pleased, though, since he considered himself a real actor, not just a singer who acts. The film provided him with plenty of dramatic opportunities and his next film, also at Fox, offered a continuation of his acting education. In *Wild in the Country*, he played a poor, uneducated young man tutored by an older woman, played by Hope Lange. Naturally, he fell in love with her and the film followed the ups and downs of their May-September romance. It should have been a good film as the script was written by Clifford Odets.

Elvis wanted to pursue a serious acting career but Colonel Tom would have none of it. Robert Mitchum wanted to cast Presley in *Thunder Road* and he was offered leads in *West Side Story* and *Midnight Cowboy*. No dice. In 1974, Barbra Streisand wanted him to costar with her in *A Star Is Born*. Presley would have excelled in any of these roles, but Parker made sure he'd never get the chance.

Instead, Presley's next film, *Blue Hawaii*, a Paramount release, followed the Presley formula. It was followed by the United Artists picture, *Follow That Dream*. He bopped back and forth between the two studios until 1963, when he landed at MGM for *It Happened at the World's Fair*. Then it was back to Paramount and on to whichever studio would pay the most for his services. Presley did manage to make some okay films along the way. At least the studios gave him some veteran directors and decent production teams, though

they kept the budgets down. Elvis also had a stable of songwriters that followed him from picture to picture and knew exactly how to showcase his talent. But for the most part, after *Viva Las Vegas*, Elvis's movies became more and more formulaic and by the end, even the songwriters let him down. By the late '60s, Elvis's career was at its lowest ebb.

The King's last film was 1969's *A Change of Habit*, featuring a young Mary Tyler Moore as a nun. The year before, after seven years off from live performances, Elvis had returned to the stage, embarking on a long period of live performances, especially in Vegas. Free from the shackles of the studios and his films' cheesy plots (and vice versa) he made a hugely successful comeback. As one friend put it, he was out of prison—the prison of Hollywood.

Viva Las Vegas may not seem that different from a lot of the other Elvis pictures but we think it's the best because of the chemistry between the leads. Ann-Margret is the absolute equal of her costar and, in fact, they seem to trade off numbers during the picture. One of the best scenes they have surrounds the song "The Lady Loves Me." Elvis and his guitar pursue Ann-Margret around the pool at the Flamingo Hotel. They end up on the high dive and both Elvis and his true love—his guitar—land in the drink. The song is a traditional musical comedy number with a good tune and witty lyrics. The two performers act as naturally as they can, camouflaging the overt sexuality that clearly came all too naturally for them. Elvis was still young and handsome and hadn't yet solidified into the persona that took over later in his career. The same could be said for Ann-Margret, and the two of them are clearly enjoying themselves—so we do, too. In her autobiography, Ann-Margret explained, "From day one, when we gathered around the piano to run through the film's songs, Elvis and I knew that it was going to be serious. That day, we discovered two things about each other. Once the music started, neither of us could stand still. Music ignited a fiery, pent-up passion inside Elvis and inside me. It was an odd, embarrassing, funny, inspiring, and wonderful sensation. We looked at each other move and saw virtual mirror images. When Elvis thrust his pelvis, mine slammed forward, too. When his shoulder dropped, I was down there with him. When he whirled, I was already on my heel. 'It's uncanny,' I said. He grinned. Whatever it was, Elvis liked it and so did I." And so do we. ■

Ann-Margret tries her best to be sexy and kittenish, two prerequisites of playing a 1960s vixen.

WE'RE NOT DRESSING

PARAMOUNT—APRIL 27, 1934

WE'RE NOT DRESSING
COMPOSER: Harry Revel
LYRICIST: Mack Gordon
DIRECTOR: Norman Taurog
SCREENWRITERS: Horace Jackson, Francis Marton, and George Marion Jr.

Synopsis

Haute society is partying on a yacht when it sinks and the bluebloods are stranded on a tropical island. Only the lowly but admirable shipmate knows how to be a survivor.

Cast

Bing Crosby.............................Stephen Jones
Carole Lombard....................Doris Worthington
Ethel Merman...................................Edith
George Burns..........................George Martin
Gracie Allen..............................Gracie Martin
Leon Errol..................................Uncle Hubert
Ray Miland.....................Prince Michael Stofani
Jay Henry....................Prince Alexander Stofani

SONGS

"Good Night Lovely Little Lady" ▪ "Finale Sequence" ▪ "It's Just a New Spanish Custom" ▪ "Love Thy Neighbor; May I?" ▪ "Once in a Blue Moon" ▪ "Sailor's Chanty" ▪ "She Reminds Me of You

Carole Lombard and Bing Crosby, marooned on a desert soundstage.

WE HEAR YOU SAY, *"WE'RE NOT DRESSING? WHAT THE HECK IS THAT?"* WELL, NOT every movie in this book is a *Singin' in the Rain* or *Funny Face*. *We're Not Dressing* is an enjoyable romp featuring an enthusiastic, game cast and wonderful songs, none of which have become standards (though "Love Thy Neighbor" was well known at the time). Gordon and Revel were terrific writers who could write effectively for both Bing Crosby and Ethel Merman, two distinct stylists. The screenplay never lags and we get lots of laughs along the way.

In the golden age of the Hollywood musical, the studios were like factories. They owned the theaters as well as the product and had to keep cranking out films to keep people in the seats. All of their employees were under contract and it was in the studios' interest to keep them very busy. So, writers, designers, directors, and others were constantly working. Cos.creenwriter George Marion Jr. had four films come out in 1934: *We're Not Dressing, Kiss and Make Up, The Gay Divorcee,* and *College Rhythm.* Unlike today, when screenwriters are lucky to have a film produced once every four or five years, writers in the 1930s and 1940s were constantly working on their craft. Their writing muscles were always in shape.

Just like songwriters of the period, screenwriters were constantly on the alert for ideas that could be worked into their plots. There were scribes that specialized in adapting stories or books into films, those that were whizzes at dialogue, and those that were thought of as gagmen, brought in to bump up the comedy. Comics such as Burns and Allen, who appear in *We're Not Dressing*, might bring in their own writers who understood their comic personae. Writers from their vaudeville years or from their successful radio shows might be hired just to work on special bits and lines.

The screenwriters at Paramount, MGM, Fox, Universal, and even Monogram were all full-time employees who worked on screenplay after screenplay. Although not all of their movies were gems—and some even stank—they were all fully professional. And a lightweight movie like *We're Not Dressing* was given the full support of Paramount's artistic and craft units. Even the second-tier films are fun to watch today, if only for a certain twist in the plot, snappy piece of dialogue, or great little sequence. It's fun to relax and go with the flow, no matter how clichéd or hokey the overall film might seem.

Even in their day, audiences knew the majority of film plots were hooey—but they didn't care. They weren't any more or less sophisticated than we are, but they went to the movies to escape and be entertained and the great screenwriters of Hollywood knew how to entertain them very well indeed. By any standards, *We're Not Dressing* is high-quality entertainment. ■

"[Norman Taurog is] a blimp-like person who issues orders kindly."

—Columnist Sidney Skolsky

RIGHT: Gracie Allen and George Burns. How they got to the island is anyone's guess.

MIDDLE: Our story gets even more confusing. An African gorilla (left) takes George's place with Gracie (right).

BOTTOM RIGHT: If you think that's crazy, here's an extraneous photo of Ethel Merman in Cole Porter's Broadway hit of 1943, *Something for the Boys*. Well, it's above her quote so we thought it would fit. Sort of.

BOTTOM LEFT: Harry Revel and Mack Gordon, songwriters extraordinaire.

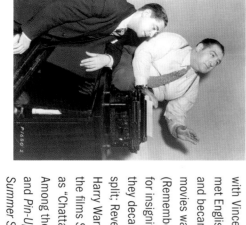

Mack Gordon and Harry Revel

A lthough Mack Gordon and Harry Revel weren't in the league with Irving Berlin or Harry Warren, they were terrifically successful songwriters. Gordon was nominated for nine Oscars, including six in a row from 1940 to 1945. He was built in the mold of another songwriter, Al Dubin, a man of giant appetites and a zest for living. Gordon's first hit, "Time on My Hands," was written with Vincent Youmans for the 1930 stage show *Smiles*. In 1931, Dubin met Englishman Harry Revel, and two years later they trekked to Hollywood and became instantly successful writing for films. Their first hit for the movies was "Did You Ever See a Dream Walking?" written for *Sitting Pretty*. (Remember, this was an era in which many significant songs were written for insignificant films.) The team stayed with Paramount until 1936, when they decamped to Fox and wrote for Shirley Temple films. In 1939, the team split; Revel retired and Gordon teamed with Hollywood's greatest composer, Harry Warren. The new duo wrote hits for Glenn Miller's Orchestra to play in the films *Sun Valley Serenade* and *Orchestra Wives*, including such smashes as "Chattanooga Choo Choo," "At Last" and "I Got a Gal in Kalamazoo." Among their other Fox film scores were *Tin Pan Alley*, *Weekend in Havana*, and *Pin-Up Girl*. Warren and Gordon also wrote the songs for MGM's *Summer Stock*.

"What the hell happened to my number?"

—Ethel Merman to a Paramount executive

WEST SIDE STORY

MGM—OCTOBER 18, 1961

WEST SIDE STORY

COMPOSER: Leonard Bernstein

LYRICIST: Stephen Sondheim

PRODUCER: Robert Wise

DIRECTORS: Robert Wise and Jerome Robbins

SCREENWRITER: Ernest Lehman

SOURCE: Based on the stage musical *West Side Story* by Leonard Bernstein, Stephen Sondheim, and Arthur Laurents

CHOREOGRAPHER: Jerome Robbins

Synopsis

Rival gangs on Manhattan's West Side fight over turf. Neither wins as the city condemns their houses and builds Lincoln Center. They shoulda stood in bed.

Cast

Natalie Wood................*Maria*
Richard Beymer..............*Tony*
Russ Tamblyn................*Riff*
Rita Moreno.................*Anita*
George Chakiris.............*Bernardo*
Ned Glass...................*Doc*
Simon Oakland..............*Lt. Shrank*
William Bramley............*Office Krupke*

Richard Beymer and Natalie Wood share a few stolen moments on a fire escape. (Only the folks on the Upper East Side have balconies.)

I T'S CHRISTMAS OR HANUKKAH OR YOUR BIRTHDAY AND YOU UNWRAP THE SOUNDTRACK TO *West Side Story* and you love it, of course. In fact, you play it over and over again. It's a wonder your mother doesn't go crazy hearing it for the thousandth time. Then you find out there's also an original Broadway cast album and you eagerly snatch it up. But when you play it, the orchestra sounds weak and the singers just don't sound like the ones on the soundtrack and the songs are in a different order. They even have some different lyrics. Or maybe you went through that whole process in reverse. The point is, whether you started out listening to the soundtrack or the original cast album, that's the one that will always be in your heart.

But, boy, it still bugs you that the film doesn't match the stage play. Is there really any resemblance at all? Few movies are completely faithful to their forebears (As noted elsewhere, *Li'l Abner* and *The Pajama Game* are the notable exceptions). Two movies adapted from Broadway musicals are distinct improvements on the originals: *West Side Story* and *The Sound of Music.*

It's no coincidence that both were directed by Robert Wise. (He also directed *Star!*— but even the exclamation point couldn't help that one, though the "Burlington Bertie" number is simple and terrific.) Each of these shows switches two songs around to great effect. The film of *The Sound of Music* puts "My Favorite Things" in the spot where the stage version has "The Lonely Goatherd" and turns the latter number into a charming puppet show. *West Side Story* swaps "Cool" and "Officer Krupke," a change that is still considered controversial to a small but fabulous segment of the population. In the film,

"Cool" comes at a tension-filled moment just after the rumble, when the gangs know that something terrible has happened but can't admit to it, so they try desperately to pretend nothing is wrong. On the stage, "Cool" is sung just before the Jets go off to meet the Sharks for the war council and have to build up their confidence. Both work—it's a matter of personal preference.

"Officer Krupke" works fine in the movie in the place where "Cool" had been in the play. As you know, *West Side Story* was adapted from Shakespeare (for those of you who live on a nonmusical planet, it's an urban version of *Romeo and Juliet*), and it's a very Shakespearean conceit to place a comic bit before a scene of great drama.

Where did the idea come from to swap the songs? When the show was trying out in Washington, the creators had talked about flipping "Krupke" and "Cool," but it was playing so well they didn't want to jeopardize its success by making such a major adjustment. They tabled the idea until the film came along—and it works.

The film includes other changes, too. "I Feel Pretty" opens the second act of the show. In the movie, it's sung earlier, and it's not as effective. In the show, only the Puerto Rican girls sing "America" but in the movie the boys

join them, racking up a new list of their own complaints about their adopted country and adding a "make-love-not-war" angle. Doing so humanizing the Shark boys and gives them more screen time. In the movie they were simply "the enemy." And speaking of new lyrics, many of the songs have revised words here and there, mainly in order to clean up what the creators felt might be offensive to moviegoers.

Whether you grew up with the original cast album or the soundtrack, you've got to admit the film version of *West Side Story* is pretty terrific stuff. ■

SONGS

"A Boy Like That" ■ "America" ■ "Cool" ■ "Dance at the Gym" ■ "Gee, Officer Krupke" ■ "I Feel Pretty" ■ "I Have a Love" ■ "Jet Song" ■ "Maria" ■ "One Hand, One Heart" ■ "Quintet" ■ "The Rumble" ■ "Something's Comin'" ■ "Somewhere" ■ "Tonight"

ABOVE: The Jets face off with the Sharks, George Chakiris (in red) stares down Russ Tamblyn (in yellow).

> "Very demanding, very demanding, very demanding, do it again, do it again, do it again—he drove the dancers out of their minds sometimes."
> —*Codirector Robert Wise on Jerome Robbins*

Behind the Screen

- The movie's opening was filmed in an area of New York that was due to be torn down to make way for Lincoln Center. The developer was paid to start the demolition on 64th Street instead of 61st, so they'd have time to shoot the film.

TOP LEFT: Choreographer and co-director Jerome Robbins shows 'em how it's done.

TOP RIGHT: They do it.

BOTTOM LEFT: Filming on the mean streets of New York City.

BOTTOM RIGHT: Sometimes you just have to improvise. Notice Russ Tamblyn, at right, who wasn't a trained dancer.

COUNTRY MUSICALS

WHILE ROCK FILMS HAVE DOMINATED THE MODERN MUSICAL, LET'S NOT FORGET about that hearty genre with a decidedly southern twang. Country musicals have always been good box office. The best of these is Robert Altman's *Nashville*, which we talk about elsewhere, but it is but one in a long line of its kind. Judy Canova and Dorothy Shay ("The Park Avenue Hillbilly") starred in a bunch of them, and they were all good fun back when country music meant southern music.

There have been a few dramatic musicals with country musicians as their subjects. *A Time to Sing* starred country favorite Hank Williams, Jr. in full on Elvis mode. The King was the natural link between country and rock music, and his films incorporated both genres, blurring the lines between them. Robert Duvall surprised his fans when he sang for himself in *Tender Mercies*. Most recently, the Academy Award–winner *Crazy Heart*, with Jeff Bridges, proved a popular hit.

Composers such as Jerome Kern and Richard Rodgers rated their own biopics and so did some country performers and songwriters. *Coal Miner's Daughter* starred Sissy Spacek as Loretta Lynn. Spacek and costar Beverly D'Angelo, who played Patsy Cline, both sang for themselves on the soundtrack. Joaquin Phoenix and Reese Witherspoon did the same in *Walk the Line*, as Johnny Cash and June Carter. Like rock musicals, country music films tend to replace traditional instrumental soundtracks with songs. *O Brother Where Art Thou* is an excellent example, and the CD released under its name was hugely successful. The movie also led to a live concert film, *Down from the Mountain*, featuring the bands and singers from the *O Brother* soundtrack.

TOP LEFT: Judy Canova in *Joan of Ozark*.

BOTTOM RIGHT: Hank Williams, Jr. in *A Time to Sing*.

BOTTOM LEFT: Sissy Spacek is Loretta Lynn in *Coal Miner's Daughter*.

WHITE CHRISTMAS

COMPOSER: Irving Berlin

LYRICIST: Irving Berlin

PRODUCER: Robert Emmett Dolan

DIRECTOR: Michael Curtiz

SCREENWRITERS: Norman Panama, Melvin Frank, and Norman Krasna

CHOREOGRAPHER: Robert Alton

Synopsis

The kids, all grown up, decide "Let's put on a show" using granddad's old songs.

Cast

Bing Crosby ....Bob Wallace
Danny Kaye..................Phil Davis
Rosemary Clooney.......Betty Haynes
Vera-Ellen ....Judy Haynes
Dean Jagger.................Major General Thomas
F. Waverly
Mary Wickes ....Emma Allen

WHITE CHRISTMAS

PARAMOUNT—OCTOBER 14, 1954

Bing Crosby, Vera-Ellen, Rosemary Clooney, and Danny Kaye sing "Gee, I Wish I Were Back in the Army."

DON'T WE ALL WISH WE LIVED IN A VISTAVISION WORLD, ACRES OF LIVING ROOMS AND bedrooms spreading out before our eyes? *White Christmas* was the first film in the new superwide aspect ratio. Clearly, it was considered an important film in the Paramount pantheon; the studio was pleased to have another in Irving Berlin's seemingly endless line of compilation films.

Way back during World War II, Berlin had had the idea of writing about a retired general who feels he has no purpose in life. He conceived it as a stage musical but Paramount, having had great success with Bing Crosby and Fred Astaire in the Berlin jukebox musicals *Holiday Inn* and *Blue Skies*, decided to option it for film. Unfortunately, Crosby lost interest and Astaire rejected the story. Crosby came back on board with a bit of cajoling from Berlin and Astaire was replaced by Donald O'Connor so the film was back on track—until O'Connor got sick. Finally, Danny Kaye took over the role and the film began shooting.

The person to watch in this movie is Bing Crosby. He believed in coming to rehearsals completely prepared, which enabled him to relax and feel secure in front of the camera. That's the key to his ability to ad-lib (and he ad-libbed a whole lot in this film) and to make the dialogue his own. He appears complete at ease and comfortable with the dancing, too, which wasn't his strong suit (watch him dance—with confidence but not much actual technique). Crosby's career was so long and so rich in experience that he could undertake anything and was game, as long as he was afforded enough rehearsal.

As you probably know, Irving Berlin had a soft spot for America, and the armed forces in particular. During World War I, he wrote *Yip, Yip, Yaphank*, which contained "Oh, How I Hate to Get Up in the Morning." For World War II, he produced the all-soldier show, *This Is the Army*. So, it seemed natural that *White Christmas* would include a subplot about a retired general and his love of his troops.

Which brings us to the problem of watching this film now. Well, it's not a problem exactly, just a sense that the it's not as affecting out of context. All films reflect the times in which they were made and sometimes, watching them now, we can't quite connect with them in the same way audiences did when they first came out. When *White Christmas* was released, the Second World War was still fresh in America's mind. Many soldiers had come home from the war wounded and others had never come back at all. Their families were still dealing with the pain and loss, and the Christmastime setting made it especially poignant.

Luckily, the performances, script, songs, and production values make the film a delight to watch even at a remove from the events it depicts. It certainly had a great impact on audiences in its time: they made it the biggest money earner of 1954, *White Christmas* represents Hollywood filmmaking at its best—funny and surprisingly touching. ■

"As I look back on my early songs, I realize I kept writing the same tune."

—*Irving Berlin*

ABOVE AND TOP RIGHT: Two beautiful couples: Rosemary Clooney and Vera Ellen and Danny Kaye and Bing Crosby.

TOP LEFT: Bing Crosby and Danny Kaye rehearse the minstrel show number

LEFT: Bing and Danny joke around on the set.

SONGS

"Abraham" ▪ "The Best Things Happen when You're Dancing" ▪ "Choreography" ▪ "Count Your Blessings Instead of Sheep" ▪ "Gee, I Wish I Were Back in the Army" ▪ "I'd Rather See a Minstrel Show" ▪ "Love, You Didn't Do Right By Me" ▪ "Mandy" ▪ "The Old Man" ▪ "Sisters" ▪ "Snow" ▪ "What Can You Do with a General" ▪ "White Christmas"

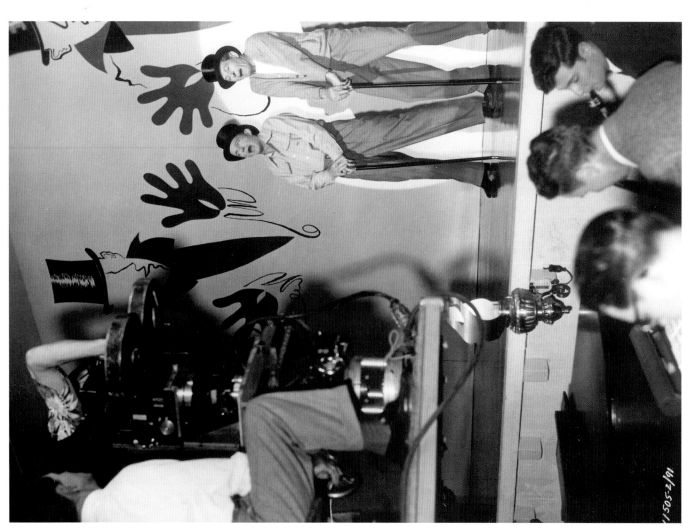

Vera-Ellen

Like Rita Hayworth and her other sisters of dance-in-film, Vera-Ellen couldn't sing but she sure could dance, and she could act as well. Audiences believed she could sing because she had a warm, musical speaking voice. Like many musical stars of the period, she found initial success on Broadway, in such shows as Very Warm for May and Panama Hattie with June Allyson and By Jupiter. Samuel Goldwyn spotted her in A Connecticut Yankee and brought her to Hollywood, where she appeared opposite Danny Kaye in Wonder Man. She partnered with Gene Kelly in On the Town and Fred Astaire in Three Little Words and The Belle of New York. She found the perfect partner in Donald O'Connor in Call Me Madam. Audiences first noticed how thin she had become in her dances with Danny Kaye in White Christmas. She retired from the movies in 1957 with the dismantling of the studio system. Vera-Ellen was sweet and elfin but she suffered fragile mental and physical health.

LEFT: Vera-Ellen takes a load off her tired feet.

ABOVE: Gene Kelly and Vera-Ellen in the "Slaughter on Tenth Avenue" ballet from Words and Music.

BELOW LEFT: Danny Kaye, Vera-Ellen, and Bing Crosby filming the minstrel number.

BELOW RIGHT: Danny exhibits some "Choreography."

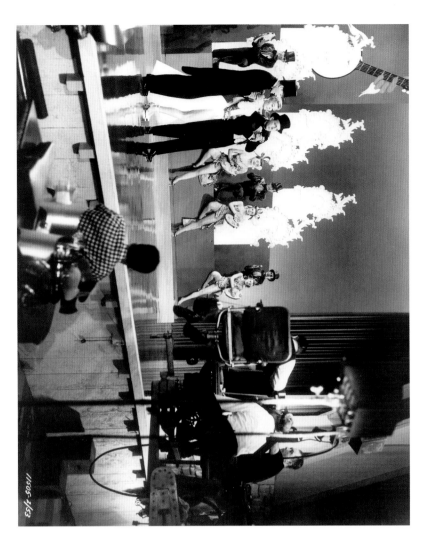

Behind the Screen

■ When Bing and Danny perform the song "Sisters" in drag, Bing is really cracking up. He didn't think they'd use that take, but they did—and the number is among the best in the film.

WHOOPEE!

COMPOSER: Walter Donaldson

LYRICIST: Gus Kahn

PRODUCERS: Samuel Goldwyn and Florenz Ziegfeld

DIRECTOR: Thornton Freeland

SCREENWRITER: William Conselman

SOURCE: Based on the stage musical *Whoopee!* by Walter Donaldson, Gus Kahn, and William Anthony McGuire

CHOREOGRAPHER: Busby Berkeley

Synopsis

Call it your typical gefilte fish-out-of-water story, set in the Wild West. Eddie Cantor tries to determine whether the Indians he encounters constitute one of the ten lost tribes of Israel.

Cast

Eddie Cantor	Henry Williams
Ethel Shutta	Mary Custer
Paul Gregor	Wanenis
Eleanor Hunt	Sally Morgan
Jack Rutherford	Sheriff Bob Wells
Walter Law	Jud Morgan
Spencer Charters	Jerome Underwood
Albert Hackett	Chester Underwood
Chief Caupolican	Black Eagle

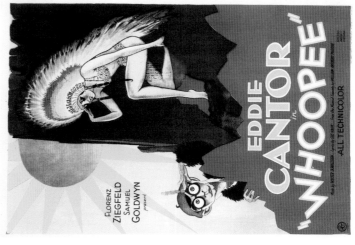

WHOOPEE!

UNITED ARTISTS—OCTOBER 5, 1930

Ethel Shutta pretends to strangle Eddie Cantor. Or does she?

WHOOPEE! IS AN HISTORIC MUSICAL, NOT JUST BECAUSE IT WAS A FAIRLY FAITHFUL adaptation of the original Broadway production featuring two of its stars, or because it was an early color film. It is significant because it was Busby Berkeley's first film. Before it, many musical numbers were shot with four cameras. The editor then edited the different shots into a final print. Berkeley decided to plot out the entire routine, use only one camera, and edit the film in the camera by breaking down the shots instead of running the sequence straight through. And for *Whoopee!* Berkeley came up with another innovation that now seems obvious. He shot close-ups of the chorus girls. When producer Samuel Goldwyn asked him why he would do such a thing, Berkeley replied, "Well, we've got all these beautiful girls in the picture. Why not let the public see them?"

The film reproduced many of Cantor's bits from the Broadway original and kept much of the show's score. It didn't hurt that Samuel Goldwyn's coproducer was the original stage producer, Florenz Ziegfeld. Yes, there was an interpolated number and the plot was tweaked, but essentially, the stage show was there up on the screen. By contrast, many films of the day either did away with the original score completely or changed the show so much that it was recognizable only by name.

Arthur Freed, who bought a lot of Broadway material to the screen, once wrote, "'Why adaptation?' somebody invariably asks. 'I thought the play was perfect. Why did you change it all around in the movie?' Undoubtedly the producer saw the stage show himself, and the chances are he also thought it was practically perfect—as a play. But if he has learned anything at all about his own business, he knows that a play and a motion picture are two separate and widely different things. A movie is a story told by a camera,

ABOVE: Christine Maple shows off her Indian regalia.

ABOVE RIGHT: Welcome to Hollywood, Busby!

RIGHT: Muriel Finley and Ruth Eddings on the arms of Eddie Cantor.

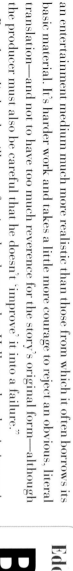

an entertainment medium much more realistic than those from which it often borrows its basic material. It's harder work and takes a little more courage to reject an obvious, literal translation—and not to have too much reverence for the story's original form—although the producer must also be careful that he doesn't 'improve' it into a failure."

Broadway die-hards will never forgive the changes that Hollywood makes in its musicals, even when they are semifaithful. But for movie audiences who never saw the original show, the only thing that matters is what's up on the screen.

Ironically, *Whoopee!* put a stop to one aspect of early movie musicals that could never again be recaptured. An early, silent French film titled *Les Revue des Revues* has an inconsequential story that serves as an excuse to film great stretches of scenes from the *Moulin Rouge!* and other live Parisian cabaret theaters. (The film shares with *Whoopee!* an early form of colorization; however, *Les Revue* is hand tinted frame by frame.) The interesting thing about *Les Revues'* glimpse into early twentieth-century live musical-stage entertainment is that such shows are really, really boring. Lavish? Yes. Lots of seminude women? Yes. But static and repetitive—almost fascinatingly so. Early film musicals producers in the United States attempted, too, to replicate what was done onstage exactly as it had been done onstage, and are likewise rather dull in consequence. But *Whoopee!* is the not-so-missing link between old-fashioned musical theater and an exciting new art form, the movie musical, whose cameramen, choreographers, and designers take the viewer far beyond the physical confines of a theatrical stage, into fantasy achievable only on celluloid. ■

Busby Berkeley

There was fun and there certainly was excitement, but what I mostly remember is stress and strain and exhaustion. I worried about being able to come up with new ideas, and then I worried about how they would go over with the public. . . . It was grueling and sometimes terrifying, because you couldn't give way to despair or lack of confidence."

Busby Berkeley is known today as a master of the moving camera and the spectacular musical number, and for his endless invention. Long pans across beautiful girls' faces, the camera tunneling through pairs upon pairs of gams, and overhead kaleidoscopic shots of gorgeous figures making geometric figures in the lens are all hallmarks of Berkeley's style. But he was equally inventive with crowds, as in the surging of the dancers in the "Lullaby of Broadway" number, the battalions of tappers in the title number of *42nd Street*, and the undulating, banana-wielding chorus of *The Gang's All Here*. He could shoot a number starting in tight close-up on Ruby Keeler's feet and pull back to reveal a huge set filled with hundreds of chorines. His vision was built upon groundwork laid by such seminal artists as John Tiller and his Tiller Girls, the Gertrude Hoffman Girls, and Russell Markert's Sixteen American Rockets, precision dancing girls. But with the "Lullaby of Broadway" and "Remember My Forgotten Man" numbers, he proved he could work serious themes into his spectacle. He moved from Warner Brothers to MGM with a side trip loan-out to 20th Century Fox for *The Gang's All Here*. When the movie musical faded in the 1950s, so did Berkeley's career. His last staging work was on *Billy Rose's Jumbo* and his last work as a director was on *Take Me Out to the Ball Game*, a film he could not complete. By that time drinking had taken its toll on his talents, and the musical numbers were left in the hands of Gene Kelly and Stanley Donen. Berkeley resurfaced as the consultant on the Broadway revival of *No, No, Nanette*, reuniting with Ruby Keeler—but more for photo calls than anything else.

Eddie Cantor

Barney Google wasn't the only one with goo-goo-googly eyes. Eddie Cantor had them, too, and he brought his eye-popping energy to every aspect of entertainment in the twentieth century. His movie career began with the film version of the stage hit *Kid Boots*. Along with his friend from New York theater, Busby Berkeley, he went on to make *Whoopee!*, *Palmy Days*, *Roman Scandals*, and *The Kid from Spain*. Cantor was a great star of the Ziegfeld Follies (the staged show, not the film) but he was an even greater star in the movies. When his screen career slowed, he turned to radio and then television. His patented hopping, clapping, and eye rolling became a trademark recognizable to all Americans. He was beloved by all and his unexpected death was a shock to millions.

WILLY WONKA AND THE CHOCOLATE FACTORY

PARAMOUNT—JUNE 30, 1971

WILLY WONKA AND THE CHOCOLATE FACTORY

COMPOSERS: Leslie Bricusse and Anthony Newley

LYRICISTS: Leslie Bricusse and Anthony Newley

PRODUCERS: Stan Margulies and David L. Wolper

DIRECTOR: Mel Stuart

SCREENWRITER: Roald Dahl

SOURCE: From *Charlie and the Chocolate Factory* by Roald Dahl

CHOREOGRAPHER: Howard Jeffrey

Synopsis

Candy baron Willy Wonka holds a contest to choose a successor to his empire—but watch out when you wish for one of those golden tickets.

Cast

Gene Wilder............Willy Wonka
Peter Ostrum............Charlie Bucket
Jack Albertson............Grandpa Joe
Roy Kinnear............Mr. Salt
Julie Dawn Cole............Veruca Salt
Leonard Stone............Mr. Beauregarde
Denise Nickerson............Violet Beauregarde
Dodo Denny............Mrs. Teevee
Paris Themmen............Mike Teevee
Ursula Reit............Mrs. Gloop
Michael Bollner............Augustus Gloop
Diana Sowle............Mrs. Bucket

Gene Wilder as Willie Wonka, in a land of pure imagination.

IT LOOKS SO EASY THAT EVERYONE THINKS HE CAN DO IT. WE'RE TALKING, OF COURSE, ABOUT making fantasy movies. There are hundreds, if not thousands, of screenwriters, directors, and producers who grew up watching *The Wizard of Oz* and thinking, "I can do that." Fantasy films are enticing. They thrive on special effects. No one can argue if the flowers are puce and the animals have twelve legs and talk in Spanish accents, because that's your imagination at work. They're fun for the whole family and, as exemplified by the likes of *Alice in Wonderland*, logic doesn't have to enter the picture at all. You're free to do whatever your coked-out/stoned/ego-ridden mind thinks up.

Take *The Wizard of Oz*. How hard could it have been to make that movie? A girl appears in a strange land, goes down a road where she meets a bunch of odd characters, and then goes home again. Simple. That's just what Darryl Zanuck over at Fox thought, so he cast Shirley Temple in *The Blue Bird*, one of the most heavy-handed fantasy failures ever. In 1976, *The Blue Bird* was remade (in Moscow) with Elizabeth Taylor, Jane Fonda, Cicely Tyson, and Ava Gardner and was even worse than the Temple version, if that's possible. Tim Burton's recent *Alice in Wonderland* (seemingly based on *The Wizard of Oz* as well as on the Carroll story) lacked the requisite magic, too, though it was a worldwide smash.

Fairy tales are favorite fantasy subjects. For example, in *Snow White and the Seven Dwarfs*, girl goes to sleep, girl is discovered by dwarfs, girl is awakened by prince, and they all live happily ever after. Even Abbott and Costello made a fantasy: the imaginatively titled *Abbott and Costello Meets Jack and the Beanstalk*, which borrowed *The Wizard of Oz*'s trick of starting in black and white and changing to color. The comparison ends there.

If you don't want to do it straight, it's even easier to mess around with an established story or characters. *Shrek* took stock fantasy characters, added knowing contemporary references and tons of attitude—and look how much money that franchise has made. (That in spite of the fact that each *Shrek* sequel has gotten more sophomoric and scatological.)

Here's the problem with fantasy: Being able to have it any way you want it can be a trap. Like good farce, fantasy requires a strict code of conduct. No one can acknowledge that anything is strange—except perhaps the protagonist (and the viewer, of course). Everything within the world of the story must be taken absolutely seriously. That's not to say that things can't be funny, but there's really no place for self-referential humor, irony, or winking at the audience (*Shrek* excepted, we guess). Groucho Marx could acknowledge the audience but only because the rest of the cast was resolutely committed to the comic situation at hand. Fantasy must inhabit its own consistent reality, even if that reality is a bit different from our own. Look at Munchkinland. The houses look like houses but with a sense of humor: the Munchkins are just like regular people but diminutive, oddly coiffed and dressed, and . . . well . . . Munchkinesque. In their world, people happen to wear hats that look like flowerpots and shop in colorful fabric stores. Fantasy is a good thing in fantasy films but, like garlic in Italian food, too much can spoil the whole thing.

Last fantasy truism before we get to *Willy Wonka*: Films aimed strictly at children may do well on DVD, where they can serve as surrogate babysitters when viewed over and over, but they don't make money in theaters. A successful children's film has to have something for everybody in the family. Successful fantasies aren't just superficial fun, and they put limits on the cuteness factor.

Oh, and one more thing. The villain should be mean. Really mean. Yes, thousands of kids have had trouble sleeping after seeing the Wicked Witch but if we didn't take her evil powers seriously, we wouldn't care what happened to poor little Dorothy (and Toto, too). Humorous baddies such as those in *Shrek* just don't really cut it. And if there's no tension between good and evil, well, there's not much of a story.

SONGS

"Candy Man" ■ "Cheer Up Charlie" ■ "I Want It Now" ■ "I've Got a Golden Ticket" ■ "Oompa-loompa-doompa-dee-doo" ■ "Rowing Song" ■ "Pure Imagination"

Behind the Screen

■ Peter Ostrum, who was excellent as Charlie, made only this one film.

■ David Seltzer rewrote Dahl's original screenplay and so angered the author that Dahl refused to see the film.

ABOVE: The Oompa-Loompas at their chocolate lake. Where's the FDA when you need it?

BELOW LEFT: Jack Albertson, Peter Ostrum, and Gene Wilder.

Willy Wonka is a fantasy film that takes itself extremely seriously, and the actions of the characters have dead-serious consequences. Wonka is a rather dour character, when you think about it. He knows that the children will disobey him when given the opportunity, succumbing to their own base natures. Each "contest winner" meets some kind of horrible fate after committing a sin of gluttony, rudeness, greed, or stubbornness. Charlie himself disobeys Wonka, but his politeness is his saving grace; a simple apology provides him with the keys to the candy factory.

The movie itself is steadfastly uncute. The Oompa Loompas are like mutated versions of the Munchkins and completely devoid of humor and sweetness. And for a lot of us, Wonka's factory is too, too much. Wonka himself is steadfastly unromantic until he opens up and sings the marvelous "Pure Imagination." It's a wonderful, unguarded moment for the character, played to a T by Gene Wilder.

Another film that exhibits unbridled imagination in the purest sense is the criminally underrated *The 5,000 Fingers of Dr. T.* Its script and lyrics are by Dr. Seuss and feature all of his characteristic surrealism, plus his rare understanding of childhood dreams and nightmares. *Willy Wonka* seems to speak directly to children in terms they understand, tapping into their sense of wonder and adventure and laying bare their impulses and their utter self-involvement. Wonka is just a grown-up child himself, who wields his power with imagination and in the end reveals his humanity by offering Charlie what every child really wants: forgiveness. ■

THE WIZARD OF OZ

MGM—AUGUST 25, 1939

THE WIZARD OF OZ
COMPOSER: Harold Arlen
LYRICIST: E.Y. Harburg
PRODUCER: Mervyn LeRoy
DIRECTOR: Victor Fleming
SCREENWRITERS: Noel Langley,
Florence Ryerson, and
Edgar Allan Woolf
SOURCE: Based on the novel *The
Wizard of Oz* by L. Frank Baum
CHOREOGRAPHER: Bobby Connolly

Synopsis

Dorothy Gale is bored of gray old Kansas, but after she gets bopped on the head she has a grand old time in the Technicolor world of Oz. Unaccountably, she still wants to go home.

Cast

Judy Garland..............*Dorothy Gale*
Frank Morgan..............*Professor Marvel,*
                          The Wizard of Oz
Ray Bolger..............*The Scarecrow, Hunk*
Bert Lahr..............*The Cowardly Lion,*
                        Zeke
Jack Haley..............*The Tin Man, Hickory*
Terry....................*Toto*
Margaret Hamilton.......*The Wicked Witch of*
                         the West, Elvira Gulch
Billie Burke..............*Glinda*
Clara Blandick..............*Auntie Em*
Charley Grapewin..........*Uncle Henry*
Pat Walshe................*Nikko*
The Singer Midgets........*The Munchkins*

ABOVE: Billie Burke, as Glinda, gives advice to Judy Garland's Dorothy.

RIGHT: Judy yearns for a world over the rainbow.

I T IS POSSIBLY THE GREATEST FILM MUSICAL OF ALL TIME. CERTAINLY, MORE PEOPLE HAVE seen *The Wizard of Oz* than any other musical and by artistic standards, it's completely brilliant. Yes, *Singin' in the Rain* is also a perfect film, but we think *The Wizard of Oz* gets short shrift because it's viewed as a children's picture. Of course, we know lots of adults who understand its brilliance. Is there any aspect of the film that is not top-drawer? We can't think of any.

And if you think it's easy making such a movie, have a look at its adaptations and sequels: *The Wiz, Journey Back to Oz, The Wonderful Land of Oz, The Wonderful Wizard of Oz,* and Tim Burton's *Alice in Wonderland* (really, check it out). They all stink.

Oz was a hit from the get-go. Reviews were almost unanimous in their praise of the film and all its elements. It was one of the top-grossing films of that golden year of movies, 1939. but. surprisingly, it didn't initially make a profit—mainly because the majority of tickets sold were children's admissions of a nickel or dime. In addition, the lucrative foreign market was undermined when war broke out in Europe. Subsequent releases and, of course, television sales earned MGM a tidy sum. And now, with the addition of video and DVD sales and marketing income, the film has proven to be one of the most profitable of all time.

ABOVE LEFT: Judy and the denizens of Munchkinland.
ABOVE: No, it's not the first day of school. It's the Singer Midgets crossing Culver Boulevard.

The road to Oz wasn't easy, as many of the histories of the film have pointed out. We've all read about how cut three times during advance screenings and how Arthur Freed fought for the song's inclusion. We've read that Buddy Ebsen's poisoning from the Tin Woodman's makeup forced him to drop out of the film. We know about the revolving door of directors, including Victor Fleming, Richard Thorpe, George Cukor, and King Vidor. Well documented, too, are the seemingly endless teams of screenwriters who took a whack at the script. And doesn't everyone know that Shirley Temple and Deanna Durbin were considered for the role of Dorothy, W. C. Fields for the Wizard, and Gael Sondergaard for the Wicked Witch? If you didn't, you do now.

Arthur Freed, who was depending on *Oz* to help him become a full producer at MGM, was looking for the perfect cast and creative team. In 1937, while he was checking out the newest shows on Broadway, he attended a musical called *Hooray for What!* starring Ed Wynn. When Freed heard the song "In the Shade of the New Apple Tree" by Harold Arlen and E. Y. Harburg, he knew he had found the perfect songwriting team. He also wanted Ed Wynn to play the Wizard but the star wanted too much money. Freed kept pestering Louis B. Mayer to let him make the movie, but Mayer and the other nabobs at MGM couldn't see a fantasy film making money. What finally got Freed the green light was the great success of Disney's *Snow White and the Seven Dwarfs* in 1938. That film showed the bigwigs at MGM that fantasy could indeed make money and could attract an audience of adults as well as children.

Here was the catch. Samuel Goldwyn owned the rights to the Oz stories, which he thought might make a good vehicle for Eddie Cantor (as the Tin Man). Twentieth Century-Fox, who had also noted the success of *Snow White*, came sniffing around as well, thinking the property would make a great vehicle for Shirley Temple. MGM eventually won the bidding war, paying Goldwyn $75,000 for the rights.

Not trusting the untested Freed to produce *Oz*, Mayer hired Mervyn LeRoy, who had had a lot of credits as a director but few as a producer. Freed was assigned to be LeRoy's associate. Although the

Behind the Screen

- *The Wizard of Oz* was one of only eight Technicolor films released in 1939.

- King Vidor directed the black-and-white footage after Victor Fleming left to take over *Gone with the Wind.*

- Bert Lahr was contracted for five weeks' work on the picture. He wound up working for twenty-six.

- Bert Lahr improvised the line, "Unusual weather we're havin', ain't it?"

- Harburg, well known for inserting his left-wing political beliefs into his lyrics, described his treatment while at MGM: "Every lyric was fingerprinted and the history of it taken and the microscopes were applied to every word to see what hidden meanings there were . . . They used to call you in at Metro and say, 'Lookit, we don't want any messages in the stuff you write. We like your stuff, we don't like your messages.'"

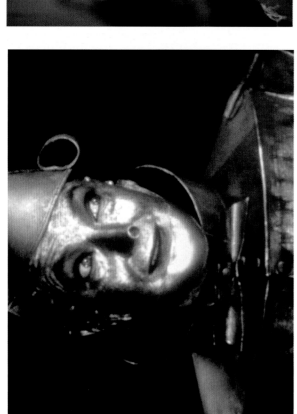

"Fun? Like hell it was fun. It was a lot of hard work. It was no fun at all. There was nothing funny about it." —*Jack Haley*

picture had been Freed's idea in the first place and he oversaw the casting and the musical aspects of the film. LeRoy took complete credit, especially after the film was a critical success.

For the role of Dorothy, Freed had Judy Garland in mind from the start. Metro had signed the youngster but didn't know exactly what to do with her. She had connected with audiences when she sang "Dear Mr. Gable," Roger Edens's intro to "You Made Me Love You," in *Broadway Melody of 1938,* so Freed had been assigned to find Garland's next property and make her a star. He immediately thought of *The Wizard of Oz.*

With a score, cast, and script in place, well, the rest was grueling work but professionally executed. MGM had to create new forms of makeup for the Cowardly Lion, Flying Monkeys, Tin Man, Scarecrow, and assorted witches and Munchkins. Seemingly endless color tests had to be made for the Technicolor part of the film. The performers, burdened by their heavy costumes and makeup, were wilting under the extraordinarily hot lights. One number, "The Jitterbug," was cut.

As we know, all the hard work paid off. Today, if a studio were to undertake *The Wizard of Oz,* the sets would all be created on computers and the Tin Man, Cowardly Lion, and Scarecrow—not to mention the Flying Monkeys and apple trees—would exist only as bits and bytes. But all the computer magic in the world cannot substitute for great acting, imaginative direction, and an exceptionally witty screenplay. *The Wizard of Oz* has all of those, as well as a brilliant score. It's a true classic.

We'll end by pointing out the true importance of *The Wizard of Oz,* for it is significant beyond its artistic merits. At the time the film was made, Technicolor was used on only a handful of films. *Snow White's* Technicolor success convinced MGM that *Oz* should also be made in color—but the hugely successful art direction and cinematography of *Oz* showed off Technicolor to its best advantage—and in a live action film. Think of the success of *Avatar* and how its 3-D effects have spurred Hollywood to embrace the format. *Oz* had the same effect and, though expensive, Technicolor was embraced for all major films. ∎

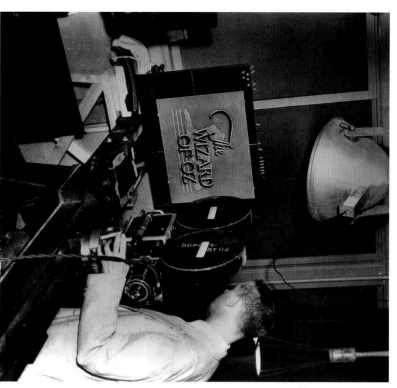

SONGS

Harold Arlen and E. Y. Harburg

Although not officially a songwriting team like Rodgers and Hart or Burke and Van Heusen, Harold Arlen and E. Y. Harburg collaborated on a number of exceptional film and stage scores. Arlen got his start as part of the Buffalodians jazz band. He joined lyricist Ted Koehler on a series of scores for Harlem's Cotton Club revues. Harburg found his early poems printed in the newspaper column, "The Conning

Tower," along with those of his friend Ira Gershwin. Arlen and Gershwin met up for the Broadway musical *Life Begins at 8:40*, which contained their first hit, "Let's Take a Walk Around the Block." After *The Wizard of Oz*, the two wrote "Lydia, the Tattooed Lady" for *At the Circus*. More hits followed for both songwriters, together and with other collaborators. Sadly, Harburg's Hollywood output doesn't equal that of other greats, perhaps because he was blacklisted in the early 1950s. Arlen wrote many film scores, most notably that of *A Star Is Born* for Judy Garland. Arlen and Harburg also wrote a Garland score for the animated film *Gay Purr-ee* in 1962.

ABOVE LEFT: Filming the opening credits.

ABOVE: Victor Fleming "directs" the Munchkins.

LEFT: Harold Arlen and E.Y. Harburg attend a rehearsal for the 1944 Broadway musical, *Bloomer Girl*.

BELOW: *Gay Purr-ee* featured the voices of Judy Garland and Robert Goulet and songs by Arlen and Harburg.

BELOW LEFT: Judy Garland in *I Could Go on Singing*.

YANKEE DOODLE DANDY

WARNER BROTHERS—JUNE 6, 1942

YANKEE DOODLE DANDY

COMPOSER: George M. Cohan
LYRICIST: George M. Cohan
PRODUCERS: Jack L. Warner and Hal B. Wallis
DIRECTOR: Michael Curtiz
SCREENWRITERS: Robert Buckner and Edmund Joseph
CHOREOGRAPHERS: LeRoy Prinz and Seymour Felix

Synopsis

Final *Jeopardy* question, category: biography. He was a Yankee Doodle, do or die; a real live nephew of his Uncle Sam; born on the Fourth of July. His mother, father, and sister thank you. Answer: Who was George M. Cohan?

Cast

James Cagney	George M. Cohan
Joan Leslie	Mary
Walter Huston	Jerry Cohan
Rosemary DeCamp	Nellie Cohan
Jeanne Cagney	Josie Cohan
Richard Whorf	Sam Harris
Irene Manning	Fay Templeton
George Tobias	Dietz
George Barbier	Erlanger
S. Z. Sakall	Schwab
Walter Catlett	Theatre Manager
Douglas Croft	oung George M. Cohan
Eddie Foy Jr.	Eddie Foy
Minor Watson	Albee Frances Langford

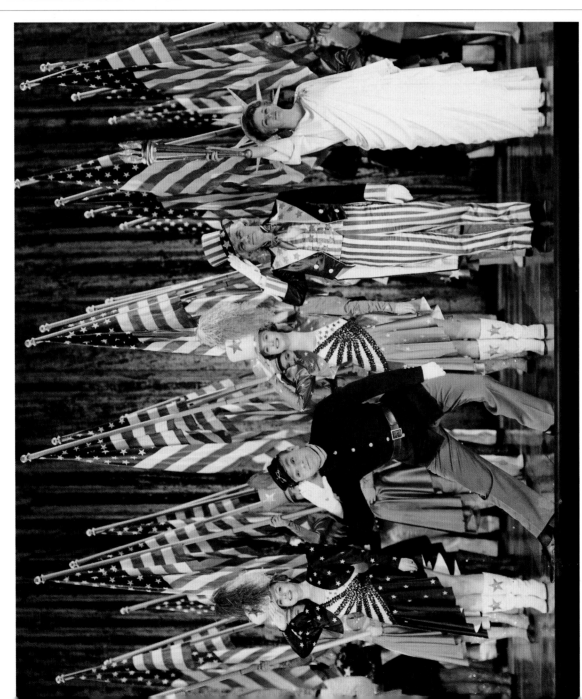

On stage in vaudeville, Jimmy Cagney as George M. Cohan and Walter Huston as George's father, dressed as Uncle Sam.

IN THE 1940S, SOMEONE HAD THE BRIGHT IDEA OF PRODUCING FILMS HONORING THE CATA-logs of famous songwriters. Warner's *Yankee Doodle Dandy* is the best of the "and-then-I-wrote" films, in part because of its sense of nostalgia. Released just before America entered the Second World War, it couldn't have been more patriotic. After all, it was George M. Cohan who had written the most popular wartime song of all time, "Over There," during World War I. And he had just recently portrayed a living president, FDR, on Broadway in Rodgers and Hart's musical *I'd Rather Be Right*, from which several numbers in the film were drawn. Yet another reason this film was such a success at the time was the absolute surprise of seeing James Cagney sing and dance with consummate style. True, he had been in *Footlight Parade* in 1933 and the forgettable *Something to Sing About* in 1937, but most people thought of Cagney as a dramatic actor, not a song-and-dance man extraordinaire.

The success of *Yankee Doodle Dandy* inspired Warner Brothers to explore other composers and lyricist's lives through what became known as biopics. Next up was the entirely bowdlerized 1946 biopic of songwriter Cole Porter, *Night and Day*, starring Cary Grant as Porter. The less said about the plot to that one, the better. A few highlights of Porter's career were touched upon, but between the facts was a ton of Hollywood hooey. Of course, few audience members knew or cared, because the film had such a great wealth of songs.

MCM got wise and decided to up the ante when they produced the Jerome Kern biopic, *Till the Clouds Roll By*, in 1946. Since they had a whole bunch of stars under contract, wouldn't it make sense to have them all show up and do a song or two in the course of telling the long story of Kern's Broadway success? Again, the plot was balderdash, but what was basically a musical revue with some pseudo-biographical scenes interspersed became a big hit. After all, who could complain after watching Judy Garland, Frank Sinatra, Kathryn Grayson, June Allyson, Dinah Shore, Cyd Charisse, Lena Horne, and other stars interpret Kern's oeuvre?

The equally preposterous *Words and Music* followed in 1948, and this time Rodgers and Hart got the MCM treatment, complete with some of the same stars—Judy Garland, June Allyson, and Cyd Charisse—plus Perry Como, Ann Sothern (who had actually starred on Broadway in a Rodgers and Hart show), Mel Torme, Vera-Ellen, Betty Garrett, and Gene Kelly. Again, the Metro class and the great songs saved the day.

Every two years, another songwriter biopic came along. In 1950, the well beginning to run dry, Bert Kalmar and Harry Ruby got biographized musically. Luckily, Fred Astaire and Red Skelton played the songwriters and they could hold their own as singers and dancers. So there wasn't the need for the all-star treatment (unless you think of Arlene Dahl, Gloria DeHaven, and Phil Regan.

as top-drawer). Yes, Vera-Ellen also appeared, dubbed as usual, as did a very young Debbie Reynolds—dubbed, too, by Helen Kane, the performer she was portraying. Whew! Anyway, producer Jack Cummings and director Richard Thorpe did a fine job on the picture.

In 1954, MCM's last songwriterpalooza, *Deep in My Heart*, premiered with José Ferrer portraying operetta composer Sigmund Romberg. This is one of the best of the biopics—though no more respectful of the facts than were MCM's previous forays. It was produced by Roger Edens, out of the shadow of Arthur Freed, and directed by Stanley Donen, who would later show his mettle with the totally delightful *Funny Face* (again with producer Edens) and a terrific cast. The MCM stalwarts were there, including Cyd Charisse and James Mitchell, Howard Keel, Tony Martin, Gene Kelly and brother Fred, Ann Miller, and Jane Powell. And it also featured pop singers Rosemary Clooney (Mrs. Ferrer) and Vic Damone. But the real delights of the film spring from opera singer turned better Helen Traubel, a real game gal who should not be underappreciated. She had a terrific rapport with José Ferrer who, for his part, didn't merely chew the scenery but practically burned up the celluloid with his manic energy. And that's a compliment. He wasn't anything like the real Romberg (though Romberg did once say that the most beautiful sound in the world was the sound of a woman's thighs slapping together). The composer liked zaftig women and Traubel was the zaftigest leading lady you could ever find.

There were other biopics, of course. One of the first came out in 1939, Fox's *Suwanee River*, which told the sad story of Stephen

ABOVE: The curtain opens to reveal American flags that seem to go on forever.

ABOVE LEFT: Director Michael Curtiz (in shirt and tie), with (standing) Joan Leslie and Jimmy Cagney and (sitting) Chester Clute, and George Tobias.

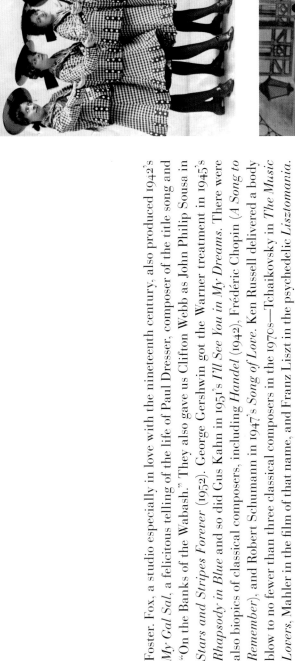

Foster. Fox, a studio especially in love with the nineteenth century, also produced 1942's *My Gal Sal*, a felicitous telling of the life of Paul Dresser, composer of the title song and "On the Banks of the Wabash." They also gave us Clifton Webb as John Philip Sousa in *Stars and Stripes Forever* (1952). George Gershwin got the Warner treatment in 1945's *Rhapsody in Blue* and so did Gus Kahn in 1951's *I'll See You in My Dreams*. There were also biopics of classical composers, including *Handel* (1942), Frédéric Chopin (*A Song to Remember*), and Robert Schumann in 1947's *Song of Love*. Ken Russell delivered a body blow to no fewer than three classical composers in the 1970s—Tchaikovsky in *The Music Lovers*, Mahler in the film of that name, and Franz Liszt in the psychedelic *Lisztomania*. Thanks for nothing, Ken.

Biopics of composers never went out of fashion. Just recently, poor Cole Porter was subjected to yet another biopic, the most misbegotten of them all, *De-Lovely* (2004), in which he was portrayed by Kevin Kline. This one attempted to tell the "truth" about Porter's homosexuality, along with other nonstarter revelations.

Composer biopics constitute a major subgenre of musical movies. But if you're taking a music appreciation course, don't count on the movie to give you anything close to the truth. ■

ABOVE: Ethel Levey and members of the chorus in the original 1904 production of *Little Johnny Jones*.
RIGHT: Jeanne Cagney, James Cagney, Rosemary DeCamp, and Walter Huston play the Four Cohans.

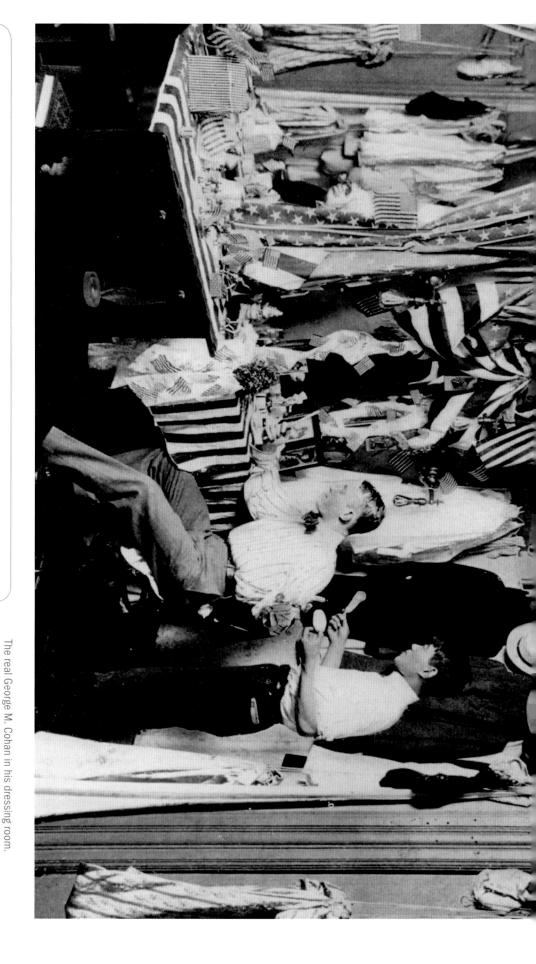

The real George M. Cohan in his dressing room.

Ray Heindorf

The Warner Brothers sound should be credited predominantly to the talents of one man, Ray Heindorf. Working first as a pit pianist in a band accompanying silent films while still in high school, he soon moved to Hollywood and worked at MGM (*Hollywood Revue of 1929*), Goldwyn Studios (*Whoopee!*), and United Artists (*Hallelujah, I'm a Bum*), before landing for good at Warner Brothers. His first job there was to provide the music arrangements for *42nd Street*. Over the next forty years, the punchy, no-nonsense arrangements, orchestrations, scoring, and musical direction of Warner movies were mostly Heindorf's doing. He could be subtle but was never namby-pamby or lightweight. Take his work on "The Shadow Waltz" or "By a Waterfall"; another arranger might have had harps glissando-ing and chords tinkling, but Heindorf's versions featured soaring strings and real depth of sound. As Busby Berkeley's cameras swooped, so did Heindorf's orchestrations. On manly films such as *The Sea Hawk* and *Kings Row*, his arrangements were masculine and full of bravado. Heindorf respected great conductors such as Toscanini but he was also a jazz buff, and in a picture such as *A Star Is Born* with Judy Garland, his arrangements could really swing. Along with MGM's Georgie Stoll, he was one of the first to insist on integrated orchestras.

SONGS

"All Aboard for Old Broadway" (M. K. Jerome and Jack Scholl) ■ "The Belle of the Barber's Ball" ■ "Billie" ■ "Blue Skies, Gray Skies" ■ "The Dancing Master" (Jerry Cohan) ■ "Forty-Five Minutes from Broadway" ■ "Give My Regards to Broadway" ■ "Good Luck Johnny" (M. K. Jerome and Jack Scholl) ■ "Harrigan" ■ "I Was Born in Virginia" ■ "In a Kingdom of Our Own" ■ "Jeepers Creepers" (Harry Warren and Johnny Mercer) ■ "Like the Wandering Minstrel" ■ "Love Nest" (Louis A. Hirsch and Otto Harbach) ■ "The Man Who Owns Broadway" ■ "Mary's a Grand Old Name" ■ "Molly Malone" ■ "Nellie Kelly I Love You" ■ "Off the Record" (Richard Rodgers and Lorenz Hart) ■ "Oh You Wonderful Girl" ■ "Over There" ■ "So Long Mary" ■ "The Warmest Baby in the World" ■ "While Strolling Through the Park One Day" (Ed Haley) ■ "Yankee Doodle Dandy" ■ "You're a Grand Old Flag"

Behind the Screen

■ Cohan had a clause in his contract that forbade the studio from even mentioning his current wife in the screenplay.

WARNER BROS: MUSICAL ENTERTAINMENT MARVEL

YOU WERE NEVER LOVELIER

COLUMBIA—NOVEMBER 19, 1942

YOU WERE NEVER LOVELIER

COMPOSER: Jerome Kern
LYRICIST: Johnny Mercer
PRODUCER: Louis F. Edelman
DIRECTOR: William A. Seiter
SCREENWRITERS: Michael Fessier, Ernest Pagano, and Delmar Daves
SOURCE: Based on the story "Los Martes Orquideas" by Carlos A. Olivari and Sixto Pondal Ríos
CHOREOGRAPHER: Val Raset

Synopsis

Fred's in Buenos Aires and broke from betting on the horses. He accepts a job pretending to be the secret admirer of Rita. You know the rest. He falls in love with her just as his fraud is revealed. Bonus: Fred in armor on a white horse.

Cast

Fred Astaire..............Robert Davis
Rita Hayworth............Maria Acuña
Adolph Menjou ....Eduardo Acuña
Isobel Elsom.............Mrs. Maria Castro
Leslie Brooks ....Cecy Acuña
Adele Mara...............Lita Acuña
Douglas Leavitt...........Juan Castro
As Themselves ....Xavier Cugat and His Orchestra

Fred Astaire with Rita Hayworth, his most beautiful dancing partner.

T HERE ARE HUNDREDS OF SINGERS AND DANCERS FEATURED IN THESE PAGES BUT, IT'S fair to say that the songs and dances they performed, while perhaps very good, didn't really matter to the story. Characters might dance to denote happiness or sadness but somehow, they were just dancing, filling in the bars of music until the song was over.

The two greatest dancers in screen history were Gene Kelly and Fred Astaire. But whereas Kelly's choreography was made up of ideas, Astaire's dances were composed of steps. In a way, the steps didn't matter to Kelly—his intention was to illustrate. Whereas Kelly was a man of power and forward momentum, Astaire was a man of intricacy. Kelly appeared to be the more athletic, bounding up and down and around his sets, but on examination, Astaire could measure up to Kelly's physical technique while demonstrating more savoir faire.

For Astaire, every movement mattered. He told stories in his dances. Just as a great song moves the plot along or reveals a change of mind or expresses a feeling, so, too, does a dance. To be sure, Astaire indulged in his share of tricks and tours de force. Think about his impromptu and wholly imaginative bullfight with an umbrella and raincoat in *Funny Face*; the dance on the walls and ceiling in *Royal Wedding*; or his waltz into the clouds

"I guess the only jewels in my life were the pictures I made with Fred Astaire." —*Rita Hayworth*

in *The Belle of New York*. But even these specialty dances somehow expressed emotions; they weren't just show(-off) pieces meant to amaze.

When Astaire partnered with someone, whether it was Ginger Rogers, Vera-Ellen, or Rita Hayworth, it was the dances that mattered. Yes, he could have a ball in a funhouse with George and Gracie, but when it came to one-on-one romance, there was no fooling around. Relationships changed between the first steps of a dance and the last. While the plots of his films may be silly, the songs a battle of "either" or "eyether," the dances are serious business. In "Pick Yourself Up," Fred might pretend not to know how to dance, but you feel him wooing Ginger with every step.

Fred's character was always in love with his costar but in almost every picture, he had to convince the girl to reciprocate. And he always won her over by dancing with her. You can see the change in demeanor, the deepening of desire, the melting of inhibitions and distrust. Step by step, note by note, a change takes place. The couple coming out of the dance is different somehow from the couple going in. "Night and Day" in *The Gay Divorcee*, "Let Yourself Go" in *Follow the Fleet*, "Never Gonna Dance" in *Swing Time*, and "I'm Old Fashioned" in *You Were Never Lovelier*—all are relationship changers.

With Astaire, it's not only the proverbial forest but the trees. Each dance is composed of steps and each step has meaning and nuance, sometimes detailed but never fussy; deftly executed, cleanly composed, definitive steps that tell

emotional stories: Fred and Vera-Ellen pulling and resisting; Fred guiding a guileless Joan Fontaine, showing her a sophisticated, adult world she never thought she could be a part of; Rita Hayworth finally giving in to her emotions during "You Were Never Lovelier."

In *You Were Never Lovelier*, the plot might be slight and veer into the realm of cliché, but the story provides a gentle hook on which to hang songs and dances of remarkable emotional depth. It's no wonder that Jerome Kern jumped up from his piano bench to hug and kiss Johnny Mercer when he first heard the lyric to "I'm Old Fashioned." As he does with all his partners, Astaire woos, cajoles, teases, and makes love through dance. *You Were Never Lovelier* is a dance film first and foremost, even if it takes thirty-five minutes to get to Fred's first dance. Dances aren't just one adjunct to the plot, the whole plot exists to be illustrated and enhanced by them.

Rita Hayworth and Fred Astaire moved in perfect harmony when they danced. She equaled him in precision, form, and grace. The audience felt secure that she was his equal, not only in terpsichorean talents but in emotional depth. That made her as great a partner for Astaire as Ginger Rogers. ∎

Rita Hayworth

Rita Hayworth was most at home on the screen when dancing. What made her a real movie star was more than her gorgeous looks, though they didn't hurt. In dramas she could come off as cool and inscrutable. She was definitely one of the greatest screen presences when she was dancing, which she had been doing since she was a child, working in her family's Spanish dance act. But Margarita Cansino had a greater future ahead of her. After a brief time at Fox Studios, she was hired by Columbia Pictures where, after learning the ropes in a series of B pictures, she became the studio's first real star. Through some wise loan-outs, she became one of the biggest stars of the 1940s ascending further in the pantheon when she joined Betty Grable as the servicemen's pinup of choice during the Second World War, earning the designation "sex-goddess." Hayworth was Astaire's sexiest partner. She was equally adept at drama (*Gilda*, *Affair in Trinidad*) and musicals (*Cover Girl*, *Pal Joey*).

ABOVE LEFT: Rita Hayworth wants to go out with Fred Astaire but Adolphe Menjou doesn't want her to.

MIDDLE LEFT: Dance seems effortless when executed by the likes of Fred Astaire and Rita Hayworth.

SONGS

"Dearly Beloved" ▪ "I'm Old Fashioned" ▪ "Shorty George" ▪ "These Orchids"
▪ "Wedding in the Spring" ▪ "You Were Never Lovelier"

"In rehearsal she would sort of walk through it. And you would say, 'I wonder if she is going to do more.'"

—*Hermes Pan on Rita Hayworth*

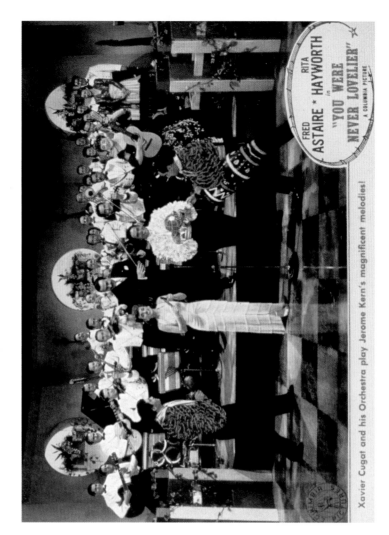

Xavier Cugat and his Orchestra play Jerome Kern's magnificent melodies!

Behind the Screen

▪ Rehearsals were held in a room above the funeral parlor of the Hollywood Cemetery. All singing and dancing would have to stop whenever a funeral was held.

▪ Fidel Castro, all of fifteen years old, is an extra in the film.

TOP LEFT: Filming the "Shorty George" number under the supervision of director George Seiter (seated in front of camera).

TOP RIGHT: Fred Astaire bops Adolphe Menjou on the head. Repeatedly. Over many, many takes, yielding many broken canes

Jerome Kern

Lyricist Johnny Mercer supposed Kern would be "quick, probably irascible, and rather conceited." The composer had reason to indulge his ego: His music was the link between European operetta and American musical comedy. His career took off in 1914 when his song "They Didn't Believe Me" became a hit. Working with lyricist Otto Harbach and librettist P. G. Wodehouse, Kern created the first intimate musical comedies. He joined forces with Oscar Hammerstein II on *Show Boat*, the musical that kicked off the full integration of song and story in musical theater. In 1935, Kern settled in Hollywood and wrote an astounding series of successful songs in collaboration with Hammerstein, Dorothy Fields, E. Y. Harburg, Ira Gershwin, and Johnny Mercer, among others. *Swing Time*, *Cover Girl*, *Can't Help Singing*, and other films all feature Kern hits. He had a sharp mind and was equally interested in all aspects of a musical production, from costumes and sets to scripts and lighting.

CHRONOLOGY

CHRONOLOGY OF THE 101 GREATEST HOLLYWOOD MUSICALS

1920s

1927 The Jazz Singer
1928 The Broadway Melody
1929 Hallelujah
1929 Sunnyside Up

1930s

1930 King of Jazz
1930 Whoopee
1930 Sun Valley Serenade
1931 One Hour with You
1933 Forty Second Street (42nd Street)
1934 Belle of the Nineties
1934 The Merry Widow
1934 We're Not Dressing
1935 Gold Diggers of 1933
1935 A Night at the Opera
1935 Top Hat
1935 Born to Dance
1936 The Great Ziegfeld
1936 Poor Little Rich Girl
1936 Rose-Marie
1936 Show Boat
1936 Swing Time
1937 A Damsel in Distress
1938 College Swing
1938 The Great Waltz
1938 Hollywood Hotel
1938 Mad About Music
1938 Snow White and the Seven Dwarfs
1939 Babes in Arms
1939 The Wizard of Oz

1940s

1940 Pinocchio
1940 Tin Pan Alley
1940 Dumbo
1941 Road to Morocco
1942 Sons of the Pioneers
1942 Star Spangled Rhythm
1942 Yankee Doodle Dandy
1942 You Were Never Lovelier
1943 Cabin in the Sky
1943 The Gang's All Here
1943 Girl Crazy
1943 Stormy Weather
1944 Meet Me In St. Louis
1945 The Harvey Girls
1945 State Fair
1947 Good News
1948 Easter Parade
1949 On the Town

1950s

1950 Summer Stock
1951 An American in Paris
1951 The Great Caruso
1952 Singin' in the Rain
1953 The Band Wagon
1953 Calamity Jane
1953 Dangerous When Wet
1953 Gentlemen Prefer Blondes
1953 Kiss Me Kate
1954 Carmen Jones
1954 Living It Up
1954 Seven Brides for Seven Brothers
1954 White Christmas
1955 Love Me or Leave Me
1955 Oklahoma!
1956 The Court Jester
1956 The King and I
1957 Funny Face
1957 The Pajama Game
1958 Damn Yankees
1958 Gigi
1959 Li'l Abner

1960s

1961 West Side Story
1962 The Music Man
1964 A Hard Day's Night (British)
1964 Mary Poppins
1964 My Fair Lady
1965 Beach Blanket Bingo
1965 The Sound of Music
1965 Viva Las Vegas
1968 Funny Girl
1968 Oliver!
1969 Goodbye Mr. Chips

1970s

1970 Scrooge
1971 Willie Wonka & the Chocolate Factory
1972 Cabaret
1972 Lady Sings the Blues
1975 Nashville
1975 The Rocky Horror Picture Show
1977 Saturday Night Fever
1978 American Hot Wax
1978 Grease
1979 All That Jazz
1979 The Muppet Movie
1979 The Rose

1980s

1984 This Is Spinal Tap

1990s

1991 Beauty and the Beast
1993 The Nightmare Before Christmas

2000s

2001 Hedwig and the Angry Inch
2001 Moulin Rouge
2002 Chicago
2008 High School Musical 3

The many moods of Judy Garland in *A Star is Born*.

INDEX

(**bold** indicates photos)

Abbott, George, 47, 62, 153, 176, 177
Abbott and Costello, 8o, 128, 137, 161, 202,
247, 266
Abbott and Costello Meet Jack and the Beanstalk, 266
Academy Awards, 23, 28, 29, 53, 65, 91, 103,
133, 146, 153, 155, 157, 158–159, 162, 169, 177,
179, 181, 185, 189, 210, 223, 226–227, 237,
240, 249, 255
Act, The, 46
Adams, Edie, 126
Adams, India, 43
Adams, Jo, 57
Adinsell, Richard, 66
Adler, Richard, 47
Adventures of Prince Achmed, The, 187
Affair in Trinidad, 277
Affair to Remember, An, 116
Africana, 33
Ah, Wilderness, 42, 133
Ahrens, Lynn, 15
Akins, Zoe, 202
Aladdin, 23
Albert, Eddie, 13
Albertson, Jack, **207**
Alexander's Ragtime Band, 19, 204, 244, 245
Ali Baba Goes to Town, 109, 287
Alice in Wonderland, 55, 260, 268
All Dogs Go to Heaven, 15
All Shook Up, 19
All That Jazz, 8–9, 39, 45
Allegro, 166
Allen, Gene, 155
Allen, Gracie, 20, **41**, **42**, 49, 113, 184, 255
Allen, Rex, 41
Allen, Woody, 8
Allyson, June, 34, 42, 56, 58, 81, 82, 83, 134
263, 273
Altman, Robert, 159, 259
Alton, Robert, 61, 77, 82, 105
Alvarez, Carmen, 127
Ameche, Don, 235, 245
American Association of University Women, 25
American Citizenship Council, 25
American Hot Wax, 10–11
American in Paris, An, 12–14, 36–55, 63, 73–75,
144, 156, 173, 204, 233
American Matchmaker, 250
Anastasia, 15
Anchors Aweigh, 17, 47, 102, 131, 226
Anderson, Eddie, **32**, 33, 224, 230
Anderson, John Murray, 118, 119
Andrews, Julie, 36, 65, **138**, **139**, **140**, 154, 173,
176, 177, **214**, **215**, **216**
Andrews Sisters, 8o, 173
Animal Crackers, 161, 184
Annan, Beulah, 38
Annie, 218, 225
Annie Get Your Gun, 34, 103, 177, 221, 225, 232
Ann-Margret, **231**, **232**, **233**
Anyone Can Whistle, 82
Anything Goes, 71, 177
Apostle, The, 208
Applause, 47, 74, 95, 152, 133, 199
April in Paris, 105, 237
April Love, 35, 153
Arden, Eve, 86
Arlen, Harold, 15, 33, 72, 109, 222, 224, 225, 229,
233, 269, **271**
Aristocats, The, 22, 140
Armstrong, Louis, 15, 33, 42, **179**
Arnaz, Desi, 177, 218
Arthur, Jean, 42
Arthur, Bea, 177, 218
Artie Shaw's Orchestra, 42
Artists and Models, 139, 199
As Thousands Cheer, 33
Asche, Kenny, 15
Ashman, Howard, 23
Astaire, Adele, 48, 49, 60, 238, 249
Astaire, Fred, 6, 13, **18**, 19, 26, 30, 39, **48**, **49**, **54**,
55, **56**, 60, **61**, **62**, 68, **75**, 77, 115, 122, 133, 142,
148, 154, 156, 186, 192, 193, 197, **198**, **205**, 207,
263, 273, 276, 277, 278
At Home Abroad, 27, 44
At Long Last Love, 208
At the Circus, 271
Athena, 8o, 45, 198, 199, 244
Autry, Gene, 141, 233
Avalon, 21, 87, 128
Avatar, 210, 270
Avedon, Richard, 60, 62
Avian, Bob, 92

Babes in Arms, 16–17, 76, 105
Babes in Arms, Strike Up the Band, 77
Babes in Toyland, 105, 247
Babes on Broadway, 77, 199
Bacon, Lloyd, 58
Badham, John, 193
Bailey, Pearl, 30
Bainter, Fay, **227**
Baker, Chet, 42
Baker, Kenny, 8o
Baker Street, 85
Ball, Lucille, 135, 177, 197, 218

Ballard, Kaye, 31
Bambi, 54
Band Wagon, The, 13, 18–19, 43, 81, 107, 205, 207, 233, 249
Baravalle, Victor, 202
Bari, Lynn, 235
Barkleys of Broadway, The, 77, 105, 207, 239, 240
Barnet, Charlie, 179
Barrie, George, 158
Barris, Harry, 119
Barry, John, 85
Barrymore, John, 80
Barrymore, Lionel, 237
Barstow, Richard, 220
Bari, Lionel, 170
Basie, Count, 42, 170
Bathing Beauty, 51, 122
Batman, 102
Batman Forever, 103
Baxley, Barbara, 158
Baxter, Warner, 45, 59
Beach Blanket Bingo, 20–21
Beatles, The, 96, 97, 98
Beaton, Cecil, 75, 154–155, 156
Beaumont, Harry, 29
Beauty and the Beast, 22–23, 53
Becky Sharp, 133
Bedknobs and Broomsticks, 149
Bee Gees, 192
Beetlejuice, 102
Belafonte, Harry, 36, 37
Belcher, Marge. See Champion, Marge
Belle of New York, The, 199, 240, 203, 277
Belle of the Nineties, 24–25, 234
Bells Are Ringing, 71, 207
Bells of St. Mary's, The, 226
Ben-Hur, 68
Bennett, Michael, 92
Bennett, Robert Russell, 202
Benny, Jack, 44, 49
Benny Goodman and His Orchestra, 110, 179
Benson, Sally, 142
Benson, Martin, 115
Bergen, Edgar, 151
Bergman, Ingmar, 47
Berkeley, Busby, 17, 35, 51, 57, 58, 59, 67–68, 69, 77, 78, 92, 100, 110, 119, 135, 148, 235, 204
Berlin, Milton, 10, 33, 34, 40, 55, 56, 63, 70, 72, 110, 204, 239, 248, 249, 260
Bernardine, 237

Bernstein, Leonard, 71, 171–172, 173, 207
Bernstein, Chuck, 11
Berry, Ken, 11
Besserer, Eugenie, 112, 113, 114
Best, Willie, 27
Best Foot Forward, 42, 105, 145
Best Things in Life Are Free, The, 107
Betty Hutton Show, The, (TV show), 225
Beware!, 231
Beymer, Richard, 236
Big Beat, The, 10
Big Boy, 83
Big Broadcast of 1937, 179
Big Pond, The, 35
Bil Baird Marionettes, 214
Bill Haley and the Comets, 11
Billy Rose's Jumbo, 11
Bird, Brad, 53
Birth of the Blues, 83
Bitter Sweet, 190
Bizet, George, 37
Bjork, 157
Black, Karen, 159
Black and Tan, 231
Black Cauldron, The, 22
Black Swan Records, 33
Blackburn Twins, 134
Blackton, Jay, 164
Blaine, Vivian, 177, 227
Blake, Eubie, 28
Blane, Ralph, 42, 104, 143, 144, 145
Blane, Susan, 187
Bledsoe, Jules, 201
Blen, Corbin, 109
Blondell, Joan, 58, 87
Bloomer Girl, 271
Blore, Eric, 248
Blue, Ben, 41
Blue Bird, The, 227, 260
Blue Hawaii, 252
Blue Skies, 19, 239, 240, 260
Bluth, Don, 15
Blyth, Ann, 191
Boasberg, Al, 161
Bob and Carol and Ted and Alice, 175
Bogart, Humphrey, 58
Boles, John, 119
Bolger, Ray, 104, 105, 177, 270
Boone, Pat, 17, 153, 186, 241
Born to Dance, 26–27, 122
Boswell, Connee, 17
Bounce, 198
Boy Friend, The, 40

Boy Scouts of America, 35
Boyd, William, 212
Boys from Syracuse, The, 134, 145
Bracken, Eddie, 15
Brando, Marlon, 43
Braselle, Keefe, 187
Brazzi, Rossano, 110
Breathless, 96
Brecher, Irving, 105, 142–143
Breen, Joseph I., 25
Bremer, Lucille, 5
Brendel, El, 236
Brice, Fanny, 42, 64, 177
Bricusse, Leslie, 15, 85, 104, 105, 210
Bridges, Jeff, 259
Brigadoon, 6, 99, 156
Bright Eyes, 111, 183, 237
Briley, Alex, 218
Bring Back Birdie, 206
Brisson, Frederick, 47
Bristolphone, 113
Broadbent, Jim, 149
Broderick, Helen, 230, 246, 248
Broderick, Matthew, 177
Bronze Buckaroo, The, 231
Brooks, Mel, 35, 161
Brown, Ada, 231
Brown, Joe E., 202
Brown, Les, 178
Brown, Lew, 82, 83, 237
Brown, Nacio Herb, 28, 29, 82, 105, 161, 205
Bruce, Virginia, 93
Bubbles, John, 33
Buchanan, Jack, 19
Back Privates, 80
Buddy Holly Story, The, 187
Buell, Jed, 231
Buffalo Bills, 152
Bullock, Walter, 111
Burke, Billie, 268
Burke, Johnny, 119, 85, 226, 227
Burns, George, 26, 41, 48, 49, 113, 184, 255
Burton, Richard, 27, 85, 177
Burton, Tim, 102, 260, 268
Busey, Gary, 159

Butch Cassidy and the Sundance Kid, 125
Butler, David, 237
Butterworth, Charles, 133
Buttons, Red, 15
By Jupiter, 105, 203
By the Light of the Silvery Moon, 107, 237
Bye Bye Birdie, 17, 20, 21, 87, 199
Byrnes, Edd, 86

Cabaret, 36–31, 40
Cabin in the Sky, 32–33, 144, 236, 231
Caesar, Sid, 86
Cagney, James, 45, 58, 64, 110, 130, 131, 156, 272, 273–274
Cahn, Sammy, 71, 158, 173, 177, 185, 226
Caine, Michael, 104
Calamity Jane, 34–35, 103, 177, 237
Call Me Madam, 177, 199, 227, 203
Callow, Simon, 94
Calloway, Cab, 42, 179, 229, 236, 234
Camelot, 27, 156, 177
Campfire Girls of America, 25
Can-Can, 122, 173, 107, 227
Can't Help Singing, 131, 136, 137, 202, 206, 220, 278
Can't Stop the Music, 192, 218
Canova, Judy, 259
Cantor, Eddie, 49, 64, 113, 177, 237, 245, 204, 265, 269
Cantor's Son, The, 230
Capitol Records, 223, 224
Capp, Al, 126
Captain January, 83, 237
Carefree, 239
Carillo, Leo, 133, 210
Carlisle, Kitty, 58, 80, 161
Carmen Jones, 36–37
Carolina Blues, 80
Caron, Leslie, 12, 13, 14, 73, 74, 75
Carousel, 116, 153, 166, 107, 176
Carr, Charmian, 214
Carradine, Keith, 158, 159
Carroll, Diahann, 37, 125
Carter, Benny, 42, 229
Carter, June, 187, 259
Cartwright, Angela, 214
Caruso, Enrico, 88, 89
Casablanca, 143
Caselotti, Adriana, 6, 22, 208
Cash, Johnny, 187, 259
Cassidy, David, 153

Cassidy, Jack, 153
Cassidy, Patrick, 153
Cassidy, Shaun, 153
Castelnuovo, Nino, 157
Castle, Irene, 249
Castle, Nick, 233
Castle, Vernon, 249
Castro, Fidel, 278
Catch Us If You Can, 97
Catlett, Walter, 225
Cats Don't Dance, 15
Catskills Honeymoon, 250
Ceballos, Larry, 110
Centennial Summer, 72, 199
Chakiris, George, 71, 72, 157, 257, 258
Champion, Gower, 51, 80, 92, 161, 202
Champion, Marge, 6, 51, 80, 92, 161, 202, 210
Chandler, Jeff, 51
Change of Habit, A, 253
Channing, Carol, 15, 71, 177
Channing, Stockard, 86, 87
Chansons d'Amour, Les, 157
Chaplin, Geraldine, 159
Chaplin, Saul, 14, 43, 55, 121, 127, 173, 216, 216, 232, 233, 234
Charisse, Cyd, 13, 19, 43, 54, 61, 10, 133, 248, 249, 273
Charnin, Martin, 217
Chase, Duane, 214
Chesterfields, 11
Chevalier, Maurice, 23, 35, 72, 132, 133, 146, 147, 174, 175
Chicago, 8, 9, 27, 38–40, 166, 193
Chitty Chitty Bang Bang, 149
Chopin, Frédéric, 274
Chorus Line, A, 28
Christie, Julie, 159
Christmas Carol, A, 104
Christmas Carol, the Movie, A, 104
Churchill, Sarah, 193
Churchill, Frank, 53
Cinderella, 22, 177
Cinephone, 113
Clair, René, 157
Clark, Ken, 110
Clark, Petula, 27, 84, 85
Clay, Andrew Dice, 187
Cleary, Michael, 53
Cleopatra, 133
Cline, Patsy, 259
Clooney, Rosemary, 26c, 261, 262, 273
Clute, Chester, 273
Coal Miner's Daughter, 259
Coburn, James, 151

Cocoanuts, 161
Cocoon, 47
Cohan, George M., 45, 64, 104, 272, 275
Cohn, Nic, 192
Gilbert, Claudette, 80
Cole, Jack, 72, 177
Cole, Nat King, 42
Coleman, Cedric, 159
Coleman, Monique, 109
Colette, 73
Colgate Comedy Hour, 129
College Coach, 58
College Rhythm, 254
College Swing, 41–42, 233
Collins, Joan, 27
Colonna, Jerry, 185
Columbia Pictures, 25, 56, 71, 80, 114, 173, 277
Columbia Records, 33
Comden, Betty, 18, 71, 81, 82, 105, 171, 172, 173, 265, 266, 267
Como, Perry, 31, 128, 134, 273
Conaway, Jeff, 87
Coney Island, 76, 227, 244
Conn, Didi, 87
Connecticut Yankee, A, 263
Connelly, Bobby, 27
Coogan, Jackie, 41
Cook, Barbara, 153
Cooper, Gladys, 138
Copacabana, 66, 218
Corey, Jill, 17
Corman, Roger, 20
Conreed, 53
Cosmopolitan Productions, 227
Council of the Methodist Episcopal Church, 25
Country Girl, The, 110
Court Jester, The, 44–45, 120
Cover Girl, 47, 173, 177, 199
Coward, Noel, 147, 222
Cowboy from Brooklyn, The, 111
Coyne, Jeanne, 122
Crain, Jeanne, 226, 227
Crawford, Joan, 43, 162, 191
Crazy Gang, 96
Crazy Heart, 259
Cristiani, Quirino, 208
Crosby, Bing, 72, 96, 119, 175, 184, 185, 224, 225, 225, 237, 239, 254, 26c, 261, 262, 263, 265, 266, 267
Crosby, Bob, 178
Cry for Us All, 121
Cukor, George, 154, 155, 174, 220, 221, 209
Cummings, Irving, 83
Cummings, Jack, 54, 120, 121, 122, 131, 107, 273
Curry, Tim, 186, 94
Curtains, 146
Curtiz, Michael, 273

Joanne Gilbert, Rosemary Clooney, and Pat Crowley of Red Garters.

A Night at the Opera by Al Hirschfeld.

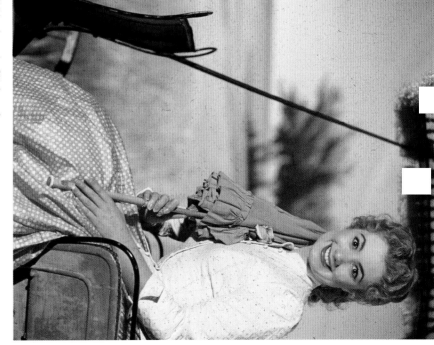

Shirley Jones in *Oklahoma!*

D'Angelo, Beverly, 259
DaCosta, Morton, 152
Daddy Long Legs, 75
Dahl, Arlene, 273
Dahl, Roald, 207
Dale, Grover, 157
Dale, Jim, 140
Dale, Virginia, 259
Dallas (TV show), 35
Dames, 59, 135, 199
Damn Yankees, 9, 46–47, 53, 177
Damone, Vic, 72, 80, 128, 273
Damsel in Distress, A, 26, 48–49, 239, 240
Dancers in the Dark, 157
Dancing Lady, 162, 249
Dandridge, Dorothy, 36, 49, 125, 235
Dangerous When Wet, 50–51
Danova, Cesare, 251
Darby, Ken, 115
Darin, Bobby, 17, 87, 128
Darion, Joe, 15
Dean, Eddie, 44
Dean, James, 164
Date with Judy, A, 108
Daughter of Rosie O'Grady, The, 107
Dave Clark Five, 97
Davidson, John, 139
Davis, Bette, 27
Davis, Johnny "Scat," 110
Davis, Sammy, Jr., 17, 42
Dawn, Allan, 13
Day, Doris, **34, 35, 47, 103, 130, 131, 139, 175, 176,** 177, 178, 237
Day, Morris, 187
Day at the Races, A, 161, 199
De Haviland, Olivia, 27
De Paul, Gene, 126
Death of a Gunfighter, 230
DeCamp, Rosemary, **274**
DeForest, Lee, 112
DeHaven, Gloria, 237
Delicious, 237
De-Lovely, 151
DeLuise, Dom, 151
DeMax, Ernest, 274
DeMille, Cecil B., **212**
Demoiselles de Rochefort, Les, 157
Deneuve, Catherine, 157
Desert Song, The, 107
Design for Living, 47, 219
Destry Rides Again, 131
DeSylva, B. G., 54, 82, **83,** 235, 237
Deutsch, Adolph, 164
Diamond, Neil, 76
Diamond Lil, 25
Dickens, Charles, 219
Dietrich, Marlene, 31, 92, 131

Dietz, Howard, 17, **19,** 37, 43, 72, 144, 265
Dimples, 237
Dirty Dancing, 45
Disney, Lillian, 210
Disney, Walt, 15, 22, 139, 140, 180–181, 208–210, 211
Disney Corporation, 22–23
Disneyland, 211
Do I Love Me?, 179
Doctor Dolittle, 85, 194, 195
Dodd, Jimmie, 56
Dolly Sisters, The, 244
Don't Knock the Rock, 11
Donat, Robert, 84
Donen, Stanley, 13, 47, 61, 62, 74, 105, 122, 153
Doran, Mary, 28
Doris Day Show, The, 178
Dorsey, Tommy, 76, 77, 179
Douglas, Stephen, 47
Down Argentine Way, 69, 245
Down from the Mountain, 259
Down to Earth, 199, 219
Dr. Jekyll and Mr. Hyde, 133
Dr. Seuss, 103, 207
Drake, Dona, 184
Drake, Tom, 143
Drasin, Tamara, 130
Dreamgirls, 39
Drescher, Fran, 11, 193
Dresser, Louise, 227
Dresser, Paul, 274
Drier Moosie, 11
DuBarry Was a Lady, 70, 77, 199, 240
Dubin, Al, 27, 38, 78, 79, 101, 255
Duchess of Idaho, 51, 230
Duck Soup, 160, 184
Duke, Vernon, 61
Duke Ellington and His Orchestra, 80, 179
Duke is Tops, The, 230, 231
Dumbo, 22, 23, **52–53**
Dumbo (animated character), **52–53**
Dunham, Katherine, 224, 229
Dunne, Irene, **200, 201, 203,** 220
Durante, Jimmy, 48
Durbin, Deanna, 21, 89, 131, **136, 137,** 108, 201

Eadie Was a Lady, 80
Earl Carroll Vanities, 226
Earl Carroll's Vanities of 1938, 33
Easter Parade, 19, **54–59,** 77, 205, 249
Eastwood, Clint, 30, 230
Easy to Love, 77
Ebb, Fred, 9, 31, **38, 40, 158**
Ebert, Roger, 243
Ebsen, Buddy, 165, 209
Ed Sullivan Show, The, 217

Eddie Cantor Story, The, 187
Eddings, Ruth, **205**
Eddy, Nelson, 21, 35, 59, 133, 190, 191, 248
Edens, Roger, 42, 54, 60, **69,** 68, 71, 82, 103, **104,** 143, 171, 172, 202, 207, 220, 270, 273
Edison, Thomas, 211
Edison Company, 204
Educational Pictures, 183
Edward Scissorhands, 103
Edwards, Blake, 40
Edwards, Cliff, 22
Efron, Zac, 17, **168, 169**
Eight Crazy Nights, 15
8 Mile, 187
El Cid, 68
Elfman, Danny, 103
Ellington, Duke, 33, 179, 294
Ellstein, Abraham, 250
Elmer Gantry, 75, 153
Eminem, 187
Etting, Ruth, 113, 130, 131, 245
Evans, Dale, 44, 243
Evans, Linda, **21**
Evans, Ray, 226
Evans, Robert, 82
Evans and Evans, 48
Evergreen, 157, 160
Every Sunday, 137, 223
Everybody Sings, 95
Everything I Have is Yours, 80

Fabian, 87, 128
Fabray, Nanette, 19, 51
Fade In–Fade Out, 109, 225
Fain, Sammy, 22, **34**
Fairbanks, Douglas, **203**
Falana, Lola, 125
Fanny, 71
Fantasia, 23, 52, 137
Farmer Takes a Wife, The, 199
Farnum, Dustin, 212
Farrar, John, 87
Farrell, Charles, 83, **236,** 237
Fashions of 1934, 68
Father of the Bride, 44
Fawcett, Farrah, 21
Faye, Alice, 49, 51, 71, 78, 101, **183,** 227, 234, 244, **245,** 246
Federation of Women's Clubs, 25
Fejos, Paul, 30
Felix, Seymour, 77, 92
Felker, Clay, 192
Fellini, Federico, 8
Felton, Verna, 22
Ferber, Edna, 201
Ferrer, José, 89, 273
Fetchit, Stepin, 91
Feuer, Cy, 31
Feuer, Ted, 71
Fiddler on the Roof, 177
Fields, Dorothy, 34, 31, **38,** 40, 45, 47, 92, 227, 237
Fields, Grace, 157, 169

Fields, Herbert, 34
Fields, W. C., 25, 175, 184, 209
Fiesta, 51
Finch, Peter, 27
Finding Nemo, 53
Fine, Sylvia, 45
Finian's Rainbow, 17, 43, 177, 197, 240
Finkelhoff, Fred, 42
Finnegan, Bill, 255
Finney, Albert, 84, 194, 195
First Traveling Saleslady, The, 177
Fitzgerald, Ella, 15
Five Pennies, The, 45
Flaherty, Stephen, 15
Flaming Star, 252
Fleischer Studios, 15
Fleming, Victor, 91, 209, **271**
Fletcher, Robert, 213
Flirtation Walk, 58, 59
Flower Drum Song, The, 13, 166, 199, 214
Flowers and Trees, 210
Flying Colors, 19
Flying Down to Rio, 240, 249
Flying High, 83
Flynn, Errol, 27
Folies Bergère, 76
Follies, 55
Follow That Dream, 252
Follow the Boys, 225
Follow the Fleet, 238, 277
Follow Thru, 27, 83
Fonda, Jane, 266
Fontaine, Joan, 26, **49, 239,** 248, 277
Footlight Parade, 35, 58, 59, 67, 110, 272
For the Boys, 188
For the Love of Mary, 137
Foran, Dick, 44
Forbes, Bryan, 97
Ford, John, 213
Forrest, George, 204
Forrest, Helen, 42
Forster, Susanna, 80
Forty Little Mothers, 29
42nd Street, 38, 45, 57–59, 110, 111, 119, 205, 275
Fosse, Bob, 8, 31, 38, 40, 45, 47, 92, 121, **122,** 199

G.I. Blues, 252
G.I. Joe, 226
Gaal, Franceska, 131
Gable, Clark, 26, **162,** 238
Cage, Ben, 42
Gamboa, Michael, 194
Gang's All Here, The, 67–68, 72, 183, 205
Gannon, Kim, 226
Garbo, Greta, 133, 147
Gardella, Tess, 201
Gardner, Ava, 202, 230, 206
Garland, Judy, 15, 17, 34, 43, 56–51, 54, 55, 63, **70, 77, 82,** 99, 103, **104, 105,** 127, 131, 137, 142, **143, 144, 145,** 108, 220, 221, 222, 225, 235, 242, **253,** 257, 249, 268, **269,** 270, 271, 273, 275
Garner, Errol, 42
Garrett, Betty, 34, 43, 172, **173,** 273
Garrett, Sam, 27
Garrick Gaieties, The, 194
Carson, Greer, 85, 139
Gay Desperado, The, 133
Gay Divorcee, 15, 323, 239
Gay Purr-ee, 95
Gaynor, Janet, 20, 83, 221, 227, **236,** 237
Gaynor, Mitzi, 110, 220
Gear, Jean, 37
Gentlemen Prefer Blondes, 70–72, 117, 123, 241
George, Florence, 41
George White's 1935 Scandals, 183
Gere, Richard, **38, 39**
Gershwin, George, 28, **49,** 60–63, 220, 249, **271**
Gershwin, Ira, 14, 43, 45, 49, 60, 70, 79, 143, 205, 213, 220, 222, 248, 249, 271, 278
Geslin, Leonard, 66–03, 95, 248
Geslie, Richard, 249, 274

Fox, Eddie, Jr., 170, **178**
Fozzie Bear (puppet), 150, **151**
Francis, Anne, 66

Hit the Deck, 26, 131, 168, 199
Hoctor, Harriet, **92**
Hoffenstein, Samuel, 132
Hodo, David, 218
Hold Everything, 33
Hold On!, 97
Hold That Good, 80
Hold That Ghost, 234
Holiday, Billie, 42, 124, 125
Holiday Inn, 239, 266
Hollander, Frederick, 41
Holliday, Judy, 71, 177, **207**
Holloway, Sterling, **141**, **225**
Hollywood Canteen, 213, 225
Hollywood Hotel, 58, 110–111
Hollywood Music Box Revue, 28, 50
Hollywood Revue of 1929, 20, 34, 115, 275
Holman, Libbie, 245
Home on the Range, 23
Honolulu, 122
Hooray for Love, 80, 234
Hope, Bob, **41**, **42**, **43**, 44, 45, 49, 51, 72, 96, 110, 154, 175, **184**, **185**, 233
Horne, Lena, **33**, **63**, 202, 220, **228**, **229**, **230**, 273
Horse Feathers, 106
Horton, Edward Everett, **69**, **248**
Horton Hears a Who, 23
Hot Chal, 27
Hot Heiress, The, 132, 134
How I Won the War, 97
How to Succeed in Business Without Really Trying, 43
Howard, Eugene, 113
Howard, Ron, 153
Howard, Willie, 113
Hudgens, Vanessa, 17, **108**, **109**
Hudson, Rock, 175, 178
Hughes, Glenn, 218
Hullabaloo, 20
Humberstone, H. Bruce, **102**
Hunchback of Notre Dame, The, 23
Hunger, The, 28
Hunter, Tab, **46**, **47**
Hustle and Flow, 159
Huston, John, 148, 218
Huston, Walter, 42, **272**, **274**
Hutton, Betty, 34, 35, **71**, **83**, 107, **224**, **225**, 232
Hutton, Marion, 178
Hyperion Studios, 209

I Could Go on Singing, 223, 271
I Dood It!, 27
I Love Melvin, 206
I Married an Angel, 77
I Remember Mama, 203
I'd Rather Be Right, 272
I'll Cry Tomorrow, 130
I'll Get By, 245
I'll See You in My Dreams, 274
I'm No Angel, 45
Ice Age, 33
Idiot's Delight, 26
If I Had My Way, 237
In Old Chicago, 183, 244
In Old Santa Fe, 273
Independent Theater Owners of America, 239
Inherit the Wind, 13
Innocents of Paris, 72, 111
Interrupted Melody, 89
Invitation to the Dance, 13, 121
Irene, 198
Irma la Douce, 71
Is Everybody Happy?, 234
Isherwood, Charles, 30, 31
It Happened at the World's Fair, 252
It's a Great Feeling, 199, 237
It's Always Fair Weather, 19, 81, 199, 207
Iturbi, José, 131, 137
Ivanovici, Ion, 173

Jackson, Calvin, 17
Jackson, Felix, 131
Jacobs, Arthur, 85
Jagger, Mick, 187
Jailhouse Rock, 148
James, Harry, **179**
Jazz Singer, The, 7, 19, 28, 29, 45, 70, 112–114, 125, 237, 250
Jean Hersholt Humanitarian Award, 85
Jean, Gloria, 201, 202, 206
Jeffrey, Herbert. See Jeffries, Herb
Jeffries, Herb, 14, 231
Jekyll and Hyde, 85
Jenkins, Allan, **110**
Jerome, M. K., 227
Jerry (animated character), **50**
Jersey Boys, 204
Jessel, George, 14
Jewison, Norman, 177
Jiminy Cricket (animated character), **181**
Joan of Ozark, 259
Johns, Glynis, **44**, 140
Johnson, Chubby, 35
Johnson, Hall, 32–33
Johnson, James P., 28
Johnson, Van, 241
Johnston, Johnny, 225
Jolson, Al, 19, 20, 49, 59, 64, **112**, **113**, **114**, 125, 173, 237, 260, 261
Jolson Sings Again, 114
Jolson Story, The, 64, 114, 125, 187
Jones, Allan, 58, 89, **161**, **200**, 201, 232

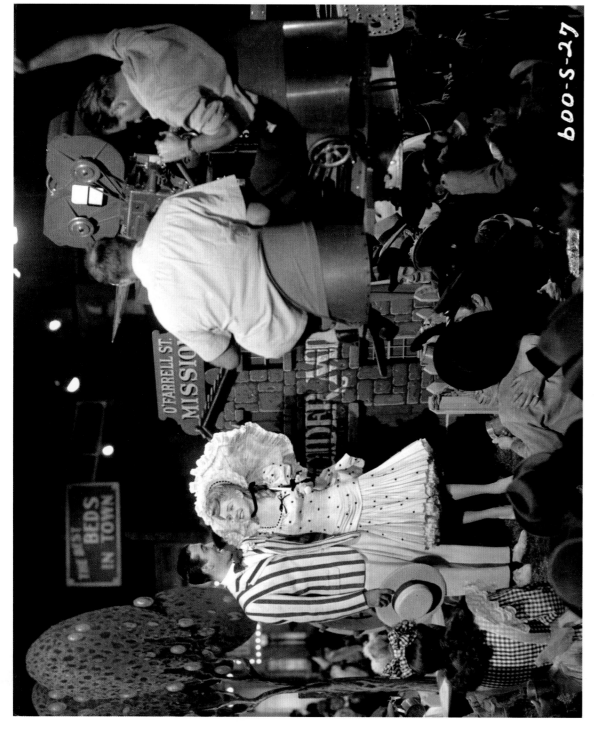

John Payne and Alice Faye filming *Hello Frisco, Hello*.

Gershwin, Leonore, 143
Gertie the Dinosaur, 208, 209
Gertrude Hoffman Girls, 205
Gibb, Barry, 87, 192
Gibb, Maurice, 193
Gibson, Henry, 158, **159**
Gigi, 54, 55, 73–75, 77, 144, 154, 156, 175
Gilda, 109, 277
Gilford, Jack, 177
Gimbel, Norman, 158
Gingold, Hermione, **74**
Girl Crazy, 63, 76–77, 249
Girl in the Pink Tights, The, 72
Girl Most Likely, 145
Girls, Les, 173, 199
Give a Girl a Break, 199
Glass Slipper, The, 75
Glee (TV show), 17, 100
Glenn, Roy, 37
Glenn Miller Orchestra, 235, 255
Go, Johnny, Go, 11
Go Into Your Dance, 59, 199
Go West Young Man, 17
God Bless You, Mr. Rosewater, 23
Goddard, Jean-Luc, 47
Goddard, Paulette, 135, **224**, **225**, 239, 246
Goffin, Gerry, 158
Going My Way, 110
Going Places, 42, 58, 111, 199
Gold Diggers in Paris, **100**
Gold Diggers of 1933, 58, 59, 78–79, 135, 249
Gold Diggers of 1935, 111, 135, 199
Gold Diggers of 1937, 111, 135
Gold Rush, 145
Goldberg, Whoopi, 194
Golden Gate Quartet, 225
Goldfinger, 85
Goldwyn, Samuel, 28, 105, 135, 203, 204, 260
Gombell, Minna, **91**
Gone with the Wind, 33, 143, 201, 209
Good News, 42, 77, 81–83, 207, 237
Good Vibrations, 19
Goodbye Mr. Chips, 27, 84–85, 194, 195
Gordon, Anita, 36–37
Goodman, Benny, 33, **179**
Gordon, Mack, 27, 42, 79, 232, 254, **255**
Gorney, Jay, 219

Gorney, Karen Lynn, **193**
Gould, Dave, 246, 249
Gould, Elliott, 151, 159
Goulet, Robert, 15–35, 271
Grabel, Lucas, **109**
Grable, Betty, **4**, 70, **102**, 135, 227, 235, 246, **244**, **245**, **246**
Grahame, Gloria, 107
Grant, Cary, **45**, 150, 272
Grant, Kirby, 141
Gravet, Fernand, **91**
Gray, Dolores, 34
Gray, Harry, 95
Gray, Margery, 15
Gray, Timothy, 145
Grayson, Kathryn, 89, **120**, **121**, **122**, 136, 202, 273
Grease, 86–87, 186, 193
Grease 2, 87, 218
Great Caruso, The, 88–89, 131
Great Mouse Detective, The, 23
Great Train Robbery, The, 141, 212
Great Victor Herbert, The, 89
Great Waltz, The, 90–91, 204, 229
Great Ziegfeld, The, 65, 92–93
Green, Adolph, 14, 18, 63, 71, 81, 82, 105, 171, 174, 173, **205**, **206**, **207**
Green, Johnny, 14, 105
Green, Joseph, 250
Green Grows the Lilacs, 129
Greenwich Village, 244
Greenwood, Charlotte, **69**
Grey, Joel, **30**, **31**, 177
Grier, Jimmie, 237
Griffith, Robert E., 47
Guest, Christopher, **242**, **243**
Guide for the Married Man, A, 13
Guys and Dolls, 43, 43, 107
Gypsy, 176

Hackett, Buddy, **153**
Hagen, Jean, 115–116
Hairspray, 17, 39, 193
Haley, Jack, **182**, **183**, 237, 270
Half a Sixpence, 69
Hall, Charles, 59
Hall, Juanita, 116

Hallelujah!, 33, 94–95, 231
Hallelujah, I'm a Bum, 134, 275
Hamilton, Margaret, **270**
Hammer, Alvin, **207**
Hammerstein, Oscar, II, 37, 116, 117, 133, 164,
166, 201, **217**, 227, 278
Hammond, Nicholas, **214**
Hampton, Lionel, **179**
Handel, 274
Handel, George Frideric, 274
Haney, Carol, 61, 121, **122**, 176, **178**
Hanna-Barbera, 15, 181
Hans Christian Andersen, 13, 45
Happiest Millionaire, The, 85, 139, 177, 218
Harbach, Otto, 278
Harburg, E. Y., 15, 33, 43, 136, 137, 202, 219, 226,
269, 271, 278
Hard Days Night, A, 96–98, 108
Hardy, Oliver, 247
Hargitay, Mickey, 24
Harkrider, John, 202
Harlem on the Prairies, 231
Harline, Leigh, 53, 181
Harling, W. Frank, 72
Harnick, Sheldon, 15
Harris, Barbara, **159**
Harrison, George, **96**, **97**
Harrison, Rex, 27, 84, **85**, 106, 154, **155**, **156**, 177
Harry James and His Music Makers, **179**
Harry James Orchestra, 42, 179
Harryhausen, Ray, 162
Hart, Lorenz, **134**, 147, 166, 217
Hart, Moss, 220
Hart, William S., 212
Harvey, Lillian, 83
Harvey Girls, The, 55, 77, 82, 103–105
Haver, Phyllis, 46
Haver, Ronald, 221
Hawkins, Screamin' Jay, **11**
Hayes, Billie, 120, 127
Haymes, Dick, 227
Haynes, Daniel L., **94**, **95**
Hays, Will, 35
Hays Code, 25, 71, 174
Hays Office, 7
Hayward, Susan, 130

Hayworth, Rita, **101**, 173, **210**, 239, 240, 248,
249, 203, **276**, **277**, **278**
Hazel Flagg, 129
Hazen, Joe, 252
Healy, Ted, **110**
Heart's in Dixie, 94
Heat's On, The, 25
Hedwig and the Angry Inch, 106–107
Heindorf, Ray, 35–47, 227, 275
Held, Anna, 24
Held, John, 91
Hello, Dolly!, 13, 42, 66, 84, 152, 168, 175,
210, 249
Hello Frisco, Hello, **101**, 183, 244
Hellz-a-poppin', 247
Help!, 97
Henderson, Florence, 219
Henderson, Ray, 82, **83**, 237
Henie, Sonja, **6**, 51, **234**, **235**
Henson, Jim, 150
Hepburn, Audrey, 36, **60**, **61**, **62**, **63**, 117, **154**,
155, **156**, 177
Hepburn, Katharine, 49, 247
Herbert, Hugh, **91**
Hercules, 23
Here Come the Waves, 226
Herman, Jerry, 210
Herman's Hermits, 97, 157
Heronymous Merkin, 27
Heyman, Edward, 226
Hi-De-Ho, 231
High Noon, 53
High School Hero, 237
High School Musical, 17, **108**
High School Musical 3: Senior Year, 108–109
High Society, 119, 199
High Spirits, 45
High, Wide and Handsome, 133, 203
Hightower, Lewis, 210
Hilliard, Bob, 35
Hilton, James, 84
Hinwood, Peter, **187**
Hirschhorn, Clive, 233
Hirschhorn, Joel, 140
His Wife's Lover, 250
Hit Parade, 103
Hit Parade of 1941, 80

Jones, Buck, 231
Jones, Chuck, 15
Jones, Shirley, 75, **152, 153**, 107, 210
Joplin, Janis, 189
Jourdan, Louis, 74
Journey Back to Oz, 268
Joy of Living, 199, 203
Jubilee, 77
Jubilee Singers, 201
Judgment at Nuremberg, 223
Jumbo, 131, 177, 199
June, Ray, 22, 40
Jungle Book, The, 22, 40
Junkin, John, 48
Juno, 121
Jupiter's Darling, 51, **131**, 199
Jurmann, Walter, 53
Just Imagine, 83, 237

Kahal, Irving, 35
Kahn, Gus, 274
Kahn, Madeline, 151
Kahn, Kitty, 42
Kahnan, Bert, 42
Kander, John, 9, 31, 38, 46, 58
Kaper, Bronislau, 53
Kasha, Al, 140
Kathleen, 183
Kaufman, George S., 101
Kaye, Carol, 151
Kaye, Danny, **44, 45, 200, 201, 202, 203**
Kaye, Stubby, **127**
Keaton, Buster, 21
Keel, Howard, **34, 35, 39, 51, 121, 122, 191, 196, 198, 202**, 273
Keeler, Ruby, 45, 49, 57, 59, 78, 79, 110, 205
Kellerman, Annette, 51, 100
Kelly, Fred, 182, 183
Kelly, Gene, 12, 13, 29, 30, 43, 45, 47, 50, 51, 54, 63, 74, 75, **102**, 105, 120, 122, 131, 157, **171, 172, 173**, 197, 199, **204, 205, 206**, 232, 233, 241, 203, 205
Kelly, Grace, 110
Kelton, Pert, 152
Kent, Walter, 226
Kermit the Frog (puppet), 150, 151, 194
Kern, Jerome, 72, 88, 133, 139, 157, 144, 160, 201, 273, 276
Kerr, Deborah, 6, **115, 117**
Kerr, John, 116
Kerr, Larry, 72
Kibbee, Guy, 58

Kid Boots, 205
Kid from Brooklyn, The, 199
Kid from Spain, The, 240, 205
Kid Millions, 135, 199
Kidd, Michael, 9, 120, 127, 199, 199, 197
Kidman, Nicole, **148, 149**
Kings of Burlesque, 80
King of Jazz, 34, 118–119, 170, 201, 204
Kings Row, 275
Kirsten, Dorothy, 88
Kismet, 35, 144, 204
Kiss and Make Up, 254
Kiss and Make Up, 254
Kiss Me Kate, 35, 68, 70–71, 120–122, 173, 202, 240
Kiss of the Spider Women, The, 40
Kitty Foyle, 249
Klein, Anne, 82
Kleinsinger, George, 15
Kleiser, Randal, 87
Kline, Kevin, 274
Knight, Hilary, 82
Koehler, Ted, 80, 111, 227, 233, 271
Konan, Jack, 149
Korjus, Miliza, 90, 91
Kostel, Irwin, 140
Kraft Music Hall (TV show), 31
Kristofferson, Kris, 85, 221
Kyser, Kay, 80, 179, 237

Laura, 133
Laurel, Stan, 247
Laurel and Hardy, 119, 161, 247
Laurenz, Arthur, 82
Laurie, Joe, 17
Lawford, Peter, 51, 81, 82, 83, 198, 241
Lawrence, Gertrude, 140, 217
Legrand, Michel, 150
Leguizamo, John, 149
Lehár, Franz, 240
Lehman, Ernest, 201
Leigh, Janet, 216
Leigh, Vivien, 201
Lemmon, Jack, 106, 125, 179
Lenbeck, Harvey, 21
Leno, Jay, 11
Leonard, Robert Z., 93, 191
Lerner, Alan Jay, 36, 43, 73, 75, 105, 127, 150, 160, 204, 215, 219
Lerner and Loewe, 43, 70, 73, 150, 160, 204, 215, 219
LeRoy, Mervyn, 203, 260–270
Leslie, Joan, 249, 273
Lester, Mark, 170
Lester, Richard, 96, 97
Let's Face It, 45, 70
Let's Go Places, 249
Let's Make Love, 72, 199
Levant, Oscar, 14, 19
Levey, Ethel, 274
Lewis, Albert, 32
Lewis, Jerry, 45, **128, 129**, 184
Lewis, Ted, 234
Li'l Abner, 83, 120–126, 197, 241, 256
Life Begins at 8:40, 105, 271
Lili, 53
Lillian Russell, 244
Lillie, Beatrice, 145
Lincoln, Abby, 95
Lindsay, Howard, 216
Liszt, Franz, 274
Listomania, 274
Little Colonel, The, 237
Little Johnny Jones, 274
Little Mermaid, The, 22, 23
Little Miss Marker, 183
Little Nellie Kelly, 87
Little Night Music, A, 27, 218
Little Old New York, 244
Little Prince, The, 9, 150
Little Princess, 227
Little Show, The, 10
Littlest Rebel, The, 237
Living in a Big Way, 13
Living It Up, 128–129
Livingston, Jay, 226
Loesser, Frank, 15, 40, 43, 79, 80, 105, 152
Loewe, Frederick, 39, 55, 150, 215
Loft, Jeanette, 118
Logan, Josh, 71
Lombard, Carole, 49, 254
Lone Star Productions, 41
Look for the Silver Lining, 107
Look Ma, I'm Dancin', 145
Loos, Anita, 17
Lopez, Francis, 157
Lopez, Vincent, 225
Lost Horizon, 27, 85, 151, 218
Love, Bessie, 82, 28
Love Affair, 203
Love Finds Andy Hardy, 77
Love in the Afternoon, 175
Love Is a Many-Splendored Thing, 35
Love Letters, 226
Love Me or Leave Me, 130
Love Me Tender, 251
Love Me Tonight, 95, 132–134
Love Parade, The, 147, 91
Love Songs. See Chansons d'Amour, Les
Love Story, 189
Love Thy Neighbor, 185
Lovely to Look At, 240
Loy, Myrna, 247
Lubitsch, Ernst, 132, 146, 147, 174, 184, 191
Luft, Sid, 221
Lullaby of Broadway, 237
Lupino, Ida, 27, 49, 133
Lupus, Peter, 123
Lymon, Frankie, 10, 11
Lynde, Paul, 21
Lynn, Loretta, 257
Lynn, Gillian, 109

MacDonald, Garry, 149
La Verne, Lucille, 210
MacDonald, Jeanette, 21, 88–89, 93, **132, 133**, 137, 147, 174, 175, **190, 191**, 248
La Verne, Lucille, 210
La and I, The, 15, 15–17, 214, 217, 227
Kiss Me Kate...
MacGraw, Ali, 189
MacMurray, Fred, 165, 139
MacRae, Gordon, 104, 107
Mad About Music, 136–137
Maggie Flynn, 53

L-Shaped Room, 75
La Verne, Lucille, 210
La Verne, Lucille, 210
Lady and the Tramp, 52
Lady Be Good!, 249
Lady Gaga, 109
Lady in the Dark, 45, 71
Laemmle, Carl, 201, 202
Lahr, Bert, 42, 105, 177, 240, 209, 270
Lake, Veronica, 224, 245
Lamas, Fernando, 50, 51, 241
Lambert, Gavin, 55
Lamour, Dorothy, 184, 185, 224, 225
Lane, Burton, 15, 40, 43, 79, 150
Lane, Nathan, 177
Lane, Rosemary, 100, 111
Lang, Walter, 110, 227
Lange, Hope, 252
Langford, Frances, 80, 100, 183, 183
Langbury, Noel, 17
Lansbury, Angela, 22, 23, 104, 140, 177
Lantz, Walter, 119
Lanza, Mario, 88, 89, 191
LaPlante, Laura, 115, 119, 201, 202
Lasky, Jesse L., 88
Last Waltz, The, 187

Magidson, Herb, 33, 226
Maguire, Father Peter, 225
Mahler, Gustav, 274
Mahogany, 158
Mako, 177, 218–219
Mame, 177, 218–219
Mamma Mia, 10, 204
Man Who Knew Too Much, The, 139
Mancini, Henry, 55, 85, 127
Mankiewicz, Joseph, 42, 43
Mann, Marjorie, 164
Manilow, Barry, 66
Marianne, 88
Mariano, Luis, 157
Martin, George, Jr., 132, 254
Martin, Dean, **128, 129**, 184
Martin, Hugh, 17, 42, 43, 83, 103, 104, 105, 143
Martin, Mary, 34, 177, 185, 225
Martin, Steve, 51, 187, 199
Martin, Tony, 74, 273
Martini, Al, 128
Marvin, Lee, 36, 84, 219
Marx, Chico, 100, 101, 184
Marx, Groucho, 100, 101, 184, 218, 267
Marx, Gummo, 101
Marx, Harpo, 128, 160, 101, 184
Marx, Minnie, 101
Marx, Zeppo, 160
Marx Brothers, 45, 48, 53, 58, 89, 100–101, 175, 184
Mary Poppins, 138–140, 170, 177
Mask of Zorro, The, 149
Mason, James, 127, 222
Masser, Michael, 158
Mata Hari, 244
Mathau, Walter, 84
Matthews, Jessie, 49, 157
Maybe, 110
Mayer, Louis B., 12, 17, 28, 88, 89, 105, 122, 137, 223, 233, 209
Maynard, Ken, 141, 212, 213
Maytime, 190, 191
McAvoy, May, 113
McBroom, Amanda, 189
McCartney, Paul, 96, 97, 98
McCav, Winsor, 268
McCracken, Joan, 42, 82
McDaniel, Hattie, 27, 33, 201
McGowan, Jack, 17
McGregor, Ewan, 148, 149
McHugh, Jimmy, 80
McIntire, Tim, 10, 11
McKean, Michael, 242, 243
McKinney, Nina Mae, 94
Mayer, Louis B., ...
Mercer, Johnny, 28, 42, 79, 103, 104, 110, 111, 126, **127, 145, 224, 225**, 226, 271, 278
Merkel, Una, 57
Merman, Ethel, 34, 59, 71, 105, 176, 177, **227**, 249, 254, 255
Merrick, David, 59
Merrill, Bob, 65, 66, 71
Merry Andrew, 127
Merry Widow, The, 131, 146–147
Mexvall, John, 201
Metro-Goldwyn-Mayer. See MGM
Metropolis, 163
Metropolitan Opera, 89, 137, 191, 223
MGM, 12, 14, 17, 19, 26, 28, 29, 33–34, 43, 50, 51, 54–55, 61, 62, 64, 74, 77, 79, 81, 84, 88, 90, 92–94, 95, 103, 105, 110, 110, 120, 122, 126, 131, 133, 139, 157, 191, 192, 199, 249, 265, 268, 202, 223, 225, 228, 230, 232, 233, 252
Mickey's Christmas Carol, 22, 104
Midnight Court, 252
Mijan, John, 24
Milk and Honey, 121
Miller, Ann, 0, 55, 80, 121, 122, 172, 173, 273
Miller, Glenn, 234
Miller, Marilyn, 33, 94, 177
Miller, Mitch, 17
Million, Le, 157
Million Dollar Mermaid, 51, 68, 100
Million Dollar Quartet, 204
Miller, Bette, 188, 189
Mills, Hayley, 80
Mills Brothers, 80
Minnelli, Liza, 30, 31, 46, 82
Minnelli, Vincente, 12, 19, 33, 73, 74, 75, 77, 103

Mr. Quilp, 219
Mr. Rock and Roll, 11
Minnevitch, Borrah and His Harmonica Rascals, 80
Miranda, Carmen, 32, 67, 69, 216, 235
Miss Jumbo (animated character), 52
Mister, Gustav, 274
Mitchell, James, 273
Mitchell, John Cameron, 166, 167
Muppets, 150–151
Mix, Tom, 212, 231
Monaco, James V., 185
Monkees, The (TV show), 198
Monroe, Marilyn, 2, 21, 66, 70, 71, 72, 117, 123
Montalban, Ricardo, 51, 241
Monte Carlo, 72, 111, 133, 147
Montgomery, George, 42
Montgomery, Robert, 26
Moody, Ron, 168, 169
Moon Over Miami, 70, 227, 240
Moonlight and Pretzels, 50
Moore, Grace, 88, 89, 147
Moore, Mary Tyler, 253
Moore, Victor, 224, 239, 240
Moreno, Rita, 115, 117
Morey, Larry, 33
Morgan, Frank, 93
Morgan, Helen, 133, 177, 201, 202, 230, 245
Morse, Robert, 177
Moscona, Nicola, 89
Mostel, Zero, 177
Mother Wore Tights, 199, 227, 244
Moulin Rouge!, 39, 148–149, 249
Movietone, 113
Mr. Big Goes to Town, 15, 199

105, 42, 43, 44, 150
Mr. Quilp, 219
Murphy, George, 80, 122
Murman, F. W., 237
Murder, She Wrote (TV show), 198
Murder My Street, 58
Muppet Christmas Carol, The, 104
Muppet Movie, The, 150–151
Munshin, Jules, 171, 172, 173
Mussel Gustav, 274
My Favorite Blonde, 45
My Gal Sal, 242, 274
My Little Chickadee, 25
My Sister Eileen, 72, 121, 173, 199
My Sons, 250
My Blue Heaven, 244
My Cousin, 88
My Fair Lady, 36, 39, 160, 117, 140, 154–156, 159
Myra Breckenridge, 25
Nagel, Conrad, 115
Nancy Goes to Rio, 108
Nash, Ogden, 61, 250
Nashville, 158–159, 259
Nathan, George Jean, 24
National Council of Catholic Women, 25
National Council of Jewish Women, 25

White Christmas

Words and Music by
IRVI...

There's No Business Like Show Business

TOP: Charlie McCarthy and Edgar Bergen make their last screen appearance in The Muppet Movie.

BOTTOM: Irving Berlin.

National Film Registry, 243
NBC Radio, 129
Nelson, Gene, **166**
Neptune's Daughter, 51, 122
Neve, Suzanne, **195**
Never Say Die, 4
New York, New York, 40
Newley, Anthony, 85, 219
Newman, Alfred, 105
Newman, Joseph M., 147
Newman, Laraine, **11**
Newman, Randy, 15
Newton-John, Olivia, **86, 87**
Nice Girl?, 137
Nicholas, Fayard, **229, 235**
Nicholas, Harold, **229, 235**
Nicholas Brothers, 228–229, 235
Nichols, Barbara, **177, 178**
Night and Day, 18, 218, 272
Night They Raided Minsky's, The, 199
Night at the Opera, A, 53, 58, 8c, 106–161, 184
Nightmare Before Christmas, The, 162–163
Nine, 39, 166, 219
Ninotchka, 47
Nixon, Marni, 6, 115, 116, **117**
No, No, Nanette, 59, 205
No Minor Chords (book), 17
No Strings, 217
Nob Hill, 244
Nolan, Bob, **212, 213**
Norman, Pierre, 35
North, Sheree, 177
Not with My Wife You Don't, 45
Nothing Sacred, 129
Novotna, Jarmila, 89
Noyes, Betty, 116
Nutty Professor, The, 129
Nuyen, France, 241

O Brother, Where Art Thou?, 259
O'Brien, Margaret, 141, **143, 144**
O'Brien, Richard, **186**
O'Connor, Donald, 49, 55, 8c, 127, 202, **206**, 260, 263
O'Neill, Eugene, 133
O'Shea, Jack, **213**
O'Sullivan, Maureen, 247
O'Toole, Peter, 27, **84, 85**
Oakes, Bill, 192
Oakie, Jack, **245**
Oders, Clifford, 252
Of Thee I Sing, 127
Ogle, Charles, 194
Oklahoma!, 43, 103, 105, 110, 129, 137, 153, 164–167
Oliver!, 84, 168–170, 177, 194, 195, 218
Oliver and Company, 22
Olivetti, Eva, 15, 201
Olivier, Laurence, 121
Olsen and Johnson, 247
On a Clear Day You Can See Forever, 66, 144, 150, 199
On an Island with You, 51
On Golden Pond, 183
On Moonlight Bay, 107
On the Avenue, 19, 58
On the Riviera, 76
On the Town, 13, 47, 55, 68, 71, 74, 155, 171–174, 207, 263
On with the Show, 29, 33
On Your Toes, 13, 105
Once, 107, 157
One Hundred and One Dalmatians, 199
One and Only, Genuine, Original Family Band, The, 139, 140, 218
One Hour with You, 111, 174–175
One Hundred Men and a Girl, 89, 137
Opposite Sex, The, 85
Orbach, Jerry, 22, 23, 38
Orchestra Wives, 199, 255
Ornadel, Cyril, 85
Orry-Kelly, 123
Osher, Moyshe, 250
Ostrum, Peter, 267
Other Side of the Mountain, The, 157
Out of This World, 121
Outlaw, The, 213
Over Here!, 193
Owen, Alun, 96, 97

Pagan Love Song, 51
Page, Anita, **28**
Page, Bradley, **213**
Page, Dorothy, 141
Page, Janis, 47, 176, **178**
Pajama Game, The, 9, 46, 47, 62, 153, 176–178, 256
Pal Joey, 101, 277
Pallette, Eugene, **40, 69**
Palmer, Peter, **126, 127**
Palmy Days, 205
Pan, Hermes, 49, **101**, 235, **246**, 249, 278
Panama, Norman, 45, 126, 127
Panama Hattie, 70, 225, 230, 263
Papa's Delicate Condition, 62
Paramount on Parade, 25, 29, 40, 43, 54, 62, 63, 74, 75, 79, 105, 110, 111, 126, 120, 147, 160, 161, 183, 184, 185, 206, 224, 225, 246, 251, 255, 260
Parapluies de Cherbourg, Les, 157

Parker, Charlie, 42
Parker, Colonel Tom, 251, 252
Parker, Eleanor, 89
Parks, Larry, 114, 125, 187
Parrish, Leslie, **126**
Partridge Family, The (TV show), 153
Passing Strange, 47
Pasternak, Joseph, 17, 54, 88, **101, 131, 136, 137,** 198, 233
Patinkin, Mandy, 210
Patrick the Great, 8c
Paul Whiteman and His Orchestra, 179
Payne, John, 41, **101, 234,** 235, **245, 246**
Pearl, Barry, **87**
Pee-Wee's Big Adventure, 62
Pendleton, Austin, 151
Pennies from Heaven, 109
Penny Serenade, 203
Pepsi Cola, 140
Perine, Valerie, **218**
Pescow, Donna, 192
Pete Kelly's Blues, 125, 179
Pete's Dragon, 40
Peter Pan, 35
Peters, Bernadette, **199**
Peters, Brock, 36
Peters, House, **191**
Peters Sisters, 237
Petite, Roland, **75**
Phantom Empire, The, 141, 213
Phantom of the Opera, The, 89, 201, 219
Phantom President, The, 194
Phoenix, Joaquin, 187, 259
Pickford, Mary, 147, 182
Pickwick, 85
Picon, Molly, **250**
Pidgeon, Walter, 105
Pied Pipers, 103
Pigskin Parade, 237
Pin Up Girl, 246, 255
Pinky, 229
Pinocchio, 23, 53, 180–181
Pinocchio (animated character), **189**
Pipe Dream, 166
Pirate, The, 13, 199, 241
Pirates of Penzance, The, 47
Pirosh, Robert, 106
Pitfall, 58
Pitt, Michael, **107**
Pixar Studios, 23, 23
Plantation Act, 114
Platt, Marc, **209**
Platters, 11
Plummer, Christopher, **216, 217**
Plunkett, Walter, 232–233
Pocahontas, 23
Pons, Lili, 26, 88
Poor Little Rich Girl, 83, 182–183
Porgy and Bess, 36, 37, 132, 133
Porter, Cole, **27, 45,** 70, 71, 72, 119, 121, **122,** 133, 145, 213, 218, 225, 240, 249, 255, 272, 274
Powell, Dick, 42, **38, 59,** 78, **79, 116, 111,** 225
Powell, Eleanor, **26, 27,** 49, 122, 230, 249
Powell, Jane, **6,** 21, 36, 8c, 83–89, 131, 136, 137, **145,** 150, 166, **197, 198, 241,** 249, 273
Powell, William, **93,** 247
Power, Tyrone, 235, 245
Preminger, Otto, 36, **37,** 133
Presentiing Lili Mars, 77
Presley, Elvis, 7, 21, 122, 131, 148, 186, **251, 252,** 259
Presley, Priscilla, 187
Pressell, Harve, 76
Preston, Robert, 152, **153,** 177
Previn, André, 17, 36, 37, 85, 156, 207
Previn, Dory, 85
Price, Vincent, 162, 163, 187
Prima, Louis, 17
Prince, 187
Prince, Harold, 27, 47
Princess and the Pirate, The, 237
Priorities on Parade, 8c
Producers, The, 101, 109
Production Code, 174–175
Pryor, Richard, **125,** 151
Pryor, Roger, 219
Pulp Fiction, 193
Purple Rain, 187

Queen Christina, 133
Queen High, 83

Radio City Music Hall, 144, 269, 218, 221
Rae, Charlotte, 126
Rafelson, Bob, 97
Raggedy Ann and Andy, a Musical Adventure, 15
Ragtime, 28, 206
Rainer, Luise, 90, **91**
Rainger, Ralph, 41, 72, 8c, 85
Raitt, John, **176, 177**
Ball, Tommy, **121, 122,** 199
Ralston, Vera Hruba, 51
Rappo, Joe, 15, 151
Rapp, Barney, 177
Rasch, Albertina, 91, 147
Ratatouille, 23
Ravenscroft, Thurl, 116
Raye, Martha, **4, 42, 43, 44,** 51, 233
Raymond, Gene, 8c
Ready, Willing and Able, 110, 199
Red Garters, 135
Red, Hot, and Blue?, 27

TOP: Esther Williams and two admirers film *Jupiter's Darling.*

BOTTOM: Zizi Jeanmarie in the otherwise lousy 1956 version of *Anything Goes.*

Elvis and Ann-Margret in a publicity clinch for Viva, Las Vegas.

Ann-Margret in the horribly cheese-ball remake of State Fair. Luckily, Oscar Hammerstein II had already passed away.

Red Mill, The, 190
Red Shoes, The, 12
Reddy, Helen, 140
Reds, 28
Reed, Carol, 168, 170
Reed, Oliver, 169
Reet-Petite and Gone, 231
Reeves, Steve, 241
Regen, Phil, 231
Reid, Elliott, 72
Reinking, Ann, 9
Reiniger, Lotte, 208
Rent, 47, 219
Republic Pictures, 41, 71, 141, 213
Rescuers, The, 22, 35
Rescuers Down Under, The, 23
Reveille with Beverly, 86
Revel, Harry, 254, 255
Revue des Revues, Les, 205
Reynolds, Burt, 218
Reynolds, Debbie, 13, 54, 80, 115–116, 145, 168.
Reynolds, Marjorie, 239
Rhapsody in Blue, 274
Rhodes, Eric, 249
Rhythm Boys, 110
Rich, Irene, 101
Rich, Young, and Pretty, 168
Richards, Cliff, 157
Richards, Martin, 46
Richardson, Frank, 256
Richardson, Tony, 90
Rickles, Don, 21
Riders of Destiny, 41
Riggs, Lynn, 129
Right This Way, 35
Rinker, Al, 110
Rise and Shine, 86
Roan Hart, 38
Ritter, Tex, 41, 212
Ritz Brothers, 229
Rivera, Chita, 38
RKO, 26, 40, 52, 55, 79, 185, 238, 239, 240, 248, 249
Road to Hong Kong, 237
Road to Morocco, 83, 127, 184–185, 237
Road to Singapore, 185
Road to Zanzibar, 185
Roar of the Greasepaint, the Smell of the Crowd, The, 85
Robbins, Jerome, 9, 107, 247, 258
Robbins Music, 172
Roberta, 130, 203, 240
Roberts, Lynn, 44
Robeson, Paul, 201
Robin, Leo, 41, 72, 79, 80, 111, 185, 227
Robin Hood, 22
Robinson, Bill, 80, 182, 228, 229
Robinson, Earl, 116
Robson, May, 45, 101
Rock of Ages, 204
Rock and Roll, Rock, 11
Rock and Roll, the First 50 Years, 11
Rock Around the Clock, 10
Rockefeller, Nelson, 209

Rocky Horror Picture Show, 186–187, 216
Rodgers, Mary, 84
Rodgers, Richard, 116, 117, 133, 134, 145, 147, 104, 166, 214, 216, 217, 259
Rodgers and Hammerstein, 43, 70, 115, 159, 194
Rodgers and Hart, 17, 28, 105, 132, 157, 272, 273
Rodgers, Ginger, 0, 27, 34, 38, 49, 50, 57, 79, 105, 185, 207, 219, 238, 239, 240, 247, 248, 249, 277
Rogers, Roy, 41, 212, 213
Rogers, Will, 237, 238
Roller Boogie, 192
Romance in the Dark, 53
Romance Scandals, 265
Romance on the High Seas, 178
Romberg, Sigmund, 89, 157, 273
Rome, Harold, 71
Romeo and Juliet, 257
Romero, Caesar, 32
Romero, George, 166
Ronell, Ann, 59, 70, 226
Rooney, Mickey, 17, 33, 34, 55, 76, 77, 40
Roosevelt, Franklin D., 69, 183
Rootie, 27
Rose, Billy, 79
Rose, David, 207
Rose, Felipe, 218
Rose, Helen, 101
Rose, The, 188–189
Rose, Shirley, 72
Rose-Marie, 74, 190–191
Rose of Washington Square, 244
Rosie Hart, 38
Ross, Diana, 124, 125, 158, 189
Ross, Herbert, 66
Ross, Jerry, 47
Ross, Shirley, 72
Rossington, Norman, 98
Roth, Lillian, 130
Roth, Howard K., 150
Royal Wedding, 0, 55, 68, 77, 127, 139, 150, 168.
Royce, Betty, 226
Rubens, Paul, 162
Ruby, Harry, 273
Ruggles, Charles, 175
Ruggles of Red Gap, 72
Russell, Jane, 70, 71, 72, 123, 241
Russell, Ken, 274
Russell, Lillian, 24, 25, 64, 245
Russell, Rosalind, 170
Russell Market Dancers, 118, 109
Ryan, Peggy, 86
Rydell, Bobby, 85, 128
Rydell, Mark, 188
Ryerson, Florence, 17
Ryskind, Morrie, 45, 101

Sager, Carol Bayer, 22
Sakow, Telly, 151
Salinger, Conrad, 105
Sam Butera and the Witnesses, 17
San Antonio, 227
Sandler, Adam, 15

Sandrich, Mark, 49
Sarandon, Susan, 187
Saturday Night Fever, 11, 86, 192–193
Say It with Music, 19, 140
Schary, Dore, 12–13, 62, 131
Schneider, Roy, 8, 9, 45
Schenck, Nicholas, 12, 95
Schildkraut, Joseph, 201
Schneider, Burt, 97
Schoenbaum, Charles, 101
Schumann, Robert, 274
Schwartz, Arthur, 17, 19, 43, 51, 72, 144, 205
Scream, 194
Scrooge, 27
Scrooged, 85, 194–195
Sea Hawk, The, 275
Seaman's Institute, 25
Sears, Ted, 53
Seaton, George, 106
Seberg, Jean, 39, 37
Second Chorus, 239, 240
Secret Garden, The, 106
Secret Life of Walter Mitty, The, 45
Seiter, George, 278
Selter, David, 207
Seitz, George, 278
Selznick, David O., 183
Senior Prom, 17
Serenade, 89
Seven Brides for Seven Brothers, 0, 13, 35, 39, 47, 121, 122, 120, 127, 131, 152, 173, 196–198
Seven Days Leave, 77
Seven Hills of Rome, 89
Seventh Heaven, 237
Sextette, 25
Shaft, 158
Shall We Dance, 239
Shane, 243
Shane, 243
Sharaf, Irene, 13, 66, 105
Sharif, Omar, 65
Shaw, Reta, 176, 178
Shaw, Dorothy, 259
She Done Him Wrong, 25, 45
She Loves Me, 140
Shearer, Harry, 242
Stevenson, Walter, 218
Shepherd, Cybill, 218
Sheridan, Ann, 27
Sherman, Al, 140
Sherman, Richard M., 138, 139, 140
Sherman, Robert B., 138, 139, 140
Sherriff, R. C., 84
Shilkret, Nat, 49
Shindone Alley, 15
Ship Ahoy, 122
Shipmates, 59
Shop Around the Corner, The, 47
Show Boat, 27, 273
Show Boat, 55, 78, 115, 160, 191, 200–203
Slow Boat, 55
230, 278
Show of Shows, The, 29, 234

Shrek, 266–267
Shubert Brothers, 191
Shutta, Ethel, 204
Shy, Gus, 82
Sidney, George, 31, 101, 102, 104
Silk Stockings, 19, 138, 170, 240
Silvers, Phil, 233
Silvers, Sid, 17
Sim, Alastair, 27
Simone, Lela, 14
Simpson, O. J., 39
Sinatra, Frank, 15, 17, 46, 42, 48, 71, 80, 102, 109, 131, 171, 172, 176, 185, 273
Singin' in the Rain, 13, 18, 19, 29, 30, 55, 81, 105, 112, 115–116, 204–207, 268
Sing Your Way Home, 220
Sing-a-long Sound of Music, 216
Sis Hopkins, 41
Sitting Pretty, 255
Sixteen American Rockets, 205
Skatetown, U.S.A., 192
Skelton, Red, 37, 50, 51, 241, 273
Skolsky, Sidney, 255
Skirts Ahoy!, 51
Sky's the Limit, The, 199, 249
Sleeping Beauty, 35, 52
Slipper and the Rose, The, 140
Small Town Girl, 108, 199
Smiles, 255
Smith, C. Aubrey, 50
Smith, Howard K., 150
Smith, Keely, 17
Smith, Muriel, 116
Smith, Stanley, 118
Snow White (animated character), 208, 209, 211
Snow White and the Seven Dwarfs, 208–211, 260, 269
So This Is Love, 80
So This Is Love, 80
Some Like It Hot, 21, 123, 199
Something for Everyone, 27
Something to Sing About, 255
Sondergaard, Gael, 209
Sondheim, Stephen, 160, 168, 217, 219
Song Is Born, A, 179
Song of Love, 274
Song of Norway, 24, 209, 229
Song to Remember, A, 274
Sons of the Pioneers, 141, 212, 213
Sons of the Saddle, 141
Sothern, Ann, 80, 135, 236, 273
Sound of Music, The, 8, 115, 117, 140, 160, 173,

175, 180, 214–217, 219, 256
Sousa, John Philip, 274
South Pacific, 47, 153, 241
Spacek, Sissy, 259
Spartacus!, 17
Spencer, Tim, 213
Spencer, Herbert, 104
Splendid Romance, The, 88
Spook, Benjamin, 209
Springtime in the Rockies, 240
Square Man, The, 212
St. Louis Blues, 187
St. Louis, Louis, 87
Stage Door, 239
Stage Door Canteen, 225
Stage Struck, 111
Stalling, Carl, 53
Stallone, Sylvester, 259
Stand Up and Cheer, 183
Star!, 140, 173, 219, 256
Star Is Born, A, 13, 26, 80, 65, 127, 226–223, 237, 252, 271, 275
Star Spangled Rhythm, 224–225
Stark, Ray, 64, 66, 71
Starr, Ringo, 96, 97, 98
Starrett, Charles, 212
Stars and Stripes Forever, 152, 274
State Fair, 43, 183, 214, 217, 226–227, 240
Staying Alive, 193, 219
Steamboat Willie, 208, 211
Steele, Tommy, 139, 177, 218
Steiner, Max, 239
Stevens, David Ogden, 22, 23
Stevens, George, 240
Stevens, James, 27, 122, 190
Stewart, Sandy, 31
Sigwood, Robert, 192
Stoll, George, 17, 275
Stockwell, Harry, 210
Stock Club, The, 83
Stone, Andrew, 229, 230
Stone, Lewis, 50, 77
Stone, Paddy, 105
Stop the World—I Want to Get Off, 85
Stormy Weather, 33, 228–230, 231, 234
Story of Irene and Vernon Castle, The, 239
Stowaway, 83
Stowkowski, Leopold, 137
Strauss, Johann, 96, 204
Street Angel, 237
Streetcar Named Desire, A, 220
Streets of Paris, The, 69
Streisand, Barbra, 49, 64, 65, 66, 71, 85, 144
Strike Up the Band, 177, 219, 221, 252
Stroue, Charles, 15
Student Prince in Heidelberg, The, 47
Student Prince, The, 89, 131, 190
Sturges, Preston, 83
Styne, Jules, 41, 43, 65, 66, 71, 72, 80, 45, 172, 173, 178, 199, 226
Sugar Babies, 55

Sullivan, Ed, 17
Sullivan, Maxine, 42
Summer Holiday, 42, 133, 199
Summer Stock, 13, 7, 131, 232–233, 255
San Valley Serenade, 234–235, 255
Sunny Side Up, 83, 236–237
Sunrise, 237
Sur les toits de Paris, 157
Susannah of the Mounties, 227
Swanee River, 234, 273–274
Swarthout, Gladys, 88
Swayze, Patrick, 45
Sweater Girl, 41, 86
Sweeney Todd, the Demon Barber of Fleet Street, 219
Sweet Adeline, 199, 203
Sweet Charity, 244
Sweet Rosie O'Grady, 244
Swing Time, 238–240, 277, 278

Take Me Out to the Ball Game, 43, 51, 207, 265
Tale of Two Cities, A, 210
Tamblyn, Russ, 106, 257, 258
Tattle Tales, 246
Taurog, Norman, 129, 137, 255
Taylor, Elizabeth, 27, 56, 133, 170, 266
Taylor, Libby, 24
Teagarden, Jack, 33
Technicolor, 270
Temple, Shirley, 71, 83, 111, 182, 183, 227, 229, 237, 238, 255, 265, 269
Tender Mercies, 259
Terrio, Denny, 103
Terror of Tiny Town, The, 231
Tewksbury, Joan, 158
Texas Carnival, 219
Thalberg, Irving, 29, 106, 101, 184
Thank Your Lucky Stars, 27, 199, 224
That Certain Age, 137
That Midnight Kiss, 89
That Night in Rio, 76
That's Entertainment III, 236
That's Right—You're Wrong, 237
Theban, Blanche, 89
Theodora Goes Wild, 203
There's No Business Like Show Business, 2, 123, 177, 199, 205, 227, 244, 245
They Got Me Covered, 237
This Is Spinal Tap, 242–243
This Is the Army, 201
This Time for Keeps, 51
Thomas, Danny, 76
Thompson, Kay, 31, 60, 61, 62, 63, 82, 104, 105, 145
Thompson, Rex, 117
Thoroughbreds Don't Cry, 76
Thoroughly Modern Millie, 140
Thorpe, Richard, 269, 273
Thousands Cheer, 13, 225, 230

Three Blind Mice, 76
Three Darling Daughters, 89, 137
Three Little Girls in Blue, 42, 76
Three Little Words, 122, 203
Three Musketeers, 97
Three Sailors and a Girl, 167, 198
Three 6 Mafia, 159
Three Stooges, 49
There's a Crowd, 19
Thunder Road, 252
Tibbett, Lawrence, 88
Till the Clouds Roll By, 18, 82, 236, 273
Tiller, John, 205
Tiller Girls, 205
Time magazine, 239
Time to Sing, A, 259
Tin Pan Alley, 19, 37, 102, 227, 244–246, 255
Tisdale, Ashley, 109
Titanic, 68
To Be or Not to Be, 147
Toast of New Orleans, 89
Tobias, George, 27, 273
Todd, Mabel, 100, 110
Toi C'est Moi, 157
Tom (animated character), 50
Tom Jones, 96
Tomkins, Don, 107
Tomlin, Lily, 159
Tonight and Every Night, 173, 226
Too Many Girls, 199
Top Banana, 46, 47, 120
Top Hat, 36, 232–233, 229
Top Speed, 246, 249
Torch Singer, 80
Torch Song, 43
Torme, Mel, 273
Town without Pity, 53
Toy Story, 23, 53, 180
Tozzi, Giorgio, 116
Tracy, Spencer, 247
Transona, 221
Trask, Stephen, 107
Traubel, Helen, 89, 273
Travers, P.L., 138, 140
Travolta, John, 86, 87, 102, 103, 219
Treacher, Arthur, 225
Trouble in Paradise, 147
Truffaut, François, 8
Tucci, Richard, 113
Tucker, Richard, 113
Turner, Lana, 51, 103
20th Century Fox, 69, 79, 111, 122, 183, 24, 229, 234, 244–245, 251, 252, 265, 269
20 Million Sweethearts, 58
Two By Two, 48
Two's Company, 27
Tyson, Cicely, 125, 266

Ullman, Liv, 218
Ulmer, Edgar G., 250

Umbrellas of Cherbourg, The. See Parapluies de Cherbourg, Les
Umeki, Miyoshi, 117
United Artists, 183, 225, 252
Universal Pictures, 25, 29, 36, 34, 54, 80, 115, 119, 131, 137, 140, 200, 260, 224, 225
Up, 23
Up In Arms, 45
Up In Central Park, 137
Utopia, 83

Vaidengo, Giuseppe, 89
Vale, John, 205
Valentine, Joseph, 137
Valez, Lupe, 32
Vallee, Rudy, 100, 177
Valli, Frankie, 87, 128
Van Dyke, Dick, 138, 139, 140, 170, 177
Van Halen, Eddie, 243
Van Heemstra, Ella, 63
Van Hensen, Jimmy, 110, 185, 226, 227
Van Riper, Kay, 17
Varsity Show, 111
Venuta, Benay, 50
Vera-Ellen, 13, 47, 172, 173, 249, 260, 201, 262, 263, 273, 277
Verdon, Gwen, 9, 19, 38, 46, 47, 92, 177
Vereen, Ben, 8
Very Warm for May, 203
Victor/Victoria, 85, 140
Vidor, King, 94, 95, 269
Vincent, 102
Virginian, The, 212
Vitaphone, 112–113, 114, 236
Vitaphone Project, 113
Viva Las Vegas, 17, 122, 251–253
Voight, Hubert, 213
Von Sternberg, Josef, 91
Von Trapp, Maria, 216, 217
Von Trier, Lars, 157

Wabash Avenue, 76, 87, 244
Walk the Line, 187, 259
Walker, Nancy, 42
Wall-E, 53
Wallace, Oliver, 53
Waller, Thomas "Fats," 8c, 229, 235, 234
Wallis, Shani, 168, 169, 170
Walston, Ray, 116
Walt Disney Studios, 35, 52, 105, 138, 180–181, 194, 208–210
Walters, Charles, 75, 77, 105, 232–233
Walton, Tony, 9
Wand, Betty, 117
Ward, Kelly, 87

Warner, Harry, 27, 28, 42, 58, 69, 72, 78, 79, 103, 111, 255
Warren, Lesley Ann, 139
Washington, Ned, 53, 81
Waters, Ethel, 32, 33, 177, 229, 230
Watkins, Maurine Dallas, 38
Wayne, John, 42, 141, 213
We're Not Dressing, 254–255
Weaver, Carl Earl, 11
Webb, Clifton, 33, 62, 274
Webster, Paul Francis, 35
Weekend in Havana, 227, 255
Weill, Kurt, 45, 71, 213, 219
Weissmuller, Johnny, 50, 234
Welcome Back, Kotter (TV show), 193
Welles, Orson, 151
West, Claudine, 84
West, Mae, 24, 25, 41, 184, 210, 234, 244
West Point Story, The, 167
West Side Story, 117, 127, 173, 196, 214, 252, 256–258
Western Electric, 112, 113
Whale, James, 201, 202
What a Way to Go, 207
What's Opera, Doc?, 52
Whatever Happened To Baby Jane, 199
Wheeler, Hugh, 38
Wheeler and Woolsey, 76, 247–248
When My Baby Smiles at Me, 227, 244
Where Do We Go from Here, 213
Where the Boys Are, 131
Where the Boys Meet the Girls, 76
Where's Charley?, 105
Whiffs, 158
White, Marjorie, 236
White, Onna, 9, 152, 169, 195, 199
White Christmas, 19, 45, 119, 265, 260–263
Whiteman, Paul, 119, 179, 234
Whiting, Margaret, 42, 111, 225
Whiting, Richard, 72, 111
Whitmore, James, 121
Whoopee!, 264–265
Why Girls Leave Home, 226
Wicked Bit of the West, The (book), 43
Wickes, Mary, 153
Wild, Jack, 169, 170
Wild in the Country, 252
Hideouts, 107
Wilder, Clinton, 61
Wilder, Gene, 266, 267
Wildhorn, Frank, 85
Williams, Andy, 82
Williams, Billy Dee, 125
Williams, Esther, 50, 51, 68, 77, 100, 122, 123, 131, 234, 235, 241
Williams, Hank, Jr., 259
Williams, Jason, 109
Williams, Paul, 151
Williams Brothers, 82
Wills, Bob, 141
Wills, Chill, 104
Wilson, Meredith, 152, 153
Wilson, P.G., 278
Wilson, Earl, 21
Wing, Toby, 58, 246
Wininger, Charles, 201, 227
Winslet, Kate, 104
Wirtz, Arthur, 235
Wise, Robert, 14, 216, 250, 258
Wister, Owen, 212
With a Song in My Heart, 136, 227
Witherspoon, Reese, 187, 259
Witett, Matthew, 149
Wiz, The, 230, 268
Wizard of Oz, The, 15, 45, 105, 111, 143, 193, 216, 230, 266, 268–271
Wodehouse, P.G., 278
Wonder Bar, 58, 68
Wonder Man, 227, 203
Wonderful Land of Oz, The, 268
Wonderful Town, 173
Wonderful Wizard of Oz, The, 268
Wood, Dee Dee, 126
Wood, Natalie, 117, 256
Woods, Donald, 203
Woodstock, 187
Woolf, Edgar, 17
Words and Music, 13, 134, 236, 263, 273
World's Fair (New York), 140
Wright, Robert, 101, 204
Writers Guild, 243
Wrong Box, The, 96
Wrubel, Allie, 226
Wyler, William, 65, 66
Wyman, Jane, 135–240
Wynn, Ed, 165, 269
Wynn, Keenan, 121

Xanadu, 219

You Were Never Lovelier, 240, 276–278
You'll Never Get Rich, 239
Youmans, Vincent, 255
Young, Roland, 175
Young, Victor, 226
Young, Waldemar, 132
Young Ladies Institute, 25
Yvain, Maurice, 157
YWCA, 25

Zanuck, Darryl, 79, 183, 229, 234, 237, 265
Zellweger, Renée, 27, 38, 39
Zeta-Jones, Catherine, 38, 39, 40
Ziegfeld Florenz, 92, 201, 204
Ziegfeld Follies, 42, 63, 82, 199, 230, 265
Ziegfeld Girl, 99
Zinnemann, Fred, 164
Zinsser, William K., 165
Zorina, Vera, 13, 225

Yankee Doodle Dandy, 45, 94, 110, 272–275
Yates, Herbert, 213
Yentl, 66, 85, 210
Fiddle with His Fiddle, 250
Yip, Yip, Yaphank, 201
YMCA, 25
Yolanda and the Thief, 13, 103
You Can't Run Away from It, 85
You Only Live Twice, 85

PHOTO CREDITS

AFD/Photofest: 150, 151, 218 bottom, 283 top; Allied Artists/Photofest: 36, 31 top & bottom; American International/Photofest: 20, 21, 123 bottom left; Cinema Center: 104, 105; Columbia/Photofest: 101 bottom right, 04, 65, 66, 168, 169, 170, 210 top left, 276, 277, 278; Columbia/Fox/Photofest: 8, o bottom; Criterion Collection: 157 bottom; Disney/Photofest: 22, 23, 52, 53, 163, 169, 138, 139, 140, 141; 46 top right, 180, 181, 208, 209, 211; Embassy/Photofest: 242, 243; Emovieposter.com: Posters on pages 16, 18, 20, 24, 26, 28, 30, 32, 34, 36, 38, 41, 44, 41, 48, 50, 54, 57, 60, 67, 84, 88, 90, 103, 106, 108, 118, 124, 127, 128, 130, 132, 139, 152, 166, 162, 164, 168, 171, 180, 182, 184, 186, 188, 190, 200, 206, 214, 228, 234, 254, 272; Goldwyn/Photofest: 179 center; Kisch/Photofest: 231; Library of Congress: 2, 7, 10 bottom left, 101 bottom left, 136 bottom, 179 bottom, 54, 50 bottom left, 75, 116 left, 131 center, 139 right (both top and bottom), 140 center, 139 right, 144 center, 145 top, 165, 167, 222 top, 223 top, 145 top, 279, 281 right, 283; MGM/Photofest: 12, 13 top, 4 bottom right, 10, 17, 48, 10 top/bottom-right, 26, 27 top, 28, 29 top & bottom, 32, 33 top, 99, 100, 101 top right, 102, 259 bottom left, 50, 51, 52 top right & bottom right, 157 top, 63, 72 top, 73, 74, 76, 77, 81, 82 left, 83 top, 84, 85 top & center, 88, 90, 91, 92, 93, 103, 104, 105 top & center, 120, 121, 122, 134 bottom, 143, 144 bottom, 145 bottom right, 146, 147, 171, 172, 173 left & top right, 190, 191, 196, 197, 208 center, 232, 233, 234 bottom left, 251, 252, 253, 256, 257, 258, 263, 293 top right, 270, 271 top, 280 left, 282, 283, 203 top, 275 top, 278 bottom left; New Line/Photofest: 106, 107; Paramount/Photofest: 15, 11, 24 top, 25, 41, 42 top, 43 center, 44, 45, 179 bottom right, 60, 61, 62, 63 bottom, 82 right, 86, 87, 124, 125, 126, 127 top, 128, 129, 132, 133, 144 top right, 158, 159, 174, 175, 184, 185, 192, 193, 203 top & center, 224, 225, 226, 260, 261, 262, 263 top & center, 266, 267, 268, 281 left, 284, 287; Pathe/Photofest: 46 center; Republic/Photofest: 259 top, 44, 49 top, 50 bottom, 203 bottom left, 212, 213 bottom, 203 bottom left, 210 bottom left; RKO/Photofest: 48, 49 top, 50 bottom, 55 left, 56 top & center, 58 center, 69 bottom, 71 bottom right, 83 bottom, 80, 107 top, 111 bottom, 250, 134 top, 137 top, 127 bottom, 131 bottom, 250, 207, 141 bottom right, 210 bottom right, 225 bottom, 236 top, 123 bottom right, 244 bottom right, 255 bottom; United Artists/Photofest: 135, 148, 149, 164, 166, 173 bottom right, 182, 183, 186, 187, 214, 215, 216, 217, 88, 189, 226, 227, 228, 229, 234, 235, 236, 237, 241, 240, 282, 285; Twentieth Century Fox/Photofest: 4, 13 bottom, 15, bottom, 36, 37, 47 bottom right, 110, 111, 207, 141 top left, 210 bottom right, 225 bottom, 236 top, 71 top & bottom center, 72 top & bottom center, 79 top & bottom right, 72 top left & bottom right, 73 bottom, 85, bottom, 226, 227, 228, 240, 282, 285; United Artists/Photofest: 135 top, 148, 149, 164, 166, 173 bottom right, 182, 183, 186, 187, 88, 180, 97, 98, 223 bottom, 204, 205, 271 bottom left, 282, 285; Universal/Photofest: 135 top, 148, 166, 173 bottom left, 212, 213 bottom, 203 bottom left, 210 bottom left; Touchstone/Photofest: 102, 179 bottom, 239, 240, 248; Twentieth Century Fox/Photofest: 4, 13 top, 14, 45, 47 top, 57, 58 top & center left, 59 bottom, 207, 141 top left, 217 top left & center left, 71 top & bottom right, 73 top, 255 bottom, 255 bottom; Warner Bros/Photofest: 100 bottom, 34, 35 top, 46, 47 top & bottom left, 57, 58 bottom, 59 top & center left & bottom right, 78, 79 top & center left & bottom right, 111, 120, 131, 138, 151, 152, 153, 154, 155, 159 top, 176, 177, 178, 203 bottom right, 226, 221, 222 center & bottom, 271 bottom right, 268 top, 272, 273, 274 center & bottom

King Vidor films *Hallelujah!* on location.

ACKNOWLEDGMENTS

Another huge undertaking, this book could never have been completed without the assistance and friendship of many people. I'd like to thank the following friends and colleagues for their help and support over the last year: Jane Powell for her wonderfully evocative Foreword (as well as her years of toil in the MGM factory); Michael Feinstein for his expert matchmaking in bringing us together with Ms. Powell; and Laura Ross, who has seen me through a series of books at Black Dog with her incisive editing and artistic input. She makes me appear to be a much better writer (and smarter) than I am. Lisa Tenaglia was an intrepid in-house editor and keeper of the schedule. Thanks too, to True Sims, Black Dog's Production Manager who has worked the impossible for us. Finally, thanks to J.P. Leventhal who has stood behind all these books. Designer Scott Citron has designed each book in the Black Dog series with an impeccable eye and a useful interest in the subjects. Richard Shearer has assisted in the layout and production of several of my books, working long hours making sense of piles of text and hundreds of errant photos.

Speaking of photos, I'd like especially to thank Howard Mandelbaum and Ron Mandelbaum of Photofest. Howard and Ron are knowledgeable, supportive, and professional. In addition to supplying the vast majority of the photos in this book, they proofread the text and pointed out many errors of fact and interpretation. Their good humor, remarkably deep knowledge, and dedication to this project make them integral to any success this book enjoys. The Photofest staff—Henry Fera, Buddy Weiss, Andy McGovern, and their colleagues—scanned, cleaned, researched, sorted, and pulled thousands of photos and I am grateful to them also. Bruce Hershenson of emovieposter.com and his associate Phillip Wages supplied many of the historic posters. Their extensive collection is remarkable and their prompt and enthusiastic response to my requests made working with them a pleasure. Additional photos were obtained from the Library of Congress's Prints and Photographs Division. Librarian Jan Grenci's professionalism, good spirits, and decidedly non-bureaucratic demeanor made searching through the Library's vast collection a pleasure.

Others who shared their knowledge, advice, and assistance include Helene Blue, Peter Filichia, Christopher Johnson, Kenneth Kantor, Barry Kleinbort, Andrew Giant-Linden, Caesar Rodriguez, and Robert Sixsmith.

Ken Bloom
New York City, August 2010

ABOVE: Not Ken Bloom, but his Aunt Bob in *Road to Morocco*.

NEXT PAGE: MGM company banquet.